THE GREAT PLAGUE
IN LONDON

GEORGE MONCK, DUKE OF ALBEMARLE

*Who remained in London throughout the Great Plague, the sole representative of
King Charles II's Government who stayed*

From the portrait by Sir Peter Lely in the Guildhall, Exeter

THE GREAT PLAGUE IN LONDON

WALTER GEORGE BELL

BRACKEN BOOKS
LONDON

The Great Plague of London

First published in 1924 as
The Great Plague in London in 1665
by The Bodley Head, London.

This edition published in 1994 by Bracken Books,
an imprint of Studio Editions Ltd, Princess House,
50 Eastcastle Street, London W1N 7AP, England

ISBN 1 85891 218 0
Printed at Thomson Press (India) Ltd.

PREFACE

THIS book tells a tragedy of the poor. A few men—very few—of birth, position, and wealth stayed in London, sharing the suffering which was the lot of all, and there are names that gained added lustre in that year of calamity; but in its immensity and in overwhelming proportion it was "the poore's Plague."

The Great Plague in London was a tragedy of errors. If only those fated people could have known!

No attempt has heretofore been made to write a full history of the Plague that desolated London in 1665. Defoe has filled the gap, and with such thoroughness that over two centuries his work has been frequently quoted as that of an historian. I have perhaps been daring. The book has to stand or fall beside the "Journal of the Plague Year," a record of fact beside a work which was given to the world as fiction.

I find myself unable to regard the "Journal of the Plague Year" as anything other than an historical novel. The circumstances under which it was written are well known. Plague raged at Marseilles in the years 1720–21; there were grave fears that shipping from Continental ports would bring infection to England, and both the Government and the public at that time showed serious alarm. Defoe found in the last visitation of Plague to London, which was still dimly in the memory of a few aged men, a fitting subject for his pen.

He used historical sources as other fiction writers have used them. The ascription of the "Journal" to a certain *H.F.*, who might be identified with Defoe's uncle, Henry Foe, can have convinced none. There is in it too much of the novelist's craft for that origin. But Defoe was extraordinarily gifted, and by combining with his simple form of narrative documents such as "the Lord Mayor's Orders," the full use made of the published Bills of Mortality and frequent mention of places familiar to every reader, and by the very confusion of his story, he has given to this imaginary journal such an appearance of truth as has deceived many. An American scholar, Dr. Watson Nicholson, who has recently been with us, has written a book upon the historical basis of Defoe to establish his conclusion that the "Journal of the Plague Year" is authentic history.

With that all too hasty judgment I disagree.

Defoe is at most a part of history, often inaccurately told; how insufficient a part to satisfy, those who persevere with this book to the end will judge for themselves. I hold that the Rev. J. Charles Cox, the learned editor of the Antiquary's Books, when he dismisses the "Journal" as "a highly imaginative work of fiction, based upon vague recollections and untrustworthy hearsay," does less than justice to the pains taken by Defoe in using such historical sources as were at his hand. Large numbers of documents and memoirs not accessible to Defoe are now available, and without the knowledge to be acquired from these no adequate history of the Great Plague in London could be given.

I have written coldly, critically, with a sobering sense of responsibility, careful before making any statement to establish its authenticity, and without resort to artifices which Defoe, as a fiction writer, was justified in employing —the frequent repetitions, the characters typical rather than individual, the piling up of one terror upon another in order to give realistic effect. It is not wholly Defoe's Plague that emerges in these pages. And yet it has seemed to me that this picture I have drawn of a city in its agony is more terrible than all that Defoe imagined. Nothing could, indeed, exceed the unexampled horror of the plain facts. The Bills of Mortality admit a loss of 97,306 lives in the year 1665, and of these 68,596 only are accredited to the Plague. London's population is likely to have fallen short of half a million at that time. I have advanced reasons for belief that these Plague figures are largely under-stated, that the Plague alone was responsible for fully 100,000 deaths—for almost all. That mass of humanity perished in a few months on the small area of ground that London of the day covered. And the proportion must be taken, not from the population short of half a million, but from a smaller population—from those who were left behind after substantially all the rich and the professional and merchant classes who were able to do so had fled from the City and its outskirts to escape the Plague.

It may occasion surprise that a writer who has enjoyed in full measure the fascination of London should have filled these grim pages ; and greater surprise that one who is not a medical man should have undertaken this task. A belief that the book as a record of things done and left undone in the panic conditions of a vast Plague will not be without value in the great profession of medicine has been with me in laborious years. I have not attempted a medical history of the Great Plague, and should not have ventured into that domain, even to the small extent herein essayed, had I not experienced the generous interest of Dr. Edwin Ash, Dr. Francis J. Allan, Medical Officer of Health of Westminster, and others, and benefited by their knowledge and advice. Sir Sydney Russell-Wells had arranged to go over the final page proofs with me in the very week of his lamented death, which has robbed them of the advantage of his revision. To all those mentioned my warm thanks are given. But for anything here said that is open to criticism the responsibility is mine alone. From Mr. A. H. Thomas, F.S.A., the Records Clerk at Guildhall, Mr. Bernard Kettle, the Guildhall Librarian, and the Library Committee I have received the willing assistance that is extended to all who seek out the story of London. The Rev. Howell Williams, Rector of Eyam, has given me valued help concerning the Plague that broke out in that Derbyshire village.

The City was not entirely immune from Plague when in 1666 the Fire destroyed the larger part of it. Restoration London I have described in detail as the flames swept over it, and for its scene and dominant characteristics the reader is referred to the earlier work.[1]

---

[1] *The Great Fire of London in* 1666, by Walter George Bell, 3rd ed. 1923.

One apology is due for this volume. Its pages are peppered with footnote references. No one is more irritated than myself by that much-abused practice. It is pedantic at best. It suggests that the author is without faith that his word would be sufficient were it not so supported; it lays him open to the charge of being anxious to show how wide his research has been. But what should I do? In my case it is a mere measure of self-defence, to establish that nothing is owing to my great predecessor, and that in method as in purpose his book and mine stand wide apart. These references, though disregarded, may have some utility by reminding the reader on every page that he has the fact before him.

CONTENTS

CHAPTER   PAGE

      PREFACE v

   I. FIRST SIGNS OF PLAGUE 1

  II. OUTBREAK OF THE PLAGUE 16

III. SPREAD IN THE OUT-PARISHES 35

 IV. FLIGHT OF THE COURT 53

  V. MEN AND MEASURES 72

 VI. PLAGUE IN THE CITY 103

VII. TOWN AND COUNTRYSIDE 136

VIII. THE GROWING BURDEN 173

 IX. LONDON DESOLATED 203

  X. THE PEAK OF THE CURVE 236

 XI. JOHN ALLIN'S LETTERS 255

 XII. DECLINE OF THE PLAGUE 266

XIII. THE OXFORD PARLIAMENT 298

XIV. THE FULL BILL 305

APPENDICES

   I. PRIVY COUNCIL RULES AND ORDERS, 1666 . . . 333

  II. POST-MORTEM EXAMINATION OF A PLAGUE VICTIM . 335

III. A HITHERTO UNPUBLISHED POEM ON THE GREAT
      PLAGUE 338

      AUTHORITIES 352

      INDEX 361

LIST OF ILLUSTRATIONS

FOLDING PLATES

FACING PAGE

A LONDON BILL OF MORTALITY OF 1665 20

PICTORIAL BROADSIDE OF THE PLAGUE 104

GEOGRAPHICAL DISTRIBUTION OF THE PLAGUE . . . 158

CHART OF MORTALITY IN THE GREAT PLAGUE . . . 238

BILL OF MORTALITY FOR THE YEAR 1665 320

FULL PAGE PLATES

GEORGE MONCK, DUKE OF ALBEMARLE . . *Frontispiece*

HOLLAR'S PRINT OF RURAL WESTMINSTER . . . 42

GRAVE OF ALEXANDER DAVIES 50

THE EARL OF CRAVEN 68

SIR JOHN LAWRENCE'S HOUSE 82

A MAYORAL PROCLAMATION 116

FRONTISPIECE TO DR. THOMSON'S "LOIMOTOMIA" . . . 128

FIGURE OF THE PLAGUE PIPER 134

PAGE OF CRIPPLEGATE BURIAL REGISTER 146

PLAGUE ENTRIES IN CRIPPLEGATE REGISTER . . . 152

ANCIENT JEWISH BURIAL GROUND 180

QUAKER BURIAL GROUND AT FINSBURY 182

DR. GEORGE THOMSON 206

RAT FLEA AND BACILLUS PESTIS 248

WILLIAM MOMPESSON, RECTOR OF EYAM 294

MEMORIALS OF THE PLAGUE AT EYAM 296

FACING PAGE

A Yarmouth Bill of Mortality 310

A Norwich Bill of Mortality 324

IN THE TEXT

Plan of the City in Squares 31

"London's Dreadful Visitation" 61

Chart showing Trend of the Plague 79

Cock Tavern Token 91

"Londons Lamentation" 139

The Plague in Cripplegate 150

The Plague in Aldgate 151

"Londons Lord have Mercy on us" 219

The Plague in Clerkenwell 272

Plague in City, Liberties, and Out-parishes . . . 273

THE GREAT PLAGUE IN
LONDON IN 1665

CHAPTER I

FIRST SIGNS OF PLAGUE

LATE into dark December nights of the year 1664 London citizens sat up to watch a new blazing star, with "mighty talk" thereupon. King Charles II. and his Queen gazed out of the windows at Whitehall.[1] About east it rose, reaching no great altitude, and sank below the south-west horizon between two and three o'clock.[2] In a week or two it was gone, then letters came from Vienna notifying the like sight of a brilliant comet, and "in the ayre the appearance of a Coffin, which causes great anxiety of thought amongst the people." Erfurt saw with it other terrible apparitions, and listeners detected noises in the air, as of fires, and sounds of cannon and musket-shot.[3]

The report ran that one night in the February following hundreds of persons had seen flames of fire for an hour together, which seemed to be thrown from Whitehall to St. James's, and then back again to Whitehall, whereafter they disappeared.[4]

In March there came into the heavens a yet brighter comet, visible two hours after midnight, and so continuing till daylight. With such ominous portents the Great Plague in London was ushered in. Report of Plague had been on the Continent. The learned in these matters

---

[1] Pepys's *Diary*, Dec. 17.
[2] John Allin's Letters, Dec. 20, in *Archæologia*, vol. 37, pp. 1–22.
[3] *Newes*, 1665, Jan. 5.   [4] Allin, Feb. 24.

held the first comet to be propitious to England, but ominous to France and Holland. The second puzzled the wisest of them. Astrologers found also in a conjunction of Mars and Saturn which had occurred in November a presage of war, pestilence, and famine.[1]

The temptation is strong to dismiss with a gesture of contempt such idle feárs and speculations, but we shall little understand London's populace in 1665 by so doing. It obscures the truth to envisage the middle seventeenth century through a medium of popular knowledge in the twentieth. The educated classes generally may have known better, though even of these a goodly part believed in portents, and they had fled before the advancing Plague—the Court, the lawyers, and an unhappily large proportion of physicians and divines. But a leaven of the bulk who remained could read and write. The printed sheet most widely circulating was William Lilly's Almanac, published each year from 1644 till his death. This and others like passed in thousands from hand to hand and were expounded, their mystifying diagrams and spells and forecasts of events satisfying minds to which greater literature was unknown.

The numerals of the year 1666, with their thrice repetition, had inspired a whole book by one Francis Potter, which claimed to prove that the three sixes together made a number " of exquisite and perfect character, truly, exactly, and essentially describing that state of Government to which all other notes of Antichrist doe agree." [2] It found a pleased purchaser in Samuel Pepys,[3] but Londoners in the Great Fire that year had no reason to bless the treble number. A prophet of the Great Plague named Edlin made a fortunate shot, actually predicting the epidemic in its correct time.[4]

But a month or two before the Great Plague appeared three hapless women had been hanged as witches. Their trial at Suffolk Assizes in March, 1665, had all the law's dread formality, and presiding was Sir Matthew Hale, whose high character made him deservedly one of the

---

[1] John Gadbury's *Londons Deliverance Predicted*, 1665.
[2] *An Interpretation of the Number* 666.   Lond. 1642.
[3] *Diary*, 1666, Feb. 17, Nov. 4.
[4] Edlin's *Prænuncius Sydereus*, Lond. 1663[-4].

most renowned of Commonwealth and Restoration Judges.
Hale made no doubt at all of the existence of witches, as
proved, he said simply, by the Scriptures, general consent,
and Acts of Parliament.[1] And if learned men rejected
portents in the skies as influencing human affairs, it was
with half reservations. Dr. George Thomson was skilled
in the medical practise of his day, and seeking to enlarge
knowledge, he had the great courage to dissect the corpse
of a Plague victim. Although impatient with many idle
superstitions held by the common people, he himself
wrote : " That comets, or blazing stars, do portend some
evil to come upon mortals is confirmed by long observation and sad experience, as likewise phenomena of new
stars, battles fought, and coffins carried through the air,
howlings, screechings and groans heard about churchyards,
also raining of blood, unwonted matter, etc., all of which,
having something *extra naturam*, are portentious and
prodigious." [2]

They who so testified their faith were able to fleck
their pages with passages in Latin and Greek, signs of
pedantic learning. Who, then, shall wonder that the
ignorant masses, in the terror and distress of a huge
public calamity, accepted comets as manifestations of
Heaven's wrath, believed that gold, if only obtained pure,
would eject all diseases from the human frame, that the
toad amulet was a charm against Plague, and unicorn's
horn a certain cure ? Any who wished to see coffins
carried in the air, to hear howlings and groans in churchyards, be sure would see and hear them. To such these
events and portents were real, terrifying. The state of
medical knowledge gave small confidence in its efficacy
to combat the death that stalked abroad. Their minds
receptive to wonders, if to little else, the untutored people
turned from medicine to the astrologers, the nostrum
dealers and the quacks who promised immunity, and in
ever increasing numbers fattened upon their fears.

There had been rumours of Plague in Holland towards
the close of 1663, and definite evidence of its spread there
next summer. Little, however, was known concerning it.
London had lost the partisan *Mercuries* and *Diurnals*

[1] Cobbett's *State Trials*, vol. 6, pp. 687–702.
[2] George Thomson's *Loimotomia, or the Pest Anatomized*, 1666, p. 66.

which had been so numerous under the Commonwealth ;
the printing press was enchained. But two newspapers
circulated, Roger L'Estrange's *Intelligencer* and *Newes*,
appearing respectively on Mondays and Thursdays each
week—actually a bi-weekly issue of one paper, with much
repetition. Each was a little quarto sheet of sixteen
printed pages (till June 1st, 1665, of eight pages) mostly
filled with advices of foreign wars and politics, the movements of the English Fleet, and some sparse home news
and advertisements. L'Estrange, himself the Licencer of
the Press and a creature of the Court, depended wholly
on Court favour for the prosperity of his enterprise, which
the franking and free postage of his newsletters made
possible. He took care to publish nothing displeasing to
Whitehall. Those who had shipping interests or correspondents on the Continent learnt from their sea-captains
and from letters that the Plague in Holland for some
months past had taken a virulent form, and the mortality
from it had been very great.

This was well known to the British Government.
Early as June 1664, persons and goods coming from
Holland had been subject to strict quarantine.[1] Ships
entering the Thames from Dutch ports were laid up at
Hole Haven, by Canvey Island. The Lord Mayor was
notified by Order in Council that should such persons or
goods be found harboured in London without certificate
of quarantine being forthcoming, he was to shut up the
houses containing them as if these were infected with
Plague.[2] In Portsmouth that summer Plague was already
seated, twenty-one deaths from it having occurred in a
single week in July.[3] The declaration of war with Holland
on February 22nd, 1665, cut off direct contact with that
source of infection ; but the peril of Plague spreading in
England no doubt had been in mind when the Privy
Council directed that the customary Proclamation for the
strict observance of Lent should not be made. Lenten collections for the relief of the poor were ordered to be taken,
the Lord Mayor and Court of Aldermen having petitioned.[4]

[1] Chester Corporation MSS. (*Hist. MSS. Comm.*, 8*th Rep.*, 387b).
[2] Duke of Buckingham to the Lord Mayor, 1664, June 27.   Original
letter at Guildhall.
[3] Marquis of Bath's MSS. (*Hist. MSS. Comm.*, 4*th Rep.*, p. 229).
[4] Privy Council Register, vol. 58, fos. 25, 61.

A Plague death in the out-parish of St. Giles-in-the-Fields figures in the Bills of Mortality in December 1664, and a second in the following February, but the bill being again clear thereafter these isolated occurrences occasioned no public concern.

In London in 1664 there had been five cases recorded by the Bills of Mortality as Plague, in the year before twelve ; others, no doubt, were concealed under names of various diseases. It is wholly a mistake, which we are prone to make after two and a half centuries' immunity, to imagine Plague as something entirely novel—so dreadful in its potentialities that report even of a single case must have given rise to widespread alarm.

The Great Plague of 1665 has so concentrated popular attention upon itself that the frequency of Plague has largely escaped notice. It was no stranger to the Londoners. For thirty years then past London had known Plague, though never with large mortality since the long visitation that reached its culmination in 1647, in which year 3,597 victims perished. Plague was then in Newgate ; the coroner refused to view the bodies of its victims, for the reason that juries were so fearful that none would enter the prison.[1]

Indeed, so persistent had been Plague since 1603, from which date weekly Bills of Mortality had been systematically compiled,[2] that only in four widely separated years in the half-century and more had London been reported entirely free from infection. That year 1603, when Queen Elizabeth died, her subjects were terribly visited. There

---

[1] House of Lords MSS. (*Hist. MSS. Comm.*, 7th Rep., 560).

[2] There is an earlier Bill of Mortality of the great year of Plague 1593, March to December ; and Dr. Creighton has printed in his *History of Epidemics in Britain*, vol. i. pp. 341–4, from the Cecil MSS. at Hatfield House, complete Bills for the years 1578–82 and January, 1583, which were obtained by Lord Burghley from the Lord Mayor of London. The preparation of Bills in times of Plague seems to have originated in a request by the Privy Council to the Lord Mayor in Oct. 1532 to furnish a return of Plague deaths, and the Bill for a single week of that year, Nov. 16th to 23rd, is the earliest Bill preserved (Brit. Mus. Egerton MSS. 2603, fo. 4). This most interesting document, showing thirty-four Plague deaths in the week and thirty-two as the " sum of other seknes," is printed by Creighton, i. 296. Apparently it is one of a series. Two other Plague bills, prepared in more clerkly fashion, are extant for August, 1535 (Creighton, p. 298), and a few memoranda of Plague bills of 1563 and 1574. But evidence of mortality in epidemics previous to 1592–3 is mostly derived from parish registers and scattered references in State papers and letters.

were 33,347 recorded Plague deaths in London : " Never
did the English nation," wrote Dekker, " behold so much
black worn as there was at her funeral.   It was then but
put on to try if it were fit, for the great day of mourning
was set down in the book of Heaven to be held afterwards."[1]
Trade wholly ceased within the City for almost half the
year, and merchants and all others of any estate fled into
the country.[2]   Elizabeth, retreating to Windsor from a
dreadful Plague in London in 1563, a thousand dying
weekly, set up a gallows in the market-place of Windsor
on which to hang all Londoners who should venture to
come there, and those bringing wares from London were
alike to be hanged thereon, " without judgment." [3]   It
was a policy of thorough wherever the Sovereign's safety
was at stake.   All acquainted with the Elizabethan stage
will recall how frequently playhouses were closed and the
companies of actors disbanded because of the Plague.
Never had two decades passed without a startling up-
growth of the death-roll in London, rising for weeks
together, four, seven, and ten times above normal figures,
thus indicating the existence of violent Plague.   It linked
back in a calamitous chain with the " Sweating sickness "
which repeatedly had afflicted the capital in King Henry
VIII.'s reign and earlier, and by which, in a single week
of the year 1485, two Lord Mayors of London in succession
had perished.   They were Sir Thomas Hills and William
Stokker, the last elected the day after the vacancy and
himself dead four days later, and with them died six
Aldermen.   In 1499 a severe Plague in London caused
King Henry VII. to retire to Calais.   Though early records
are few, scattered references to Plague in London are
sufficiently numerous to suggest that for centuries back
years were rare which did not show some manifestation of endemic disease, with at intervals violent
outbursts in epidemics ; but these are beyond my present
purpose.

In a register of burials of the City church of St. Peter
Cornhill, at the close of the entries for the stricken year

[1] Dekker, *The Wonderfull Yeare* 1603.
[2] Letter by East India Committees to their servants in the East,
Dec. 1603.   W. Foster, *The East India House*, p. 57.
[3] Lambeth Palace MSS. (Stow's *Memoranda*, Camden Society).

1593 the searcher comes unexpectedly upon these lines, penned in a neat Elizabethan hand—

> " In a thousand five hundred ninety and three
> The Lord preserved my house and mee
> When of the pestilence theare died
> Full manie a thousand els beeside."

The clerk of St. Peter's wrote that, satisfied that he should himself be alive. He placed just above the figures of the whole year's mortality : that in London and the out-parishes 15,003 persons had perished of Plague.

The migrations of Parliament are little known, and they are significant. It had been adjourned from Westminster in July, 1467, after several Members of the House of Commons had died of the Plague. King James I.'s earliest Parliament met at Salisbury, and the Law Term was kept at Winchester, where Sir Walter Raleigh was arraigned and received sentence for high treason under which fifteen years later he suffered. The Parliament of King Charles I. on his accession year was adjourned to Oxford. The High Court of Justice sat at Reading. Neither Parliament nor the Judges would dare assemble at Westminster, all London being fearfully stricken with Plague in those years.

The long visitation of 1640–47, when in eight years Plague claimed 14,420 dead (so recorded, and no doubt under-estimated) among the capital's small population, was to those living in Restoration London a comparatively recent memory. The older folk had more terrible memories of the epidemic of 1625. Many recalled with a shudder the ill omens of that year when King Charles I. stepped up to the Throne, which the frightful record of 41,313 dead from Plague in London within twelve months made grimly memorable. The City was one wide mortuary ; a reeking prison house of the living, the dying, and the dead. That was the worst Plague that London had ever experienced, save only the Black Death in the Middle Ages, for which figures are wanting ; [1] it has been roughly computed that

[1] London owes its possession of Charterhouse to the Black Death. A meadow was opened for huge pits into which the City's dead were cast, and afterwards a chapel stood there for those who came to pray for the souls of their relatives ; the chapel swelled into a monastery, which became in the whirl of events a ducal town house and lastly Thomas Sutton's famous foundation for poor brethren and scholars.

by the Black Death one-third of the country's entire population was swept away.

I am content to give a single record of the visitation of 1625, not from London, where scores of homes were swept clear of every living person, as this one, but taken out of the church registers of Malpas, in Cheshire. Ralph Dawson figures among the first six of his family buried within eleven days ; he came from London in mid-July sick of the Plague, and died in his father's house, infecting the whole household. The seventh entry tells of a surprising example of a man's fortitude when awaiting death—

. . . Richard Dawson, (brother to ye above named Thomas Dawson of Bradley) being sicke of ye plague and perceyveing he must die at yt time arose out of his bed and made his grave, and caused his nefew John Dawson ' to cast strawe into ye grave, which was not far from ye howse, and went and laid him down in ye said grave and caused clothes to be layd uppon him and soe dep'ted out of this world ; this he did because he was a strong man and heavier than his sayd nefew and another wench were able to burye, he died about ye xxiii of August. Thus much was I credibly tould, he died 1625.

John Dawson, sonne of the above mentioned Thomas, came into his father when his father sent for him beinge sicke, and haveing layd him down in a dich died in it, the XXIX daye of August 1625 in the night.

Rose Smyth, servant of the above named Thomas Dawson and last of yt household died of plague and was buryed by Wm Cooke the Vth day of September 1625 near unto the sayd howse.

Till 1665 came to give new experience to England of Plague's possibilities, the fateful epidemic of the year 1625 was always known as " the Great Plague," and as such it figures in contemporary literature and reference.

That name was to be handed on to a calamity far more terrible ; a calamity, indeed, that seemed to concentrate in a few brief months all the malignity of which Plague had been capable over half a century. It made the disaster much the worse that London was ill-prepared, and until realization of the full horror confronting them was borne home, the bulk of the people were stolidly indifferent. The Great Plague fell upon them unexpectedly. London, it was true, had in no single year over the past thirty years been entirely immune from Plague, but since 1648 it had been hardly appreciable—a case here, another there, never swelling into epidemic, and if noticed at all soon forgotten. The few precautions usual even in those careless days had been neglected. It had been better for London had the Londoners then living seen much more of Plague—or nothing; always the crowded, insanitary, timber-built town and its festering suburbs harboured the pestilence in some obscure corner. Look for the Plague's first signs, and one must look among the poor, whose squalid conditions of life when herded together in undrained and dirty tenements and hovels, or underground cellars, offered to it a ready lodgment. Even in the Great Plague no magistrate succumbed, and the deaths were not in large proportion among the parish officials who remained at their posts throughout the anxious months. The little body of doctors and apothecaries who courage-ously stayed to labour among the Plague-stricken paid a greater sacrifice.

And London had learned nothing. Sanitary science had not been born. Foul streams like the Fleet, defiled from every overhanging house and neighbouring alley, were no better than open sewers, and in parishes aligned upon the banks of these pestilent watercourses [1]—St. Bride's, St. Sepulchre's and St. Andrew's Holborn notably, and St. Giles's Cripplegate by the water-soaked moor—the Plague mark is most darkly drawn. Laystalls of rotting town refuse, the sweepings of streets, houses and middens, were piled high near inhabited quarters, poison-ing the air. The dead were buried thickly in graveyards surrounding the City churches; the living drew from wells water for household use which had percolated through the graveyards. At St. Clement Danes, St. Bride's, Cripplegate (Crowder's Well) and many more City places, each of the parish wells now closed, but commemorated by surviving pump or lettered tablet, is a churchyard well.

[1] Wherever in mediæval London there was running water, or for that matter stagnant water, the " houses of office "—closets—were built over, as affording the easiest way of performing the withdrawals now effected by water carriage and a drainage system ; and in parts of Restoration London the practice had not fallen into disuse.

London, it is true, had better water. Much of the town benefited by the New River service, brought in from Hertfordshire by Hugh Myddleton in King James I.'s reign. Spring water from Tybourne and the brooks could be drawn at the conduits that stood in the more important City streets. The riverside quarter depended largely on a supply raised direct from the Thames. There were many private wells. The streets were better kept than in Queen Elizabeth's and King Charles I.'s times, though alleys in wet weather often remained ankle deep in mud and foul water, and in the wider ways after every rainstorm, the water streamed from the house roofs upon the cobble stones and ran out to the kennels. But the value of fresh air and cleanliness in the person and the house was little understood. Confined wooden buildings, with projecting upper stories that almost met over streets and courts of but a few feet width, prevented healthy circulation of the air.

Let us realize that the picturesqueness of the timber-built city of gables and steep roofs, red-tiled, did not apply to the conditions of life for those who dwelt within the houses. They lived out of the picture that we vizualise. The thin framework of the front and rear, filled in with laths and made rain-tight with roughcast plaster, harboured dirt and damp. The method of frame building should have afforded ample opportunity for good lighting, but the rooms behind the attractive casement windows were in fact dark—dark and low. The house drained at best, and if at all, into a cesspool. It was rat-haunted as a matter of course.

The charm of Old London, as seen in prints and models, must not blind us to its many detractions. The un-cleanliness of the city differed little, if at all, from that of most Oriental towns to-day. One detects a touch of exaggeration in the author of "The Golden Coast," 1665, when comparing London with villages of Guinea that could be smelt leagues out at sea, but that such a com-parison should have been made suggests much. In an earlier age Cardinal Wolsey when passing about the town had the habit of holding to his nose an orange, in which pungent spices had been inserted, to keep back the smell that filled the streets ; and to this day there is borne in an ancient City custom observed each year a remembrance of their filthy condition. The Vintners Company, when going in procession from the hall in Vintry to service at church, sends ahead the Tackle Porters, wearing white aprons and wielding new brooms, to sweep a path clean before the Master and Wardens. It was an actual necessity in mediæval times to brush aside the mud and mire that fouled the streets before the fur-robed officials could make their progress unbesmirched.

In the period known for convenience as the Restoration, English practical medicine, hitherto obscured by the prestige of Continental professors, was to take its great modern start ; but as yet medical science crept painfully along the path of progress. In all that concerned Plague, its causation, its treatment and the conditions which favoured its spread, the doctors groped blindly in utter bewilderment. Light seemed to have broken in after the frightful visitation at King Charles I.'s accession. In 1636 the College of Physicians condemned as " Annoyances " likely to foster the spread of Plague the neglect in cleansing sewers and town ditches, the presence of standing pools of fœtid water, uncleanliness of the streets, the toleration of laystalls so near the living quarters, especially on the City's north side, the overflowing of the churchyards with Plague burials and use by the poor of rotting food.[1] The same annoyances remained in 1665. None can read without a feeling of despair the prescriptions which, at the instance of the Privy Council, the College issued in the English tongue for public use at the outbreak of the Great Plague ; [2] they are pathetic in their hopeless inadequacy.

Each visitation was met as had been the last. Plague was the will of God. The fatalism of the East seemed to have settled upon our people—or, at least, upon the masses who looked to the heavens for signs and portents, and frightened themselves with the mad-brained stuff poured out for them by the astrologers and quacks. Dr. Nathaniel Hodges wrote with a spice of humorous truth, that " the mischief was much more in the pre-

[1] College of Physicians MSS. (*Hist. MSS. Comm.*, 8th Rep., 229a).
[2] These are reprinted among *A Collection of Very Valuable & Scarce Pieces*, etc., London, 1721.

dictions of the star-gazers than in the stars themselves." [1]
The well-to-do had an old and tried expedient for salvation
in time of Plague, better than any doctor's potions—to
fly into the country away from it. The ruling classes,
the pious who in simple faith accepted Plague as the just
vindication of God's wrath upon the nation's sins, the
illiterate and the dumb neglected masses alike seemed
numbed by their helplessness in the presence of a calamity
which none could understand. It has significance that
when the Great Plague of 1665 struck London, it was not
to the gains won from experience over half a century that
the authorities turned for powers and guidance, but to an
Act passed by the first Parliament of King James I.[2]

Nothing is more necessary, if we are to take the true
measure of the Great Plague, than to know London's
population. The inquiry is beset with difficulties. There
can be little doubt that the population has been over-
stated by modern writers. In 1631 a census taken by
order of the Privy Council of men, women, and children
within the City and Liberties returned a total of 130,178,[3]
and on the basis of the deaths that year as recorded in the
Bills, the inhabitants of the out-parishes gave an additional
40,000, together 170,000 ; but with the bulk of the populace
illiterate, it may be imagined that the census was far from
full. John Graunt, an original Fellow of the Royal
Society, and the first man in this country to investigate
vital statistics scientifically, estimated in 1662 that the
City, Liberties, Westminster, and out-parishes contained
384,000 persons. As he used the births and deaths given
in the published Bills of Mortality, this is probably an
under-statement. In 1665 his estimate, made on a
different basis, was "not above 460,000." [4] Count
Cominges, the French Ambassador, declared that the
best informed spoke of a London population (in 1665) of
600,000,[5] but he passed on mere speculation ; there were
others, and among them City Aldermen, who in their

[1] Hodges' *Loimologia*, p. 5.
[2] *Statute 1st James I*, ch. 31.
[3] The return, giving the separate figures for each ward, is printed by
Graunt in his *Observations on the Bills of Mortality*, 3rd ed. 1665, p. 173.
[4] *Ibid.* p. 124 and p. 161 Appendix.
[5] " Relation de l'Angleterre en l'année 1666 " (Bibliothèque Nationale,
Paris, MSS. Fr. 15889).

ignorance counted London's population by millions.[1] Norwich, in that age the second most populous city in the kingdom, was known twenty-five years after the Great Plague to contain 30,000 inhabitants. Bristol, which came third, had 25,000.[2] The preponderance of London over rival cities was even greater than it is to-day.

No doubt there had been large accessions of traders and craftsmen who flocked to the capital to profit by the luxury which the Monarchy revived. It is rash to dogmatize, but after study of all available sources, I have become convinced that the population of London in 1665—City, Liberties, Westminster, and out-parishes—fell short of half a million.

None can tell the particular parish in which the Great Plague first appeared. The knowledge is not of momentous importance. As with all previous visitations, the infection began in the out-parishes, or suburbs, and only after slow progress made became lodged in the City. The first cases figuring in the Bills of Mortality of December and February in St. Giles-in-the-Fields do not stand alone. There were others about the close of 1664 in Westminster, where two or three persons in one family died suddenly, attacked by like symptoms which to Dr. Nathaniel Hodges manifestly declared their origin as Plague ; [3] and Boghurst says that Plague had appeared in St. Giles-in-the-Fields, St. Clement Danes, St. Paul Covent Garden, and St. Martin-in-the-Fields in the three or four years preceding. He had been so informed by people who themselves had it in their houses.[4] Dr. Hodges expressly asserts that the first cases were in Westminster, but the link with the fearful visitation of the next year is not strong. If Plague was already seated in London, it was kept down by the rigours of an unusually severe winter.

Hard frost came on in December, 1664, and for three months of the New Year rarely lifted. Pepys, up till two

[1] Graunt, pp. 119, 120.
[2] J. G. Muddiman, *The King's Journalist*, p. 3. The rise in importance and population of the great industrial and shipping towns of the North, Manchester, Liverpool, Leeds, Sheffield, and others, came long after the Restoration. Edward Chamberlayne, F.R.S., in *Angliæ Notitia* (3rd ed. 1669, p. 79), basing his calculations upon the numbers of houses in each parish, estimated the population of England at 5,446,000—far less than that of Greater London to-day.
[3] *Loimologia*, p. 5.   [4] *Loimographia*, p. 26.

o'clock on Christmas Eve, when he was called by the
bellman, went on to Tower Hill in the still, cold air to see
the comet, concerning which all tongues were agog, but
had no fortune. In January Evelyn coached through
Kent in " excessively sharp frost and snow " ; the 6th
February, his fellow-diarist writes, all men declared to be
òne of the coldest days they had ever experienced in
England. In two separate months ice blocked the
Thames, stopping the river traffic.[1] But Plague occasion-
ally showed its head even through the frost. There is
Dr. Hodges' testimony that very few died that season,
but he himself in January attended a case in which the
Plague spot was apparent ;[2] the patient recovered. John
Gadbury, the astrologer, who lived by Aldersgate, had
Plague during Christmastide, and he tells that Josiah
Westwood, his own surgeon, in the continuance of the
frost attended patients in whose condition he recognized
Plague. They obtained cure, " the air then being so
friendly to nature, and an enemy unto the Pestilence."[3]
Other indications suggest that instances of Plague were
not uncommon, but in the cold the disease never became
severe, and the deadly symptoms afterwards so familiar
were suppressed. Nothing of this was disclosed ; it is
worth mention, in view of the charges afterwards made of
so many false declarations of death, that none of the three
Westminster cases given by Hodges figures as Plague in
the Bills of Mortality.

If, by the circumstances of the visitation, no first case
can positively be traced, there is no difficulty in determining
where the first outbreak of the Plague in epidemic form
occurred. It was in St. Giles-in-the-Fields. Living in
that parish and labouring among the Plague-stricken poor
there was a worthy apothecary named William Boghurst.
In his healing work he courageously encountered the
gravest perils, and escaping infection himself, he wrote a
little brochure which is valuable for the careful observations it records.[4] Boghurst recalls that in the summer

[1] Rugge's " Diurnal " (Brit. Mus. Addit. MSS. No. 10,117, fo. 131).
[2] *Loimologia*, p. 6.
[3] Gadbury's *Londons Deliverance Predicted*, 1665.
[4] *Loimographia, an Account of the Great Plague of London in the Year*
1665. Ed. by J. F. Payne, M.D., for the London Epidemiological Society,
1894.

before the Great Plague smallpox was so rife in St. Giles's that between the church and the pound, a distance not above six score paces, about forty families were afflicted by it. Also that summer flies pestered the houses in such multitudes that they lined the walls, and where any thread or string hung down, it was presently thick set with flies like a rope of onions. Ants covered the highways, swarming so thickly that a handful at a time might have been taken up, and the croaking of numerous frogs was loudly heard even before the ditches sheltering them could be seen.

The influence of climate upon Plague is still imperfectly understood. The Great Plague occurred in a year of drought so severe that Richard Baxter, the divine, declares the winter, spring, and summer to have been " the driest that ever man alive knew, or our forefathers mention of late ages ; so that the grounds were burnt like the high-ways where the cattle should have fed. The meadow grounds where I lived (Acton) bare but four loads of hay which before bare forty." [1] The level of saturation in the ground fell unprecedentedly low. Long after the frost ended the conditions continued dry, no rain falling except a slight sprinkling at the end of April [2] till a few days of broken weather came in August,[3] followed after three weeks' interval of increasing heat by the torrential rains that put out the fires lighted in the London streets in September, in the groundless belief that they would destroy infection latent in the air.

[1] *Reliquiæ Baxterianæ*, 1696, p. 448.
[2] Boghurst's *Loimographia*, p. 29.
[3] Pepys's *Diary*, Aug. 13.

CHAPTER II

THE frost broke as soon as March was out, and epidemic Plague at once appeared. It is useless to search the Bills of Mortality for it ; a dozen adequate reasons existed why the dreaded disease should be concealed, and was in fact concealed. Plague was mostly among the poor, and knowledge of it first came to the overseers by the necessity of giving parish relief to the sufferers and their dependents. If a doctor in his practice attended a case that he recognized as Plague, he was under no duty to notify. Indeed, until the magistrates some weeks later took control there was no authority to be notified. If fatal results attended infection then, strange as it must seem to ourselves, that was not the doctor's concern.

In the upheaval of the Commonwealth, the control of the College of Physicians over the Faculty of Medicine had loosened. Early after the Restoration that learned body had strengthened its position and discipline and enlarged its depleted funds by admitting seventy doctors who had practised without its qualification.[1] Many practitioners had not received a college training. Apothecaries performed the duties of doctors. The distinction between the man qualified by knowledge and experience and the pretentious quack was less sharply drawn than in later times. Although never a year passed without isolated cases of Plague occurring in London, many doctors practising had not seen Plague. They might have suspicion, but lacked conviction. Were the hard central spot and scarlet ring about it—the " token "—present on a corpse, the sure sign of Plague, the doctor, though

[1] Munk's *Roll of College of Physicians*.

16

he had been attending from the first, was not called upon even to certify death.

We are confronting conditions wholly alien to everything accepted to-day, and warning may be repeated of the futility of observing the Great Plague through the medium of the twentieth-century knowledge and practice. Notification of death, now so exact, was the most careless of matters. None expected it of the doctor. Relatives were under no obligation to make known to any public authority the loss of a life. It was no national or county or civic officer's duty to ascertain death; in fact, no man's job. It was a woman's job—that of the " searchers of the dead."

They were women who filled the gruesome office, and those so employed were illiterate, without knowledge of disease, usually aged, and circumstances made them habitually dishonest. They gave the information to which every statement in the Bills of Mortality is traced back.

It was the parish which appointed " searchers," two or more in number, and as the office carried the right to exact a small fee, always it was given to a pauper woman who without such support would have become chargeable to the poor rate. The parishes were careful of their expenditure, and that was an economy.

Nothing looks more imposing than the long rows of names of diseases, and figures against them indicating the deaths from each, in the printed Bills of Mortality of the seventeenth century till after the Great Plague had passed. As vital statistics they are largely worthless, at best a rough guide. Some deaths were surely recorded— for instance, " Executed and pressed to death." The latter was, of course, the hideous practice of *peine forte et dure* within Newgate upon felons who refused to plead at trial. " Drowned," " shot," " fell from a ladder "—these offered small scope for mistake. But the rest give little ground for confidence. The procedure of notification was this. Intelligence of a death came to the parish church by a message for the bell to toll or for the sexton to prepare a grave. Hearing the toll, or receiving word from the sexton, the " searchers " would go out to the house of bereavement, to exercise their right of viewing the body and receiving a fee.

c

The Quakers, Jews, Anabaptists, and other sectaries refused to notify their deaths to a Church with which they had nothing in common, or to ask for tolling of the bell. They buried their own dead, and mortality among them mostly, and in the earlier stages of the Great Plague wholly, escaped record in the Bills. A solitary exception I was surprised to find in the burial register of the City church of Allhallows Bread Street, where the parish clerk made this entry of tragedy among Quaker neighbours—

Aug. 16.—Mrs Clements wife of Jacob Clements in the ground   plague.
Sept. 1.—The sonn of Mr Clements at the quakers new ground   plague.
Sept. 3.—Mr Jacob Clements att the quakers ground plague.

In Plague time the searchers lived as outcasts from the community they served, performing duties hazardous to themselves as to others. They were required to lodge at a place appointed, not going abroad more than was necessary, and then only in execution of their duty. They were to absent themselves from their families, and always to avoid the society of others. In their walk they should keep as far distant from others as might be, carrying in the hand a white wand by which pedestrians should know and avoid them. To do that they took oath.[1] Upon these ancient matrons devolved the task of examining by what disease death occurred. They reported to the clerk of the parish, who each week returned a list of deaths to the Company of Parish Clerks at their hall in Brode Lane, Vintry. The Company in turn gave the information to the Lord Mayor, by whom, when Plague roused public interest, it was passed on to the Minister of State. From the material so derived the Bill of Mortality was made up and printed. Sometimes the women searchers learnt the doctor's opinion, at others they were given the cause of death by relatives, but often they depended upon their own crude observation of the corpse, which to an unskilled eye can have indicated little. They relied largely upon

[1] John Bell, *Londons Remembrancer*, 1665. The searchers' oath as administered when Plague broke out in Colchester in July is preserved (Brit. Mus., Stowe MSS. 840, fo. 46). They swore to report the cause of death " honestly, unfeignedly and impartially," to the best of their skill.

signs, which after a little experience gained sufficed for a rude classification.

John Graunt, the statistician, writing four years before the Great Plague, scoffs at the frequency of consumption in these women's reports. " The old-women Searchers (says he) after the mist of a Cup of Ale, and the bribe of a Two-groat fee instead of one given them, cannot tell whether this emaciation or leanness were from a Phthisis or from a Hectick Fever." [1] I imagine that few people realize how casual was registration, not only in the seventeenth century, but through much of the eighteenth and, although improved, even into the nineteenth century, and how long was the dependence upon the parish clerks and " searchers of the dead " for vital statistics. The old-women searchers, with their right of intrusion into the house of bereavement, exercised their office down to the passing of the Registration Act. [2] The date of the Registration Act was 1836. Venereal disease, a frightful scourge, even with those who died out of the lock-hospitals in Southwark and at Kingsland, [3] was in Restoration times habitually concealed as ulcers and sores, and only by the clerks of St. Giles-in-the-Fields and St. Martin-in-the-Fields was honestly returned, those being the two parishes in which lay the vilest and most miserable houses of uncleanness. [4] It was simple to dissolve doubts by calling a case " fever."

The burial register of St. Paul Covent Garden has these entries—

April 12. — Margarit Dau of Dr John Ponteus Bu[ried] Church pla.

May 13.—Mrs Bowler Bu Church yard plage.

[1] John Graunt's *Observations*, p. 46.

[2] John Tilley, Clerk of the Parish Clerks Company, giving evidence before the Select Committee on Parochial Registration in 1833, said : " The office of searchers is confined to two old women, generally paupers, who are legally entitled to ask a fee of fourpence, and on their hearing from the parish clerk that there had been a death in any house they go and demand a sight of the body. Being very needy people, they are open, of course, to any fee that may be given them to dispense with their office altogether. If instead of fourpence they get a shilling or half a crown, they go away without looking at the body."

[3] Both were " outhouses " of the great medical foundation of St. Bartholomew's Hospital, Smithfield, in charge of assistant surgeons borne on the hospital staff. Probably these places were originally leper houses.

[4] Graunt's *Observations*, p. 46.

Neither of these Plague cases figures in the printed Bills of Mortality, obviously in this instance by wilful concealment of the parish clerk who himself entered them in the register. The Bills represent the parish as free from fatal Plague till late June. Few of the earliest cases were notified.

The Bills of Mortality must not be read as are the returns of our own Registrar-General, or allowed authenticity they do not possess. They were in origin essentially a warning of the existence of Plague in London. They first gave the sum totals of the dead, and Plague or no Plague ; only later were the statistics of separate diseases introduced. Death mattered little two and a half centuries ago. In Plague time, the temptation to bribe the searcher or parish clerk to make a false report was terribly strong. Human nature asserted itself. Could it humanly be expected that the widower should resist temptation, knowing that were the truth exposed, neighbours would shun him and his motherless children for fear of infection ? Later, when epidemic spread, how should a family be expected to disclose Plague, knowing full well that all would be shut up together in the infected house for forty days, all closely confined with any fresh cases of Plague that might break out amongst them ? That was the practice ; the law allowed it. " Bring out your dead ! "— London came to know that cry too well. Whose fortune could be worth such a fate ? That the Plague return should be falsified in many thousands of instances was inevitable. The return of 68,596 in the visitation of the Great Plague in 1665 probably is short of the truth by fully twenty-five thousand, by wilful or ignorant misdescription and unrecorded burials in the cemeteries and the ghastly Plague pits.[1]

The cases came slowly into the Bills of Mortality. The

[1] Even in the total number of burials recorded in the confusion of the Plague, the church registers of an individual parish rarely agree with the returns made in the Bills of Mortality for that parish, the register's numbers being often the larger. The burial register of St. Giles-in-the-Fields contains no entries between May 13 and June 22, when they are continued by another hand, after some pages left blank. It is surmised that the clerk, whose duties brought him into close contact with those who came direct from infected houses, himself died of Plague, and that the burials recorded on loose slips till another clerk could be found were never entered.

	Bur.	Plag.		Bur.	Plag.		Bur.	Plag.
St Alban Woodstreet	11	8	St George Botolphlane			St Martin Ludgate	4	4
Alhallows Barking	13	11	St Gregory by St Pauls	9	5	St Martin Orgars	8	6
Alhallows Breadstreet	1	1	St Hellen			St Martin Outwitch	1	
Alhallows Great	6	5	St James Dukes place	7	5	St Martin Vintrey	17	17
Alhallows Honylane			St James Garlickhithe	3		St Matthew Fridaystreet	1	
Alhallows Lesse	3	2	St John Baptist	7	4	St Maudlin Milkstreet	2	2
Alhallows Lumbardstreet	6	4	St John Evangelist			St Maudlin Oldfishstreet	8	4
Alhallows Staining	7	5	St John Zachary	1		St Michael Bassishaw	12	11
Alhallows the Wall	23	11	St Katharine Coleman	5		St Michael Cornhil	3	
St Alphage	18	10	St Katharine Crechurch	7	4	St Michael Crookedlane	7	4
St Andrew Hubbard	1		St Lawrence Jewry	2		St Michael Queenhithe	7	6
St Andrew Undershaft	14	9	St Lawrence Pountney	6	5	St Michael Quern	1	
St Andrew Wardrobe	21	16	St Leonard Eastcheap			St Michael Royal	2	
St Ann Aldersgate	18	11	St Leonard Fosterlane	17	13	St Michael Woodstreet	2	1
St Ann Blackfryers	22	17	St Magnus Parish	2		St Mildred Breadstreet	2	1
St Antholins Parish			St Margaret Lothbury	2		St Mildred Poultrey	4	3
St Austins Parish			St Margaret Moses			St Nicholas Acons		
St BartholomewExchange	2	2	St MargaretNewfishstreet	1		St Nicholas Coleabby	1	
St Bennet Fynck	2	2	St Margaret Pattons	1		St Nicholas Olaves	3	1
St Bennet Gracechurch			St Mary Abchurch	1		St Olave Hartstreet	7	4
St Bennet Paulswharf	16	8	St Mary Aldermanbury	11	5	St Olave Jewry	1	1
St Bennet Sherehog			St Mary Aldermary	5	1	St Olave Silverstreet	23	9
St Botolph Billingsgate	2		St Mary le Bow	6	6	St Pancras Soperlane		
Chrits Church	27	22	St Mary Bothaw	1		St Peter Cheap	1	1
St Christophers	1		St Mary Colechurch			St Peter Cornhil	7	6
St Clement Eastcheap			St Mary Hill	1		St Peter Paulswharf	5	2
St Dionis Backchurch	2	1	St Mary Mounthaw	1		St Peter Poor	3	2
St Dunstan East	7		St Mary Sommerset	6	5	St Steven Colemanstreet	15	11
St Edmund Lumbardstr.	2	2	St Mary Stayning	1		St Steven Walbrook		
St Ethelborough	13	7	St Mary Woolchurch			St Swithin	2	2
St Faith	6	6	St Mary Woolnoth	1	1	St Thomas Apostle	8	7
St Foster	13	11	St Martin Iremongerlane			Trinity Parish	5	3
St Gabriel Fenchurch	1							

Christned in the 97 Parishes within the Walls —— 34   Buried —— 538   Plague —— 366

	Bur.	Plag.		Bur.	Plag.		Bur.	Plag.
St Andrew Holborn	432	220	St Botolph Aldgate	238	212	Saviours Southwark	160	12
St Bartholomew Great	58	50	St Botolph Bishopsgate	288	236	S. Sepulchres Parish	403	27
St Bartholomew Lesse	19	15	St Dunstan West	36	29	St Thomas Southwark	24	21
St Bridget	147	119	St George Southwark	80	60	Trinity Minories	8	5
Bridewel Precinct	7	5	St Giles Cripplegate	847	572	At the Pesthouse	9	9
St Botolph Aldersgate	70	61	St Olave Southwark	235	131			

Christned in the 16 Parishes without the Walls —— 61   Buried, and at the Pesthouse —— 2861   Plague —— 2139

	Bur.	Plag.		Bur.	Plag.		Bur.	Plag.
St Giles in the fields	204	175	Lambeth Parish	13	9	St Mary Islington	50	45
Hackney Parish	12	8	St Leonard Shoreditch	252	168	St Mary Whitechappel	319	27
St James Clerkenwel	172	172	St Magdalen Bermondsey	57	36	Rotherith Parish	7	2
St Kath. near the Tower	40	34	St Mary Newington	74	52	Stepney Parish	371	27

Christned in the 12 out Parishes in Middlesex and Surry —— 49   Buried —— 1571   Plague —— 1244

	Bur.	Plag.		Bur.	Plag.		Bur.	Plag.
St Clement Danes	94	78	St Martin in the fields	255	193	St Margaret Westminster	220	19
St Paul Covent Garden	18	16	St Mary Savoy	11	10	whereof at the Pesthouse		13

Christned in the 5 Parishes in the City and Liberties of Westminster —— 27   Buried —— 598   Plague —— 488

A LONDON BILL OF MORTALITY.   (OBVERSE)

second and third for the year were reported together in
the week April 18th to 25th, both from St. Giles-in-the-
Fields—not before. Next week the Bill was again clear,
but the first complete week in May, the 2nd to 9th, showed
nine Plague deaths. Three were in St. Giles's, and Plague
had crossed into the neighbouring parish of St. Clement
Danes, wherein were four deaths. Two houses were shut
up in Drury Lane.[1] Plague crept with slow and halting
progress along Holborn and down Chancery Lane [2] to the
Strand, a dread, invisible thing. A victim was claimed in
St. Andrew Holborn, a parish standing part within and
part without the City Liberties ; and—most significant—
a Plague death occurred in the heart of the City itself, at
St. Mary Woolchurch Haw, where to-day the Mansion
House stands.[3] Hodges infers that Plague was carried
there by some timorous persons who had moved out of
Westminster into the City.[4] The Quakers have a contemporary record that the first Plague death within the
City wall was in Bearbinders Lane, at a house a few doors
distant from that of Edward Brush, who was the first
Quaker to be transported to the plantations under the
persecuting Conventicle Act.[5]

Next week the recorded mortality from Plague went
down to three, and in the following week, from the 16th to
23rd May, it rose to fourteen, a case being through Temple
Bar, in the Fleet Street parish of St. Dunstan's West. In
the last week of May there were seventeen cases.

The Bills are, in truth, a most delusive guide. The
people had been stolidly indifferent when first the Plague
spread, deceived by concealment and evasions, seeing little
beyond what they were accustomed to in the three isolated
deaths reported till May. Keen distress had been
occasioned by the prolonged frost, which had thrown
thousands of the poorer workers out of employment, and
made pitiful their struggle for existence ; the contribution
for relief being insufficient, the Lord Mayor before the
thaw came issued a precept to the City Companies requir-

[1] John Allin's letters, April 27.
[2] Allin, May 26.
[3] See *London's Dreadful Visitation ; or a Collection of all the Bills of
Mortality for this present year*, London, 1665.
[4] Hodges' *Loimologia*, p. 2.
[5] George Whitehead's *Christian Progress*, p. 300.

ing a charitable collection to be made amongst the Livery-men.[1] When spring, fine, warm, and dry, changed the whole face of Nature, and brought forgetfulness of the sharp winter which had entailed great suffering and affliction chiefly upon the poor—the herald of the most tragic summer London had known—the evidences of Plague were obvious to the dullest. The red cross of Plague was marked upon more doors in the mean alleys, giving its significant message. Then alarm grew apace ; the people, as always, magnified the things which before had seemed so small. They knew better than they were told.

They knew there was Plague in London, already so swollen that these few foolish returns gave a fantastic misrepresentation of it. Neighbour talked to neighbour ; that was the common channel of information when few could read and write, and be sure this exchange of news did not minimize the Plague's gravity or extent. Why had comets appeared in the sky ? The very stars in their courses betokened evil about to fall upon the city.

Most unhappily it had become a received notion among the masses that Plague broke out in England once in twenty years, as if it were something inevitable. The cycle had come round, and people terrified one another with remembrances of the last long visitation of the pestilence,[2] with its 3,597 dead of Plague in the year 1647.

Even while the public knew nothing, the ruling authori-ties had awakened to the prospect of a grave outbreak of Plague. In part deceived themselves, they cannot be acquitted of a share in wilful concealment, which fear of disorders alone can have excused. In its persistence, and the disturbing spread outwards from the first centre of infection, this visitation differed wholly from the isolated cases of previous years. War being declared with Holland, Parliament had met to vote money for the vigorous prosecution of hostilities, and when March had passed was well content to disperse, there being indications of Plague in the town's outskirts. It was prorogued till June, and then again until August, on this last occasion

[1] Jupp and Pocock, *Carpenters Company*, p. 127.
[2] *Loimologia*, p. 3.

with an intimation from the King that if the pestilence had by that time subsided he would gladly meet the two Houses again, to make report upon the war's progress. But if the infection unhappily increased, members would be notified by Proclamation whereby they should have no need to hazard themselves.[1]

One imagines that Charles had small hope. London by August had become so transformed as to be almost unrecognizable as the capital to which the Restoration had brought reinvigorated life and prosperity. The Royalist emigrés whose return had set an example for licentiousness of manners, a profusion of luxury and the squandering of fortunes with a recklessness unknown in dour days of the Commonwealth, were again sent scattering by an enemy more potent than Cromwell; and the merchant class following them in the flight, they left a town in part depopulated and in extreme poverty. The Plague enlarged with slow and measured progress, irresistible and in its nature the more alarming because without any set-backs, till with the heat of summer it developed the capacity for destruction of human life on the vast scale which has made this visitation of 1665 memorable for all time as the Great Plague.

In April, when still the Bills of Mortality indicated only three deaths from Plague in the four months of the year then passed, the Privy Council directed the Lord Chief Justice to give orders to the justices of the peace of Middlesex that all houses suspected of infection be examined. Where Plague was found they should shut them up. The reference to the Chief Justice notified Plague in St. Giles-in-the-Fields and other out-parishes.[2] A week later (May 4th) an order to the City and Liberties of like effect was made by the King's Bench. Constables were to act promptly in shutting up infected houses, and to prohibit all persons from conversing with those within.[3]

The Chief Justice and the magistrates met in conference, and authority was given to the latter to use all means that should be deemed expedient to stay the contagion.

---

[1] Clarendon's *Life*, ed. 1827, ii. 352–3.
[2] Privy Ccl. Reg. 58, fo. 114.
[3] Addit. MSS. 4182, fo. 15.

Had three deaths since December represented the toll of Plague in London—all the public were told of—then that action was inexplicable. As many had occurred in years when none troubled about them. London had not known epidemic Plague for close upon twenty years ; there was no reason for these few isolated cases to excite fear—if they represented the fact. The magistrates knew that the Bills were falsified. The measures betoken alarm. Plague mortality was always in exceedingly high percentage of the numbers of persons attacked ; and that such far-reaching powers should have been given is sufficient refutation of the Bills. A few days after the justices were authorized by warrant to purchase ground for the erection of pest-houses, and to open byways giving access thereto.[1] In the years of immunity no provision of the kind had been attempted.

April was not out before the town had witness of the deep-seated hostility which the practice of shutting up infected houses with the people within them was to bring about. Among the first houses so sealed in St. Giles-in-the-Fields was one in certain New Buildings, showing the sign of the Ship. The parish officers chalked the red cross of Plague on the door, and affixed thereon a printed paper. A riotous assembly of neighbours obliterated the cross and tore down the paper, then forced open the locked door and allowed the inmates to go freely into the street. Severe punishment overtook those of the rioters who fell into the magistrates' hands.[2]

Ignorance on the part of the authorities as to the inevitable results of their own chief measure of prevention, and the open hostility of the populace to the measures undertaken, both served the same end. The Plague enlarged.

The King and those about him on May 12th arrived at a momentous decision. They entertained no illusions. A Privy Council Committee was appointed, to meet without delay next morning, charged " to consider of the best means of preventing the spreading of the infection of the Plague," to revise all former orders made to that purpose, and to make such new orders as should seem most expedient. Epidemic Plague admittedly was in London.

[1] *State Papers (Domestic)*, 1665, p. 432.
[2] Privy Ccl. Reg. 58, fo. 118.

They were Charles's most trusted advisers who were chosen for this task. Monck Duke of Albemarle had given the King his Throne, and next to the monarch himself was the one outstanding figure among the public men of the time. His participation would have assured importance to any committee. Henry Benet Lord Arlington was Secretary of State. Wriothesley Earl of Southampton held the troubled office of Lord Treasurer. The Earl of Manchester was Lord Chamberlain ; and besides these forming the Committee of Privy Council were the Duke of Ormonde, the Earl of Bath, the Comptroller, the Vice-Chamberlain, and Mr. Secretary Morice, numbering nine in all.[1]

The Committee called physicians into consultation, and a week later made a first report. It directed an additional pest-house to be built in St. Giles-in-the-Fields. There were but two other recommendations then made to the magistrates : that the number of alehouses to which persons resorted in infected areas should be lessened, and that the laws against harbouring " inmates " be strictly enforced — the overcrowding of the squalid dwellings built thick and close in poor quarters on the town's outskirts.[2]

L'Estrange's *Newes* was already printing by May 18th the advertisement of " An excellent preservative against the Plague Pestilence," to be obtained, price two shillings and sixpence, from a quack named R. T. Rooks at the Lamb and Inkbottle in St. Paul's Churchyard—the first of a lengthy series of such mendacious advertisements.

The outbreak occurring in St. Giles-in-the-Fields, was upon the highest land about London as at that time limited, where St. Giles's Church crowned the slow ascent from the River Thames. It had chosen for its appearance no low-lying, water-soaked soil wherein fever might first be expected. None had greater reason than the Lord Mayor to watch with growing anxiety the spread of Plague into the adjacent out-parishes. These had been the first infected at previous visitations, and always from them the infection had travelled back into the City. Sir John Lawrence, Alderman of Queenhithe Ward, had been

[1] Privy Ccl. Reg. 58, fo. 142.
[2] *Ibid.* 58, fo. 143.

placed in the Mayoral chair in the previous October.[1]
No warning shadow of the impending calamity had
darkened his entrance to office, with ceremonial which
had been unusually brilliant. King Charles II. had paid
him the signal honour of himself watching Lawrence's
pageant, the Queen being with him, though it was a foul
rainy day, and he had dined at the Lord Mayor's feast.
Evelyn was there, much impressed by the greatness of
the company at Guildhall, for besides the King at the
upper table were Count Cominges, the French Ambassador ; Hyde, the Lord Chancellor ; George Villiers Duke
of Buckingham ; Albemarle, Southampton, Arlington,
Ormonde, and the rest of the Great Officers of State—the
circle immediately about the King.

My Lord Mayor came twice up to us, first drinking in the
golden goblet his Majesty's health, then the French King's as
a compliment to the Ambassador ; we returned my Lord
Mayor's health, the trumpets and drums sounding. The cheer
was not to be imagined for plenty and rarity, with an infinite
number of persons in that ample hall. The feast was said
to have cost £1,000. I slipped away in the crowd, and came
home late.[2]

The Plague-threatening, but while still no City parish
save Woolchurch reported infection, the Lord Mayor in
May issued a Proclamation for care of the streets. From
their neglected state danger arose. The inhabitants were
directed each morning to water, sweep, and cleanse the
streets before their doors, removing all dirt and rubbish.
That was, not alone at Plague times but at all others, a
private and not a public duty, householders being required
to maintain the cobble pavement each from his own house
front to the middle of the street, and to be responsible for
its condition, though there were scavengers and rakers
to remove the most offensive matters from the public
ways and the houses. After a fortnight's lapse came
another Mayoral Proclamation, complaining that the
streets were lying more filthy and noisome than before.

[1] Lord Mayor's Day was moved on to November 9 when eleven days
were taken out of the calendar, on the belated change made in 1750 from
the Old to the New Style. The reform still met with much ignorant
hostility, and a popular cry was, " Give us back our eleven days ! "
[2] Evelyn's *Diary*, 1664, Oct. 29.

The Aldermen of the different wards were charged to see to it, and to report all persons failing in this duty, that they might be punished.[1]

A foul passage along the bed of the last remnant of the ancient town ditch behind Christ's Hospital was closed as a measure of precaution.[2]

Still the Plague leapt up, and always the fated parish of St. Giles-in-the-Fields bore the larger burden of it. In the first week of June the figures in the Bills of Mortality —whatever their worth—more than doubled ; forty-three deaths from Plague, of which St. Giles's contributed thirty-one. The second week, ending on June 13th, these figures were nearly trebled ; 112 deaths from Plague, towards which St. Giles's gave the melancholy number of sixty-eight. The third week of June, St. Giles's mortality from the pestilence over-topped the hundred. None now could question the prevalence of Plague. The parish to-day takes roughly the shape of a carpenter's square, or letter **L**, with the Seven Dials at the bend, stretching far along the Tottenham Court Road in one direction, and down the length of Holborn towards the City to Great Turnstile ; but at the time of the Plague it bulked larger in area before Bloomsbury had been taken from it. Bloomsbury was green meadow land, with as yet but a single resident of note, Wriothesley Earl of Southampton, the Lord Treasurer, who had built his great house there. New Oxford Street had not been cut out, and St. Giles's Church, now sheltered and remote from the roaring traffic, stood conspicuously upon the highway that ran by Holborn and Broad Street and High Street into the road, lined with flowering hedges, that led to Tyburn. In years later than Charles II., felons going out to their doom on the triple tree customarily received at St. Giles's Church door their last glass of ale.

St. Giles-in-the-Fields remained right up to the month of August the darkest Plague spot upon London's map, when pre-eminence in this monstrous horror was taken by another parish of St. Giles—that by Cripplegate. June opened with torrid heat, the worst condition for spread of Plague. " The hottest day that ever I felt in

[1] Guildhall " Journal " 46, fos. 59b, 60.
[2] Guildhall " Repertory " 70, fo. 134b.

my life," Pepys jotted down in his diary of the 7th of the month, and he remained in his garden till midnight watching the vivid lightning. The mortality from infection in this ill-fated parish alone was then three times as great as that in all the rest of London.

The sad experience made St. Giles-in-the-Fields a source of hatred. "That one parish of St. Giles at London hath done us all this mischief," Sir Thomas Peyton wrote with bitterness at a later stage of the epidemic.[1]

The parish officers had yet to learn the advisability of timely provision for the relief of those infected, and of keeping check upon "inmates"[2]—the lodgers herding in the poorest quarters whose squalid conditions of life made them the first likely victims of Plague. Lying out west of the City, St. Giles's in its populated part was essentially a town area, built about Holborn as its main street. It had in Whetstone Park the most notorious of the Restoration resorts of ill-fame; and there and elsewhere its streets were thick and foul with the filth, the profligacy and misery that then and long afterwards made the St. Giles's Rookery a byword and disgrace to London till its clearance, less than a century ago. Difficult in any case, the situation was made worse by the migration of the derelicts, the needy and the destitute of other parishes into the slum areas of St. Giles's. The poor in their fœtid slums the Plague struck first and fiercest and with the greatest persistence. It was to earn the ominous name of "the poore's Plague."[3]

If Plague could be strangled in its hotbed, in St. Giles-in-the-Fields it was to be found. The magistrates sought to isolate it. By their orders, constables of the different parishes encircling St. Giles's set warders at all roads leading thereto. They suffered no vagrant or loose persons to pass out from St. Giles's, or others suspected to come from infected houses or alleys.[4]

As a measure of quarantine the step was wise, and had it been taken when first the frost broke, London might have been saved much distress. In a detached rural

---

[1] *State Papers (Domestic)*, 1664–5, p. 504.
[2] Vest. Mins. July 3, 1666.
[3] Hodges' *Loimologia*, p. 15.
[4] Privy Ccl. Reg. 58, fo. 187.

The Diseases and Casualties this Week.

Abortive	4
Aged	45
Bleeding	1
Broken legge	1
Broke her scull by a fall in the street at St. Mary Wool-church	1
Childbed	28
Chrisomes	9
Consumption	126
Convulsion	89
Cough	1
Dropsie	53
Feaver	348
Flox and Small-pox	11
Flux	1
Frighted	2
Gowt	1
Grief	3
Griping in the Guts	79
Head-mould-shot	1
Jaundies	7

Imposthume	8
Infants	22
Kingsevil	4
Lethargy	1
Livergrown	1
Meagrome	1
Palsie	1
Plague	4237
Purples	2
Quinsie	5
Rickets	23
Rising of the Lights	18
Rupture	1
Scurvy	3
Shingles	1
Spotted Feaver	166
Stilborn	4
Stone	2
Stopping of the stomach	17
Strangury	3
Suddenly	2
Surfeit	74
Teeth	111
Thrush	6
Tissick	9
Ulcer	1
Vomiting	10
Winde	4
Wormes	20

Christned	Males	90		Buried	Males	2777		
	Females	81			Females	2791		Plague—4237
	In all	171			In all	5568		

Increased in the Burials this Week ———— 249
Parishes clear of the Plague —— 27   Parishes Infected —— 103

The Assize of Bread set forth by Order of the Lord Major and Court of Aldermen,
A penny Wheaten Loaf to contain Nine Ounces and a half, and three
half-penny White Loaves the like weight.

THE SAME BILL OF MORTALITY. (REVERSE)

parish it might have been effective. Unhappily, St. Giles's situation was the worst possible. How should they prevent the egress of Plague—carried none knew how—from a parish almost shouldering the City and its crowded skirts, with streets of poor houses continuous with those of the City? Even as the warders were attempting a sanitary patrol of St. Giles-in-the-Fields, Plague was newly asserting itself in St. Martin-in-the-Fields, in St. Andrew Holborn, and in St. Dunstan-in-the-West. It had got round to Cripplegate, where late in May a house was closed and the red cross marked on the door [1]—forerunner of the frightful visitation in that parish. A death was reported at Whitechapel, and another from distant Islington.[2]

It was a large churchyard, that of St. Giles-in-the-Fields, and still it is among the largest in London. It did not afford space, nor was there time, for the decency of single burials. The Rev. Robert Boreman was rector of St. Giles's. His name commands respect, for he had the courage and fortitude to live and work among his parishioners throughout all the tragic months when Plague desolated his parish. His sexton was John Geere. The time had come for Geere to set labourers to open a pit, and it was in St. Giles's churchyard that they dug. It was, in fact, the first of five pits that were excavated in the churchyard, and were filled to overflowing before the Great Plague in London had passed over, leaving these livid scars. They were great pits, dug deep in the soil, long and wide. For the digging the parish paid £4 9s.[3] Labourers' wages were then one shilling and sixpence for a long day's toil. Bearing that in mind, one takes a mental vision of these pits' cavernous extent, of the depth whereon a thin overlay of earth concealed so much horror.

Forbear to look too curiously into those shuddering Plague pits, and there came to be so many of them elsewhere. A single passage from a contemporary letter tells enough—

Carts are the beare[r]s, wide pits are the graves. The carkasses of the dead may say with the sons of the prophets, "Behould the place where we lye is strait for us," for they are not allowed to lye single in there earthen beds, but are

---

[1] Allin, May 26.   [2] *Bills of Mortality.*   [3] Ch'wardens' Accts.

piled up like fagots in a stack for the society of there future
resurrection.[1]

The alarming rise of mortality in a badly infected parish
may be illustrated by the weekly figures in St. Giles-in-
the-Fields, taken from the published Bills. For three
months before the Great Plague came, the average weekly
number of burials in St. Giles's had been nineteen, and
the previous year fifteen—

For The Week Ending.			Deaths from All Causes.	Of These Attri- buted to Plague.
May 30	.	. .	53	9
June 6	.	. .	74	31
,, 13	.	. .	120	68
,, 20	.	. .	150	101
,, 27	.	. .	185	143

A month later the highest mortality above shown
had doubled ; in St. Giles's parish 370 perished in the
week ending July 25th, and of these deaths, 323 were
attributed to Plague. For every three persons buried
in normal times the ill-fated parish that week was burying
seventy-three. St. Giles's had no worse record than this.
A bellman had gone round the streets with the burial-cart,
notifying the presence of each load of death ; but so many
died that the constant clang only filled the people with
fears, and in mercy the bell was silenced.[2] The Plague
in St. Giles's reached the top of its curve. It spread from
this first centre of infection east and south over the out-
parishes, thence in its onward stride carrying a great
burden of death to the City's northern outskirts by
Clerkenwell and Cripplegate to Bishopsgate, and across
the river settled over Southwark, before the City within
the walls was grievously visited.

We have become so accustomed to thinking of the
Great Plague *in London* that probably few realize how
vast was the tragedy outside the City. Of the 97,306
recorded deaths from all causes in the Plague year, no
fewer than 40,748 occurred in the out-parishes, the
remainder being within the City and its Liberties, a proportion of eight to eleven. That the out-parishes, thinly

[1] John Sturgeon to Sir Robert Harley, Portland MSS. (*Hist. MSS.
Comm.*, iii. 292).

[2] Hearne to Blythe, July 18, in Clare College MSS., Cambridge.

peopled for their area and enjoying fresher air, should
have suffered so severely seems inexplicable—until it is
explained. For to the citizen of King Charles II.'s Restoration the City with its Liberties was London. The City
had the Cathedral of St. Paul and the one hundred and
nine parish churches; it had some fifty-three Companies'
halls, headquarters of the craft gilds; it had Guildhall;
it had the Exchange, then London's chief mart, and the
various public buildings, the shipping interests of the
Thames—all was concentrated there that goes to make
a capital city, self-governed. I have said elsewhere that

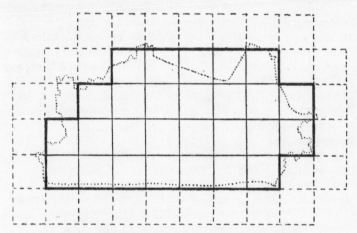

ROUGH PLAN OF THE CITY IN EQUAL SQUARES.
The City's actual ground plan is shown by the dotted lines.

nearly everything we know to-day as London save this
central spot was green fields.[1]

The explanation is, of course, that population spreading
outwards from a centre increases in rapid ratio as the
radius expands. A diagram here printed makes this
clear. The City with its Liberties is roughly represented
in outline by the thick line, the plot being divided into
twenty-seven equal squares. The belt represented by
broken lines outside the thick outline contains twenty-
eight squares of equal size. In other words, a belt no
wider than the distance between Temple Bar and St. Mary

[1] *The Great Fire of London in* 1666, 3rd ed., 1923.

le Strand Church drawn around the City's boundary has more area than is required to contain the whole mass of houses and population that is contained within the City and Liberties, Cathedral, Guildhall, churches, markets and all else.

That is obvious, yet who would give significance to this narrow external belt ? It seems a mere fringe, though in fact it has the larger area. To the average mind the solid, central block in this rude map, stretching wide about the towering Cathedral on the hill, would represent London.

Under pressure of population London had spread out, spreading not far, but here and there for this little space. It followed from the method of London's growth, first from within the City wall out into the Liberties, then an out-thrust into the county parishes, that population was thickest, not at the centre, but in this outer fringe— because it was thickest where the poorest classes were thickest. It is general report that London was unusually crowded with the poorer classes, to whom the revived luxury of the rich gave a livelihood. The City itself harboured numbers of them, in decaying houses, in cellars, and in alleys down by the waterside ; but multitudes of the poorest people failed to find accommodation within the walls, where generally space brought better reward from shops for handcrafts and the sale of goods and from warehouses. They herded thickly in the Liberties and the slums they created about the outer edge ; at St. Andrew Holborn, St. Giles's and neighbouring western parishes, in Clerkenwell, Cripplegate, Whitechapel, and Ratcliffe, and across the river at Southwark and Bermondsey.

The Liberties had themselves been the suburbs of London till the break-up of the religious houses, and by hasty building in Elizabeth's and James I.'s reigns upon the forecourts and rear gardens of the ecclesiastical mansions they had become as densely built as the walled City. But the Liberties, if stifling by the close contact of too many people, were old enough to be opened up for trade by streets. The out-parishes, where they touched the Liberties, had not this small advantage of space and air. They had no main arteries besides the country highways into London, which made the one thread of communication. Left and right of these, the low overhanging wooden houses, ill-kept, dark and congested, covered the ground in seemingly impenetrable rookeries of filthy courts and blind alleys. Back-to-back building was customary, to save cost and space, and none thought ill of it. Many dwellings—the majority hereabouts, indeed—were weather-boarded ; and to an observant eye they presented a drab of exposed wood unrelieved by paint, the pitch that was the sole covering worn away, and crevices in these fragile walls and decay in the roofs let in damp and rain.

To such conditions of life thousands of Londoners were condemned. We have no slums like these, for in the most sordid quarters of East London to-day there are at least a pure water supply, and drainage, and refuse removal. The foul habitations on the town's outskirts, knowing nothing of these advantages, are amongst the most ominous things in the Plague story. The City's government by Lord Mayor, Aldermen and Common Council, far short as it fell of such sanitary ideas as this generation holds, did not reach out to them. The out-parishes stood apart, each separate parish self-controlled by its own vestry and its vestry-appointed officers, and subject to no central authority. None troubled about drainage for these town slums. Each house sheltered many poor families in tenements, in various stages of dilapidation. In places the squalid dwellings stood upon ground whereon, till the populace spread outwards, had been heaped the City's laystalls. Finsbury Fields for centuries had been " a common laystall of all filth that was to be voided out of the city." [1]

The greatest toll of Plague outside the City was in the streets immediately contiguous to it ; in St. Giles's at places no more rural than Holborn and Drury Lane, in St. Martin's at Long Acre, which became heavily infected,[2] and in St. Clement Danes at Clare Market (Aldwych and Kingsway), a stone's throw from Temple Bar. If now I seem insistent upon this aspect of the outer ring of London, its neglect and poverty and squalor, and shall return to it again and again, the reason will become apparent.

[1] Stow's *Surveigh of London*, 1598.
[2] Heathcote MSS. (*Hist. MSS. Comm.*, p. 199).

North and west St. Giles's Church overlooked open meadows and hedges. Long years afterwards the parish maintained this rural character ; a trim Georgian farm-house survived, embedded in the back premises of Messrs. Heal & Sons in Tottenham Court Road, till the year 1912. A foul water ditch early in the Plague was ordered to be cleansed, lest the stench arising should spread infection.[1] Its situation was about St. Martin's Lane, where still was open land. But the parson found his parishioners pressed most thickly towards the City ; the parish had few fashionable residents. Near Drury Lane's exit to the Strand stood the great house of the Earl of Craven, but Drury Lane had thus early the poverty which remained its distinctive characteristic till the last Westminster improvement in our time.

Towards Westminster in one direction and Shoreditch in another the town spread more distantly, and the communities congregated there gave great black spots to the Plague map. The huge parish of St. Margaret West-minster, now much cut up, stretched undivided back from the church and the Thames bank through Knights-bridge, to include much of Kensington ; and east of the City, Stepney was another area of enormous size, extending from Shoreditch to Blackwall, with sea-faring interests and population straggling along the riverside. West-minster comprised, besides St. Margaret's, the four parishes of St. Martin-in-the-Fields, St. Paul Covent Garden, St. Mary Savoy and St. Clement Danes, the first alone lying distant from the City boundaries. The other twelve out-parishes in Middlesex and Surrey included, besides Stepney, land stretching away to Islington, Hackney, the big expanse of Lambeth, Newington, and Rotherhithe.

It proved greatly prejudicial to the outer areas that collective supervision was wholly lacking, save such as could be exercised by the justices of the peace. In national emergency these were accustomed to receive instructions from the Privy Council. The cleavage from the City was distinct, and only for statistical purposes was the Greater London of that day comprised within the Bills of Mortality.

[1] Privy Ccl. Reg. 58, fo. 143.

CHAPTER III

SPREAD IN THE OUT-PARISHES

MEDICINE had produced Harvey, whose great discovery of the circulation of the blood had won acceptance by the Faculty; but it is, perhaps, characteristic of an age when men of serious mind accepted comets as influences in human affairs, that it was not to the learning of the College of Physicians that the authorities first turned when seeking relief from the Plague, but to an arch quack.

James Angier, a Frenchman, made the preposterous claim that his remedies had stopped the infection at Lyons, Paris, Toulouse, and other cities. He succeeded in deceiving Lord Arlington, the Secretary of State, and the Privy Council. The Middlesex justices were approached, and their permission being given, Angier's assistant on the 8th June entered the shut-up house of Jonas Charles in Newton Street, St. Giles-in-the-Fields (lying south from Holborn), after four persons had died therein, showing Plague spots. Eight others remained alive, of whom two were infected.

The remedy was that of fuming—the burning of a strong-smelling disinfectant of brimstone, saltpetre, and amber,[1] which in the belief of the time was effective in killing the poison of Plague wherever lodged. After fuming, no other person died in this Newton Street house. A like result attended the experiment in other dwellings.

Eight justices attest receiving these facts by witnesses. Jonas Charles, the householder, offered himself to enter any other infected house and administer the remedy.[2]

[1] " Paid to Mr. Angier the ffumor by order of the justices of the peace, £20." St. Giles's Ch'wardens' Accts. See also Kemp's *Brief Treatise*.
[2] *Newes*, June 29.

King Charles and the Privy Council obviously were impressed. The Solicitor-General was charged to report what countenance his Majesty might properly give to Angier, to ensure the distribution of his Plague cure for the benefit of the public, and what reward be made to him.[1] The Council caused advertisement to be published of six addresses at which Angier's fume could be obtained,[2] and, moreover, burdened the Lord Mayor and Aldermen of London with the quack. They were ordered to give Angier all due encouragement freely to make and distribute his medicaments, and at their own cost to requite him for his good service in so dangerous an undertaking.[3]

In the disillusionment which quickly followed, the Privy Council accepted the advice of the College of Physicians, whose nostrums, it has to be confessed, gave little better result. They were to learn that no medicine could eradicate Plague.

The College, at the Privy Council's request, undertook a revision of the rules and prescriptions drawn up by physicians at former epidemics of Plague. Alert in their work, they had their report ready in twelve days. It prescribed medicines for the rich and for the poor, directions for compounding them being issued to the public in English and advertised ; and, furthermore, the report made several practical recommendations to the authorities. None should be permitted to travel in the kingdom without certificate of health ; all needless concourses of people should be prohibited ; the poor to be relieved and put to work ; beggars not suffered to go about ; the sale of corrupt food restrained ; streets and houses, " as diligently and carefully as may be," to be kept clean ; liquid refuse of the houses to be removed otherwise than by being thrown into the open street kennels ; medicinal fumes to be burnt within doors. It was advised that slaughter-houses be removed outside the City, that the burials of infected persons take place beyond its limits, and that quicklime be used to ensure rapid destruction of corpses dead from the Plague.[4]

[1] Privy Ccl. Reg. 58, fo. 187.
[2] Newes, June 29.
[3] Privy Ccl. Reg. 58, fo. 210.
[4] *Certain Necessary Directions for the Prevention and Cure of the Plague*, 1665.

At their own charge, the College of Physicians left a stock of medicines with their apothecary and chemist, William Johnson, at Amen Corner, to be dosed out to patients and delivered at the infected house of every family that was poor and necessitous. In particular, for preventing infection, there was commended as a thing necessary for all people to take the Spiritus Antiloimoides, or Antidote against the Plague.[1] Johnson had been handing out his specifics, by charitable gift or sale, but a few weeks when the Plague took him.[2]

The advisability—at any rate—of segregating Plague cases had been in the minds of the ruling authorities from the early visitations. Back in King Henry VIII.'s reign it had been done by closing them in the infected houses. Wolsey gave orders that dwellers in such houses should keep within doors, and put out wisps as a mark to the street.[3] The shutting up of houses had been the practice in London certainly since the year 1518,[4] but with the common prevalence of Plague and the passage of time more than this was considered necessary, and in Elizabeth's reign pest-houses were established, not only in London but in country towns where Plague raged. It was in the magistrates' power to cause sufferers to be removed to them,[5] and by this means the few sporadic cases occurring in uneventful years were kept in check and prevented from spreading contagion. But unfortunately such provision was never adequate. Epidemic no sooner broke out than the panic measure of locking in the sick and the healthy together in their dwellings was at once resorted to.

All through the terrible story of the Plague rises again and again the cry of these prisoners held fast in the infected houses.

The parish of St. Giles had no pest-house. At the Plague visitation with which King Charles I.'s reign had gloomily opened there was a common building known as the London Pest-house, that served as a hospital for nine

[1] Advertisement in *Intelligencer*, June 26.
[2] Tillison to Dean Sancroft, Sept. 14.
[3] *Letters and Papers Henry VIII.*, vol. 2, pt. 2, no. 4125.
[4] The familiar period of forty days is given in the first set of Plague orders that survive in the Guildhall archives, bearing date 1543, when the wisps set out are replaced by the Plague cross marked at the doors.
[5] *House of Commons Journals*, ii. 273.

out-parishes,[1] and on the approach of the long but less harmful Plague of 1640–47 had been acquired by St. Giles's for its own patients. In subsequent years of comparative immunity the building had been converted into a workhouse,[2] and was no longer available. Nor had St. Giles's claim to send its stricken sufferers to the pesthouses of Westminster or the City. From the first—there was no option—they were sealed up in their houses, behind doors held fast with staple and padlock, which opened for the passage out of the dead, and but rarely for the emergence of the living and the cured. That was their fate.

Peremptory orders were given to St. Giles's to build a pest-house. The rector and churchwardens answered the Privy Council that they had no ground remote from houses that was suitable for the purpose, but they had found in a meadow at Marylebone, known as Mutton Field, a favourable site. The owner was willing to sell. Marylebone's inhabitants, the village (as it then was) being still healthy, stoutly opposed the dumping down of such a building in their locality.

In view of St. Giles's emergency, which was, in plain truth, that of London, the Privy Council swept all obstruction aside, in part placating the protesting parish by an undertaking that should any of Marylebone fall sick of the Plague, they should have the benefit of this pest-house alike with the inhabitants of St. Giles's.[3] The building was rapidly constructed. Like others, it was timber framed upon a foundation course of brick. A well was sunk to give a water supply to the inmates, and the place walled in. A surgeon named Fisher was appointed.[4]

The justices also ordered St. Martin-in-the-Fields to provide a pest-house. It was erected on five acres of ground called Clayfield in Soho Fields,[5] to which at that time the parish stretched out. Hyde's great house in Piccadilly, then building—the " Little Dunkirk " of his calumniators—seems to have been the nearest neighbour. Dr. Tristran Inard, a physician, became master of the

[1] *Bills of Mortality*, 1625.
[2] Parton's *History of St. Giles's*, 1822.
[3] Privy Ccl. Reg. 58, fos. 167, 170.
[4] St. Giles's Ch'wardens' Accts.
[5] Privy Ccl. Reg. 58, fo. 171.

pest-house, and in addition to receiving fees amounting to £170,[1] in part obtained reward when not attending there by treating patients at his private dwelling in Long Acre, where also his Grand Preservative, or Antidote Epidemical, was to be obtained at a very reasonable price.[2] Additions made this Soho pest-house the largest of those in London, accommodating ninety patients, and at the height of the visitation it served not only St. Martin's parish, but St. Clement Danes, St. Paul Covent Garden and St. Mary Savoy as well.[3]

The dying and the dead made close neighbours. Near by this pest-house, as near by the others, a rough cemetery was marked out in the fields, enclosed with palings, for interment of those who succumbed ; and when deaths in the out-parishes became so numerous that the church-yards were choked, others were brought there, and in the worst weeks of Plague great pits were dug in the ground, into each one of which twenty, thirty, or forty corpses were consigned at night time by the carts.[4]

There were in all five pest-houses about London during the Great Plague of which record survives, one being a detached place that served the far-spreading out-parishes on the City's eastern side, then constituting the Tower Hamlets, and to which cases out of the Tower of London were also taken.[5] Its location I have not found. Most were newly built in great haste as the Plague enlarged. The only pest-houses separately returning Plague deaths in the Bills of Mortality were those of the City of London and Westminster, and deaths in these others either are not recorded—a most likely case—or they are comprised in the parochial returns.

From the first centre of infection in St. Giles-in-the-Fields the Plague spread outwards like the points of a star, arrested where meadows lay north and west, but following unerringly the lines of population. You may

[1] St. Martin's Ch'wardens' Accts.
[2] Advt. in *Newes*, July 20.
[3] Earl of Craven to Privy Council, Feb. 19, 1666.
[4] Rugge's " Diurnal," fo. 147.
[5] *Petition of Charles Wilcox* (Brit. Mus. Library, Press-mark 816 m. 9). Defoe's statement that " In all this dreadful visitation there were but two pest-houses made use of, viz. one in the fields beyond Old Street and one in Westminster," is but an example of his all too frequent inaccuracy.

trace in the Bills its slow progress in St. Martin-in-the-Fields, which in a long arm included the Royal Palace of Whitehall, in St. Clement Danes at the City's western gate, and in St. Andrew Holborn, the parish part without and part within the City Liberties. In no week after May opened was St. Clement Danes reported clear of infection, and in all the parishes the rise in the general mortality largely above what was normal indicates but too plainly the presence of concealed Plague. Before St. Martin's Church stood the stocks and whipping post, new painted and furnished the previous year.[1] The whipping post (or perhaps a successor) still may be seen in the crypt of Gibbs's church by Trafalgar Square, a relic of barbarous punishments common to Restoration London and long afterwards.

Plague remained from its first definite indications in April and throughout May almost wholly in the outparishes which constituted western London. In the City Liberties it was negligible; within the City wall no case of Plague death save the early one in Woolchurch occurs in the printed report till the second week of June, when there were two deaths by Crooked Lane, near Old London Bridge. The Court journalist of the day, Roger L'Estrange, made much of the fact when compelled at length in his news-sheet to acknowledge the appearance of Plague in the capital. " There are such reports," he wrote in the *Intelligencer* of June 5th, " spread abroad of the multitudes that die weekly of the Plague in this town, that for better information I shall very briefly deliver the truth of the matter. There have died 3, and 9, and 14, and 17 in these four weeks (43 in all) and none of these within the walls, and but five parishes infected out of one-hundred and thirty." This small return for the complete month seemed not alarming.

A week or two later, as Plague increased, a noted astrologer set out on his travels.

Lilly had prevision to quit London—warned by information derived nearer, I fancy, than the stars. He read the future, and people resorted to his lodging not alone to learn Fate's decrees, but also to find preservatives or cure; for he made some pretension to medicine as well, and

[1] Ch'wardens' Accts., 1664.

five years later obtained license from the Archbishop of Canterbury to practise it. That license was then and long after in the Primate's gift.[1] Many of Lilly's visitors were the very poorest. To those infected and judged not likely to die he ordered cordials, and caused them to sweat, whereby he claimed that many recovered. The landlord of his house was filled with fears of this invasion —" I nothing at all," declares Lilly. " He was desirous I should be gone ; he had four children ; I took them with me into the country and provided for them." The kind act redounds to the astrologer's credit. Six weeks later the landlord, his wife, and his man-servant were all dead of the Plague.[2]

Although Westminster stood adjacent to the out-parishes that first were most heavily infected, and St. Margaret's boundaries ran with those of St. Martin-in-the-Fields, yet that far-spreading parish remained in health till late in May. Plague then appeared in Long Ditch.

This was a squalid quarter near the Abbey, built along the ditch that in an earlier age had made Thorney an island. Westminster grouped closely about its famous Abbey. It had the Parliament House, not the centre of activity that it is to-day, with the infrequent and short sessions that served for King Charles II. It had Westminster Hall. We know that famous Hall as enjoying a quietude that seems heavy with the stilled throbbings of the centuries, but for Restoration London it was a lively resort, its vast roof sheltering not alone the judges and lawyers and suiters, and all the business of the law, but stalls of the booksellers, the law-stationers and seamstresses,[3] and a mart for dealers in toys and small wares as well. Samuel Pepys was a frequent purchaser of haberdashery at the stalls. He eased a parched throat at Heaven

[1] It is not revoked, though never practised. Late as 1922 sympathisers with Sir Herbert Barker, the eminent bone-setter, made application to Dr. Randall Davidson that he should be so licensed, but the Archbishop tactfully refused to re-assert the power.

[2] William Lilly's *History of his Life and Times*, ed. 1715, p. 95.

[3] Thus Wycherley's *Plain Dealer :*

" In Hall of Westminster,
Sleek sempstress vends amid the courts her ware."

and Hell, two taverns so named that buttressed the Hall on either side.

We have appropriated the Abbey to London, but it was different then—the Abbey that is the most glorious of our ecclesiastical buildings, lacking then, as now, the sky-aspiring spire that alone is wanting to crown its complete dignity. Westminster was still a little place, and most of what we know by the name was fields. Old Westminster lay wholly within sound of the Abbey bells; it was poor; it was low-lying, much of it built upon marshlands—the floods had been in Westminster Hall, covering its floor—and the houses had no drainage save to the open ditches which intersected so much of the surrounding land. These last received every imaginable pollution. At the length of a few short alleys and courts beyond the Abbey boundaries, and poor streets like Petty France, Westminster ended abruptly. It had evil-living, evil-smelling, dilapidated slums overrunning the ancient Sanctuary, but a stone's-throw distant from the splendour of the Court and the solemn Abbey. Beyond, a wide expanse of green meadows through which the Tyburne flowed to the Thames, well shown in Hollar's drawing, stretched away to the distant village of Chelsea.

The foul town ditches have a bearing upon this narrative, for wherever found there is traced a deepening line of Plague. That had always been the same, and wonder arises that in the recurring Plagues the matter did not receive more attention. A poor captive in the Fleet Prison, by the stinking Fleet Ditch, had made complaint to Thomas Cromwell, Henry VIII.'s Minister, begging consideration for his sufferings, " and the Plague with which Fleet Street is sore infected, to my no little danger." [1]   Often stagnant, and rarely scoured in summer, the watercourses made the adjacent locality unhealthy. It was into one of these open Westminster ditches that Nell Gwynne's infamous mother slipped, and in her helpless state lay there and drowned, mourned by none in the world save poor Nelly. The Mill Ditch (Great College Street), another of Thorney Island's boundaries, had been filled in, but others remained to poison the atmosphere and lower the vitality of the inhabitants, whose chance

[1] *Letters and Papers Henry VIII.*, vol. 5, No. 1868.

Totehill fields

S.t James his Westminster

S.t Peter's London

HOLLAR'S VIEW OF TOTHILL FIELDS

Showing the rural conditions of Westminster at the Restoration

of longevity at best was small in the noxious condition of the poorer streets and dwellings.

Westminster was isolated in a manner that would seem most strange to-day. King Henry VIII., having seized York Place from Wolsey, had much extended its ground ; the tall Holbein Gate and the King Street Gate, placed across the broad thoroughfare from Charing Cross at the limits of the Royal Palace of Whitehall, asserted its privacy, but did not secure it. Annoyed by so many funerals passing his windows to St. Margaret's church-yard, Henry VIII. had cut out of that parish St. Martin-in-the-Fields, hitherto dependent, giving to it its own burial ground. St. James's Park at the Restoration stretched along the north side of the way from Charing Cross behind the King Street houses, with only a circuitous road around its skirts. There was no Embankment to Westminster, no bridge thrown across the river, and the sole direct access from London was that past the Palace. The highway to Westminster was the Thames.

Already Westminster had seen the beginning of great changes, which in the lapse of time were to incorporate its life with that of London. It was Royal and ecclesiastical, but the City, and not the immediate surroundings of the Royal Palace, was the traditional place of residence of the noble families. Roger North has told that in the year 1641 his father's house in King Street, Westminster, "though but a sorry one," was remarkable for being the first brick house there, standing in lonely isolation.[1] King Street, now encompassed within the great width of Parliament Street, became at the Restoration the capital's most fashionable quarter. New ground was broken, mansions were built or in the building, and away on a spur Pall Mall was being laid out and the beginning of St. James's Square.

"The poore's Plague," true to its name, had little concern with these. Its victims were found where squalor, dirt, and neglect made for pestilence a fitting home in the reeking, overcrowded alleys. Long Ditch was inhabited by the poorest people. There a woman named Marie Gale was the first infected, and was taken to the pest-house. Neighbours knew that Plague had come among

[1] *Life of Sir Dudley North.*

them when a watchman was placed at the door, locked and guarded to keep in other inmates, lest by going abroad they should spread the pestilence.

A few days after Marie Gale's seizure her child was stricken. Then to the pest-house went Nicholas Stow and his wife. They recovered, and they remained at the pest-house throughout all the year and till the Great Plague died out by exhaustion next year, tending the sick who soon after their arrival came in an increasing stream. It was not till three weeks later that Plague deaths in the parish of St. Margaret's began to figure in the Bills of Mortality, first seven together, sharply rising the next week to twenty-six.

After Long Ditch, Plague came to Bell Alley, a stifling cul-de-sac built about with old, decaying wooden houses, separated by a mere thread of broken pavement, where to-day Parliament Square stands in austere dignity. Infection ran through the alley; a family named Hardcastle were taken away to the pest-house. The locked doors, the red cross rudely painted thereon, the supplication, " Lord have mercy upon us ! "—these sights became increasingly familiar to all who walked in Westminster's darker ways; and those whose affairs took them wider afield about London began shudderingly to see such Plague signs in many new places. Pepys records the shock given by his first acquaintance with them on June 7th—

This day, much against my will, I did in Drury Lane see two or three houses marked with a Red Cross upon the doors and "Lord have mercy upon us!" writ there; which was a sad sight to me, being the first of the kind that, to my remembrance, I ever saw. It put me into an ill conception of myself and my smell, so that I was forced to buy some roll tobacco to smell and to chew, which took away the apprehension.

The overseers of Westminster reported Plague in Thieving Alley, a passage skirting the Sanctuary to the north-west—with unaltering persistency, always it first raised its head in the town's most disreputable and dirtiest quarters. Also there were " several visited " at Knightsbridge, at that time a remote hamlet. By mid-June Plague had become firmly lodged in St. Margaret's parish, and a first list of those receiving relief at the pest-house numbers twenty in all, several being children.

The Great Plague but repeated an experience with which Westminster was sadly familiar. The visitor who seeks the quiet shelter of the Abbey Cloisters may stand upon a stone which is said to cover the remains of twenty-six monks who perished in the Black Death in the fourteenth century. Canon Westlake has pointed out that from 1570 to 1666 (three years' records are missing) Westminster had in forty-nine out of the ninety-four years a story of Plague, intermittent indeed, and often negligible, but sufficiently continuous to overshadow the brighter years. In the register of 1603, the fateful initial " P " figuring before over 900 burials testifies to the severity of that year's visitation ; and the actual numbers were probably far greater. In the Plague of 1625 alone some 1,500 victims of this one large parish perished.[1] In the records of these earlier visitations may be traced the practices for combating Plague which were followed with sheep-like fidelity when the greatest epidemic of all swept over the harassed population in the year 1665. Experience had taught but little—very little. Preventive treatment and cure had made small advance since Elizabeth, or even Henry VIII. The best teaching of the time counselled flight. Kemp urgently advised this course, and only to those who through poverty, or want of friends in the country, or business that could not be abandoned, were compelled to stay recommended medicine to fortify the body against Plague as a last resort.[2]

The burden of directing administration fell upon the magistrates, those for Westminster and Middlesex in the out-parishes and the Lord Mayor and Aldermen within the City. South London beyond Southwark was not infected till later. The powers they exercised were rooted in the Statute 1st James I. chap. 31, and by this authority came the appointment of all those officials with gruesome duties whose activities the Great Plague made unhappily familiar. A vital clause ran :

It shall be lawful for justices of the peace, mayors, bailiffs and other head officers aforesaid to appoint [within their several jurisdictions] searchers, watchmen, examiners, keepers

[1] Rev. H. F. Westlake, *The Church of St. Margaret Westminster.*
[2] W. Kemp, *Brief Treatise of the Nature and Cure of the Pestilence,* 1665. The advice was as old as Hippocrates.

and buriers for the persons and places respectively infected
as aforesaid; and to administer unto them oaths for the
purpose of their office of searchers, watchmen, examiners,
keepers and buriers, and give them other directions as unto
them for the present necessity shall seem good in their
discretions.

That " present necessity " was the furious Plague which
had accompanied King James I. to the English Throne.
Plague had been so persistent in England that the Act,
although intended for a limited term, had never lapsed.
Infected persons attempting to go abroad should be forced
by violence to keep their houses. If one infected, having
any sore upon him uncured, so escaped out and conversed
in company, then he became felon, " to suffer the pains
of death as in case of felony " ; if without sore upon him,
he should be punished as a vagabond and bound to good
behaviour. It is right to say that the penalty for felony
or vagabondage was not, in fact, inflicted upon the many
maddened victims who in the greater visitation of 1665
broke out or were found wandering. This little advance
had been made in humanity towards the Plague-stricken.

The Act was primarily one for charitable relief, which
when tested by the Plague of 1603–4 had hopelessly broken
down. Where towns and places visited—so said the preamble—could not sufficiently relieve their infected poor,
these wandered abroad, infecting others. To prevent this
evil, the mayor, bailiff, or magistrates as the authority
might be, should levy from time to time upon all houses
and land within the infected place such reasonable tax as
was thought fit for relief of the Plague-stricken poor.
They should distrain upon and imprison those who failed
to pay. Where such an internal tax did not give adequate
relief (the common experience) then upon certificate by
the authority, any two justices of neighbouring counties
might assess the inhabitants of such counties within five
miles of the place infected, at such reasonable weekly
tax as they should deem fit.

By such methods, assisted with widespread charity,
the severe financial strain created by the Great Plague was
met. Parliament at no time made a grant, nor did the
profligate finance of King Charles II. even attempt help
to the capital in its distress. A small sum diverted from

the Highways Stock by way of loan for relief of the first poor families and persons afflicted [1] would hardly merit mention were it not that alone it represented all Government effort.

That in brief was the law. Orders made from time to time by the Privy Council and by the King's Bench Judges gave precedents for putting the law into force, but had not in any material respect modified it. In the critical appearance of the Great Plague, there should be no questioning the magistrates' authority. It was definitely asserted and made plain by an Order in Council directing all churchwardens, constables, headboroughs and other parish officials to render full account to the justices of moneys received by them by way of rate or contribution. The magistrates were further authorized to make choice of three or four substantial persons in each parish to be their assistants.[2] In Westminster these valued assistants became the " examiners," and they are met with elsewhere. They account for all money spent.[3]

The justices of Westminster and Middlesex, when the severity of the outbreak could no longer be concealed, levied a special poor rate. One small benefit resulted from Westminster's long inheritance of Plague. Like the City of London, it possessed a permanent pest-house. A structure had been erected in 1638 in the extensive Tothill Fields, of which to-day Vincent Square, where the boys of Westminster School play by immemorial right, alone gives a refreshing sight of green turf, the rest being built upon. Vincent Square stands upon a burial ground of the Great Plague, and in excavations not only were heaped bones found in disorder, but broken clay pipes thrown into the pits by the buriers, who for disinfection incessantly smoked at their ghastly work.

This pest-house was a mere collection of wooden sheds, and in the records figures as " the sheds." After the outbreak of the prolonged visitation of Plague of 1640–47,

[1] Privy Ccl. Reg. 58, fo. 90.
[2] *Ibid.*, fos. 207–8.
[3] " The Account of Michael Arnold and Nicholas Hobman, Churchwardens of ye Parish of St. Margte in Westminster of all their Receipts and Disbursements in Relation to ye Poor Visited of ye Plague within the sayd Parish in the Yeares 1665 and 1666." MS. in Westminster City Hall.

more extensive building was undertaken.[1] Therein the
Plague patients lingered and many died, behind doors
which, alike with those of the sealed houses in street after
street, were crossed with ochre—the red cross that in
Queen Elizabeth's reign had been blue,[2] and now bearing
below the supplication, " Lord have mercy upon us ! "
The pest-house, but little used before 1665, had fallen into
disrepair. First by the magistrates' orders a ditch was
cast about it, further to isolate the building. Ten new
rooms were added, and also further sheds. It being still
wholly inadequate, on part of the ground fresh levelled a
" New Pest-house " was raised, for building which John
Goodchild, the carpenter, received £93 5s. That was
sufficient sum in Restoration times for a fairly spacious
wooden annexe.[3] The pest-house was placed in charge
of Dr. Grant, a French physician.[4]

It was but sorry accommodation for the stricken living ;
there was none ready for the dead. The last bad visitation
of Plague in Westminster had filled the graveyard about
the New Chapel (to-day Christ Church) and the parish
could do no better when the Great Plague came than
utilize the open spaces of Tothill Fields, where only after
hasty burials had begun an area was walled in and isolated
by a ditch dug around it, across which a bridge was thrown.[5]
Pepys records being " much troubled " at this scandal,
that " none but such as are able to pay dear for it " could
secure burial in consecrated ground ; [6] and he tells of a
poor woman scolding the master of a house that a kins-
woman of hers dead of the Plague should not be buried
in the common land, but decently interred in the churchyard.[7] The Plague pits were held in horror by the poor,
who strove to prevent burial of their dead therein till
despair of any escape from the Plague save by death made
most callous and indifferent. They were dug chiefly

[1] " Rec. out of the black chest at several tymes for the building of
the new pest houses, £200." (St. Margaret's Ch'wardens' Accts., 1642.)
[2] " Item, to the paynter of Totehill Streete for payntinge of certain
blewe crosses to be fyxed upon sundrie houses infected, vjd "—St.
Margaret's Ch'wardens' Accts., 1563. There are many like entries later.
[3] St. Margaret's Plague Accounts ; also Vest. Mins., July 14.
[4] Rugge wrongly describes Dr. Grant as master of the Soho pest-house.
[5] St. Margaret's Plague Accts.
[6] *Diary*, July 18.
[7] *Ibid.*, July 22.

in fields and waste lands, and lacked the sanctity and sentiment attaching to the more customary places. The Bishop of London held himself bound by the Church's laws to refuse to consecrate land that could not be dedicated to such use in perpetuity ; [1] and that was impossible.

The bodies were committed at night without any rite, with no minister of religion attending to do his office, and any who by mischance were near by when, lit by the flare of torches, the dead carts emptied their ghastly loads, fled precipitately from a sight that must have strained the strongest nerves. The flares lit up a scene that is best left to the imagination.[2]

The fashionable folk who fled from London were subject to a good deal of merited obliquy. To their credit be it said that at least a goodly number recognized their obligation to the poor, tied to the town by poverty, who remained to suffer and die. They were, too, prompt in giving assistance. In St. Margaret's parish the receipts spent in relief totalled £1,652, and of this sum no less than £1,117 came by contributions ; the rate compulsorily levied provided only £402. Anne Hyde, the romantic Duchess of York, the Earl of Craven, and Lord Newport were distinguished by their benefactions to the out-parishes first visited. In June, soon after Plague appeared, Dr. Busby, the famous headmaster of Westminster School, then flogging his way to immortality, gave £15 (and later an additional £10) for relief. It was Dr. Busby of whom the doubtfully veracious story is told that he refused to take off his hat before King Charles II. in the presence of his scholars, lest they should think there was any man greater than himself. He removed Westminster School during the epidemic, for such boys as did not return to their homes, to a house at Chiswick which had been attached to the foundation since Elizabethan times and was used by scholars who remained in residence during the holidays, and afterwards became a country residence for the head-master. They went there by boat along the river, avoiding the dangerous streets.

[1] Earl of Craven to Lords of the Council, Feb. 19, 1666.
[2] Defoe's ghastly scenes at the open plague pits appear to have been derived largely from George Wither's long poem, *Britains Remembrancer*, which is a description of the Plague of 1625. It served for other parts of Defoe's narrative, as did Dekker's *Seven Deadly Sins of London*.

The Dean and Chapter of Westminster at the same time provided £20 that a surgeon might be paid to attend the poor. Dr. Dolben, the Dean, personally contributed £40. Sir Heneage Finch, the Solicitor-General, gave £40 ; the Archbishop of Canterbury from Lambeth Palace sent £30. The sympathetic Bishop of Bangor was instrumental in raising £66 for Westminster's needs ; and Mr. Thompson, Bailiff of the Hundred of Ossulston, in which so much of the City of Westminster stands, sent £30. Money was, of course, both greater in value and scarcer than it is to-day. Among the receipts figures this pathetic item—

> Robert Crosse, being moneys left when
> he dyed, leaving 2 children upon the
> parish   .   .   .   .   .   . £1. 13s. 7½d.

A custom grew up that was honourable and fitting in those sad times. Display in great funerals was out of place when death was the common lot. Instead of spending money in lavish ostentation, the well-to-do who suffered bereavement made contributions to the poor visited by the Plague, and St. Margaret's received upwards of £130 for relief from this source, in sums rising from as little as 10s. given at the burial of a child. Alexander Davies, scrivener, fell an early victim to the Plague in Westminster on July 2nd, and his enclosed tombstone in St. Margaret's churchyard, just by the railings and pavement by which so much traffic passes, is the solitary one remaining there to mark this land as a burial ground. In the St. Margaret's accounts is this entry—

> At the Buryall of Alexander Daveis Esqre being
> ye Charitable Benevolence of his Widdow   .   £10.

That name has an enduring place in London's story. His widow was Mary Davies, one of a family of twelve daughters and three sons of a poor Rector of St. Clement Danes. It was their daughter, another Mary Davies, whose inheritance of the fields upon which Belgravia and other quarters of fabulous wealth are now built, and subsequent marriage with Sir Thomas Grosvenor, brought a great fortune to the house of the Grosvenors, Dukes of

GRAVE OF ALEXANDER DAVIES

The railed tomb in St. Margaret Westminster Churchyard—the solitary one remaining—is familiar to passers by. Davies, whose daughter brought the Belgravia lands to the Grosvenor family, died of the Plague

Westminster—a romance of London and of the peerage that Mr. C. T. Gatty has delightfully told.[1]

That the magistrates, spurred to action by frequent letters from the Privy Council, kept the parish officers alive to their duties we know from the latter's accounts. They bought " a board to carry the dead on." Then the dead becoming too many to be so carried, St. Margaret's obtained a cart, " to carry ye dead visited corpses to ye graves," for which ten shillings' hire was paid each week. As still the mortality from Plague leapt upwards, the parish fitted up its own dead cart. A Sedan chair, with straps, was acquired to convey afflicted sufferers to the pest-house. That was a common means of carriage adopted by other parishes.

This hospital soon became full—the only institution that served as such [2]—and the shutting up of so many infected houses involved a number of purchases, of padlocks, hasps, staples, and nails. Henry Weedon, the smith, received £3 11s. for 108 locks obtained at a single purchase, there was a larger second purchase, and many others like. They were for fastening in the infected, making sure that none entered or came out of the closed-up house without consent of the warder. He kept the key, and was sworn under penalty to admit none save the examiner, doctor and nurse, and in the last extremity those dread officials, the searchers and bearers of the dead. There were physic and drugs for doctors' and apothecaries' use entered upon the bills.

Pails were bought for carrying water into the enclosed houses, for the imprisoned residents were locked even out of reach of their own wells ; " fume " to burn as disinfectant, and lime for the same purpose ; powder and shot for killing dogs. The dog killer received 4s. for burying 353 slaughtered dogs. Time after time the bill is presented by Francis Brockhurst for shrouds for the dead ; no less than £60 13s. was paid to him for that

---

[1] In *Mary Davies and the Manor of Ebury*, 1921. Smyth, who records in his *Obituary* the deaths of so many of his contemporaries, says that Alexander Davies " died in Westminster of plague, but not so recorded."

[2] The medical hospitals of St. Bartholomew's and St. Thomas's appear not to have accepted Plague cases recognised as such, and not without ample reason, but their qualified staffs did good work among the Plague-stricken in the city.

service. For St. Margaret's before the Plague left it
had 4,700 dead. The authorities held true the old
adage that prevention is better than cure, and they distributed four quires of copies of Dr. Coxe's " Divertions
against ye Plague "—precautions thought to be desirable
according to the best knowledge of the day.

There is an item among these Plague accounts the full
significance of which is grasped slowly—

Pd to Mr Mann for links and candles for ye night
    bearers . . . . 18s.

Why should they want candles ? When darkness fell
over London and on till past midnight at the height of
the visitation, often the streets resounded with the cry,
that hushed all who heard it, " Bring out your dead ! "
From some of the dark houses marked with the Plague
cross came no response. The bearers, leaving the dead
cart in the street, entered, and searching about with
lighted candles in the ghastly rooms they learnt why there
had been no answer to their cry. It was not unusual
to find that the whole household had perished.

At times the words of the inked line excite a shudder.
What could be a more dreadful introduction to the world
than is indicated by this—

To Jane Allway for her Extraordinary Paynes in
    delivering 4 Women in Childbed visited of ye
    Plague . . . . 10s.

Or again, the story of bereavement told in these few
sentences—

Item given to severall poore people at the pest
    howse and to take away to [two] orphants from
    thence [1] . . . . 10s.

To Anthony Halfield his children and hee being
    all sick [at margin, "dead."] [2] . . . 12s. 6d.

Item paid to John Alordin towards the buriall of
    his wiffe being poore and ded of the sickness and
    having 4 more in family . . . . . 11s.

Item paid to helpe buery John Alordin and his kins-
    man both of the visitation [3] . . . . 2s.

[1] St. Margaret's Plague Accts.
[2] St. Clement Danes Ch'wardens' Accts.
[3] St. Martin's Ch'wardens' Accts.

CHAPTER IV

FLIGHT OF THE COURT

TALK of the Plague was the common burden of the coffee houses, dividing interest with rumours that the Dutch sail had set out to sea. Remedies were advocated, canvassed, rejected, " some saying one thing, and some another." [1] Who should decide? The poor were committed by their poverty to stay in London, whatever fate betide; to the well-to-do and the rich there was a means of prevention common to all previous visitations, that experience had taught to be more effective than medicine. They could fly from the infected town before the Plague. They took that precaution with no unnecessary delay.

Not actually the first, but the second of Pepys's many references to the Plague jotted down in his " Diary " was concerned with the flight. Plague was outside his interests till the movements of the fashionable world amidst which he lived attracted his attention. Lord Sandwich had gone to sea, expecting contact with the Dutch fleet; " but my poor lady, who is afraid of the sickness and resolved to be gone into the country, is forced to stay in town for a day or two or three." [2]

It was then but May, as a dry spring, delayed by the long frost, opened in full beauty. The flight from London had already begun—furtively, and perhaps a little shame-faced. Many families hastened away on the first alarm, arousing the somewhat contemptuous wonderment of neighbours. These had seen no reason as yet to fly the danger. The nobility resident in the country learnt from their correspondents of the peril in London. They found it convenient to postpone a visit to town.

[1] Pepys's *Diary*, May 24. [2] *Ibid.*, May 28.

Old folk whose memories went back forty years to the Plague epidemic of 1625, and who noticed the likeness of the premonitory signs, in their letters from London foretold a terrible summer.[1]

The presence of the Court in London assured a brilliant season for those who moved within its charmed circle, despite growing forebodings on account of the Plague. People of all conditions thronged the playhouses.[2] The axe which fell when King Charles I. was brought upon the scaffold at Whitehall did more than take a King's life. It made a cleavage in the centuries-old tradition of London which the ensuing years of the Commonwealth left so wide that never since has it been bridged. Few of the Royalist families who had returned with King Charles II. took up residence in the City in the dwellings of their ancestors, finding their cramped discomfort unsuitable, or finding them converted into tenements. The Earl of Arundel's house at Lothbury, the Bishop of London's ruinous Palace by St. Paul's Cathedral, the big house near the Royal Exchange which had sheltered La Motte, Lord Rivers' residence and many more had already undergone this fate ; and the Marquis of Winchester's town house, wherein the Spanish Ambassador had been lodged, had given place to a new street.[3] Inigo Jones, in the reign of the first Charles, began street architecture in London by building in Lincoln's Inn Fields the first houses on a concerted plan, so designed that to the ordered beauty of the whole each individual dwelling should contribute. About Covent Garden broad new streets had been laid out, more convenient than the City's narrow ways for the coming and going of the carriages of the nobility and their guests— there was Charles Street, and Henrietta Street, named after the Royal House. Living there when the Great Plague struck London were many of the noble families. The Earl of Bedford had his great house on the north side of the Strand, and against its wall fruit and vegetables for sale were already being exposed by countrymen, there free from interference by the City's market officials—the beginning of Covent Garden market. In the Piazza resided

---

[1] Clarendon's *Life*, ed. 1827, ii. 352.
[2] Rugge's " Diurnal," May.
[3] John Graunt's *Observations*, etc. 1665, p. 110.

the Earl of Oxford, head of the ancient line of De Vere,
the proudest family in the peerage. Neighbours there
were the Duke of Richmond, Lord Newport, Lord Lucas,
Lady Abergavenny and many more ; in Henrietta Street
lived Sir Edward Grant ; in Charles Street, Sir William
Gideon.[1]

The Restoration sent the world of fashion trekking
farther west than Covent Garden or the Savoy, another
favoured quarter, to St. Martin-in-the-Fields and Westminster. The old City of London of closely built streets
stood unchangeable ; the transplantation to the West-end
made fast progress. New mansions stood one after another
upon the few principal streets. Westminster, as Canon
Westlake has said truly, is a modern city,[2] though the
saying seems paradoxical ; its old life was about the Abbey.
Past Whitehall Palace, by which the tall Holbein Gate
rose as a dividing symbol, the highway west was continued
by King Street. This was Westminster's most fashionable
locality, and there were the town houses of Monck Duke of
Albemarle and of the tragically fated Duke of Monmouth,
Charles's natural son, then but recently acknowledged
and ennobled. Near neighbours were the Earls of Lincoln
and Tirconnell and Sir John Cotton in St. Margaret's
Lane ; and also in Westminster had settled Lord Fitz-
william, the Earls of Derby and Manchester, Lord Grandi-
son, Lord Scudamore, and Lady Knightley,[3] to name but
a tithe of the nobility there. St. Giles's had few residents
of quality, but the Plague, spreading outwards from
it, moved first into those western out-parishes wherein
fashion had chosen to reside. Behind and about the
stately mansions were some of Westminster's most squalid
alleys, and in them Plague found lodgment and flourished.

The juxtaposition of mansion and slum, the consorting
together of rich and poor, was nothing uncommon ; it
had been traditional in London from time immemorial.
The sharp division of west from east came later into
London's life.

For ten weeks after the frost broke the City within
the wall remained substantially immune from Plague—

[1] St. Paul Covent Garden Ch'wardens Accts.
[2] H. F. Westlake, *The Story of Westminster*.
[3] Assessment for the Poor in St. Margaret's Plague Accts.

a long spell. A case or two occurred, the sufferer being taken to the City pest-house, or some poor corpse brought out for burial, but for three weeks till mid-June the Bill had been wholly clear. Then several cases of infection were reported together, and among the first houses that Plague entered was that of Dr. Alexander Burnet in Fen-church Street, by St. Gabriel's Church. Burnet was Pepys's physician and near neighbour. His serving man, William Passon, was stricken with pestilence, and in a few days was dead. Report got abroad—none knew how—that the man's end was not by Plague, but that Burnet himself had murdered him ! The rumour ran further, that the doctor had been committed to Newgate for the crime. So persistent was this calumny that Burnet posted a bill on the Exchange and inserted adver-tisement in the *Intelligencer*, setting out the pest-house master's certificate that the man's death was from Plague.

Dr. Burnet figures first on the roll of medical heroes which the Great Plague was to fill. He knew the danger, not only to himself but to others. On the discovery of Plague he caused himself to be shut up in his own house, that contagion might not spread, gaining thereby great goodwill among his neighbours. Patients found his door locked. He spent his quarantine uneventfully ; in August the house was re-opened, and he resumed practice.[1]   On August 25th Burnet died from Plague,[2] with other physicians struck down about the same time.

To outward appearance the City was undisturbed. The red cross of Plague was marked on a few doors, but a wayfarer must needs go into the meaner courts to find these, and places known to be infected the passer-by shunned. "It broke the trade of the nation," Bishop Gilbert Burnet afterwards wrote of the pestilence,[3] but London's commerce was still unaffected. There was stir on the high-roads. The King's highway, badly kept indeed, and not without perils, meant much to England in that age of revived luxury and extravagance. It was her most democratic institution, the common resort.

[1] Pepys, June 10, 11, July 22, Aug. 25 ; *Intelligencer*, July 17. See also p. 203, *post*.

[2] Smyth's *Obituary*, " ex-peste," and Pepys.

[3] Burnet's *History of His Own Times*.

When everything went by road that could not be confided to the broad Thames, Royal and ducal carriages and the merchant's goods, the carrier's waggon and the pack-horse, the solitary horseman and people tramping on foot more miles than would now be thought agreeable, the roads out of London rarely lacked animation ; but their accustomed traffic was much swelled. The stage coach had been introduced towards the end of the Commonwealth, but had hardly yet won popularity. The nobleman of the Restoration and his family travelled from seat to seat with several coaches, six-horsed as a rule, and a large number of men-servants on horseback, and waggons conveying many things that would not to-day be moved, a long retinue. Numbers made him safe against the hazards of the road, and the men-servants not infrequently gave a shoulder to heave the coaches out of the deep ruts.

Signs were not wanting of how soon the pestilence was to throw out of gear the entire trade and administration of the capital. Still the Court remained at Whitehall. Parliament having risen in April, no need pressed any of the well-to-do to stay, save those in immediate attendance upon the Court, or others whose mode of life required that they must themselves be wherever fashion consorted. But the Plague was disturbing to those who lived a life of pleasure and irresponsibility, and the discomfort experienced by its near presence gave place to alarm. Numbers, increasing each week, found excuse to join the exodus from London that as June advanced became general. On June 21st Pepys found " all the town almost going out of town, the coaches and waggons being all full of people going into the country." Next day he sent away his mother, Margaret Pepys. Late at the posting-house, she lost her place in the crowded coach, " and was fain to ride in the waggon part." [1]

As the month drew on apprehension grew at Court, excited by the successive Bills of Mortality. Till the Plague's influence became marked, the deaths in London from all causes had rarely exceeded 380 a week, save for a period in January-February when swollen by " fever." For ten successive weeks, March to May, they had not

[1] *Diary*, June 21 and 22.

touched 400 a week, the actual figures of the Bill
being—

			Year 1665. All Deaths in London.
Week ending March	21	. . . .	363
,,	,,	,, 28	353
,,	,,	April 4	344
,,	,,	,, 11	382
,,	,,	,, 18	344
,,	,,	,, 25	398
,,	,,	May 2	388
,,	,,	,, 9	347
,,	,,	,, 16	353
,,	,,	,, 23	385

and to May 30th, 400. London's death rate over the
previous year had averaged 352 a week. The Plague
made such vast accessions to the roll that it is well to
have these figures lodged in mind.

The Bill appeared on Thursday of each week, a single
fly-sheet compiled and printed by the Company of Parish
Clerks. Any who paid a penny could purchase it, or
paid 4s. for the year's subscription. Its contents
were bad, and promised worse. Plague, that in the
first week of June had taken toll of 43 deaths (so
attributed), enlarged its inroads, finding in the second
week 112 victims. The purchaser who scanned the Bill
for June's third week there read of a mortality in London
numbering 615, and of these 168 cases were marked as
from the contagion. The deaths from Plague, so recently
counted in tens, and now by hundreds, on this progressive
scale would soon rise to thousands, unless the progress
was checked. Pepys, going by water to the Royal Palace,
saw the streets about Whitehall " full of waggons and
people ready to go out of town," and learnt that each day
the Plague made fresh inroads in that end of the town.[1]

The nobility's country houses were made ready for
their reception. The Rev. Thomas Vincent, an ejected
City parson, took note that " the great orbs begin to move
first," and his reproving eye discerned the change in
Westminster's leisured life : " few ruffling gallants walk
the streets ; few spotted ladies to be seen at the windows ;
a great forsaking there was of the adjacent places where

[1] *Diary*, June 29.

the Plague did first rage." They left the roses and the gay flowers to wither in the gardens.[1] Sir Robert Long, Auditor of the Exchequer and himself an emigrant, expressed the panic fears then prevailing in a letter of instructions given to his clerk—

I pray you use all possible care to preserve yourselves and my house. Send for things to burne, and make use of them dayly; lett noebody stirre out, nor any suitors come into the house or office. Lett everyone take every morning a little London Treacle, or the kernell of a walnutt, with five leaves of rue and a grayne of salt beaten together and rosted in a figg, and soe eaten; and never stirre out fasting. Lett not the porter come into the house; take all course you can agaynst the ratts, and take care of the catts; the little ones that will not stirre out may be kept, the great ones must be kiled or sent away.[2]

The constant passage of state coaches of the nobility and of laden carts travelling outwards by every road, testified how rapidly the western environs were being left empty of people of note, though not by the poor. They were numb and dumb. The Church collection plate gives a measure of the emptiness of Westminster of all but the poor. The offertory on June 18th at St. Margaret's Church had been £13 9s. Rarely thereafter did it realize one-third as much, though all the circumstances impelled generosity in giving, a common sum being a poor £2 or £3 for the fashionable parish church, and less for the Abbey and New Chapel.

I turn back to the City for a moment to tell one of the most moving stories of the Great Plague. In Gracechurch Street, when it raged its worst, was a house shut up, in which were imprisoned a saddler, " a very able citizen," his wife, and a last surviving child. They had seen their family of children, one by one, carried off by the Plague, the little corpses passed out successively to the buriers coming at night with the dreaded dead-cart. The couple, despairing themselves of escaping alive, had no desire save for the safety of their last living offspring, and with the connivance of a friend they devised a stratagem. From a window of the house of infection they lowered

---

[1] Vincent's *God's Terrible Voice*, 1667, pp. 26–7.
[2] Long to Burgess, July 5, in *Archæologia*, vol. 37, p. 6.

the child, stark naked, into the arms of their friend waiting in the street below to receive her, and he, having put the little one in fresh new clothes, conveyed his charge to Greenwich and safety.

The magistrates, moved to compassion in stern times, on learning the sad facts broke their strict rule by permitting the child to be received in the town.[1]   This incident of the Plague forms the subject of a well-known picture in Guildhall Art Gallery, which has been often reproduced.

The legal Inns were close about the City, though never have they been within its jurisdiction.   The lawyers were quick to take alarm.   Plague had periodically visited the Inns of Court, and their practice invariably had been to fly from the pestilence.   On notice of suspicious sickness commons, moots and readings were postponed ;   and when the Great Plague came the readings for the next vacation were at once discharged,[2] and barristers and students betook themselves to their country houses or homes of parents and friends.   That order went out in Inner Temple on June 11th, in Middle Temple and Lincoln's Inn on June 13th, at Gray's Inn about the same time. A week or two later the Inns were virtually emptied.

Residents of Lincoln's Inn had noticed with concern the Plague's slow encroachment down Chancery Lane, past their ancient turret gate, still standing.   The Parliament of the Inn on May 26th took decisive measures. Order was made that any stranger occupying or lodging in a member's chamber should forthwith be ejected.   The servants must strictly keep watch and ward day and night. They should allow no stranger access to a member unless accompanied by a warder to his chamber.   At ten at night the gates should be locked against all persons without exception.[3]   This done, the gentlemen of the law themselves retired into the country, leaving Lincoln's Inn deserted save by the servants.

When they returned next February a porter at the gate had died.   John Davyes, " the wash-pot," had his place.[4] Middle Temple was fortunate in that James Buck, their

[1] Pepys to Lady Cartaret, Sept. 4.   *Diary*, Sept. 3.   The circumstances were told to Pepys by Alderman Hooker.
[2] W. Paley Bailden, *Black Books of Lincoln's Inn*, iii. 47.
[3] *Ibid.*, p. 48.   [4] *Ibid.*, p. 49.

stout-hearted Sub-Treasurer, offered to stay in the dangerous time, and the Benchers of the Inn left all things in his care.[1] Still Plague got in amongst the skeleton

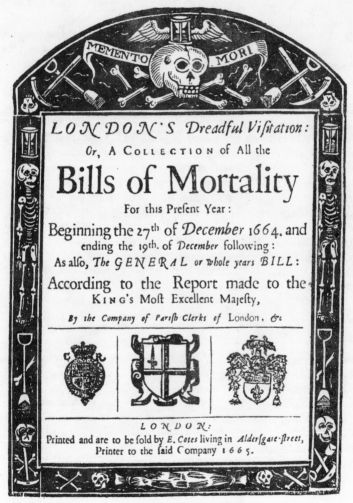

LONDON'S *Dreadful Visitation:*

Or, A COLLECTION of All the

Bills of Mortality

For this Present Year :

Beginning the 27th of *December* 1664. and ending the 19th. of *December* following :

As also, The GENERAL or *whole years* BILL :

According to the Report made to the KING's Most Excellent Majesty,

By the Company of Parish Clerks of London, &c

LONDON :

Printed and are to be sold by *E. Cotes* living in *Aldersgate-street*, Printer to the said Company 1 6 6 5.

A CHARACTERISTIC TITLE PAGE.

companies remaining to keep ward. In the little church-yard of the Temple, which the two societies share, twelve

[1] Hopwood, *Middle Temple Records*, iii. 204.

were buried between August and November, all dead of the Plague, among them being Henry Chilton, the faithful Steward of Inner Temple, and the assistant-clerk of the Temple Church. A Captain Gyfford and a stranger lodging with him were brought out dead from the former's chamber in Middle Temple Lane, and one Musgrave, a stranger, perished in Essex Court.[1] The worthy Buck survived to receive his merited reward from those of lesser courage than himself.

The divines and doctors, from whom a good example might have been expected, were not the last to leave. Edward Cotes, the printer of the Parish Clerks Company, whose "London's Dreadful Visitation" contains the Bills of Mortality compiled in the Plague year, closes his foreword to the "Courteous Reader" with a pious hope that in like emergency "neither the physicians of our souls or bodies may hereafter in such great numbers forsake us."

The doctors followed their patients, though a number there were who stayed, and their names it is an honour to mention in the subsequent pages. Not a few among these paid the supreme sacrifice for their zeal and devotion, and in medicine's roll of heroes, so rich in sacrifice, are none more worthy. Sir John Alston, the President of the College of Physicians, went out of London. Dr. Sydenham—a great name in seventeenth-century medicine —afterwards wrote a short treatise on the Plague which he did not stay to see. These and others whose practice was among the wealthy classes had the poor excuse that their patients having gone into the country, they must needs go to them.

The College of Physicians was deserted by the Faculty. Its buildings stood at Amen Corner, where to-day the Canons of St. Paul's have sheltered residence, and in the rooms left empty of all but Dr. Merritt, the Harveian Librarian and Keeper of the College, Fate played a queer prank.

Dr. Merritt had not long been alone when the increasing inroads of the Plague upon the City began to alarm him ; or, as is perhaps more likely, alarmed his family beyond endurance. He, too, fled into the country, feeling confident that his deserted charge would be safe, for the

[1] Inderwick, *Inner Temple Records*, iii. 446.

governing body of the College, after anxious consideration and discussion, had placed all the household silver and money, amassed over a long period of time, in a strong iron treasure chest, and this they concealed in a place thought to be secret and secure. Thieves in the last days of June broke in and robbed the treasure chest of its entire contents, worth £1,000—of course, a larger sum than those figures represent to-day.[1]

Plague caused the Royal Society to discontinue its meetings at Gresham College in Bishopsgate at the end of June. Most of the members went into the country. The publication of "Philosophical Transactions" was suspended till November, and not until March 14th next year were the Fellows summoned to take up the broken thread of their discussions.

Roger L'Estrange, in his newspaper, the *Intelligencer*, again sought to allay the rising alarm. It had been made the business of several people, he represented, to report the mortality to be much greater and the sickness more general than these were. He gave the June figures last published, finding reassurance in that out of 130 parishes within the Bills of Mortality—many City parishes cover only a few odd acres—but nineteen in all were infected, and that two-thirds of the whole number dead of Plague were from one western out-parish, that of St. Giles-in-the-Fields. But such consolation was futile. A Plague victim had been struck dead in Fenchurch Street. Another had died in Broad Street.[2] A bit-maker's shop in the open street before St. Clement Danes Church, at the gate of the City, was shut up and its door marked with the red cross.[3] How should the Plague be kept out?

The last gaol delivery at Newgate was made in June, though none could foretell that it would be so; the Judges, the Lord Mayor and certain Aldermen attended the opening of the trials. A shivering wretch, indicted

---

[1] "Annales" of the College of Physicians. Munk, *Roll of the College of Physicians*. Large as was this loss, the cup of bitterness was filled brimful next year, when the entire buildings of the College of Physicians in Amen Corner were destroyed in the Great Fire of London, only the "Annales" and a few valued relics and books from the medical library being saved.

[2] Pepys, June 15.   [3] *Ibid.*, June 26.

for blasphemy and in fear of its terrible penalties, looked so sickly when brought from his cell to plead that the Court, suspicious of the cause, sent for the master of the City pest-house. Stripping the man, he found the Plague sore upon him.[1] The trial collapsed.

No other delivery was taken during the year. Sessions at Old Bailey were, indeed, opened and held formally before the Lord Mayor and two or three Aldermen in October and December, and in January 1666, each being instantly adjourned, possibly to the relief of the culprits awaiting trial, though they stood in grave peril of death by Plague in Newgate, or by the dreaded gaol fever. The Sessions at Hicks Hall, Clerkenwell, were similarly adjourned.[2] The Great Plague drove out of London the law tribunals, with so much else. By bringing about a cessation of their sittings, it eliminated one cause of death from the Bills of Mortality. It stopped executions in London. From January to June in the stricken year no month had passed without them, but from July's entrance till the February following there was not a single hanging. Harsh as was the criminal code, Restoration times had not the entire callousness for human life of later days, and in these first six months of 1665 but twenty-one felons suffered on the gallows. It was the multiplication of crimes made capital and greater brutality in the administration of the law that made the reigns of the Four Georges the real hanging days.

The hot summer months were close at hand. In all heavy visitations they had left the blackest mark upon the Plague map, the mortality curve climbing to its peak in August and September.

The Queen-Mother, in indifferent health, on June 29th left Somerset House for France to drink the waters. The King accompanied her to Dover. After the Royal leave-taking the Sovereign proceeded to the Nore, to visit the Fleet assembled there that had fought the victorious engagement off Lowestoft on the 3rd of June, when the Dutch were completely defeated, and Opdam, their Admiral, perished as his flagship blew up after receiving a fortuitous shot from the Royal Charles. The ships made a fine spectacle—" the most glorious fleet that ever spread

---

[1] Addit. MSS. 4182, fo. 21.
[2] *Middlesex County Records*, iii. 372.

sails " it appeared to Evelyn's admiring eyes.[1] The Lord Mayor, Sheriffs, and Aldermen of London had hastened to congratulate the King, assuring him of their readiness on all occasions to lay their lives and fortunes at his feet, and Waterman and Doe, the Sheriffs, received knighthood.[2]

National exultation was at full tide at so great a victory in the first battle of the War, the enthusiasm in London much damped by growing fears of the Plague. At the public thanksgiving in the metropolitan churches, a collection was made by the King's order for the relief of the Plague sufferers.[3] The gallant Admiral Sir John Lawson, who had received mortal wounds in the action and died at Greenwich, was brought for burial late at night on July 2nd to the City church of St. Dunstan-in-the-East, "without any company at all," Pepys says, and in a grave unmarked.[4] There could be no thought of memorials in the time of Plague.

King Charles, with the Duke of York, who had been again at sea, returned to Whitehall in the first days of July.[5] The Plague deaths recorded in the Bill of Mortality then awaiting them were alarming—not yet, perhaps, desperately alarming. The last Bill issued in June showed a total of 267 deaths from Plague, four only being within the City walls. There were 55 returned from the Liberties, but still the western out-parishes remained the hotbed of infection. The one tragic parish of St. Giles-in-the-Fields had buried that week 143 Plague victims— more than one-half of the total accounted for in all London.

The next Bill showed that in seven days (June 27th to July 4th) the Plague deaths had leapt up to 470. In the Royal parish of St. Martin's the numbers, till then inconsiderable, had trebled. Plague had found lodgment in the fashionable King Street, several houses being marked

---

[1] Rugge's " Diurnal " ; Evelyn, June 30 ; Pepys, June 24, July 4.

[2] Addit. MSS. 4182, fo. 20b.

[3] Privy Ccl. Reg. 58, fo. 178.

[4] In the contemporary *Poems on State Affairs* are these lines :

> " He led our fleet that day, too short a space,
> But lost his knee, since died, in glorious race :
> Lawson, whose valour beyond Fate did go,
> And still fights Opdam in the lake below."

[5] *Newes*, July 6.

F

with the red cross close to the Palace gates.[1] A hasty
decision for the Court to move out of London was taken.

On July 6th a Royal Proclamation was published. It
did not minimize the peril. The people were told that
by spread of the disease into remote parts of England,
a general and most dreadful visitation threatened. A
day of solemn fast and humiliation before God to avert
the disaster was appointed, to be observed throughout
the country first on Wednesday, July 12th, next on
Wednesday, August 2nd, and thereafter on the first
Wednesday in every month until the contagion should
cease. Collections were to be made for the relief of
sufferers by the Plague, the public being exhorted to give
freely. All places uninfected were directed to send their
contribution to the Bishop of London for distribution.

The same day it was ordered that the High Court of
Admiralty be adjourned to Winchester, there to sit in the
Guildhall.[2]

This was disconcerting, it being the first movement of
any established authority away from the advancing
Plague. Quickly other news followed which made a much
deeper impression upon the public mind. Whitehall was
left empty. The Londoners learnt on July 7th that the
King had gone to Isleworth.

No accusation of undue precipitancy in flight can
properly be made against the Court. Whitehall had
maintained calm, and the Privy Council had sent out
successive orders for precautions against the Plague, while
as day succeeded day ever greater had swelled the exodus
of those who lived around and moved within the Court
circle. It had been anticipated that the King would
quit London, and for that step the public were prepared ;
many blamed him for not leaving the peril behind earlier.[3]
It is possible that he had intended to remain with his
people, for every indication points to haste in the decision.
Orders to the Lord Chamberlain to have rooms prepared
for the King's use at Sion House, the Thames-side seat
of the Duke of Northumberland, were given only the

---

[1] Pepys, June 28.

[2] Privy Ccl. Reg. 58, fo. 201.

[3] Le Fleming MSS. (*Hist. MSS. Comm.*, p. 37), Capt. Stewart's MSS.
(*ibid.*, p. 111), also Clarendon.

previous afternoon. Twice the Council met there, but the stay at Isleworth was short, and on July 9th the Court moved up-river to Hampton Court.[1] The Duke of York and Prince Rupert accompanied the King.[2]

Public business being urgent, his Majesty ordered further sittings of the Privy Council at Sion House, in order that those coming out of infected London might have no pretence for presenting themselves at Hampton Court.[3] The old Royalist Dean of Westminster, Dr. Dolben, took opportunity of a visit to Hampton Court to collect there a sum of £26 for relief of the sick in St. Margaret's stricken parish.[4] The courtiers, the vicious, mad circle by which Charles surrounded himself, driven by Plague's spectre from their accustomed haunts and daily round, were by no means happy at Wolsey's riverside palace; it was dangerously near London; they were fearful of infection even from one another; their one inquiry from all comers was how the Plague progressed.[5]

Charles left for consideration at Hampton Court how his movements should be planned for the summer, and before his departure thence for Salisbury had determined ultimately to meet the Parliament at Oxford. Money for the Dutch War must needs be voted. Both Houses had been prorogued till August, but that Plague should die down so rapidly as to make Westminster safe for their assembly none could now expect. Accordingly the King made known his intention further to adjourn the Parliament to assemble at Oxford on October 9th, intimating that all members save the few in office required for the formalities of adjournment would be absolved from attendance.[6]

London, fearful of the worst, was thus cut adrift from the ruling authorities. The City, jealous as always of interference by the Crown, had its Lord Mayor and Aldermen to exercise executive power, and placed confidence in them. But the out-parishes were beyond civic

[1] Privy Ccl. Reg. 58, fo. 201, *passim*.
[2] *Intelligencer*, July 16.
[3] Clarendon's *Life*, ed. 1827, ii. 404.
[4] St. Margaret's Plague Accts.
[5] Pepys, July 10.
[6] Clarendon's *Life*, ii. 405. Clarendon gives the dates of the Parliament's adjournment inaccurately.

control or concern. They were left at a loose end, in no
one's especial charge. Quickly the omission was detected.
A Council at Hampton Court on the 9th July directed,
" that Sir William Wheeler, Sir William Playter, Thomas
Warton, Richard Jegon, Joseph Ayloff, Edmond Warcupp,
Edmond Bury Godfrey, James Underwood, and Peter
Sabbs, justices of the peace, be and are hereby desired to
remain and continue at their habitations in the City of
Westminster and the out-parishes during the time of this
visitation, to the end that the people may be better
governed, and such orders observed in this sad season as
are necessary." The King promised that he would take
very particular notice of their service and submission to
his desire. The justices were given wide powers.[1]

Nothing could have been more lamentable. The
safety of the King was the highest object of State. A
demise of the Crown at such a time, and in the circumstances of the time, must greatly have accentuated the
troubles due to the Plague, the heir being the King's
brother James, in whom no public confidence was placed.
The withdrawal of the Court to a locality more healthy
than was Whitehall, when Plague was stalking through
the streets about the Palace, was a measure fully justified.
It would be hyper-critical to cavil. But no excuse is
possible for the abandonment of the stricken capital by
those to whom its welfare should have been a first consideration, with a callous indifference to its fate that must
for ever remain a black stain on Charles's Government.

Few can then have imagined that the Court which
left London in the first days of July would not return until
the February of the following year. The thing that would
seem incredible were it not unhappily true, is this. In
that fateful interval of seven months, wherein 100,000
persons died, thrice only did the Privy Council, sitting
with the King, concern itself with the Plague. In two of
these three instances [2] the concern shown was solely to
secure from infection the place wherein the Sovereign and
the Court happened to be lodged !

The effect of the withdrawal of the Court has no
parallel in similar circumstances should such arise

[1] Privy Ccl. Reg. 58, fo. 207.
[2] *Ibid.*, fos. 240, 257.

THE EARL OF CRAVEN

Whose fine example encouraged London's Plague-stricken poor, and widespread charity did much to relieve their necessities

to-day, when public government, centralized at Westminster, would go on undisturbed. Had Parliament
been in session, it would have been futile for control.
The government was personal. The Privy Council, in
the most desperate domestic crisis that the capital had
known, delegated its responsibilities to a small committee,
and of that committee, numbering nine, Lord Arlington
(Secretary of State), the Lord Chamberlain, Lord High
Treasurer, Comptroller, Vice-Chamberlain, and Mr. Secretary Morice followed the King. Its activities quickly
thereafter ceased ; its members being scattered, it faded
away rather than underwent formal dissolution.

King Charles was not wanting in personal courage, as
a year later he was to prove in the flaming streets of
London during the Great Fire, but his indolent and easy-
going nature in the crisis of the Plague wholly lacked
initiative. That the King was seriously troubled in mind
by the calamity and its results to the State, at a time
when the Dutch War called for the full energies of his people,
many indications suggest. But it was the object of the
few statesmen at Court not to display concern to the
frivolous and irresponsible entourage gathered closely
about the monarch, amid whom they were isolated.

The situation was saved by the fortitude of one man
to whom Charles already owed much. Peril could not
dismay the stout courage of Monck Duke of Albemarle.
As soon as the Court's departure was decided, Monck let
it be known that he would stay at the Cock-pit in St.
James's Park, sharing the lot of the afflicted people whatever might befall. No words can over-estimate the value
of his fine example and good work. His prestige stood
without parallel ; in no other man was public confidence
reposed in equal degree. The very fact of his presence
gave assurance that order would be maintained, and
obedience exacted.[1] As Plague decimated London's
population, and decimated again, he stayed, the sole
representative in London of the Government. His part
in the west end of the town (the Lord Mayor in the City
was little interfered with) was that of a benevolent dictator,
a somewhat awesome, mysterious figure, wielding unlimited
powers, as seen by those tragic, Plague-stricken subjects

[1] Clarendon's *Life*, ed. 1827, ii. 404.

over whom he ruled. His ministers were mere justices of the peace, his office that of Custos Rotulorum of Middlesex. I do not find that additional authority was conferred upon him by Royal Sign Manual or warrant. It was enough that no man questioned it.

The Earl of Craven, Monck's most active lieutenant in the Plague, played a man's part. Old friendship linked these two. William, first Earl of Craven, the son of a Lord Mayor of London, had shared King Charles's exile. Throughout the Great Plague he exerted himself unceasingly, keeping open his house in Drury Lane, where he sheltered numbers of distressed people whose presence alone was a peril; and he distributed constantly the larger part of his revenue to supply the necessities of the sick and the perishing.[1]   Lord Brouncker, recently chosen a Commissioner of the Royal Navy, until the Navy Office was removed to Greenwich stayed at his town mansion in the Piazza at Covent Garden, with infection close at hand, for in one of the great houses within two doors of his the inhabitants were shut up.[2]   Archbishop Sheldon at Lambeth, and Dr. Symon Patrick, Rector of St. Paul Covent Garden (and later Bishop of Ely) also remained, fearless amidst the population's fears, and many another made good his claim to remembrance in that time, like the Rev. Thomas Vincent. Especially I would give a place of honour to Sir William Lawrence, the always courageous Lord Mayor. Their names brighten a record that necessarily is steeped in gloom.

The unsavoury story of the Court's remissness is best finished and dismissed here. At a Council at Whitehall on the 16th May, 1666, the King received from the justices of the peace he had delegated to stay during the Plague the report of their work. Three alone sign, Warcupp, Godfrey, and Jegon. In recognition of " their well-deserving and great service at that time of eminent danger," and as " a testimony of his princely bounty," Charles ordered that to them, to three doctors and apothecaries recommended, and to seven others, silver plate of a total value of £200 should be distributed, with inscriptions upon each piece denoting the King's free gift and the recipient's merit.[3]

---

[1] Dr. Thomas Skinner's *Life of Monck*.   [2] Pepys, July 6.
[3] Privy Ccl. Reg. 59, fos. 22, 23.

They had dared much ; they had done the King service, with death always before their eyes, as Plague, stalking from door to door, struck down its victims in sheaves, and from the absent monarch their reward was £200 in silver plate.

To the Lord Mayor—nothing.

CHAPTER V

MEN AND MEASURES

AN authentic history of the Great Plague in London has been wanting. In its absence we have drawn all our ideas of that tragic time—it would be small exaggeration of language to say, all our knowledge—from Defoe's vivid "Journal of the Plague Year," which two centuries' test has placed amongst English classics.

His book is built upon the "Orders Conceived and Published by the Lord Mayor and Aldermen of the City of London concerning the Infection of the Plague, 1665." These he prints in full. With sure instinct, Defoe realizes their value in winning the reader's confidence for his narrative. They cover in most editions ten pages, and in reality they give much more to the work. Defoe's historical accuracy has a resourceful protagonist in Dr. Watson Nicholson, an American scholar recently in our midst, who says concerning these Orders—

But their importance is by no means to be measured by the space they occupy ; for out of these Orders Defoe evolved a considerable proportion of the remainder of his history. This he accomplished in a manner so skilful as to elude one who reads the "Journal" for pleasure alone; but when subjected to the scrutiny of the historian it immediately appears what Defoe has done, and how he did it. In the first place, he restated, either in a contracted or expanded form, in his own manner, practically every one of these Orders, some of them several times. . . . So, also, all the records respecting the searchers and watchmen, shutting up and marking of houses, burial of the dead, forbidding the use of hackney coaches, keeping the streets clean, killing dogs and cats, regulations concerning public houses, prohibiting public plays, duties of the Lord Mayor and Aldermen, etc., etc., are but repetitions and variations of these Orders.[1]

All this is true, and is plain as light to the attentive reader of Defoe's book. As a statement of Defoe's method, I find no fault with it. The astonishing thing is that Dr. Nicholson apparently does not realize how opposed such work is to the historical method, and how well calculated it is to destroy all confidence in the result. A writer setting out boldly to establish that Defoe's " Journal of the Plague Year," given to the world as fiction, is actual history, one would expect to inquire how far the Saddler's narrative fits in with the ascertainable facts. Defoe bodily lifted his " Orders Conceived and Published " from a reprint by one J. Roberts in 1721, contained in his collection of " Very Valuable and Scarce Pieces." It came conveniently in time to his hand. The date 1665 is an addition, by Roberts the printer, and is not the only one. For purposes of realism and heightening effect, Defoe has forged the signatures of the Lord Mayor and Sheriffs to a document that in fact never bore those signatures—

> SIR JOHN LAWRENCE, *Lord Mayor.*
> SIR GEORGE WATERMAN, } *Sheriffs.*
> SIR CHARLES DOE, }

The last two names should have excited suspicion in a knowledgeable critic. The Sheriffs do not countersign the Lord Mayor's Orders. That would be a duty quite outside the scope of their independent office. Incidentally, the Lord Mayor does not sign them either. Roberts's print does not bear the signatures.

The " Orders Conceived and Published " were, save by this reprint, unknown to Defoe. I have traced them back to the original print,[2] which as already indicated is without date. Not in the title page, preamble, the body of the document or imprint does any date appear. The only suggestion of origin is in the imprint—" Printed by Joseph Flesher, Printer to the Honourable City of London." Flesher printed during the Plague, and relinquished his

---

[1] *The Historical Sources of Defoe's " Journal of the Plague Year,"* by Watson Nicholson. Boston, Mass., and London, 1919.

[2] British Museum Library Pressmark 1167 a 21. Guildhall Library, so richly equipped in London books, has also acquired one of the few copies extant.

office in August, 1670. Flesher's print may safely be attributed to the period of the Great Plague, and there I leave it for the moment.

Defoe assumes, wholly without warrant, that these authorized and printed Orders were necessarily carried out. If they fail, the bed-rock splits and collapses underneath the imposing fabric of Defoe's " Journal." The Orders were not carried out in many—indeed, most—particulars, and those of vital importance, and in consequence he has left to us a delusive though admittedly virile picture of London under the Plague. It may be that he knew nothing of the conditions of civic and parochial government in the early years of King Charles II. The more simple explanation is that he was entirely careless, realizing that his sole purpose was to interest people in a fictional work dealing with the last great visitation of Plague in England, at a time when the public mind was sorely excited by the terrible Plague that raged at Marseilles and claimed its victims by thousands, which there were grave fears would be brought to our shores. Defoe, though he made incursions into history, was not an historical writer. The pity is that this book of his about the Great Plague the public for two centuries past should have insisted on reading as history.

No condemnation of his method in an historical writer can be in terms too severe—a claim not made by himself, though so often advanced on his behalf by others. The appearance of these Orders so early in the book, their full transcription, page after page, the prominence given to them, their obviously official character, set up in the reader's mind a conception that is false which he never loses throughout the narrative ; and Defoe has deceived himself. The most liberal constitutions in the world are those of the Central American Republics. No happy race of contented men has lived under a constitution so thoroughly democratic, so careful of the equal rights of all, so deeply rooted in abstract justice, as that of Mexico under the long ascendancy of Porfirio Diaz. Its sole fault was that it was paper only, and the Dictator accepted that as its worth.

As well should the historian visualize Mexico's idyllic political conditions from this paper constitution ; as well, in intoxication of delight, write the state of freedom in Soviet Russia from Lenin's manifestoes ; as well draw the strong character of the ex-Kaiser Wilhelm II. from that monarch's own martial utterances. The process would be the same as that which Defoe has used in the smaller matter of picturing London on the basis of these Plague Orders.

The Plague Orders which Defoe has given as of the year 1665 are not even of that date. They are the Orders of 1646, nineteen years before the Great Plague. The long Plague which had begun in London in 1640 continued with slowly increasing severity for seven years. It was drawing towards its climax and its close when, in the autumn of 1646, the dominant House of Commons directed the Lord Mayor in the City and the magistrates in the out-parishes to see that the customary measures of shutting up infected houses, marking doors, and watching be enforced, and at the same time gave command that " the late Orders and directions concerning the Plague "—they were late even then—be forthwith printed and put into execution.[1] The Orders issued by the City in 1665 are identical with those so authorized in 1646, save only a few additions, altogether not thirty lines. For instance, hackney coaches had been placed on the London streets between the two Plagues, and a clause directed that such coaches in which persons had been conveyed to the pest-house should not be used again until properly aired. Otherwise the Orders are the same.

They make a comprehensive code, and in the light of the time a very efficient code. It is plain that where they vary from the practice hitherto accepted they embody the results of experience gained in dealing with Plague. The Orders represent an ideal to be sought ; the one fault in their framers is to have been blind to human nature and to the panic conditions created by Plague, when so many of those in authority, so many doctors, surgeons and magistrates, had fled from the City, and the body of Plague swelled up to such monstrous size that the few people left in authority could not cope with it.

It had been precedent back to the reign of King Henry

[1] Letter of Aug. 20, 1646, signed by H. Elsynge, Clerk of Parliament, prefacing the official print of the Plague Orders of that year.

VIII. as a measure of quarantine to shut up infected houses with the people within them for forty days after death or recovery. In these Orders of 1646, reissued for the Great Plague, the period was reduced to four weeks—twenty-eight days—a humane concession in the long term of irksome imprisonment. Yet when the Great Plague came it was the forty days' term that was everywhere imposed.[1] It is of the utmost rarity to find even a reference to the month's period, so completely was it set aside and forgotten.[2] In the acute apprehension of Plague and the presence of the most terrible epidemic they had known, the authorities went back to the practice of their forefathers. The time when people by hundreds each day, and soon by a thousand a day, were dying of Plague was thought no time to flaunt the medical wisdom of a century and more past, and to try humane experiments at the risk still further of increasing the public peril of life. The repeated orders that came from the Privy Council in the early stages of the Plague of 1665 were to shut up the infected houses with more and ever more rigour.

The framers of the Plague Orders contemplated surgeons having each quarter of the City in their keeping, who should visit and search all infected persons. It was expressly ordered. In two fearful weeks of September, when Plague overspread the whole capital and 16,549 persons admittedly died, there were not surgeons enough left in London to go round one-tenth of the numbers stricken and dead. The surgeons were directed to notify the women searchers of the dead of all Plague deaths, "forasmuch as there hath been heretofore great abuse in misreporting the disease." For each Plague victim so certified the surgeons were to receive one shilling. Nothing indicates that they had this mortality fee. Repeated complaints were made by the Lord Mayor of misreported Plague deaths, and consequent falsification of the Bills of Mortality, by ignorance of the searchers.[3] I shall show that the medical service was mostly voluntary and largely casual. So much in the Great Plague was casual.

[1] Earl of Craven to the Privy Council, printed p. 315, *post*. Hodges' *Loimologia*, p. 7. *The Shutting Up Infected Houses*, 1665, p. 10.
[2] There is a reference to " a month or forty days " in *Golgotha*, 1665.
[3] See p. 131, *post*.

The Orders direct the Alderman and Common Councilmen of the Wards to meet weekly to report on matters perilous for the spread of Plague. Guildhall directed the wardmote inquests to assemble weekly for the purpose,[1] the Commoners, not receiving the express injunction given to the Aldermanic body to stay, having in no small proportion joined in the flight out of London.

Many circumstances combined to make a comprehensive and efficient system for fighting Plague at that time impracticable; and in this regard nothing was more detrimental than the parochial character of London government, the sharp division between City and out-parishes, and the subdivision of the small area of the City and its Liberties into no fewer than 113 separate parishes. Each had its separate officers, locally appointed. Each was jealously individualistic. The parishes of the Liberties, as distinct from the walled City, had the larger areas, the least prosperity and the greatest need. Linking the groups was only the authority of the Alderman in the City Ward and of the justices in the out-parishes. Had Plague recurred in London on a like scale after the visitation of 1665, none can doubt that for the emergency the whole method of attempting to grapple with a great national calamity by parochial responsibility, necessarily inefficient and obstructive, must have been swept aside. The age of King Charles II. knew nothing better.

In another most essential matter these Plague Orders are far more enlightened than was the actual practice followed. They offered relief to the householder by allowing him to move by night a sick person to another house. Choice was permitted an owner of two houses to remove either his sound or his sick to the spare house, so keeping them apart. These are in direct contradiction of the practice pursued by the magistrates from the first, and render nugatory the one argument left to those who stoutly defended the shutting up together of the sick and the whole in infected houses, that the passage of large numbers of sick through the streets would scatter infection. Had liberty to separate the sick from the healthy in fact

[1] Mayoral Proclamation, July 4.

been enjoyed and practised,[1] there can be little doubt (with our present knowledge) that the Plague might have been restricted, and many thousands of human lives that perished have been saved. The panic of Plague and the tendency that is entirely human to resort to measures of the utmost severity in the effort to stifle it are matters which the code shut out from consideration.

The " Orders Conceived " gave liberty to inmates (lodgers) to leave a house wherein infection occurred providing they first obtained certificates of health from the examiner of the parish. That liberty was not conceded in the Great Plague. The house was shut up on discovery with all families remaining in it, and by common experience the Plague destroyed all. The importance of the office of examiner contemplated by these Plague Orders and the failure generally to create it I come to later.

It is essential to an understanding of the Great Plague in London to put out of mind, as of practical application, the comprehensive code of Orders that is an obsession with Defoe throughout his book. The shock of Plague was too great, and its effects too convulsive, to condone any considerable tampering with the measures that throughout long experience had been considered necessary for meeting it. A body of precedent had grown up, going back through the Plague statute of James I. to the reigns of Elizabeth and Henry VIII., and it was from this precedent that in time of crisis guidance was sought. The whole system of treatment was rooted in error, had grown up in error; and though, as successive Plagues came and passed, in the orders drawn up one may detect advances towards the light, the despairing thing was that when confronted anew with the gaunt spectre the authorities never looked forward, but always back.

Neither law nor civil administration, nor medicine itself, had any real enlightenment. For sixty years past there had been no attempt at statutory legislation for combating Plague, though in that time London and the Kingdom had been visited with epidemics by each one of which tens of thousands of people had perished. Dr.

---

[1] It was sometimes done by stealth. Boghurst instances a case where the inhabitants of a house, " for fear of being shut up," removed a Plague-stricken man to another house in the middle of his sickness. (*Loimographia*, p. 46.)

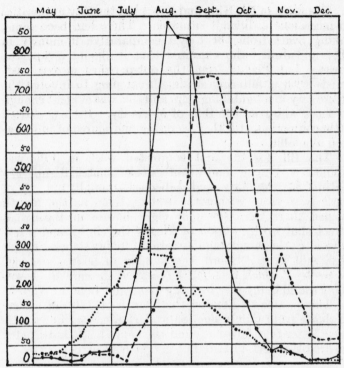

CHART (ALL DEATHS) SHOWING TREND OF THE PLAGUE FROM
WEST TO EAST.
Based on the Bills of Mortality, 1665.
Dotted line, St. Giles-in-the-Fields.
Solid line, Cripplegate.
Broken line, Stepney.

Creighton has rightly pointed out [1] that the recommendations of the College of Physicians in 1665 are but the
recommendations of the College of Physicians in 1636
repeated, with but insignificant change; and the civic
authorities, like the doctors, as sheepishly followed upon
the lines of what had been done at former Plague
epidemics,[2] displaying neither initiative nor insight.

[1] *History of Epidemics in Britain*, i. 646.
[2] Guildhall possesses in the Letter Books, Repertories and Journals
circa Henry VIII., Elizabeth and James I., a number of orders given and
regulations made for dealing with earlier Plagues. The calendars prepared and published by the City Corporation have not yet reached these
reigns. A useful abstract of these City Plague Orders is contained in
Brit. Mus. Addit. MSS. 4376.

The flight of the King and Court left the City authorities to face alone a difficult situation.   There had been some, taking heart from the City's comparative immunity in May and June, who expected that it should escape the worst ; but Plague from the out-parishes moved eastwards with unfaltering stride, threatening to involve the entire City in a tightening grip, and this was evident enough to those who read the Bills of Mortality.   If these carried little conviction, still they were the one source of information available.

The Bill for the first completed week in July was ominous.   Plague had that week snatched up 279 victims in the City and Liberties, though but 28 of these were from within the walls.   Even as the month opened there were seven or eight houses in Basinghall Street shut up by reason of Plague therein [1] ; and a few days later the increasing desolation forcibly struck Pepys's observant eyes.   " Lord, the number of houses visited," he wrote, " which this day I observed through the town, going round in my way by Long Lane and London Wall." [2]

There came to London this month of July an undergraduate from Cambridge, Samuel Herne, who in an intimate letter tells how he found the capital.   It anticipates events by a week or two, but is best read here—

London, July the 18 1665.

HONOURED SIR
Blessed be the lord I got to London safe on wensday by eleven of the clock : and there is but very little notice tooke of the sicknesse here in London though the bills are very great there dyd threescore and 18 in st giles in the feilds since the bill ; and 5 in one hour, in our parish since, it spreads very much ; I went by many houses in London that were shut up ; all over the city almost ; nobody that is in London feares to goe anywhere but in st giles's : they have a Bellman there with a cart ; there dye so many that the bell would hardly ever leave ringing and so they ring not at all : the citizens begin to shut up apace ; nothing hinders them from it for fear of the houses breaking open : my fathers has been shut up about a weeke ; but theyr is hardly an house ope in the strand : nor the exchange : the sicknesse is at Tottenham high crosse but Mr Moyse would not have you let his son know. it is much at hogsden [Hoxton] ; so that I saw them as I went in the road,

---

[1] Pepys, July 1.   [2] *Ibid.*, July 6.

ly in a small thackt house, and I beleeve all most starved so great a dread it strikes into the people : I taryd In london till thursday in the afternoon, because the tide would not serve. but then went to Wandsor . . . It is very credibly reported that de Ryter is beat and taken or sunke. one wensday night such news came from hampton Court. the sickness is at Richmond and we beleeve the King will reside not there long.

thus with my humble service to you and Mr Blith Jun
I Rest your Obedient pupill
SAM : HERNE.

For his Honoured Tutour
    Mr Samuel Blithe fellow of
    Clarehall In Cambridge.[1]

Guildhall had not been idle, or blind to the peril threatening the City. On June 19th the Lord Mayor sent copies of Plague Orders to each Alderman, with a precept thoroughly to peruse them and to cause them to be put in operation.[2] Presumably these were the " Orders Conceived and Published " that Flesher had printed, but the Guildhall archives contain nothing by which they can be identified. The civic Court of Requests was closed the same month, lest resort thereto should spread infection.[3]

King Charles, before his departure from Whitehall for Hampton Court, received the Lord Mayor, consulting with him upon the measures to be adopted in the City.[4]

Albemarle's courage never faltered. Edward Bury Godfrey, a conscientious justice, has remembrance by his violent death at the time of the Popish Plot—his body run through with his own rapier and left in a ditch at Primrose Hill. Warcupp, the Westminster magistrate, had associations with the Court, being Cup Bearer to the Duke of York. He did good service in London throughout the whole of the Plague, then fell upon evil days. He used Lord Arlington's name when, for a money payment, negotiating the pardon of one Burton, summoned by Proclamation for not returning from beyond the seas, and on the transaction being disclosed asserted that Arlington

---

[1] This letter is printed by Mr. J. R. Wardale, M.A., Fellow of Clare College, in his *Clare College Letters and Documents*, Cambridge, 1903. Samuel Herne became a Fellow of Clare College, of which the recipient of his letter, Dr. Blythe, was later the Master.

[2] " Journal " 46, fo. 60.

[3] " Repertory " 70, fo. 136b.

[4] Clarendon's *Life*.

was privy to it ; for which "scandalous defamation" of
the Secretary of State he was banished for ever from the
Court, committed to the Fleet Prison, and put out of the
Lieutenancy and the Commission of the Peace.[1] Apart
from these and Lord Craven, the magistrates to whom
supreme control in the out-parishes of London was given
have little personality. It is possible that that of Sir John
Lawrence, the Lord Mayor, has not had full appreciation.

He was a masterful man. He imprisoned a civic officer
who spread abroad news of the week's mortality from
Plague before the Bill had come to the Lord Mayor.[2]

John Lawrence was of the family which has left to us
the Lawrence Chapel in Old Chelsea Church, wherein
many of its members are buried. He had been sworn
Alderman of Queenhithe Ward in 1658. Later that same
year he became Sheriff, and he was one of the first two
civic dignatories knighted by King Charles on his Restoration.[3] In such circumstances a loyal adherent of the Court
party might be expected. He was not that.

Lawrence's politics at the time of the Plague had not
the ascerbity of later years, when he had become the stal-
wart leader of the party in opposition to the Court in civic
affairs, and was attacked with venomous animosity by the
creatures of Whitehall.

A curious manuscript survives that was written in
1672, secretly to give King Charles II. knowledge of the
characters of the Aldermen of the City, as read by a
Court partisan. Its violence and bigotry attest this
writer's worthlessness as a judge of men, and if I repeat its
libels it is not because they are true, but because they are
revealing. Of Lawrence, the manuscript says that he
"hath always three or four busy turbulent fellows to cry
him up in all parts of the City, and to assist him in all
popular elections." It asserts that "he hath put all
affronts and indignities imaginable upon all those persons
that have been willing to venture their lives and estates in
any military employment for his Majesty." As a parting
shaft, this critic declares that all Lawrence had gained by

---

[1] Privy Ccl. Reg. 59, fo. 104.
[2] Symon Patrick to Mrs. Gauden, Dec. 5.
[3] Genealogical MSS. Collections relating to Lord Mayors in Bishopsgate Institute Library.

House in Great St Helens formerly the Residence
of Sr J.^{no} LAWRANCE, LORD MAYOR of LONDON A.D. 1665

SIR JOHN LAWRENCE'S HOUSE IN GREAT ST. HELEN'S

treacherous compliance with the Dissenting party he had
lost by " impious and insolent behaviour " towards almost
all he had come in contact with. He says of another
Alderman that " he for a while was guided by Sir John
Lawrence, who led him astray." [1] Now a venomous
opponent does not say such things of a man of straw.

Look between the lines, read the mind of this Court
libeller, and there lurks there a man whom he fears—a
strong man.

Lawrence was ejected from his Aldermanry eleven
years later, after judgment given against the City in the
Writ of Quo Warranto proceedings,[2] and his seat filled by
a Court placeman. Everything we know of him indicates
a fearless, independent man, and well it was for the City's
rule and orderliness that in these desperate months of the
Plague its chief magistrate had strength and personality.
He worked quietly, and was little interfered with. Lawrence in his Mayoral year was also Master of the Haberdashers Company. He had nine daughters, and a son who
died in infancy. He lived in Great St. Helen's, Bishopsgate,
in a house that survived more than a century after the
Great Plague, bearing upon its decorated front the date
1662 and his arms and those of the City of London. An
old print of it is here reproduced. Defoe very likely
preserves a memory of the time when he says that
Lawrence had a low gallery built in his hall, whereon he
appeared to receive the people of all sorts and conditions
who came to see him, secure himself from contact and
contamination. The tradition of his benevolence has been
handed down. No man could have stayed in London as
he did, not absenting himself for a day, without realizing
the worthlessness of riches unless they could be used in
relieving the wretchedness about him.

The tablet of his wife Abigail is in Great St. Helen's
Church, but nothing of Lawrence himself, who also lies
there, save his arms on the highly decorated sword-rest
and the entry in the burial register—

1691[2]. Jan. 29. Sir John Laurence.

The Sheriffs' office made them less conspicuous in the

[1] Rev. Alfred Beaven, *Aldermen of the City of London*, ii. 186, 188.
[2] When in 1685 the City's Charter was restored, Lawrence was rein-
stated in his Aldermanry, and he died on Jan. 26th, 1692.

Plague, but the Court libeller above quoted in a reference to Sir George Waterman hits off a character in a sentence that is true of so many others that I cannot resist temptation to repeat it : " He employs abundance of time, but does no business."

On July 5th it was ordered by the Court of Aldermen, the Lord Mayor presiding, that no Alderman should move out of the City or remain away from it without leave given by the Lord Mayor or the Court on reasonable cause. Aldermen then absent were required to return forthwith and fulfil the duties of their office.[1] It is their creditable record that these duties were performed unfalteringly.

The Court of Aldermen had met that day, with premonition, if not actual knowledge, that the King and the Royal Court were about to leave London. They had then framed an additional set of orders, " as a further means (by God's blessing) than what is before directed to obviate the increase of the Plague." These were supplemented by occasional orders from time to time.

The Court of Aldermen at their meeting on July 5th had tightened the regulations upon inn-holders and tavern-keepers, who during the infection were forbidden to receive or entertain any save travelling guests, and those with sobriety and moderation. Strangers desiring to eat or drink should receive their wants at the doors, and residents in the locality of an inn should send for their requirements, to be consumed within their own dwellings.

Other regulations made were these :

Wardmote inquests to assemble weekly to report nuisances such as were most perilous for the infection, and to inquire into all offences and disorders committed in taverns.

None to sing or cry ballads in the streets, or to hawk goods.

All inmates or under-sitters (lodgers) of houses within the City to be ejected, these having been found to be a principal means of increasing the infection.

All grammar schools, writing schools, and other schools for the teaching of youth of either sex to be broken up and discontinued till Michaelmas next, " especially dancing

---

[1] " Repertory " 70, fo. 141.

and fencing schools, and all meetings there to be utterly prohibited."

Careful watch and ward to be constantly kept at the gates and Thames-side landing places to prevent the ingress of all vagrants, beggars, loose and dangerous people from the out-parts into the City and Liberties, such persons to be apprehended and punished.

It being dangerous for the spread of the infection that people resort to the Mayor's and Sheriffs' Courts at Guildhall, no trials at law to be held or inquests (requiring jurymen) to be summoned till the contagion be abated.

Dogs, cats and " other vermin " killed or left dead in the streets to be carried away by the rakers.

Aldermen and other officers acting in execution of orders made for the prevention and cure of the Plague to be defended and indemnified by the Court of Aldermen in any controversy that arose.

Churchwardens, constables and others to prevent the profanation of the Lord's Day by disorderly tippling, gaming, labouring, and rowing upon the River Thames.[1]

These public regulations touched the daily life of every citizen. They were issued in a Mayoral Proclamation, and were read on the following Sunday from the pulpits of all the City churches. The orders were quickly supplemented by a provision aimed to prevent infection coming in by the river, watermen being forbidden to bring to the City from adjacent parts any infected persons, or vagrants or suspected people.[2] Again there was the attempt to isolate the City against infection by warders at the gates and landing places, as earlier the out-parishes had attempted to isolate themselves by drawing a cordon around the parish of St. Giles-in-the-Fields; and again the precaution was taken too late. The Plague had already entered.

London for many months thereafter, while Plague raged, presented the surprising spectacle of a capital without law tribunals, with no gaol delivery; the ordinary activities of government paralysed into inaction, and its

[1] *Mayoral Proclamation, July* 4 (Brit. Mus. Pressmark 21, h. 5, No. 33) and Guildhall " Repertory " 70, fos. 139, 141. The " Repertory " dates these orders a day later than the printed Proclamation and the entry is incomplete, a blank being left in the pages which was never filled. There are a few textual discrepancies.

[2] " Repertory " 70, fo. 143b.

whole energies diverted to combating the Plague and alleviating the resulting distress. The magistrates dealt out summary justice upon wrongdoers. It is curious how false tradition lingers. That attractive spot at Hampstead, "Judges' Walk," you will be told locally received the name from the circumstance that in the year of the Great Plague the Judges, driven out of London, held the Assize there, beneath the shade of a giant elm. There was no Assize.

The most pressing requirement was some medical provision. Public health—at least out of Plague time—was not a matter of civic concern. The Medical Officer of Health did not exist. His services were urgently needed, and already the Court of Aldermen had considered what should best be done to provide physicians, surgeons, and apothecaries to visit and prescribe for the Plague-stricken poor, and had been in communication with the College of Physicians.

A small committee set up, consisting of two Aldermen— Sir William Turner and Sir William Peake—the Sheriffs and the Sheriffs-Elect, made recommendation for the appointment " at present " of Dr. Nathaniel Hodges, who practised at Walbrook, and Dr. (afterwards Sir Thomas) Witherley, of Hatton Garden, for the prevention and cure of the Plague within the City and Liberties. The College of Physicians had at the outset advised that six or four doctors at least be chosen to apply themselves to the task, and that to each doctor there be assigned two apothecaries and three surgeons. If any died by the Plague, their widows should have pensions during life.[1] Drs. Hodges and Witherley were asked to consult together without delay, and thereafter to advise the committee as to such means as they conceived would be most expedient to stop the Plague.[2] These two, as heads of the service, had direct contact with the civic rulers throughout the visitation.[3]

The result was the immediate appointment of two other practitioners, Edward Harman, of Finch Lane, and Thomas Gray, of Temple Bar, to be employed under direction of

[1] *Certain Necessary Directions*, etc. 1665.
[2] " Repertory " 70, fo. 144.
[3] *Mayoral Proclamation*, July 13 (Brit. Mus. Pressmark 21. h. 5, No. 34).

Drs. Hodges and Witherley for the cure of the Plague. They were to be paid out of a rate to be raised for the relief of the infected poor, sums of £30 each on appointment, £30 each more at Michaelmas, and £40 each at Christmas if, as the conditions grimly stated, " they or either of them shall be then living and continuing in the service." [1] Still the medical staff numbered but four.

Voluntary assistance augmented the little band as the rapid spread of Plague in the City made plain how large was the work to be done. Before a bad July merged into what should prove a far more desperate August, the civic authorities were able to organize a medical service to attend the infected poor in the various wards. To their enduring honour, doctors offered themselves for the perilous work without fee. The Court of Aldermen, bearing a lasting record that they did " well approve and kindly accept " these proposals, made the following apportionments of areas :—

Dr. John Glover, for the Wards of Cordwainer, Cheap, Walbrook, and Cannon Street ;

Dr. Humphrey Brookes, for the parishes of St. Helen Bishopsgate, St. James Duke Place, St. Katharine Cree, St. Andrew Undershaft, St. Katherine Colman, Allhallows Staining and St. Olave Hart Street ;

Dr. Barbone, for the parishes of St. Dunstan's West, St. Bride, St. Martin Ludgate, and St. Anne Blackfriars. [2]

Two other doctors were quickly enrolled in the healing work, both having made a like gratuitous offer, and in addition to their labours elsewhere in the City

Dr. Brookes [3] took medical charge of St. Benet Gracechurch parish ; and

Dr. Parker charge of the Ward of Cripplegate Without (where the worst Plague in the City raged) and the parish of St. Stephen Coleman Street. [4] A petition subsequently made shows Dr. Parker to be dead and his good services unrequited, but whether or not dead of the Plague is not disclosed. [5]

---

[1] "Repertory" 70, fo. 147. For their fate see p. 206, *post.* Gray was a surgeon of Bart.'s, Harman perhaps an apothecary.

[2] "Repertory" 70, fo. 150b, 151.

[3] There appear to have been two doctors of this name.

[4] "Repertory" 70, fo. 152.

[5] *Ibid.*, 76, fo. 272b.

Gladly I add to these Dr. Nicholas Davis, of Austin Friars, and Dr. Edward D'Awtry, or Deantry,[1] living in Broad Street, whose spheres of labour cannot now be ascertained. Both were presented by the College of Physicians to the Lord Mayor and Court of Aldermen for prevention and cure of the Plague, they having volunteered for that dangerous service, as they simply stated, " upon principles of honour and conscience."

The City, wherein so rarely a year passed without cases of Plague, possessed a permanent pest-house. It stood isolated beyond the northern Liberty by Old Street, near the west end of St. Luke's Hospital site, where still a part of the old pest-field exists in a rear garden. Long afterwards the place was kept in remembrance by Pest House Row, built on the site in 1737. Its origin may be traced back to the many Plagues which afflicted Elizabeth's London. Seven Aldermen had perished of the " sweating sickness " in the first year of her reign ; and after twenty-five years' experience of Plagues Elizabeth was moved to protest her surprise that no pest-house or hospital had been built by the City of London, although other cities of less antiquity, fame, wealth, and reputation had provided themselves with such places, whereby the lives of the inhabitants had been in times of infection chiefly preserved.[2]   Fleet-wood, the Recorder of London, asked to advise the Privy Council, had proposed that the Queen, by Prerogative, should appoint a " Harbourer for the Plague," with power to take up lodging in any newly-built house, therein to place and cherish the Plague-stricken until they be whole.[3]

The necessity could not be long disregarded when London was terribly visited by Plague in 1592, and the City raised the money and built a pest-house. Sir Walter Raleigh had been engaged in a successful privateering venture against Spain, and the Livery Companies which had taken shares in the enterprise were called upon to contribute one-third of their clear gains for the purpose.

---

[1] Dr. D'Awtry I cannot trace except by the announcement made in the *Intelligencer*, Aug. 7, 1665, and it seems likely that this contains a misprint, Edward Deantry, M.D. Oxon., Hon. F.R.C.P., being intended. See Dr. Clippingdale's letter in *British Medical Journal* for Feb. 16, 1909.

[2] Lords of the Council to the Lord Mayor, April 21, 1583, printed in Overall's *Index to Remembrancer*, p. 336.

[3] Clode, *Early History of Merchant Taylors*, ii. 296.

The sum so raised proving insufficient, the contribution had to be supplemented by a "benevolence" in each ward.[1]

Little is known of the City pest-house at the Great Plague. It was a timber structure, as were so many dwelling houses of the time, and in its primitive arrangements far apart from a hospital as we conceive it to-day. As contagion grew ever more threatening, additional accommodation was given by large sheds erected around the building.[2] Nathaniel Upton was master of the pest-house. Probably he had medical qualifications, but there is nothing to show it. Often he was called into the City to certify, after examination, deaths from Plague—

> Paid Mr Upton Master at the pest-house for comeing twice into Bearebinder-lane to view the bodies of two dead boys [3] . . 10s. 0d.

The practice of the pest-house keeper was to extract fees from such parishes as sent their infected poor to receive his attentions.

Additional bedding and equipment as required was sent in at the City's cost,[4] and when the great spread of Plague filled all his beds, Upton was ordered to take no more than forty shillings for each person received.[5] Apparently the one sum sufficed for all charges and costs till death or cure relieved the pest-house master of further responsibility. His trade was a gamble with death. How many beds the City pest-house contained is unknown, but from the fact that in no single week of the Great Plague did more than twelve deaths occur there,[6] the number cannot have been large.

Long before the Plague became seated within the City's wall the pest-house by Old Street had filled from the Liberties, and the ghastly policy of shutting up the sick with the healthy was pursuing its devastating course. It was the experience of St. Giles-in-the-Fields over again,

---

[1] Dr. Reginald Sharpe, *London and the Kingdom*, i. 551–2.
[2] "Repertory" 70, fo. 135. In this work and in essential equipment £220 was spent (Guildhall Library MS. 359).
[3] St. Mary Woolchurch Haw Ch'wardens Accts.
[4] "Repertory" 70, fo. 143b.
[5] *Ibid.*, fo. 152.
[6] *Bills of Mortality*.

but upon an enlarged scale. There the Plague still piled up unceasingly its awful tale of dead. In the five weeks that in the Bills comprised the whole month of July, St. Giles-in-the-Fields lay prostrate under the visitation, when into its great pits were hurried no fewer than 1,391 corpses, and in a single week 370. What wonder if, with fearful vision, men foresaw an early time when St. Giles's should stand depopulated, a waste of desolate houses, all the inhabitants being dead ? London City, its own fears increasing daily, lay within sight and sound of all this woe.

In July the Great Plague in the City may be said to have begun. Till then the Plague stood at the door, a spectre menacing evil. Its dread possibilities the merchant citizen had fully grasped, but his habit of mind was to consider civic London as an entity complete of itself, and he learnt that the deaths from all causes in the City and Liberties for the week ending July 4th did not exceed 453. The balance that made the sum total that week upwards of one thousand occurred in the out-parishes beyond the Lord Mayor's jurisdiction. None could harbour any longer a false sense of security, or be blind to the immediate peril, when in a fortnight the City's own mortality doubled, and but a fortnight later the figures so grossly swollen doubled again. It was the cumulative effect of the weekly Bills that struck terror.

As in the thermometer the rise of the mercury in the column tells of increasing heat, so these figures, eagerly scanned by all, disclosed the tendency of the Plague, always upward. The printed Bills for the month showed this :

CITY AND LIBERTIES.

For the Week ending	Deaths from All Causes.	Of these were Attributed to Plague.
July 4	453	189
,, 11	559	279
,, 18	876	472
,, 25	1,451	823
Aug. 1	1,767	1,101

It was common report that in one day of mid-July as many as one hundred houses were shut up in the single parish of St. Andrew Holborn,[1] on the City's edge.

[1] Sir George Sitwell, *Letters of the Sitwells and the Sacheverells*, i. 64.

The poor rate made in ordinary course was quickly exhausted by the unprecedented burden thrown upon it; and in July a special rate was ordered by the Lord Mayor and Court of Aldermen to be levied in every ward, for the relief of the infected poor in the City and Liberties.[1] Urgency was impressed in the speedy collection of the sums due; the Aldermen were required to report those failing to pay, that proceedings be taken against them.[2]

A devout Puritan element in the City long survived the Restoration, and religious fanatics of many sects. These, finding the heaviest mortality to be among the unconsidered poor and those of vicious life, took heart of grace, and as Richard Baxter remarked, "began to be puffed up and to boast of the great difference that God did make." [3] They were to learn that there should be no Passover, as with Israel; no blood sign upon the lintel and door-posts or saintliness of life within be sufficient to ward off the swift angel of death. The Plague made no distinctions.[4] Like the fashionable western outskirts before it, the City in July began rapidly to empty of its wealthier people. Merchants where possible sent their families away, and as alarm grew apace took themselves the first opportunity to follow. The world of fashion found it far easier to uproot itself than did the world of commerce, and there were many who stayed throughout the height of the infection in August and September, till the worst was over. Looking down the long lists of burials in the City church registers, a week's return swollen into many pages

COCK TAVERN TOKEN.

where before a few lines had sufficed, now and again the searcher comes upon the names of some merchant of substance and often wife and child, and against them the fatefully significant letter "P." These had ventured to take the risk, and had perished.

The taverner of the Cock in Fleet Street—the sign

[1] "Repertory" 70, fo. 144b.
[2] "Journal" 46, fo. 60b.
[3] *Reliquiæ Baxterianæ*, ed. Sylvester, 1691, part 3, p. 1.
[4] Cf. Vincent, p. 27. Boghurst's *Loimographia*, p. 25: "As far as I could discern the difference of the two, more of the good died than of the bad."

is still borne there—advertised his absence in the *Intelligencer*—

This is to notify that the master of the Cock and Bottle, commonly called the Cock Alehouse, at Temple Bar, hath dismissed his servants, and shut up his house, for this long Vacation, intending (God willing) to return at Michaelmas next, so that all persons whatsoever who have any accompts with the said master, or farthings [tokens] belonging to the said house, are desired to repair thither before the 8th of this instant July, and they shall receive satisfaction.

How quickly the Plague mortality leapt up as the area of infection extended is best illustrated by taking the London of the Bills of Mortality as a whole. I have before recalled that the deaths from all causes over the previous year averaged 352 weekly. These were July's figures :

CITY, LIBERTIES, AND OUT-PARISHES.

For the Week ending	Deaths from All Causes.	Of these were Attributed to Plague.
July 4	1,006	470
„ 11	1,268	725
„ 18	1,761	1,089
„ 25	2,785	1,843
Aug. 1	3,014	2,010

The mortality ascribed to Plague, three only in the first four months of the year, had been 43 in May, in June (four weeks) 590, and rose in four complete weeks of July to 5,667.

The figures used are from the only source available, and for reasons already explained there must be added many other deaths that are not recorded. The apportionment to Plague is wholly unreliable. It stretches human credulity to believe that a capital whose normal weekly death rate, when fully populated, had been but 350, should when Plague-stricken and partly depopulated, have lost in the one week ending the 1st August 1,004 of its inhabitants by deaths other than Plague, besides 2,010 from the infection. Or to take another instance equally enlightening, who shall believe that in the City and Liberties, where the pre-Plague mortality averaged 205 weekly, there died in the week ending the 25th July 628 persons from causes other than Plague ?

It is preposterous. The City, like the out-parishes, was concealing the ravages that Plague made.

A chance meeting by Pepys with the Parish Clerk of St. Olave Hart Street, and the scrap of conversation preserved, tells much. "Asking how the Plague goes, he told me it increases much, and much in our parish; 'for,' says he, 'there died nine this week, though I have returned but six.'" Pepys held it "a very ill practice," making him think there was the same deception in other parishes, and therefore the Plague was much greater than people believed it to be.[1] That was in August—not in the first fright of Plague, but fourteen days before it reached its highest incidence in London.

What was there one could believe? If dishonest, the Bills of Mortality gave sufficient warning. The citizen Rugge asserts that 1,800 families moved away in July.[2] Wherever there was high land overlooking London, at Hampstead and Highgate on the north and Shooter's Hill south-east, from there the highways out of the capital were to be seen thronged with vehicles of every description, and horsemen riding away from the City that soon should be overspread by death from street to street, as the better-class merchants followed in the flight which the fashionable world had led.

It was a crying scandal of the time that great numbers of these emigrants, whether of fashion or business, in their haste to put the Plague behind them and find a safe refuge left no bounty for their poorer and less fortunate neighbours, and, moreover, left the pest-rate unpaid. They could not be traced. There were those who remembered their duty. "If the rest," wrote L'Estrange in his news-sheet, "that have withdrawn themselves would follow that copy, and contribute liberally to the relief of the parties they have forsaken, it would certainly be, under God, the most sovereign means imaginable of putting a stop to the progress of this grievous sickness." He spoke of persons insensible of a common calamity; of Christians incompassionate one of another; and many who had made money or found pleasure in the town now abandoning it without leaving so much as a morsel of bread for the relief of the distressed.[3]

[1] *Diary*, Aug. 30. [2] Rugge's "Diurnal," July.
[3] *Intelligencer*, July 24.

Van Gogh, the Ambassador, reported to the States-General that great and mean fled the City. Foreign merchants and residents sought their passes and joined in the exodus, " there being no manner of trade left, nor conversation, either at Court or on the Exchange." London's great commerce dwindled away. Bills of exchange were no longer accepted on the mart, none knowing what might befall, or where the creditor should be found when payment fell due.[1]

Stephen Bing, a Petty Canon of St. Paul's, from the heart of the City was a witness of the flight—

The increase of God's judgment (he wrote) deadens people's hearts so that trading strangely ceaseth. They shut up their shops, and such a fear possesseth them as is wonderful to see how they hurry into the country, as though the same God was not there that is in the city. Those that are living and lived in the great sickness time [the last grievous Plague visitation] knew nothing the like, even when there died four thousand a week. I pray God to prevent a sad sequel. Great complaint there is of necessity, and needs must it be the more when the rich haste away that should supply the poor's want.[2]

The panic and the Plague came into the City together. The flight was so fast that for most of July the houses left empty and forsaken by their owners were more numerous than those marked by the red cross, where the Plague had entered.[3] There were yet many intending to fly, both in the out-parishes and the City, who lingered too long and fell victims to the Plague before they could get away.[4] For weeks the tide of emigration flowed by every outlet from London towards the country, the smaller traders who were fortunately circumstanced following in the steps of the rich merchants. It was checked at last by the refusal of the Lord Mayor to grant further certificates of health, and by the effective opposition of the neighbouring townships, which in self-defence set armed guards upon their roads and formed a barrier around the stricken capital.

The first of the appointed days of fast and humiliation for the Plague was observed in London on the 12th of July, with strictness and solemnity, the people crowding

[1] *State Papers* (*Domestic*), 1664–5, p. 488.
[2] Bing to Dean Sancroft, July 27.
[3] Vincent, p. 28.   [4] Boghurst, p. 70.

the churches.[1] The Lord Mayor and Sheriffs with a
goodly company of Aldermen, and a vast congregation,
attended at St. Paul's Cathedral.[2] A special form of
Common Prayer for use was prepared by the Primate.
The Litany has the passage : " For there is wrath gone
out against us, and the Plague is begun. That dreadful
arrow of Thine sticks fast in our flesh." [3]

In many of the City's short streets when alarm was
universal were not more than eight or ten houses remaining
open,[4] the neighbouring merchants or tradesmen having
sought the country. They left their unemployed journeymen and servants to swell the crowded populations in the
poorest quarters. That was the awful tragedy of the
Plague. In these circumstances it was inevitable that
the Plague, instead of relieving the poor streets, should
add to their congestion. Poverty, increasing as the
pestilence increased—the poverty to which the short-
sighted parsimony of the parish officers contributed, in
paying no more than a starvation wage to those they hired
for perilous services—drove the people into congested and
insanitary areas of the outskirts, where alone they could
secure lodging in decaying wooden houses built about the
narrow and filthy alleys. There Plague found all the
material it required to thrive upon. It made the task
of combating epidemic immensely difficult. Roger
L'Estrange, who had little vision, and may be said to
express the opinions of the well-to-do classes, in his
newspapers rails repeatedly against the poor for bringing
disease upon themselves by their environment and habits.

The statements of this contemporary writer merit
attention, though the conclusions we draw from them are
not his :

The last week's Bill of Plague amounts to 1,089, of which
number 867 died in ten of the out-parishes, and even of them it
may be fairly established that poverty and sluttishness hath
destroyed the one-half. Within the walls of the City there died
only 56, and very few of those but in the close and blind alleys.
—*Newes*, July 20.

The weight of this heavy judgment hath hitherto fallen only
upon the poor, who are either crowded up into corners or

[1] *Newes*, July 13.   [2] Bing to Sancroft, Aug. 3.
[3] A printed copy of the Order of Service is in Lincoln's Inn Library.
[4] Rugge's " Diurnal," July.

smothered for want of air, or are otherwise lost for want of seasonable attendance and remedies.—*Intelligencer*, July 24.

In the City (that is to say, in the close and filthy alleys and corners about it) the Plague is very much increased, but in the broad and open streets there is but little appearance of it. . . . The main part of the rest [dead from Plague] is within half a score of the out-parishes ; and those, too, in the sluttish parts of those parishes where the poor are crowded up together, and in multitudes infect one another.—*Newes*, Aug. 10.

I am warranted by good authority to advertise, that partly by taking cold, and small drinks in the heat of the fever ; partly by putting off their sweats too soon ; and in part by rising and exposing themselves to the air before the sweats are well over, some thousands of those who have perished in this dreadful mortality have in all appearances hastened their own destruction.—*Newes*, Aug. 17.

Not alone was such herding of the poor deplorable ; it was true. Against these examples L'Estrange, near the close of epidemic, found satisfaction that " In this raging pestilence it hath pleased God to spare those public ministers, magistrates, and officers upon whose lives the peace and order of the government so much depend, insomuch that I do not find this visitation to have taken away any person of prime authority and command." [1] The poor were blameworthy ; how much better was the sensible behaviour of the rich ! His mind seemed impenetrable to the fact that it was the action of these same better classes in leaving their workless dependants to be crowded together in the " sluttish parts " that gave the Plague such a wide and congenial field for working devastation.

In the streets the quacks were about, pushing their wares under notice of each passer by. They promised immunity and cures. On shuttered shops their claims were vaunted. Their bills were on every post. Country readers of L'Estrange's weekly *Newes* gained their first knowledge that Plague was abroad in London from advertisements of quack medicines five weeks before it had mention as news. [2] John Sly—befitting name—at the sign of the Blazing Star within Aldgate sold an excellent drink of sovereign virtue, used in the last great Plague and approved by eminent physicians. [3] Dr. Trig's

---

[1] *Intelligencer*, Oct. 23. [2] *Newes*, May 18.
[3] *Ibid.*, July 20.

" great cordial " was commended, having wrought famous
cures at London's previous visitation.[1] That was a
favourite trick, to claim for the lauded specific past
services which none could deny.

In St. Paul's Churchyard were the little shops of the
stationers and booksellers. They made under the Cathedral's shadow a centre for the unholy trade. At Richard
Lowndes' sign of the White Lion was procurable the
approved antidote or pectoral, prepared by eminent
physicians in the great year of contagion 1625, and then
taken with great success.[2] Henry Eversden, of the Greyhound, offered Dr. Theodore de Medde's famous Anti-
pharmacon at the low price of threepence. That appealed
to the needy ; for the well-to-do he had the more potent
Universal Elixir at 2s. 6d. the 5-ounce glass.[3]

The flight of so many doctors who should have watched
over the people's lives gave opportunity to these impostors,
and they made sad havoc both of bodies and purses,
selling their stuff at an extraordinarily dear rate. One
vended pills, as worthless as the rest, at 2s. 6d. the
single pill, another plasters at 5s. apiece.[4] These their
credulous dupes eagerly bought. No reason existed to
fear the Plague were a tithe of the pretensions justified.
A charlatan styling himself Constantine Rhodocanaces had
that admirable preservative against Plague " wherewith
Hippocrates, the Prince of all Physitians, preserved the
whole land of Greece." [5] The poor, nerve-shattered
citizen, chilled with fear, had but to walk below stairs at
the New Exchange in the Strand, to where Mrs. Anne Loves
traded beneath the sign of the Black Boy, to obtain from
her a pomander, prepared according to the prescription of
Dr. Clayton, King Charles I.'s physician,[6] which had
magical effects.

Any who called upon Gabriel Bedel and Thomas
Collins, whose stationers' shop was by Middle Temple
Gate in Fleet Street, could obtain there the Avrum Velans
sive potabile, being the true philosophical preparation
of potable gold, distilled by a pure crystalline and innocent
spirit. The price was high, £5 sterling per ounce, but

[1] *Newes*, July 13.   [2] *Intelligencer*, July 17.
[3] *Newes*, July 22.   [4] Boghurst's *Loimographia*, p. 75.
[5] *Newes*, July 13.   [6] *Intelligencer*, June 3.

remedy sure.[1]   Austin, the versifier of the Great Plague, lashes out at the stationers for their avarice in lending their shops for the purpose, and taking a share in the disgraceful plunder of the quacks.[2]

There was no escaping them.   They thrust into every hand some trash or other under a pompous title.[3]   A cure seller named Matthews had a pill to promote sweating, containing helebore, opium, and other ingredients, which Boghurst, the apothecary, declares choked people.   Gray, of Gutter Lane, Cheapside, gave purging pills to all who came to him ; and wholly unskilled men, without knowledge of Plague or any observation of it, had audacity to write out prescriptions for a fee, and to induce vomiting or undertake bleeding.[4]   " Preposterous physic killed many." They carried their imposture to the bedside, and by peering into chest, arms, and groin for buboes or " tokens " gave such fright to the sufferers as hastened the end.[5]

A tradesman, Francis Hall, at the Green Dragon in Cheapside, offered an electuary at twelve pence an ounce, and a drink at 3s. 6d. the pint, which he laid claim to expose " by order and appointment of his Majesty, the College of Physicians London, and by their special care and advice."   Thomas Williams, " of the Society of rare and well meaning Chymists," compounded medicines for the cure and prevention of Plague, without benefit to himself and for the public good [6]—but at a price.   A yet more audacious quack, styling himself Dr. Stephanus Chrisolitus, " a famous physitian, lately arrived in these parts, having travelled in several countries which have been infected by the Plague," offered a sure palliative.[7]   It is the old, old story of human credulity upon which these leeches fattened.   The tricks of the quacks are as ancient as Hippocrates.

The frightened poor bought freely from them, paying money for what was at best useless and at worst poisonous, and the harm they wrought was second only to the Plague itself.   " Hardly a person escaped who trusted to their delusions," says Dr. Hodges.   " They are traitors ! " he

[1] Newes, July 13.   [2] Anatomy of the Pestilence, 1665.
[3] Loimologia, 21.   [4] Loimographia, p. 75.
[5] Ibid., pp. 25, 30.   [6] Newes, July 20.
                        [7] Ibid., June 1.

declares passionately of those who terrorized the people
with apprehensions of Plague. Their medicines added to
the numbers of the dead; and he rejoices that these blowers
of the pestilential flames were themselves caught in the
common ruin, and by their death in some measure excused
the neglect of the magistrates in suffering their practise.[1]

Most unhappily a report got abroad that venereal
disease gave immunity from Plague. It was the most
tragical teaching, how originated none knew, for in the fear
that became universal there were those ready to accept
any risk that promised life. Its results beggared in horror
the worst effects of the Plague itself. Hodges says the
report was about the town by common fame. " Wicked
and impious was the consequence," he adds. " The
greatest aggravation to this misfortune was, that the very
taint which was to defend against another had it in its
nature to be more forcibly attracted by it ; so that the
rash adventurer was soon brought to a bitter repentance
for his experiment, by sinking immediately under the
pestilential contagion at its first stroke." [2]

A startling adventure, not a little ridiculous, befell
Sir Anthony Browne, with his brother and some friends,
when riding in a coach in the narrow lanes of Essex. They
overtook another coach, its curtains closely drawn. A
young man of the party, believing there might be some
lady travelling who would not be seen, in a spirit of
gallantry leant from his vehicle and thrust his head into
the lady's window to gaze. There, lying back, was a
woman looking very ill, and in a sick dress (" and stunk
mightily, which the coachman also cried out upon," adds
Pepys, who tells the story). Hastily they let the sick
patient get on ahead, and some people, coming up, told

---

[1] *Loimologia*, pp. 21, 22, 206.

[2] *Ibid.*, p. 77. Kemp, who declares the report to have been
" less unfortunate and wretched than devilish and wicked " (*Brief Treatise*,
p. 57) and Boghurst (p. 55), among the medical writers of the time, also
refer to it. The false promise of immunity evidently became widely
circulated. Hodges mentions " a few instances " where both poisons were
in a great measure cast off together ; and there is the curious statement
by Boghurst, for what it is worth : " Of all the common hackney prosti-
tutes of Lutener's Lane, Dog Yard, Cross Lane, Baldwin's Gardens,
Hatton Garden, and other places ; the common criers of oranges, oysters,
fruit, etc. ; all the impudent, drunken, drabbing bayles and fellows, and
many others of the Rouge Route, there are few missing " (*Loimographia*,
p. 96).

the party that she was a maid of Mr. Wright, a neighbour, who was being carried away ill of the Plague. The gallant who had thrust himself so near to contagion was frightened almost out of his life, and fear made him ill.

That was the climax to a whole comedy of errors, very typical when everyone's nerve was at breaking strain. The maid, taken ill of Plague, had been removed to an outbuilding. In the absence of a nurse appointed to look after her there, she escaped through a window and ran away. The nurse, returning, and getting no answer to her repeated knocks, believed her charge was dead. She told the master of the house so. He and his lady were much disturbed, for no villagers would touch a Plague corpse, and he went into Brentwood to obtain assistance in the burial, but none in the town would help. On the way back over the wild common he encountered the girl— and believing it to be her wraith, was more alarmed than ever. Finally she was taken and put into the pest-coach to be carried to a pest-house.[1]

Left in London when most men of affairs had gone was Samuel Pepys, always a lover of good company. He had sent his wife to Woolwich, his mother having already been despatched into the country, and himself lingered behind, a lone, somewhat pathetic figure. Mid-August was past when at last the raging Plague roused the authorities to the grave danger of any longer conducting the business of the Navy Office from Seething Lane, by the Tower, and it was removed to the Manor House at Greenwich,[2] where the new lodging little pleased Pepys, " it being in the heart of all the labourers and workmen there, which makes it as unsafe as to be, I think, in London." [3]

As the weeks passed, he experienced increasing depression in the stricken City. Lady Cartaret had given him a bottle of Plague water as a specific [4]; it did not raise his spirits. " The season growing so sickly, that it is much to be feared how a man can escape having a share with others in it, for which the Lord God bless me ! or make me fitted to receive it." [5] That was the thought given to his "Diary" on July 3rd. Before the month was out the Plague had got into Pepys's own parish of St. Olave Hart Street.

[1] Pepys, Aug. 3.   [2] State Papers (Domestic) 1664–5, p. 518.
[3] Diary, Aug. 19 and 21.   [4] Ibid., July 20.   [5] Ibid., July 3.

"It is got, indeed, everywhere; so I begin to think of settling things in order, which I pray God enable me to do, both as to soul and to body." [1]

All his accustomed haunts were desolate. The gaiety and chatter of Whitehall had departed, the empty Palace being left under guard of a few soldiers. Nothing of the stir of life animated Westminster, its offices, wherein he had picked up the news and gossip of brighter days, now tenanted only by clerks. In leisured moments what should a man do? St. James's Palace had been closed on the Duke of York's flight with the Court. He could not walk in St. James's Park, the gates having been made fast against all comers since Plague first appeared in Pall Mall. [2] He sought distraction at Vauxhall's gay gardens, but could sight not one guest there, "the town being so empty of anybody to come there." "I went by coach home," he tells on July 22nd, "not meeting with but two coaches and two carts from Whitehall to my own house that I could observe, and the streets now mighty thin of people." [3] He deemed it "a very dangerous passage nowadays." The hackney carriages, a popular means of travel about town since the Restoration, were generally shunned through fear of infection by previous passengers. Pepys had himself an alarming experience. Driving from the Lord Treasurer's house in Bloomsbury down Holborn into the City, he noticed the vehicle going slower and slower till finally it came to a stop, and the coachman got down hardly able to stand, saying he was suddenly struck very sick, and felt almost blind. Hastily the diarist changed to another coach, "with a sad heart for the poor man, and for myself also, lest he should have been struck with Plague." [4]

Within shelter of his own door he was not care free. "Will is come in thither and laid down upon my bed, ill of headache, which put me into extraordinary fear; and I studied all I could to get him out of the house," Pepys adds naïvely. [5] A visit to the Royal Exchange, where most of the merchants congregated, disclosed little business doing, and very thin attendance. [6] The Exchange was

---

[1] *Diary*, July 26.
[3] *Ibid.*, July 22.
[5] *Ibid.*, July 29.

[2] *Ibid.*, July 5.
[4] *Ibid.*, June 17.
[6] *Ibid.*, July 16.

closed at the end of July for cleaning and repairs,[1] and in the slackness of all commerce in London was not reopened till two months later.[2]

A resultant tragedy of the Plague I will not pass unnoticed, the dumb victims of the universal death. Ever since London became a city, and the dog became the friend of man, the capital had possessed many dogs—the trades-man's best protection against thieves when the watches were so inefficient. In Plague times none were seen. It was a heritage from Elizabethan Plagues that on the appearance of contagion all dogs and cats should be killed. Popular instinct, on no sure ground, held them in fear as carriers of infection, and they were slaughtered by hundreds and the bodies buried.

A customary payment to the dog-killers was twopence a body.[3] St. Martin's took for this service a man with the then ominous name of Crumwell, whose repeated charges figure in the accounts. The City, with perhaps unconscious irony, delegated the task of clearing its streets of dogs in the Great Plague to the Common Hunt; it paid for the service £36 10s.; [4] and that sum, at twopence per head, represents 4,380 unhappy dogs slain by the public slaughterers in the City alone. May they rest in peace!

[1] *Newes*, Aug. 3.
[2] Rugge's "Diurnal," Sept. 28.
[3] "Repertory" 70, fo. 136b.
[4] Guildhall Library MSS. 359.

CHAPTER VI

PLAGUE IN THE CITY

TO picture the City in the grip of Plague we can first turn to pictures; men lived through the time and left testimony that will fill in what remains wanting by the artist's shortcomings. Hogarth alone could have suggested to us the dramatic quality of those fearful months, and by brush or graver have implied the sufferings of a people Plague-beleaguered in the capital. Restoration London had no Hogarth. A popular broadside had vogue, printed when the pestilence was dying down and people took a morbid interest in recalling its terrors. This has some crude illustrations, here reproduced.

Its value is that it is contemporary. The first drawing takes us to an infected house, into the sick-room. Two persons are lying in one bed together, with a figure (perhaps a doctor) approaching them. In a second bed, alone, is another Plague-stricken, and a woman who may be presumed to be the nurse-keeper is bringing a dish. A sufferer is vomiting. Others, recovering but lame by reason of their Plague sores, walk with sticks about the room. Conspicuous in the foreground a body is laid out, awaiting the bearers, and close at hand is the coffin that will contain it.

All this in one room! Perhaps the draughtsman has crowded his objects too closely to get all represented, but what he has expressed is true. And it is the same with the next picture.

This shows a row of timber-framed houses, like those of any of the larger London streets. The dwellings are shut up, with the red cross marked on the locked doors and the bill " Lord have mercy upon us ! " beneath. Watchmen, armed with halberds, stand on guard before. The drawing suggests that the occupants of the neighbouring houses have fled. In the open street a dog-killer follows his calling, licensed to slaughter any dogs that he meets. The canine bodies are carried away by the raker, here seen trundling a wheelbarrow's load of them. Along the street two women searchers approach, bearing white wands in their hands. That is the mark of their office. It warns passers by to keep distant from them, lest infection pass. Bearers are seen conveying in a Sedan chair a Plague patient to the pest-house. Fires burning in the street (that was done in September) are correctly placed before every sixth house.

These are the incidents of a typical street scene of London during the Great Plague, repeated at a hundred places and times.

Other drawings illustrate the bearers carrying bodies of Plague victims, both coffined and uncoffined, to a large churchyard outside the City wall, in which several pits have been dug, and also to Plague pits in the fields. Those uncoffined are merely tied by head and feet in coarse shrouds, a common practice, though at the height of the visitation corpses were often delivered over naked. The bearers hold red staves, as a warning to avoid them. An open dead-cart is heaped with coffins, and following is a hooded dead-cart. The flight from London by road and river, the country guards stopping travellers to inspect their certificates of health, a crowd of mourners following a funeral, despite strict prohibition, and finally the return after the Plague—all are pictured in this broadside woodcut.

The stricken months made these officers and appliances of the Plague service sadly familiar. On the appearance of Plague in the out-parishes, the magistrates had first been charged to discover and shut up infected houses. In the City, when Doctors Hodges and Witherley were appointed physicians in the Plague service, two Aldermen were also selected to attend to the care of the infected ; [1] the ultimate responsibility in supervision rested, as was to have been expected, with the Alderman of each ward.[2] By that time there were certain superior

[1] Hodges' *Loimologia*, p. 14.
[2] All Mayoral Proclamations were addressed to the different Aldermen personally, as being the proper officers to see the orders were carried out.

FACSIMILE REPRODUCTION FROM A PICTORIAL BROADSIDE OF 1665 [-6] IN POSSESSION OF THE AUTHOR

John Dunstall fecit

parish officers known as " Examiners." [1] In those " Orders
Conceived and Published " upon which Defoe built up his
" Journal of the Plague Year," the examiner has importance ; he is the first officer mentioned ; his duty is clearly
set out, " to inquire and learn from time to time what
houses in every parish be visited, and what persons be
sick, and of what diseases," and where Plague was found to
order the constable to shut up the house. That was his
office, and the whole of his office. No word of giving relief
is there. Defoe's Sadler himself served as examiner for
two months, the term of the " Orders Conceived," and he
explains its shortness and the frequent changes made as
due to the always present peril of infection.

The discovery of Plague would be, to our ideas,
obviously the first and most important measure. Negative
evidence is the least satisfactory of evidence, but I have
not found that during the Great Plague such an officer
was commissioned specifically to search for Plague in the
dwellings. I have found much to suggest that there was,
in fact, no such officer during the Great Plague, and that,
so far as discovery was performed, the duty fell upon the
overseers of the poor. There comes into vision here and
there a parish official called the " Examiner." The Lord
Mayor in July sent orders to the different parishes, " to
charge persons convenient for the better attendance and
burial of such as are now sick, or may die "—which is not
the same thing. These were styled examiners.[2] At
St. Giles-in-the-Fields, Mr. Mann and Mr. Middlemore
were appointed " examiners for the relief of the visited
poor " [3]—not, it will be noticed, for their discovery. It
is in the largest parishes alone, with the rarest exceptions,

[1] In St. Margaret Westminster the first examiners were Joseph Bonner
and Christopher Sheene. On August 14th John Eley and James Harper
were the examiners. Plague was then so heavy in Westminster that
additional examiners were appointed, John Fells and John Grubb, and
also Daniel Booker and John Smyth. Not until September 25th do new
names appear, when John Hinder and Philip Gavell were working with
Fells and Grubb. On October 12th William Stanton and Ralph Fancott
appear as examiners. The four last named—Fells and Grubb, Stanton
and Fancott—the others having by that time disappeared, carried on till
the year was out, when expenditure in relief became so small that Mr. Hobman, the churchwarden, thereafter, rendered the account alone (St.
Margaret's Plague Accounts).

[2] St. Thomas Apostle Vest. Mins., July 26.

[3] St. Giles Ch'wardens' Accts. 1665.

that this official is met with.   In many City parishes the churchwardens and constables continued to perform all duties.[1]   Plague commonly became known by the demand for parish relief or the calling in of a doctor, and often by discovery of the searchers of the dead.   Nor have I found that the examiners were frequently changed.   Save under exceptional circumstances, a change was rare.

In the wide parish of St. Margaret Westminster the examiners undertook the distribution of relief, and they account for money so expended (as at St. Giles-in-the-Fields),[2] duties till then carried out by the church-wardens.   They first came into office on July 24th, when Westminster for two months had been infected, and violent Plague raged.   Two examiners served from August 14th, and two others from October 12th, till the year was out.   There is nothing that shows, nothing to suggest, that they accepted the hazardous task of searching out Plague in its hotbeds.   Discovery seems to have been as casual as was notification of death, and largely left to chance.

Defoe's sadler-examiner, nosing out Plague in 1665 in the interest of public health, is a figure of fiction, invented by him out of the " Orders Conceived and Published." The examiners of the Great Plague were superior relief officers, a check made advisable by the greatly augmented expenditure distributed.

The searchers' office has already been explained, and undesirable as were the women chosen to fulfil it, they were not the most undesirable characters whom the hard necessities of a Plague service, filled in emergency, brought into intimate contact with the sick and the dying.   In their isolation the imprisoned families fell dependent upon the watchman for every need.   Liberty was given him to fetch and carry.   He made their purchases at the shops and market stalls remaining open, took messages to the doctor and brought the medicine, and was their one means of communication with the world shut out.   When so absent he kept the key of the house, securely locked, in his possession.

---

[1] St. Augustine Vest. Mins., July 13.
[2] See also Ch'wardens' Accts. of St. Anne and St. Agnes, St. Martin-in-the-Fields, and others.

It was duty which none save those driven by want
would take. The parishes, anxious as in the selection of
women searchers to save their money, first appointed their
pensioners to earn the poor wage paid. They had been
directed by the Privy Council so to act in any shortage
of fit persons for the task, and to any who refused such
employment they were to deny further relief.[1] Honest
service in the watchman became of first importance both
to the afflicted families and to the community, whose
guardian against infection he was ; and it was seldom
given.

What fate befell the shut-up families, the stricken, the
dying and the whole all cooped in behind locked doors, a
contemporary writer has tersely described—

No drop of water, perhaps, but what comes at the leisure of
a drunken or careless halberd bearer at the door ; no seasonable provision is theirs as a certainty for their support. Not
a friend to come nigh them in their many, many heart and
house cares and complexities. They are compelled, though
well, to lie by, to watch upon the death-bed of their dear relation,
to see the corpse dragged away before their eyes. Affrighted
children stand howling by their side. Thus they are fitted by
fainting affliction to receive the impressions of a thousand
fearful thoughts, in that long night they have to reckon with
before release, as the family, so dismally exposed, sink one
after another in the den of this dismal likeness of Hell, contrived
by the advice of the English College of Doctors.[2]

He asks how four or five of the most skilful and hardiest
physicians would expect themselves to fare, shut up together
in a poor house as they had advised for others, with none but
an ignorant old woman for nurse, having no maintenance
beyond what the parish allowed, and the searchers and
surgeons who had visited others coming to them ; so used
till forty days or a month after the last man stricken died ?
" Do they not think in their consciences that, with all
their skill, their carcases would all, or most of them, be
carried away in the night-cart ? " Recovery (or death)
and forty days thereafter was the term of immurement.
Should a second case of Plague occur under the roof, the

[1] Privy Ccl. Reg. 58, fo. 187.
[2] *Golgotha ; or a Looking-Glass for London*, 1665. I have slightly
altered the ill-arranged and punctuated text, in order to make the passage
intelligible.

period from that recovery was advanced forty days, and so on remorselessly, till to those confined there can have been small prospect of release save by death,[1] which was, indeed, the common deliverer.

The nurse-keepers were charged with duties that made their influence stronger than that of the watchmen for good, and unfortunately also for evil. Their place was in every locked house. It startles a little to find a first reference to them as " dirty, ugly, unwholesome hags ! "

The most vitriolic passages which during the Great Plague pen put to paper, the fiercest denunciations of any individuals, are unhappily given to them. They are painted as monsters of iniquity. It would be happy to believe the charges incredible. They are too persistent and definite to be untrue ; and when this character is allotted to the nurse-keepers by persons so fair minded as Dr. Nathaniel Hodges and by the Rev. Thomas Vincent— to name but two—it becomes evident that, in at least a great number of instances, the one who should have been the sick man's best friend was in fact his worst enemy. All things considered, perhaps this is no cause for wonder. Thoughts of ministering angels, the patient, skilled nurses who stand by our sick-beds to-day, must be swept out of mind. They were not these.

In pre-Reformation times the women who tended the sick were sisters of religion, as largely is the case in Roman Catholic countries to-day. Sisters they remained ; they had, perhaps, more intuition than knowledge ; and the records of St. Bartholomew's Hospital in Smithfield make it plain that in Restoration times ability to toil at the wash-tub and in fashioning and mending the hospital's linen—tasks which occupied many of their hours—were considered not secondary to skill in bedside ministration. It was not until the middle seventeenth century that women named as nurses first came upon the staff of Bart's, as helpers to the sisters. The first nurse to be promoted sister was Margaret Whitaker in 1652, after five years spent in the hospital.[2]

The nurse, so called, of the Great Plague, a wholly illiterate person, had no skill, and in most cases no

[1] Hodges, p. 7.
[2] Sir Norman Moore's *History of St. Bartholomew's Hospital*, ii. 764.

character. The profession of nurse in the modern sense did not exist. She took to her perilous service by no love for alleviating the sufferings of the sick, no thought of a career for herself, but from sheer desperation, poverty, and want. The wage paid by the parish was but 5s. to 8s. per week, and largely she was forced to rely for livelihood upon her opportunities for peculation and theft. There existed no body of instructed women, fitted by high character or by training, from which nurses for tending the Plague patients could be drawn. Some few who had rude experience as midwives were most favoured for employment. Thereafter any woman whose need forced her to accept the task of nurse-keeper was chosen to serve.

It is depressing to know that the Great Plague, which cannot have passed without many heroic deeds performed —it must have produced heroines and heroes—has left us the record of very few of them. That was of the character of the visitation. It brought under notice much that was evil in human nature ; but the very circumstances of the time created concealment of good that it would be more pleasant to dwell upon. Long study of our newspapers to-day by a detached observer from Saturn would lead him to the conclusion, from the persistency of crime to which so much space is daily given, that the English character was largely criminal ; from the long columns of divorce reports, that English marriage bonds were a failure ; that with factory explosions, street accidents and fatalities so frequently reported, life was held cheaply on this planet. The historian, dependent upon written and printed sources for knowledge of events that passed two and a half centuries ago, must have the same suspicion that would break in upon this imagined visitor from Saturn, that he knows only a part. He must maintain a constant check upon himself, lest he hands on a representation which is in essentials false.

The nurse entered with authority. The household could not eject her ; and the parishes, anxious to hire anybody, were little concerned for the good character of those they employed. Many, no doubt, became hardened into callousness by the frequent scenes of death. Others, evil, abandoned, and criminal women of a rough and licentious age, finding their means of livelihood gone, accepted employment as nurse-keepers with no better object than to profit by the opportunity to plunder the dwellings, even expediting death where it served their ends.

The Rev. Thomas Vincent declares that the stricken Plague victims were more afraid of the nurse than of the Plague itself.[1]

Dr. Hodges in his practice among the sick entered scores of the shut-up houses, and his contact with the nurses, and the horrors that he knew and witnessed so filled his mind that he has no word to say of them save in hot indignation.   He tells of nurses who were " struck down from Heaven in the perpetration of their crimes," and particularly of one amongst many who, as she was leaving the house of a family, all dead, laden with her robberies, fell dead under her burden in the streets.   He recalls the adventure of a worthy citizen.   Suspected to be dying, he was beforehand stripped by his nurse, but being fated to live came a second time into the world naked.

Lest I should be thought to exaggerate, let Dr. Hodges speak for himself.   This is testimony by a skilled medical man, to whose high character his own unremitting attentions to the Plague-stricken poor and the good words of his fellows bear witness—

But what greatly contributed to the loss of people thus shut up was the wicked practices of the nurses, for they are not to be mentioned but in the most bitter terms.   These wretches, out of greediness to plunder the dead, would strangle their patients, and charge it to the distemper in their throats.   Others would secretly convey the pestilential taint from sores of the infected to those who were well.   Nothing, indeed, deterred these abandoned miscreants from prosecuting their avaricious purposes by all the methods their wickedness could invent. Although they were without witnesses to accuse them, yet it is not doubted but Divine Vengeance will overtake such wicked barbarities with due punishment.   And so many were the artifices of these barbarous wretches, that it is to be hoped posterity will take warning how they trust them again in like cases.[2]

The writer of "The Shutting Up Infected Houses," a contemporary pamphlet, asserts that " Infection may have

---

[1] *God's Terrible Voice in the City*, 1667, p. 30.
[2] *Loimologia*, pp. 8, 9.

killed its thousands, but shutting up has killed its ten thousands."

Little is it considered (he goes on to say) how careless most nurses are in attending the visited, and how careful (being possessed with rooking avarice) they are to watch the opportunity to ransack their houses ; the assured absence of friends making the sick desperate on the one hand, and them on the other unfaithful. Their estates are the Plague most die on, if they have anything to lose, to be sure those sad creatures (for the nurses in such cases are the off-scouring of the city) have a dose to give them; besides that it is something beyond a Plague to an ingenious spirit to be in the hands of those dirty, ugly, and unwholesome hags ; even a hell itself, on the one hand to hear nothing but screeches, cries, groans, and on the other hand to see nothing but ugliness and deformity, black as Night and dark as Melancholy. Ah ! to lie at the mercy of a strange woman is sad ; to leave wife, children, plate, jewels, to the ingenuity of poverty is worse ; but who can express the misery of being exposed to their rapine, that have nothing of the woman left but shape ? [1]

A versifier of the day, William Austin, in his "Anatomy of the Pestilence," 1666, sums up the characters of the sick attendants—the watchmen, nurses, and pretentious quacks —in a style reminiscent of Chaucer's "Canterbury Pilgrims," but unhappily without a spark from the fire of that poet's genius—

NURSES.

" Her politics are not from Aristotle,
But from the grave, the purse, the bag and bottle.
Though she may take many a preservative,
Quick silver's that which keeps her best alive.
Her hands to take are nut-hooks, and her feet
As ready are to run for winding sheet.

*   *   *   *   *

" He'll ne'er give out she killed him : for 'tis said
He's to be always silent when he's dead.
And while he lives, nurses he'll never nurse,
Knowing few good, most bad, and many worse.
Quietly he'll conclude she's such a thing
About his person as is plague-sore ring."

It was " the poore's Plague " that the richer classes flying from it left behind—ominous name, and so true. In order to know the full horror of these shut-up houses, one must realize how mean were the sums that public

[1] *The Shutting Up Infected Houses Soberly Debated,* 1665, p. 9.

opinion of the age accepted as sufficient for poor relief,
and by what trifling reward men and women were lured
to perform perilous services in the Plague time. That is
difficult over the gulf of two and a half centuries. London
had become a city of the poor ; a population still counted
by hundreds of thousands, governed by a ruling class and
their officers who can have numbered together, of those
remaining, but a few hundreds. There was a Poor Law
well adapted to grinding down the faces of the helpless, a
criminal code and the prisons for any troublesome ; and
the times condoned, and indeed expected, that the inexorable laws of supply and demand should operate in their
cruellest form.

Those who paid the poor relief alone were concerned in
its levy and distribution. The public spectacle of a person
or family dying of starvation was not to be tolerated, but
actual starvation being held off, how near to it the recipients
of relief came was not a matter which excited much concern. If relief kept the recipient alive, it was all that the
steel-like hardness of the age expected. The prepon-
derating masses of labourers and artisans, little cared for
and unrepresented, had no part whatever in civil or
parochial government.

No charge of especial inhumanity lies against the ruling
class at the Restoration. They acted according to the
light at that time. The parsimony of the parochial
authorities almost defied belief. For those locked and
imprisoned in the infected houses and forbidden to go out,
or for fear of infecting others to follow their trade and
earn a livelihood, a common rate of relief given to adults
was sixpence a day for all necessities,[1] two, three, or four
children being relieved as the equivalent of one adult. It
was perhaps just possible to maintain life on this dole.
The allowance was not always so much.

Ordered, that Goodwife Stapleton and her 3 children being
shut up in her house should be allowed 5s. a week towards
their maintenance during the time of their confinement,
beginning June 12.[2]

[1] " That ye p'sons infected in this parish with ye Plage be alowed each
person 6d p[er] diem ; And 10s. a weeke ye nurse and 12d. a day ye
warder " (St. Mary-at-Hill Vest. Mins., 1665, Aug. 25). This was when
wages for labour in the Plague services had risen.
[2] St. Benet Paul's Wharf Vest. Mins., June 11.

The payments made in the Plague service were as little generous. Bearers employed in carrying infected patients to the pest-houses and by night collecting the dead for the pits, most hazardous work, were paid 7s. a week. The watchman outside the infected houses had the same reward. These rates varied by a shilling more or less in the different parishes. The buryers working at the fearsome Plague pits fared a little better, receiving 1s. 6d. a day. By September, men hired for digging the pits for St. Bride's parish had to be tempted by wages of 2s. and 2s. 2d. a day, to which ultimately a free breakfast was added.[1]

There was for thousands no alternative to accepting this service but actual starvation, the ordinary channels of employment having dried up. The spectre of starvation stood always before the helpless masses of the poor. That fear it was that enabled the different parishes to give all services in the emergency of the Great Plague at a cost that must seem to ourselves almost ridiculous. It alone explains the trifling expenditure with which the Great Plague was met. The populous parish of St. Clement Danes, having 1,967 deaths that year in the Bills (1,319 attributed to Plague) spent in all £633 15s., this sum including voluntary contributions from its fashionable residents.[2] The far-spreading parish of St. Margaret Westminster (4,710 dead) disbursed £1,714.[3] In the difficulty of filling all the offices, women were occasionally employed as " watchmen " outside the infected houses—

Item, Paid to a poor woman for watching, 3s.[4]

The fearful peril to life by Plague was well understood, and there were few so foolish as Theophilus Garencieres, a physician dwelling in Clerkenwell, who had the hardihood to assert : " The Plague is one of the easiest diseases in the world to be cured, if it be taken within four hours or six at most after the first invasion, otherwise and for the most part mortal. If people would only observe this rule, I would undertake, by the grace of the Almighty and without bragging (I believe most men that know me will believe me) to cure nineteen of twenty." [5] That was

[1] Ch'wardens' Accts.   [2] *Ibid.*   [3] Plague Accts.
[4] St. Katherine Cree Ch'wardens' Accts.
[5] *A Mite Cast into the Treasury*, 1665.

I

written in the early days, and Clerkenwell told another
tale. One Stokes, an apothecary, who was equally
contemptuous, himself fell a victim of Plague.[1]

The theory for the shutting up of houses with the sick
and the healthy together was that Plague contagion was so
universal that anyone who came near an infected person
almost of a certainty took infection himself; if allowed to
go free among his fellows he constituted a public danger.
Medical opinion upon its advisability was divided. The
evil policy had long precedent supporting it, and had,
unfortunately, the approval of the College of Physicians.
As a body, the magistrates were insistent, and their action
was supported by the highest authorities at Court; the
Privy Council sent repeated commands to them to enforce
the shutting up of infected houses with more, and ever
more, rigour. The middle class was doubtful, and uncon-
vinced. The poor, upon whom the chief burden fell, were
bitterly hostile to their imprisonment. They could not
understand. Ignorant, unthinking, passionate, with that
incipient tendency towards rebellion so often found among
the poor, they sought by escape and every other possible
device to defeat the end aimed at.

In attempting judgment upon the College of
Physicians, set aside the medical knowledge of to-day.
Necessity, not choice, was the deciding factor. No means
were available for segregation beyond the pest-houses,
with their ridiculously few beds. It was London's
immeasurable misfortune that no man arose strong enough
to command that a whole quarter of the town, or an outside village, should be cleared of its inhabitants, isolated,
and made a refuge camp for the sick. The Great Plague
produced no man of strength and vision.

The magistrates professed to take long views. They
held that the welfare of the individual must give place to
the welfare of the community. No means served except
shutting up the houses for stifling the contagion in its
seat; and pressing a simile beyond its just application,
they succeeded in persuading many frightened people not
yet infected that there was no cruelty in taking off a
mortifying limb to save the whole.[2] What could be of
more immediate service than securing those families who

[1] Boghurst, p. 72.   [2] Hodges, p. 10.

were healthy from infection, though hardship thereby fell upon particular persons ? It was appealing argument, and that the traditional policy in all past Plagues in England.

Intended to confine the Plague, this practice had two results. It spread the Plague abroad. It brought about on a wholesale scale concealment of Plague and falsification of the Bills of Mortality. A third result—the one that mattered—was that it raised the death-roll in the closed-up houses, enlarging it perhaps by four and five times what need have been had facilities existed for the removal and segregation of the sick, or had the removal from them and their Plague-bearing surroundings of the healthy been permitted and practicable. In human error are few things more tragical.

The inevitable happened. Where Plague broke out in a house, those who could do so promptly fled. Scattering, they took the sources of contamination amongst those who received them. This a writer of the time freely avows—

So dreadful it is to us to be shut up from all comfort and society, from free and wholesome air, from the care of the physician and the divine, from the oversight of friends and relations, and sometimes even from the very necessities and conveniences of Nature, that we run as far in the city and country as our feet can carry us, leaving wives and children to the parishes, empty walls and shops to creditors, scattering the infection along the streets as we go, and shifting it from lodging to lodging with ourselves, till at last we drop in some alley, field or neighbour village, calling the people round about by the suddenness of our fall to stand awhile astonished at our deaths, and then take their own ; each man fearful of us frighted from his own house, killing his whole town by surprising them unprepared.

See, see, we infect not our next neighbours, and this sickness spreads not so much in any one place, but we carry it from place to place, running from our home as from our places of torment, and thus the roads are visited, and men travel the same way to the country and to their long home. Thus the contagion hath reached most places round the city, which is now as it were besieged.[1]

A watchman came, the doors were padlocked, and the red cross was marked thereon, when often the inhabitants

[1] *The Shutting Up Infected Houses*, 1665, pp. 5, 6.

had gone. Only a devoted parent, sister or son, or some faithful servant, remained with the sufferer. The ungovernable fear of Plague finds illustration in a complaint from Wiltshire, that Mr. Richard Constable, " a gentleman of good and plentiful estate," on Plague appearing in his house at Mildenhall abandoned it with the greater part of his family, " taking no care of the sick people left therein, but leaving them wholly to the charge of the parish." [1] None traced the wanderers. It was no one's concern to do so. Each tenement in London's mean alleys, where Plague most violently raged, harboured four or half a dozen families. When a single person became sick, every family in the crowded house must be shut in as constituting a common danger. Flight gave the one hope of life.

Maybe the authorities were cheated. A Plague case was returned by the old woman searcher, bribed for the purpose, as of some innoxious disease, and the corpse buried. The residents went on living in the house, which received no disinfection or airing, till two or three others were struck down, and further concealment was futile.

Dr. Hodges, whatever his first opinions, became convinced of the evil of shutting up the sick and the whole together, a practice which he has characterized as "abhorrent to religion and humanity." Although he was the City's medical adviser, his influence was powerless to remove the pressure exerted from the highest quarters. A deplorable evil was that the shutting up of an infected house made the neighbours right and left fly in fear, and sufferers perished for want of help. " I verily believe," he adds, " that many who were lost might have been now alive, had not the tragical mark on the door drove proper assistance from them." [2] Any who, on a mission of mercy, had attended a sick person realized full well the risk they ran of being themselves enclosed, if the fact became known to a magistrate. Few were willingly so daring. [3]

Boghurst, the apothecary, who had large experience of Plague, is equally emphatic. " As soon as any house is infected, all the sound people should be had out of it, and not shut up therein to be murdered." [4] The Plague

---

[1] Salisbury Corporation MSS.
[2] *Loimologia*, pp. 9, 11.
[3] *Golgotha*, 1665.
[4] *Loimographia*, p. 99.

By the Mayor.

To the Alderman of the Ward
of

S a farther means (by Gods blessing) then what is before directed to obviate the increase of the Plague within this City and Liberties, you are to put and cause to be put in present and effectual execution, within your Ward, the several Orders following, devised and enjoyned by me and my Brethren, in the Court of Aldermen, in that behalf.

1. That no Vintner, Inholder, Cook, Ordinary-keeper, Seller of Strong-waters, Ale-house-keeper or Coffee-house-keeper, shall henceforward, during the Infection receive or entertain any person or persons (not of their own Families) to eat or drink in their houses or shops, (save onely the travelling Guests of Inholders with sobriety and moderation.) But that others who want these Accommodations may receive the same at the doors, or send for (as they need) them to their own dwellings or lodgings.

2. That your Wardmote-inquest do enquire weekly of all Offences and Disorders committed in any Tavern, Inne, Ordinary, Ale-house, Coffee-house, or other place of common entertainment, contrary to the Order before mentioned, or otherwise against the Laws and Customs of this City ; and likewise of all other Offences within their enquiry, especially Nusances, and such like, as are most perillous, and make due presentment thereof unto you, that thereupon present course may be taken for correction and punishing of the person offending contrary to Law.

3. That present and especial course be taken to avoid all houses within your Ward of Inmates or Undersitters, which have been a principal means of increasing the Infection within this City and parts adjacent.

4. That none be suffered to sing or cry Ballads in the Streets, or to sell, by way of Hawking, any Goods or Commodities whatsoever.

5. That all Grammar-schools, Writing-schools, and other Schools for the teaching of youth or Children of either sex, be broken up and discontinued till Michaelms next, unless the Court of Aldermen shall otherwise order in the mean time; and especially that Dancing-schools, and Fencing-schools, and all Meetings there, be utterly prohibited and prevented until the said Court take other order therein.

6. That a carefull Watch and Ward be constantly kept at the Gates and Landing-places, to restrain and prevent the ingress of all Vagrants, Beggers, loose and dangerous people, from the out parts into this City and Liberties, and to bring to punishment such as shall be apprehended doing the same, according to Law.

7. That Doggs, Catts and other Vermin, kill'd or lying dead in the Street be duly carried away (as the soil and other filth) by the Raker of every Ward.

8. That the Churchwardens, Constables and other Officers, (whom it concerns) be very active and diligent to search for, discover and punish all unlawfull and disorderly Tipling, Gaming, Labouring, Rowing upon the River of Thames, and other Offences whatsoever, to the breach and prophanation of the Lord's day, And to employ their utmost endeavours for the due and religious observation thereof.

And, for better notice of these Orders, you are to send Copies thereof to the Ministers of the several Parishes within your Ward, who are desired to read the same in their Churches the next Lord's-day.

And hereof fail you not, as you mind the Health and Welfare of the City. Dated at the Guild-hall, London, the fourth day of July, 1665.

Weld.

Printed by *James Flesher*, Printer to the Honourable City of LONDON.

MAYORAL PROCLAMATION DURING THE PLAGUE

treatment was obstinately perverse, hence the vast loss of life. When what was wrong (as modern knowledge has taught us) could be done, wrong was done.

Always there were self-denying men and women, from Church and Dissent alike, ready at humanity's call to enter the Plague-infected houses and bring comfort and relief to the sick and the dying. They gave a fine example of Christianity in contempt of peril. The Quakers have an honourable place in this work.

There is a letter which throws light upon the sufferings of their little community. It was written to Margaret Fells by Ellis Hookes, the first Recording Clerk and Registrar, who manfully stuck to his post in London, in November, when the Plague was mostly spent—

Deare M. ff.—My deare love is unto thee and to all thy deare children and ffamily, and Anne Travers deare love is to thee. There 3 been buryed out of our ffamily in a months time, and her Child has had the distemper, but is recovered againe. Deare Margaret I have been preserved well, but soe as a brand is pluckt out of the fire, soe has the Lord delivered me. For I have often laid downe my head in sorrow and rose as I went to bed, and not slept a wink for the groanes of them yt lay a dyeing. And every morning I counted it a great mercy that the Lord gave me another day. And I was made a strength and a help to poore Anne, who has also been well hitherto.

They keep us out of our meeting at the bull [Bull and Mouth Tavern] on ye first and fourth dayes but on ye fifth dayes wee meet within.

Last first day they carryed Ester Bidle and another woman to prison for speaking in the streets, and struck Ester over the face with their halberts. Our meetings are quiet everywhere else.

ffriends are generally well, both in prison, in the shipp[1] and at Newgate, and those that are at liberty; and not above 1 a day buryed, whereas there used to be 16 or 18 and sometymes 20 a day burryed, for severall weekes it was soe. These are a list of ye names of ym that died in Newgate and in the shipp, which yet remains where it did . . . Christo : Dickenson who was the gravemaker for ym was the last yt died.[2]

Deaths falling sixteen to twenty a day, and that for

---

[1] These were Quaker prisoners on board the Black Eagle, lying in the Thames. See p. 217, *post*.

[2] Swarthmore MSS., iv. 121, at Devonshire House, Bishopsgate.

several weeks together, in a community which can hardly have numbered above 4,000 in London, is a terrible proportion. The Quakers had their own burial ground, their grave-maker, their dead-cart—the parish dead-cart upon its rounds would make no distinction of faiths in disposal of its fearsome loads.

The persecutions continued in all that time of calamity. The Friends' meetings, held despite the Plague, were violently scattered. Many arrests resulted ; the meeting room at the Bull and Mouth in Aldersgate Street was boarded up by the justices to exclude the Friends, but they assembled in the street. The Quakers undertook the support of their widows and orphans, and once each week assembled for receiving information and dealing with the cases presented, Friends in the country freely contributing to a fund.

In the fearless work of administering relief to families in the shut-up houses are three outstanding figures. On May 18th the City Marshal, breaking into the Friends' meeting at Gracechurch Street, there arrested Alexander Parker and George Whitehead, who were sent to Newgate. They were shortly after released. Whitehead then went into the country on religious service, but news of the sufferings of the Friends in London brought him hastening back, and he and Parker laboured in the capital throughout the period of the contagion. They were joined by Gilbert Latey, the Strand tailor. He had taken country lodgings when the Plague threatened to become virulent, but abandoned all intention of flight.

Latey worked chiefly among his own people in the western out-parishes beyond Temple Bar, taking charitable relief and ministering to the sick and the dying. " Many had running sores upon them," says his biographer, " but still the Lord was with him to preserve him in continued health." [1] He himself became infected in October, and recovered. George Whitehead and Parker had the larger field. The former has told himself that he never left his lodging in Watling Street for meetings without carrying with him his nightcap, not knowing when he might be arrested and clapt into goal. He frequently visited Newgate, the Gatehouse at Westminster, and the White Lion

[1] Hawkins, *Life of Gilbert Latey*, 1707, pp. 63–4.

prison in Southwark, there praying by the beds of the sick and the dying. He entered the infected houses, and testified to death-beds of which he was a living witness. " In all the time," he writes simply, " the Lord preserved me by His power, through Faith, from that infectious distemper." [1] No man had undertaken graver risks.

The figures of July, bad as they were, inspired dread less by their own magnitude than by their tale of the Plague's irresistible growth. Worse was always followed by worse. The Bills of Mortality carried no conviction, and each man made to them his own mental additions as his fears dictated. The week's Bill was to be obtained for a penny, and what was read as successively the fly-sheets came out was that Plague had :

> In the first complete week of July taken 725 lives ;
> In the second week had taken 1,089 lives ;
> In the third week had taken 1,843 lives ;
> In the fourth week had taken 2,010 lives.

Little did the citizens then realize that a time lay but a few weeks ahead when July's mortality from all causes would not fill the tale of Plague in a single week.

Figures have been given, the most inadequate of symbols, that alone convey but little. In a town which to-day contains a population of 5,000,000, and upon whose main arteries west to east houses are continuous for thirty miles, it is difficult for the imagination to shrink sufficiently to visualize the little capital of King Charles II.'s early years, a walled City—the " one square mile "—with suburbs nestling close about it, when the West-end had not yet spread up the Haymarket, and St. James's Street was but beginning to lose its character of a rural path from the Palace to open fields ; and Lord Chancellor Hyde, in Piccadilly, was building next the site of the present Burlington House the last town mansion in London, with outlook over the country scene, determined that none should be farther out than he.

Vauxhall had but three years before been moved up river, where Samuel Pepys and kindred spirits made

[1] Letter addressed " To the remnant of Friends and chosen of God," in Whitehead's *Christian Progress*.

" mighty merry." Till then the popular resort for the fashionable monde had been Spring Gardens at Charing Cross, most flourishing in King Charles I.'s reign, and there under the trees many an amorous intrigue had been conducted and men played on the bowling green and at the butts—at Charing Cross! London covered but small ground. Now the European War, with its serried ranks of graves counted in millions, each marking a life cut off, has entirely altered our conceptions of massed death. What trifles seem the few tens of thousands of the Great Plague! But we must strive to recover the perspective, and to see in them, as the Londoner of the Restoration saw in them, the losses of a capital the remaining population of which can little have exceeded 350,000 souls.

As Plague settled down upon London, the reaction was at once apparent. London City had been a busy thriving place, the houses jammed into every available corner, with narrow streets insufficient for circulation, and population packed tight, as was customary in every ancient walled town. Its manufacturing business and transport would have been impossible without the Thames. It was the financial capital of the Kingdom; it had the great commerce; its merchant adventurers led in all enterprise; its shops attracted the custom of, and set the fashion for, the world of wealth and fashion. But with these diverse interests London also was the Kingdom's greatest industrial city, and was also that which necessarily we find it somewhat difficult to appreciate—an industrial city without machinery, all the processes of manufacture being slowly and laboriously accomplished by hand. That involved a large preponderance of artisans, craftsmen, unskilled labourers and servants in its population, poorly paid, and without employment quickly made destitute. They were not grouped in factories, answering a morning bell, but for the most part toiled at their crafts in the thousands of small houses and yards. They made the helpless masses of the poor when the Plague came, they and their wives and many children and dependents—and when the truth is known, actually not many others.

There was no house that was not full of people, for merchants and tradesmen, whether in big business or small, lived over counting-house or shop, with their families, apprentices, servants, and often journeymen, a numerous community—till the merchants began to fly before the Plague. The breweries in Thames Street, and tanneries, dye-works and others, occupying space, additionally cramped the accommodation for those living within the confines. It was a picturesque city, mostly of gabled houses, timber built with rough-cast walls, the storeys as they rose projecting outward, one beyond another, to give weather protection ; the streets narrow and winding ; insanitary without a doubt, but even in that respect healthy in contrast with the reeking outskirts.

The Plague altered the whole course of its life. The transformation was made complete when the hurried flight from London had ended—made more quickly than war or famine could have effected it.

In normal times the City's activities had started early. The night-watchman carried his dim horn lantern and called the hours. He had hardly crept home when the street criers were about, offering fish, eggs, milk and cream, and provisions for the morning meal. At six o'clock in summer the City apprentices brought down their shutters with a clatter, and standing at the shop doors made their appeal to the passers-by, " What d'ye lack ; what is't ye lack, ladyes ? " That cry had resounded through London for many centuries.[1] As the day progressed the streets grew increasingly lively with the presence and cries of itinerant sellers of all kinds, the vendors of small, unconsidered things, too trifling to excite attack by the jealous trade guilds. In Charles I.'s reign, as I have recalled elsewhere, the obstruction caused by baskets and stalls was such that it had been proposed to tax vendors and pedlars with the double purpose of providing the King with revenue and keeping down a nuisance.

From the near villages around London country women brought in their produce. They settled at every street corner post to sell. The handyman moved about, ready to cut wood or cobble shoes, the dealer in " small-cole " carried in a sack upon his back, the barterer of " green

---

[1] It was a learned Bachelor of Divinity, one Alexander Gell, who was sentenced to lose his ears and be degraded from the ministry, for giving his opinion of King Charles I. that he was fitter to stand at a Cheapside shop with an apron before him, and say " What lack ye ? " than to govern a kingdom (Ellis's *Original Letters*, iii. 276).

broomes " for old shoes or kitchen stuff, and a hundred others. No hour passed till nightfall when people in plenty were not about. Little wheeled traffic stirred on the cobble stones, or was there need for it, when the house-wife carried her own marketing, tramping along with basket slung across her arm, to visit the meat, fish, fruit, and herb markets, and at these made the more considerable purchases required for the daily fare. City streets were not meant for heavy traffic. The larger loads from the Thames' quays were carried by carts licensed by the Wood-mongers' Company, which enjoyed a monopoly of such transit, and the vehicles were severely restricted in number.

The Plague was quickly to extinguish most of these activities. It made every one suspicious—suspicious of intimate friends as of strangers, of resorting to market places, of shops and streets, of goods bought ; suspicious even of the very air lest it should bear infection. Self-preservation became every man and woman's consuming interest. Large families were deemed most acceptable to the Almighty. With what pride, on the monument of the City merchant, Sir Richard Hayward, in the tower of St. Alphage London Wall are arrayed the carved and painted figures of his two wives and his sixteen children ? There are many like elsewhere. The parent of the large family was the most anxious of men. Infection of one involved the closing in of all, and that was death.

The street cries were no longer heard as the small sellers disappeared, the poorest alleys in which they found lodging being the first to harbour Plague. If any person had entrance to the taverns it was furtively, under the host's suspicious eye. The doors should have been shut. The schools kept enforced vacation that at regular hours had brought the clatter of children's feet on the pavements, and their laughter and play. A paralysis crept over the City. The quacks, offering sure cure for all, were unable to cure themselves, and when Plague had taken many of them and the untruthfulness of their boastful claims to stay the infection were exposed, they, too, faded out of sight. London, noisy at all other times, became strangely quiet, few people caring to linger in the dismal streets as they exchanged news and fears. In horrible contrast with the growing pestilence in the town was the magnificence of the summer, day after day the constant sunshine, the heat, the unchanging blue sky.

Famine London happily was spared. There was that year greater plenty than usual of most produce, the encircling fields and market gardens being planted for a full supply, when with diminished population and absence of the wealthier classes the demand was reduced. The sun ripened an abundant crop in the orchards, fruit being at so low a price that the poor surfeited upon it.[1] Bread was moderately cheap, and no actual shortage occurred, the penny wheaten loaf being of 10 oz. weight from April till June came in. Thenceforward, throughout the dreadful Plague months it remained at $9\frac{1}{2}$ oz. for the penny, never varying till in November the larger $10\frac{1}{2}$ oz. loaf was restored.[2]

London's healthiest area the Bills show to be that within the wall. Less than one-sixth of the Plague mortality occurred in the City within the wall—the area stretching from Ludgate east to the Tower, from the Thames north to Cripplegate, the City which contained Guildhall, the Exchange, the Cathedral, the Companies' halls, the immense preponderance of the churches, all the big trade, most things that mattered. It suffered to but one-third the extent of the Liberties, to but one-third the extent of the out-parishes and Westminster. A City parish, St. John the Evangelist, returned no single case of Plague, and in that respect stands unique; St. Benet Sherehog allowed but one; St. Matthew Friday Street had six. The Plague deaths in the year's epidemic, as given in the Bills of Mortality (much under-stated) totalled :

9,887 within the City wall ;
28,886 in the Liberties ;
21,420 in the Out-parishes ; and
8,403 in Westminster ;

making together an acknowledged loss by Plague of 68,596 lives in London.

False deductions have been drawn from these figures. Look behind them, and you may see a movement that was perhaps the most significant thing in the Great Plague in

[1] Hodges, pp. 20, 21.
[2] The prices of bread as fixed by the Lord Mayor each week are given in the printed Bills of Mortality.

London, and in large measure was responsible for heaping up the huge mortality. In the houses abandoned by merchants and tradesmen a trusted servant was often left in charge, the others being sent adrift ; as often the houses were emptied and closed up, all those engaged in carrying on the trade being discharged, and these were condemned in the absence of other employment to sink lower and lower. They had no place of refuge save the poor lodging to be obtained in the town's outer ring, already badly infected, and in its squalor inviting Plague.   From the City within the wall was constant migration to the outskirts and a lessening population ; in the Liberties and beyond the ravages of Plague in reducing population were made good by new accessions, a circumstance which goes far to explain its long persistency therein.

The City's deliberate policy contributed to that end. It was City law, did any resident take in a lodger during the infection, that his house should be shut up, guarded and watched as if it was infected with Plague.[1]   The Aldermen, each jealous for the health of his own ward, saw to it that householders did not encourage the peril of poor lodgers ; when these migrated to the pest-ridden outskirts his concern ceased.   The times were callous.   What should the wretched inmate do ?   He could not follow the example of the rich and fly from the town.   He must get in somewhere.   Attempts repeatedly made to clear the City of lodgers were ineffectual, as were all such efforts by whoever made, but they did reduce the bulk of the City's mortality, at the cost of increasing that of the out-parishes.

The Plague's approach was insidious.   The sufferer rarely knew when first the infection was upon him, and not infrequently it happened that the real nature of the sickness was determined only after the Plague had far developed.[2]   It was not uncommon for the victim, attaching little importance to a slight indisposition, suddenly to awaken to the dreadful realization that this was the Plague.

Most persons first noticed a chill to creep over them, which produced a cold shivering in a very short space.

An unnatural feeling of horror came, a great fear, accompanied by shaking and trembling, which the

[1] " Journal " 46, fo. 61.   [2] Thomson's *Loimotomia*, p. 52.

physicians have remarked threw the patient into a condition that made him least able to resist the disease. It might pass away in half an hour. It might endure for four or five hours. After the horror came nausea and vomiting, the retching being at times so severe that the patient, wholly exhausted thereby, quickly died. This was the first dependable sign of the Plague's attack.

Others upon seizure became comatose, and slept as if dosed with an opiate. Many in the midst of their employment, or when talking with friends, would suddenly without reluctance fall into profound sleep, and if not roused, they died.[1] These first symptoms were succeeded by headache, that became so intolerable that many fell early into a frenzy. Bleeding was favoured by few. Boghurst in his practice urged as a first principle " the total avoiding of bleeding, purging and vomiting as most pernicious and destructive, by what means soever secured." [2] A high fever soon assailed the sufferer. Plague, when greatly virulent, might kill before the fever developed, or any external mark of infection be given,[3] but of those who survived all earlier symptoms none escaped the fever. It put to rest any doubts the doctor may have held. Yet, so many were the variations of the malady, the fever might be low and concealed, though the usual indications of a fever's accession were apparent.

The medical treatment on attack was by heaped blankets and internal medicines to encourage copious perspiration. The sufferers were rigidly kept in bed, and any who became delirious were tied down. Sleep being feared during " the sweats," the patients were forcibly kept awake, and if at later stages a little sleep was allowed, they were roused every four hours to take medicine. Blisters were applied, and the parts so treated were not permitted to heal until the malignity of the disease was spent, apparently with the idea that the Plague would escape through that channel. A marvellous assortment of drugs was poured into the patient. Those used by Dr. Hodges were mostly fresh indigenous herbs, and he mentions angelica, rue, veronica, scabius, pimpernel, ivy berries, balm, gentian, juniper berries and many more. He

---

[1] Boghurst's *Loimographia*, p. 34.　　[2] *Ibid.*, p. 78.
[3] Allin to Fryth, Sept. 20.

writes scornfully of the Oriental bezoar, powdered unicorn's horn, and powder of toads, which many thought efficacious.

The diet given was light and generous—eggs, strong broths, and good wines where means allowed ; but of the usefulness of gold boiled in the broths Hodges has " nothing to say."

None could foretell the recurrence of convulsive and febrile paroxysm. It made the patient's plight worse that he stood in need of close watching by the nurse, and this the ignorant and undesirable women pressed by poverty into the service were not able or willing to give. Hodges declares that violent palpitation of the heart was a significant warning of approaching death ; and he even gives the case of a Plague victim, who died quickly thereafter, whose palpitation was so loud that he and others could hear it at some considerable distance.[1]

The delirium was the cause of the sights and sounds about the town that were so distressing to those compelled to endure them. They made the Plague most horrible. A sharp cry of a man or woman in agony, the scuffle in a room, the throwing open of a window from which plaintive calls or some unintelligent message reverberated down the street, caused the passer-by to shudder and hurry along. He could give no help. A door would suddenly be thrust open, and some poor Plague victim, wild-eyed, emerge. He had broken his bonds by the unnatural strength given by fever, and would run staggering about the streets or market-place, if not confined by force, clothed only in the bed shirt, or even naked. Soon, tired out, he fell down with giddiness, wholly ignorant of his condition or where he was.[2] Not uncommonly the effort was the last, and the man expired on the stones. " The Plague," Hodges declared, " seemed to have complicated in its production everything of a poisonous and destroying nature."

It was rarely longer than two or three days after the attack when the visible signs of Plague appeared on the body. The " blains," so-called, were like blisters on the skin, obscurely ringed about. If no worse signs followed, the patients might entertain hope.

" Buboes "—hence the term, bubonic Plague—were

[1] *Loimologia*, p. 106.   [2] *Ibid.*, p. 96.

tumour-like outgrowths most commonly found under the arms and in the groin, and less frequently behind the ear, two, three, or four in number, and varied greatly in size. They were also called botches. If the growth failed to break naturally, the surgeon opened it by incision. Unhappily the rising of Plague buboes was attended by such severe pain, and a feeling as of intolerable burning as the time for suppuration approached, that the sufferers often became raving mad. Incision by the knife and the subsequent cleansing, of course without anæsthetics, were so extremely painful that patients collapsed under it. If the buboes failed to rise and break, there was little expectation of life. As they broke, the fever declined.

With carbuncles, another common eruption in Plague, mortification had always to be dreaded. The surgeon, by cauteries or the lancet, opened the carbuncle, a task necessitating the greatest care, or gangrene destroyed the patient.

These were the common concomitants of the Plague as it developed towards recovery or death. But the sign most feared was that to which the people gave the name of " the tokens." The devout and the superstitious accepted them as God's sign—" the heathen are afraid of Thy tokens." Some called them " God's marks." [1] They were the almost certain forerunners of death. Medical observation agreed that very few with these marks upon them recovered health. " The tokens " were spots upon the skin, breaking out in large numbers, varying in colour, figure, and size. Some, where they had run together, became as broad as a finger nail, others were small as a pin's head, till they enlarged and spread. The colour might be red, with a surrounding circle inclining towards blue; in others a faint blue, the circle being blackish; others again took a dusky brown tone. Often the flesh was found to be spotted when no discoloration was visible on the skin. No part was immune from these round spots, though the neck, breast, back, and thighs were the most common places for them. " The tokens " sometimes were so numerous as to cover all the body.

It was " the tokens," so universally dreaded, that gave to the Plague the name of " the spotted death."

[1] Richard Kingston's *Pillulæ Pestilentiales*, 1665, p. 14.

They customarily appeared after two to four days' progress of the disease, but might rise without any previous warning of infection. A woman, the only one of her family left alive and thinking herself perfectly well, perceived the pestilential spots on her breast and shortly thereafter died. A young man of good constitution, unexpectedly finding " the tokens " upon him, believed them not to be the genuine marks, he being otherwise in such vigorous health, yet within four hours death confirmed the physician's diagnosis.[1]

Dr. Hodges mentions as being most strange in his first experience that many persons came out of delirium as soon as " the tokens " appeared, believing that they were in a recovering and hopeful condition. The poor sufferers did not know their fate. He recalls the case of a maid who had no idea that she was attacked by Plague, her pulse being strong and senses perfect, and she complained of no disorder or pain, but on examining her chest he discovered " the tokens " there. Within two or three hours she was dead. " The tokens " sometimes first became visible after death.[2]

The results of a single post-mortem examination of a Plague victim have come down to us. Dr. George Thomson, in his time greatly daring, made it. No need is served by giving here the gruesome details of this piece of morbid anatomy ; [3] enough to say that the dissection showed that the Plague produced far-reaching changes in the internal organs, as well as affected the surface of the body by the multitude of blue or black spots containing congealed blood. In fact, no organ was found to be free from changes which suggested that its structure had been materially altered by the poisons circulating through the body. No discovery could be made of any particular organ

[1] Hodges, pp. 49, 50.

[2] The most detailed observations of the Plague are by Dr. Nathaniel Hodges in his *Loimologia*, written in 1665–6, and the *Letter to a Person of Quality*, dated May 8, 1666, the last being printed in *A Collection of Very Valuable and Scarce Pieces*, 1720. Dr. Thomson, in *Loimotomia*, 1666, is wordy but much less informing. Boghurst may also be read with advantage, Allin only with great caution. Later medical writers upon the Plague in London have been mostly dependent upon these three first-named sources.

[3] Dr. Thomson gives a detailed report of the post-mortem examination in his *Loimotomia, or the Pest Anatomized*, 1666, pp. 69–77, which I have reprinted in Appendix II.

The Manner of Diſſecting

the

PESTILENTIALL BODY.

FRONTISPIECE OF DR. THOMSON'S "LOIMOTOMIA"

From the copy in possession of the Author

so affected that it might be considered as the original seat of the disease, or of infection. What was found pathologists of to-day recognize as the changes associated with any severe toxic infection in which the whole system has been subjected to high fever and intense poisoning for a few hours, or days, if life lasted so long.

As the number of infected houses to be marked grew large, the authorities had resort to the printing press. A poster was prepared for affixing to the doors, bearing a conspicuous cross over the length and width, and bearing also the familiar words " Lord have mercy upon us ! " In the four quarters formed by the limbs of the cross were printed directions for managing the patient, and regulations for the visits of the doctor and for the supply of medicines, food, and water.[1] Printed bills for the purpose had been used as early as Queen Elizabeth's reign.[2]

The Goldsmiths' Company on May 29th had made fitting observance of the anniversary of King Charles II.'s happy return to his people. The Court of Wardens approved this bill of fare, which has some interest as the detail of a feast of two and a half centuries ago—

Westfalia hams
With pidgeons and chickens boyled
Rost befe, and one piece for breakfast
Lamb pastie
Green geese, three in a dish
Rost capons, two in a dish
Rost chickens
Tarts
Sparagrasse [3]

There was no more feasting. The Lord Mayor prohibited all public festivities, entertainments, and assemblies of people, for fear of contagion spreading. Even at the election of Master and Wardens within the several Companies, the year's great day—that, too, went without the customary banquet.[4] The Carpenters' Company had

---

[1] A contributor to *Notes and Queries*, 2nd Ser., ii. 108, saw one of these posters in Guildhall some seventy years ago, but on a subsequent visit found that it had disappeared, and it is not in the collections to-day.

[2] St. Martin-in-the-Fields parish purchased forty bills on the 10th August, 1593, at a cost of 18*d.* for posting on the doors of infected houses (Ch'wardens Accts.).

[3] Prideaux, *Goldsmiths' Company*, ii, 154.

[4] Heath, *Grocers' Company*, p. 124.

election in private, "without a sermon, music, or other ceremonies, only a cup of wine and a Naple biskate." The honours were indeed shorn. No summons went out to any of the Livery or commonalty to assemble in Hall, where on necessary occasion the Master, Wardens, and some few of the assistants alone foregathered to pay the benefactors' gifts and the doles to widows and poor people, this being done with as little concourse as possible.[1]

An assessment upon the Companies for relief of the poor stricken by the Plague quickly followed. This supplemented the unspent poor-rate, and with receipts from the special pest-rate and voluntary contributions and collections made a sufficient sum with which the first charges in the City were met. There was no demand upon the City Cash till August closed.[2] In the extreme need of money, the Lord Mayor on July 28th issued a Proclamation to the Companies, requiring that each should devote to the relief of its poor members one-third of the sum economized by lapse of the customary dinners and entertainments. The Proclamation made plain how vast already was the distress in London, instancing "the great multitudes of poor persons who, by reason of the infection, have their houses shut up and are restrained from their daily trades and labours whereby to maintain themselves and families by means thereof, and by the bitter cessation of trade do endure great wants and extremities."[3] This but followed precedent, a similar request having been made at the visitation of 1625,[4] in the epidemic of 1603, and earlier in that of 1593.[5]

The Companies had also orders to make search in their records,[6] and the Aldermen in the Ward Books,[7] to ascertain what moneys had in 1625 or other year of great sickness been paid towards the relief of the infected. Always the authorities, in their uninspired efforts to combat the Plague, followed precedent. The reverence of Law and Parliament for precedent was not greater.

---

[1] Court Minutes printed in Jupp & Pocock's *Carpenters' Company*, pp. 127-8.

[2] Guildhall Library MSS. 270.   [3] " Journal " 46, fo. 61.

[4] Dumville Smythe, *Girdlers' Company*, p. 161.

[5] Clode, *Memorials of Merchant Taylors*, p. 151 ; *Early History of Merchant Taylors*, ii. 309.

[6] Jupp & Pocock, *Carpenters' Company*, p. 129.

[7] " Journal " 46, fo. 61.

The behaviour of the poor, against which L'Estrange in his newspapers so continually railed, added to their perplexities. It had been remarked at the last bad visitation in London that " there is a strange opinion here among the poorer sort of people, who hold it a matter of conscience to visit their neighbours in any sickness, yea, though they know it to be the infection." [1] Their habits were ineradicable. They strove in every way to conceal Plague in their midst ; they visited houses known to bear infection, careless of the risk to themselves and others ; even the red cross of Plague on the door did not keep them out when a watchman could be bribed or persuaded to violate his duty. They had, as have so many of the poorest to-day, that deep-seated love of a display of pomp and extravagance over their dead—the enjoyment of a wake.

Funeral processions, the consorting together of relatives and friends in the house of death, were obvious perils, and had been legislated against. None should follow a corpse to the grave. It was absolutely forbidden.

Lawrence, the Lord Mayor, in mid-July found it necessary to give explicit directions to the Aldermen of every ward—

Whereas several persons who died last week were, from ignorance of the searchers, reported to die of other diseases [than Plague] and great audiences assembled at their burial, which may prove a great cause of spreading the contagion, you are to take more effectual care for preventing all public burials within your ward for the time during the infection, according to former orders on this behalf.[2]

Nothing proved effectual to stop the practice. Long as the Plague lasted there was this attendance of poor mourners, openly defiant. In the worst weeks of September, when authority partially broke down and license prevailed, new and more stringent orders were issued by the magistrates. They could not be enforced. " But Lord," Pepys wrote in his " Diary " on Sept. 3rd, a Sunday, " to consider the madness of the people of the town, who will, because they are forbid, come in crowds along with the dead corpses to see them buried." Three days later

[1] Gawdy MSS. (*Hist. MSS. Comm.*, 10th Rep., pt. 2, p. 163).
[2] Mayoral Proclamation, July 13 (Brit. Mus. Lib. Pressmark 21. h. 5 (34).

he watched in broad daylight two or three burials from Bankside, " one at the very heels of another, and doubtless all of the Plague, and yet at least forty or fifty people going along with every one of them." The practice carried infection over whole parishes.[1] The folly of it is writ large in the Bills of Mortality.

The dead cart carried its loads to the pits after nightfall, till a time came " when the nights, though much lengthened, are grown too short to conceal the burials of those that died the day before." [2] Pitiful calls from the windows of " Pray for us ! " to passers-by, none would wish to prevent. The Plague, in some phases, struck down its victims suddenly ; they expired in the street ; some fell dead at the scales in the market-place, when buying the necessities for supporting life.[3] Parish constables were within call quickly to remove the horrid sight from the public gaze—

> Item. Paid for the buryall of a man found dead
> in the streete . . . . . . 4s. 6d.
> Item. Paid for the buryall of a boy found dead
> in the streete . . . . . . 4s.

The churchwardens of St. Katherine Cree met these " items " together, and every parish made many like payments. Occasional opportunity came to the parish officers to augment their little stipends—

> To John Burge, Cons[t]. and ye Beadle for carry-
> ing a visited Woman out of ye parish [4] . . 2s. 6d.

Such ghoulish work was going on everywhere. " Sick " —" sickness "—" visited "—these were terms in habitual use for the pestilence. No sooner was a Plague victim seen helpless in the street than the beadle or constable's first thought was to hustle him or her out of the parish, that the cost of relief and burial should not fall to its charge. Often the victim, realizing suddenly that the Plague was upon him, was in extreme distress and physical pain. Another, with whom the disease was far advanced, staggered about, raving incoherently—perhaps escaped from the nurse-keeper. No matter. He must be moved,

[1] *Newes*, Aug. 31.   [2] Pepys to Lady Cartaret, Sept. 4.
[3] Sir W. Rider to Pepys, Aug. 20.   [4] St. Margaret's Plague Accts.

pushed, or carried over the boundary and dumped into the next parish, that the poor two-and-sixpence or seven shillings, the price of humanity towards him or a grave, might be saved. The parish which unwillingly received him was just as anxious to pass him on to their neighbouring parish. It happened not infrequently that in the hands of one or another the poor Plague victim fell and died on the cobble stones. These entries below are from St. Paul Covent Garden—

To a poore man sick of ye Plague to get him out of the p'ish	1s. 0d.
To two sick beggars to get them out of the p'ish	6d.
To a sick woman to get ye p'ish freed of her	1s. 0d.
To one Sick of the Plague in the street	1s. 0d.

The churchwarden of St. Alphage London Wall when logging up his payments was even more engagingly candid—

Item. Given to a man to carry away a sick man for feare hee should dye in the streete within this parish	1s. 0d.
Item. Paid for carrying a sick man out of the parish to prevent further charge	1s. 0d.

The brutality of it all certainly did not disturb the penmen who have left these cold records.

Let us frankly understand that the impulse in the administration of poor relief two and a half centuries ago was not humanity, but economy. Humanity had nothing to do with it, no place in the code, no uplifting part in its work. It was not alone the Plague sufferers whose lives were held as nothing against a few pence chargeable to parish funds. How often in these written books of payments in other years have I found the little sums entered, of rewards of sixpence or one shilling made " for getting a big-bellied woman out of ye parish," or " carrying a woman greate with childe " beyond the boundary—in dozens, aye, a hundred cases—lest the birth in some shadowed doorway, which might give the mother a little shelter from wind and driving rain, should cast the cost of the waif upon the parish. Sometimes by sixpences and shillings one seems to trace the progress from parish to parish, till at last the burdened woman falls. I take in the

Great Plague a gruesome case from St. Mary Woolchurch Haw, the more inhuman because here the expectant mother was herself Plague-stricken—

Pd. Gilbert Rigbie for getting a woman out of the parish ready to fall in travaile at Mrs Clay's door and for brooms . . 1s. 8d.

Pd. Chiurgeon for Eliza Hog who fell at Mrs Clay's doore and broke her skull . . 2s. 6d.

Pd. Edward Phillips for two to looke to hir and her child while she lived . . . 10s. 0d.

Pd. to the searchers, to the bearers, to the gravemaker and other conveniences for her buriall and her boy afterwards . . 16s. 0d.

Pd. the Coroner for hir and spent on witnesses £1 1s. 0d.

Who does not feel maliciously glad that in this instance the parish failed to save its money ? There are 130 parishes comprised in the Bills of Mortality, and here I have drawn upon the records of but four.

A more grateful task is to lift a familiar incident of the Great Plague out of fiction into the domain of truth. A piper, stupid with drink, fell asleep in a London street. In the morning the dead-cart came along, late about its work as these were. It was nothing uncommon to find some victim struck down by Plague lying stark before the dark doors. The bearers hooked the man into the cart, already piled high with bodies that had been collected, and the cart trundled away to the Plague pit. With the jolting and jars over the cobbled streets, the then half-sobered piper awakened, as daybreak brought the first shafts of light into the sky. He raised himself upright, dragged his bagpipes clear, and began madly to play.

Leading the horse and walking by the side, the bearers in the dusk could see little of the movement in the cart. But hearing the uncanny music proceeding out of the load of dead, they bolted in terrible fright, afterwards reporting that they had taken up the Devil in the form of a man.

For nothing has Defoe been so much discredited as for this picaresque story. His assumed disbelief has been condemned as part of his artistry. Critic after critic has fastened upon it as a case where a too lively imagination has descended to mere buffoonery. Yet I find the incident told by Sir John Reresby in his Memoirs, under date in

FIGURE OF THE PLAGUE PIPER

At Welcombe, the seat of Sir George Otto Trevelyan, Bart., at Stratford-on-Avon

1665, in words that in substance are identically as I have given them.[1] Reresby died in 1689, his memoirs were not committed to print until 1734, and Defoe can by no possibility have seen them. Reresby gives his assurance that the incident occurred in London. No doubt it was thought too good to be forgotten by those who lived through the Great Plague, and this is one instance where Defoe has repeated (with small embellishment) what was told to him by a survivor.

In the garden terrace of Welcombe, the seat at Stratford-on-Avon of Sir George Otto Trevelyan, there stands to-day a sculptured figure of a piper in costume playing his bagpipes, and swung at his side a keg of liquor, and at hand his dog, illustrating this story. The group was at one time in possession of John Duke of Argyll at Whitton, and after his death passed to Stowe, and it is catalogued in the Stowe sale of 1848.[2] It is believed to be the work of Caius Gabriel Cibber, the famous sculptor of the Restoration, and it is likely that the subject appealed to his whim rather than that the statue was commissioned by the sobered and afterwards enriched piper, as the legend associated with it asserts.

It is a striking piece of work. Sir George Trevelyan thus described it to me : " The clothing—the cut of the coat tails and the breeches—when examined close by is very characteristic of the period. The sculpture is very bold, very plain and simple, very English ; and many times better than anything which the artist's sensational son did in Literature."

[1] *Memoirs of Sir John Reresby*, ed. by J. J. Cartwright, 1875.
[2] The migrations of this statue may be traced in *Notes & Queries*, 11th Ser. v. 64, 153.

CHAPTER VII

TOWN AND COUNTRYSIDE

THE country knew that the shutting up was ineffectual, that people already Plague-stricken or in incipient stages of the disease made their escape. London had become a Plague centre from which only peril radiated. Scotland took decisive measures for its protection.

Immediately news of the Court's departure reached the North, the Council for Scotland issued at Edinburgh on July 12th a Proclamation prohibiting trade and intercourse with London or any part of England where the pestilence had already appeared or might in future appear ; and the prohibition, thrice renewed, lasted to the summer of 1666. Ships at sea laden with goods from such places were made to perform quarantine. Goods passing by land were detained at the border till license for entry was given.

The ultimate effect was an interdiction of all trade between Southern England and East Coast ports and Scotland. So complete was the surveillance that merchants from London already on their journey when the Proclamation was published were stopped at the border, and before they might enter Scotland were compelled to resort to a country house allotted to them, there to spend forty days, undertaking not to go near any town or village.[1] All persons thereafter coming from England were held at the border and required to converse with none till the Sheriffs or magistrates had approved their certificates that their towns of origin were free from Plague, signed by the Mayor, Aldermen, or justices.[2] At Haigh, Scottish

[1] *Acts of Privy Council for Scotland*, 3rd Ser. ii. 78.
[2] *Intelligencer*, July 24.

merchants returning were confined to their houses for a month.[1]

These measures were justified by their results. Badly as English towns suffered by contagion brought from London, in all Scotland there was no Plague.

In vain Sir John Lawrence, the Lord Mayor, strove to keep open channels for intercourse between London and the surrounding and distant counties. For better security, he ordered strict inspection within the City and Liberties of all goods brought in or taken out by country carriers. It was published that nothing should be delivered to or received from any infected place or person.[2] That satisfied none—the dread of Plague was overwhelming.

London was at open warfare with the countryside. Always there were people seeking the safety of the country. Neighbouring towns and villages posted armed guards to keep watch at their entrance roads, and these turned travellers back. It was soon made plain that no assurance by certificates of health would be accepted. Albemarle's and Craven's signatures carried authority which none dared dispute. Lord Montagu of Beaulieu has among his papers a document endorsed " A passe in the plage tyme," signed by Lord Craven and addressed to mayors, constables, headboroughs and others whom it may concern, which in peremptory terms required that William Wynde, esquire, and his man be allowed to pass to Newbury, Berkshire, they themselves and the house from which they came and all persons therein being free from infection [3]; though at the date borne, July 17th, the parish of St. Clement Danes from which they set out was itself heavily infected. Other magistrates' names had not such weight.

Little as was the value attached to certificates of health by those who read them, they were quickly forged, and the officers of City parishes gave public notice that they would sign and issue none other than printed certificates, and these to residents personally known to them alone.[4]

Pepys, whom business took down Thames and into Essex, was aghast at the fear in which the people lived.

[1] *State Papers (Domestic)*, 1664–5, p. 484.
[2] *Intelligencer*, July 17.
[3] Lord Montagu of Beaulieu's MSS. (*Hist. MSS. Comm.*, p. 167).
[4] *Intelligencer*, July 16 ; *Newes*, July 20.

" But Lord, to see among other things, how all these great people here (at Dagenham) are afraid of London, being doubtful of anything that comes from thence, or any that hath lately been there, that I was forced to say that I lived wholly at Woolwich." [1]

" I am troubled at it, and wish myself away," he jots down a few days later. " But some cause they have ; for the chaplain with whom, but a week or two ago, we were here mighty high disputing, is since fallen into a fever, and dead." [2]   Riding from Deptford to Dagenham, on all the road he met people walking to and fro, whose one inquiry was how the Plague progressed in London, " a sad question to be so often asked me." [3]   The country was as cruel to its own Plague victims as to others.   That is an illuminating passage in Samuel Herne's letter, already printed, where he pictures the plight of the infected at Hoxton, then a pleasant rural village away north-east of London, as from the road he saw them lying together in a small thatched house and he feared almost starved for want of provisions, so great was the dread of the people to go near anyone Plague-stricken.

Suspect to all, travel-stained, tired and dispirited, the flying Londoners were kept outside towns and forced to find refuge in the fields.   A few, the most fortunate, carried tents.   Others crept for cover beneath trees and hedges, into cow-byres and dirty hovels of the farms, [4] where the farmer's consent could be obtained or his anger dared, till as distance from the capital increased they found, if never welcome, at least better shelter.   There were some hideous tragedies, inevitable in the circumstances.   The fine weather that prevailed through the summer happily favoured the refugees.   They escaped the chilling wet and resultant fever ; but townsmen and women were little hardened to sleep amid the dews upon the ground, or in close hovels fouled by the pollution of cattle. Ill-nurtured and exhausted, in the last stage of distress, some among them died where they lay under the skies. The countrymen slunk away, fearing infection if they touched the bodies, and these were left unburied, a prey to dogs and crows. [5]

[1] *Diary*, July 17.   [2] *Ibid.*, July 28.   [3] *Ibid.*, Aug. 3.
[4] Rugge's " Diurnal," fo. 143.   [5] Boghurst's *Loimographia*, p. 54.

" I well remember," Sir Edward Southcote wrote to his son, " when I was five years old, the time of the Great Plague by the smoking of the houses with pitch, and the dismal stories that were brought in of people lying dead on the highway that nobody durst bury." [1]

A pamphlet circulated, first printed at the Plague visitation of 1641, which under the title of " Londons Lamentation " sought pictorially to distinguish between the good treatment given by the capital to the Plague victims, and the harsh brutality of the countryside. To a City churchyard the dead are brought from their beds for

FROM TITLE PAGE OF " LONDONS LAMENTATION," 1641.

decent burial in graves, coffined and under a pall, mourners following. That was London's charity. In contrast, " the Countries Crueltie " is illustrated by travellers fallen by the highway and in fields, whose corpses the heedless countrymen drag by the heels and cast into ditches. At two and a half centuries' distance the admission may be made that the county magistrates had adequate reason for the precautions they adopted. The lurking peril was the greater because unseen. There were cases reported, and accepted as authentic by medical authority of the time, of travellers who had come out of infected

[1] Southcote " Memoirs " in Woodchester Priory MSS.

places into the country upon whom the evident signs of Plague developed a month or two after.[1]

A man who had set out from London to Dorchester died within a mile of that town after four days' sickness. He had been refused entrance to the town; his only refuge available was a poor hovel on a farm, wherein he lay down and expired. Unwilling either to handle the corpse or to enter the infected place, the people of Dorchester boarded up the little structure and dug a deep pit, into which hovel and corpse together were tossed and buried.[2] The dread was universal.

Dorset has a worse memory of the Great Plague. It was carried to Poole, report said, by goods contained in a pedlar's pack. The magistrates were able to stamp out the pestilence by removing the sick to a pest-house at a distance from the town. They had difficulty in finding anyone to serve as nurse there, and had resort to engaging in that capacity a young woman then lying in the gaol under sentence of death, on a promise made to her to use their influence to secure a pardon. The nurse performed her risky duty and escaped infection, and quickly after the pest-house emptied she was barbarously hanged by the mayor.[3]

In pathos of human suffering a case at Southampton excels. Plague was virulent there in July, and town guards were posted to prevent ingress and egress, yet some crept out. The bodies of a man, a woman, and a little child lay on the open downs two miles away. The woman, the last survivor of the three, had scratched with her hands a shallow hole for her husband, and therein had half buried him.[4]

The Plague was in Dover, taken there, the people believed, by a servant girl from London, and that year and the next 900 died of it. The contagion far overspread Kent. A place on the hillside at Dover, facing the pier fort, was long known as " The Graves " from the number of Plague victims buried there, mostly uncoffined.[5]

The justices of Surrey locked the wells of Epsom, a

---

[1] Hodges, p. 57.   [2] Newes, Sept. 25.
[3] Dr. Mead's *Short Discourse on the Plague*, 1720, pp. 117-9, 149.
[4] Addit. MSS. 4182, fo. 28.
[5] Halsted's *Kent*, iv. 48, 97-8.

popular resort by Londoners for the healing waters, set a watch about the town, restrained the inhabitants from receiving any lodgers, and permitted no coaches or waggons with passengers or goods from infected places to enter.[1]

Ipswich, then a town and port of great importance as a chief victualling centre of the Royal Navy, admitted no strangers till their certificates of health and the goods they brought had been examined. It became badly Plague-stricken.[2] Leicester employed four watchmen to prevent entry of persons travelling out from London until the Mayor and Aldermen approved.[3] The Mayor of Bath required of any person coming from an infected place a certificate that he had been twenty days absent from it. Coaches, waggons, and carriers' horses, with the goods they brought, were kept outside the city and forbidden entrance till they had forty days' airing. Bath impoverished itself by locking its famous bathing pool, to discourage fashionable town visitors from coming to the Spa.[4] At Lichfield a careless fellow entertained an infected person in an alehouse, and the master of the house was a few days later dead of Plague.[5]

Letters from London were held in universal suspicion, as a possible vehicle for carrying infection. Few cared to receive them, anxious as was the whole country for news how the capital fared. John Allin's correspondence[6] is a valuable record of the time, but his temper was sorely tried by the reluctance of his friends at Rye to reciprocate by answering him. "Surely, if my friends be afraid of my letters, I would not be afraid of theirs," he wrote in protest.

The Letter Office had a courageous public servant in James Hickes, the acting postmaster—a fine character. From the time of the fight at Edgehill he had carried King Charles I.'s foreign letters from London to Oxford at great risk of life, and though taken more than once by the Parliamentary Army, he had never been surprised to the loss of one letter. He stuck to his duty in London in all the months when Plague was raging about him, and

---

[1] *Intelligencer*, July 24.
[2] *Newes*, July 13.   Add. MSS. 4182, fo. 31.
[3] Leicester Corporation MSS. (*Hist. MSS. Comm.*, p. 439).
[4] *Intelligencer*, July 24 ; *Newes*, Aug. 3.
[5] *Intelligencer*, Oct. 23.   [6] See Chapter XI., *post*.

between twenty and thirty of the postal servants died.[1]
The volume of the post became so reduced that he made
complaint that at the year's end the officers would not
clear £10 of their salaries. Had the contagion been
catching by letters, he wrote in August, contemptuous of
the popular fears, they who handled them would all have
been dead long since.[2]

A favourite means of disinfecting letters during the
Plague was to air them over a bowl of vinegar, and orders
that this practice should be followed were sent to provincial
postmasters. Mails from the North before entering London
were aired at Hounslow.

No letters save those for actual delivery in the City
and Westminster were received in London, others which in
ordinary circumstances would have passed through being
diverted by a widely circuitous route so as to avoid the
infected capital.[3] Horse and foot posts accepted packets
from none save the town or village watchman, that contagion might not be carried, and made deliveries to them
alone. Late in the autumn, when Plague broke out at
Sherborne, Dorset, the postmaster there was given
peremptory orders to move out his office to some safe
rural place, and not to return to the town till it was free
from infection.[4]

Yarmouth had the Plague even before London, and
the county magistrates in panic not only set guards to
prevent those of the town coming out, but forbade butchers
and other market people to carry in produce. Starvation
confronting them, the townsmen appealed to the Privy
Council, which directed the justices to find some means to
prevent Plague spreading and yet allow the town to be
provisioned.[5]

The Plague got into the Isle of Wight, Newport, the
capital, being infected by a traveller. The Mayor shut up
the house wherein the man died ; two women, by changing
and airing the sheets of the bed, took the infection and
died, and such was the fear of touching the corpses that

[1] Hickes's Petition to the King, in *State Papers* (*Domestic*), Addenda,
1660–70, p. 577.
[2] Hickes to Williamson, Aug. 14.
[3] Sir Philip Froude to Williamson, Aug. 5.
[4] Lord Arlington to Bennett, postmaster at Sherborne, Nov. 11.
[5] Privy Col. Reg. 58, fo. 136.

the householder himself was compelled to bury both in his garden.[1] A month later (October) there was revived alarm by the bold action of two young seamen from the Fleet, who, at a despairing mother's request, at dead of night ventured into Southampton, broke open a locked house wherein all were lying dead of Plague save one girl, and brought this last survivor down by water to Cowes, where ultimately she was discovered.[2]

In Northamptonshire, where Plague was especially prevalent in towns along the great arterial highways, and in Cheshire, to which county the Plague reached, the justices not only closed the inns but pulled down their signs, that there should be no encouragement to people to foregather and spread infection.[3] There was Plague as far north as the Tyne, the towns upon which were said to have been infected by coaling ships returned from the Thames.[4]

At Gloucester an agitated Mayor would not permit pipes of port from London to be brought into the city till he had had them drawn through the River Severn. After some experience of this the wine importers angrily protested. Leave was then given to disinfect the casks by pouring water over them.[5] Amid a multitude of counsels none knew the best course to take.

There is no need to look so far away from London. The deplorable case of Coombe Farm illustrates the actual peril of contagion against which these towns guarded. This Kentish holding was a few miles out of Greenwich, back from the road that led to Woolwich, the single house standing remote from all others in an unprotected and desolate spot. The farm had been much molested by passing beggars, and rather than endure trouble from them and their petty thefts, the farmer had allowed them to lie at night in his barns. Plague came there in August, brought by some vagrant wanderer. On the 22nd of that month, a coffin with a man dead of the Plague lay out in a meadow, to which it had been carried after dark. The parish, too frightened to handle the corpse, had made no

[1] *State Papers (Domestic)*, 1664–5, p. 548.
[2] *Ibid.*, 1665–6, p. 35.
[3] *Cal. of Treasury Books*, 1660–7, p. 710.
[4] *Newes*, Oct. 19.
[5] Boghurst's *Loimographia*, p. 54.

effort at burial, but a watchman kept guard day and night, that none should come near.

Fierce dogs were thereafter left loose on the farm to scare away future beggars, but infection having got in, it desolated the place with the fearful speed which made the appearance of Plague so terrible. By the 4th September—in thirteen days—twenty-one persons at Coombe Farm were dead of the Plague.[1]

Abroad, France refused entrance to its ports to any vessels coming from England, on pain of death to the ship-masters.[2]

The Dutch in their struggle at sea gained renewed confidence from London's plight, and a September *Utrecht Couranter* was pleasant enough to say : " The English nation is now brought so low with the Plague that a man may run them down with his finger."

The City's worst experience of the Plague was in St. Giles Cripplegate. That is the largest City parish, containing the whole Ward of Cripplegate Without [3]—the one instance in which ward and parish are coterminous ; and in Restoration London it covered yet larger space. It had areas outside the City's boundary and jurisdiction, the " lordship." So early as Elizabeth the evil state of the skirts of the town by overcrowding with the poorest people had engaged attention in a Royal Proclamation :—

The Queen's Majesty perceiving the state of the City of London and the suburbs and confines thereof to increase daily by access of people to inhabit the same . . . and there are such great multitudes of people brought to inhabit in small rooms, whereof a great part are seen to be very poor ; yea such must live of begging, or of worse means ; and they heaped up together, and in a sort smothered with many families of children and servants in one house or small tenement ; it must needs follow, if any plague or popular sickness should by God's permission enter among those multitudes, that the same should not only spread itself and invade the whole city and confines, as great mortality should ensue the same, but would be also dispersed through all other parts of the realm, to

[1] Pepys, Aug. 21, 22, Sept. 4.
[2] *State Papers* (*Domestic*), 1664–5, p. 571.
[3] Cripplegate Within and Without are to-day merged in a single ward, under one Alderman.

the manifest danger of the whole body thereof. For remedy
whereof, etc.[1]

no building in London on new foundations should thereafter be permitted.

That was the first futile effort made—the first of many
—to restrict the size of the capital; and when, eighty-five
years later, the Great Plague came additional areas were
built upon, accretions to the ancient City. Largely by
reason of its wide expanse, Cripplegate was fated to show
a greater death-roll than any other City parish. It was
exceeded only in the far-spreading out-parish of Stepney.
But other causes made it inevitable that Cripplegate
should suffer with exceptional severity. Its lands came
up to the City wall, standing wholly outside.

In its western extension, Cripplegate had some remains
of magnificence. Bridgewater Square marks the site of
the mansion, with orchard, of the Earls of Bridgewater,
destroyed by fire in 1687. Two sons of the then Earl
perished in the flames. Prince Rupert's town house had
for many years stood in Beech Lane [2]; but the fashionable
residents since the King's return had mostly drifted towards
Westminster, leaving a toiling population here herded
together. The weaver's industry spread into Cripplegate;
with these craftsmen were many printers and others engaged
in small trades, and pipe makers, pedlars, labourers and the
like, whose uncertain means of livelihood made necessary
a cheap lodging, best obtained outside the City wall.

Cripplegate was part built upon London's ancient fen,
overlooking the reclaimed marshland which stretched
east along the City wall and north—to-day's Finsbury and
Moorfields. London of the Middle Ages had known all
this area as actual wet marsh. The Walbrook stream,
rising in Hoxton, never had been allowed sufficient unob-
structed passage through the wall and the City to the
Thames, and flooded this land. Moorfields had given a
water surface for winter skating. A Mayor's Court record
of 1301 shows the City officials making their inspection in
a boat.

The marshland had been ineffectually drained in the

---

[1] *Royal Proclamation*, 1580, July 7.
[2] Sir John Baddeley, *Cripplegate Ward*, p. 129. Its " shadow " was
standing in 1808, when Malcolm (*Londinium Redivivum*) mentions it.

year 1411, and two other attempts at drainage followed in the reign of King Henry VIII. Centuries' accumulations of the rubbish and debris of the City thrown down upon it, and some preparation of the ground under James I. and the Commonwealth, had gradually raised the level. Although a fen no longer, the land remained pitted with depressions and shallow ditches. Water lay stagnant at the bottom of these, loaded with the filth and pollution of the time. Always Cripplegate had been a bad quarter for fever. The ancient Crowder's Well, much used by residents, was in the churchyard, close by the present parsonage. The extreme virulence of Plague wherever polluted watercourses or ditches are traced, or water-logged ground lay open, is too persistent to be mere coincidence.

The Plague found nothing wanting at Cripplegate. The City had a great laystall at Moorfields, the accumulated garbage and decaying vegetable matter raked from the streets rotting there in the sunshine—the same laystall against which the College of Physicians thirty-five years before had lodged its protest. Foul ditches were upon one hand, this heaped pollution on the other, and adjacent a big population was massed about the few narrow streets that threaded a honeycomb of dark, overshadowed alleys—a place of concentrated squalor, dilapidation, dirt and neglect such as, happily, is unknown in London by the living generation.

The first entries of Plague in the Cripplegate burial register are these—

> June 2. Bennet wife of Phillip Puller in Creswell St., plague.
> „   2. John Barker, weaver in Old Street, plague.

and a third on June 6th. For eleven days thereafter the parish was clear, when two more deaths are recorded, the outlying Old Street again providing one, and the entire month's mortality from Plague figures as twenty-nine, half a dozen being on the last day of the month. The Plague was soon firmly installed in Old Street and other parts of the lordship, it being complained that the parish authorities shut up houses in the area under jurisdiction of the City Alderman but let the infected of the outer part go freely about.[1]

[1] Addit. MSS. 4182, fo. 29.

PAGE OF CRIPPLEGATE BURIAL REGISTER, AUGUST 1665

Nicholas Pyne was parish clerk. Each week he took to Parish Clerks Hall Cripplegate's return, to be included in the printed Bills of Mortality, and each week the figures showed the Plague leaping up; from 49 deaths recorded in the first week of July to 114—then to 208—next to 302. Already Cripplegate in the numbers of its Plague victims had assumed the lead over all the parishes in the City and Liberties that had been earlier infected. That month its Plague burials reached 691.[1] On two days alone, the 28th and 31st, St. Giles's buried 54 and 56 acknowledged Plague victims; and report ran that one dreadful night of July, a Sunday, above 100 corpses were hurried to the graves and pits.[2] As with many of the crowded parishes of London, previous Plagues had stuffed the burial grounds full, and one in Whitecross Street, much used, had the year before been closed.[3] The chief recourse was to the Plague pits.

Lest a continuous recital of figures be wearisome, I have here reproduced a single page of the register of August, making appeal to the eye. It contains thirty-six entries, a death in every line, and of these all but five are given as Plague—the three entered as " spotted fever " and one as " fever " probably conceal Plague. The page contains but a section of a single day's entries, on August 13th.

The deaths in this one parish for the month of August fill ninety-nine and one-half similar pages.

In one day, August 18th, St. Giles Cripplegate buried 151 of its parishioners. That was its dreadful record for a day, never exceeded. In the burial register each has a line, giving name, and often place and trade, save that occasionally no more is written than " a stranger," " a man "—these unidentified. Elsewhere I have reproduced a page from the burials of September 1st, which with the names of many unconsidered people, weaver, " soldjer," dyer, water-bearer and the like, includes these—

John Waters, Chyrurgion, plague.
Isabella, dau : of Edw : Bolnest, Dr. Phisicke, plague.

A full year's mortality in St. Giles Cripplegate in 1666

---

[1] Burial Register.   [2] Addit. MSS. 4182, fo. 25b.
[3] Vest. Mins. 1664, June 4.

numbered 776—fewer than the deaths of a single week while the pestilence ran its course.   For decency of burial, Cripplegate purchased four church coffins at a cost of £1 6s., these being used again and again for the transference from the house of death to the grave, and returned to the church.   Most churches at the time had among their properties a coffin, so used.

The Vicar of St. Giles Cripplegate was Dr. John Pritchett, a notorious pluralist.   On his death, when reputed to be a very rich man, he held with Cripplegate his Bishopric, the living of Harlingdon, Middlesex, and a stall in St. Paul's Cathedral.[1]   He gained no honour in the Plague.   He was among the first in flight, and never returned in all the months that the infection raged, leaving his City parish in the charge of Thomas Luckeyne, his curate.   When informed in August by Luckeyne that the parish clerk had died at his post, he wrote to him from his retreat, directing that the place be sufficiently supplied, and pending a new appointment the curate was to take the fees for his pains.[2]   A generous soul !

Nicholas Pyne had compiled his successive weekly returns, tramping himself with them across the dismal City streets to Parish Clerks Hall in Vintry, and always they showed that same upward tendency—356 dead of Plague[3] in the week to August 8th, 521 more to swell the toll in the following week.   Then the Plague entered his house and laid him low.   He was buried on August 21st, and in the register his death is attributed to dropsy. The same day his wife Elizabeth died and was buried, and again the death cause is dropsy.   Who believed it ? Old Smyth, the obituary compiler, who lived in Cripplegate and with better information logged up the deaths of his friends and any others of note, simply enters " pest."

The parish paid one year's wages of Ferdinando

---

[1] Sir John Baddeley, *Church and Parish of St. Giles Cripplegate.*
[2] Vest. Mins., Sept. 4.
[3] The concealment of Plague in Cripplegate was attempted in the most barefaced manner.   In this particular week of August the mortality returned was 691, and Plague was credited in the Bill with only 356 of these deaths—in other words, one-half of the deaths were passed off as due to ordinary diseases.   The true proportion is more likely to have been 656 dead from Plague.   Till the Plague became marked, Cripplegate's mortality, already swollen much above normal figures, had averaged 28 a week.

Sothern, the sexton, to his widow. His work invited infection, and he died on July 5th after a day or two's sickness, believed to have been Plague, but not so returned.[1] The register again says dropsy! On October 7th Henry Barret, the Clerk of the Lordship, died of Plague.

St. Giles Cripplegate, despite its vicar's bad example, had the fortune to be served by better men than he. The parish had four churchwardens, one of them being Edward Gervise (or Jarvis), a broker, and I take it that two of these fled before the Plague, for two others performed their work, Thomas Blizard, a coppersmith, and James Vurles, who figure in the register as " churchwardens in being." In the dreadful months the parish lost three of these, Gervise and Blizard within two days of one another in August, and Vurles later, all by the Plague.[2] New wardens were appointed for the broken term. Mr. Luckeyne, the curate, survived. It was impossible that one man, however willing, could in the fearful conditions of Cripplegate minister to the whole of that large parish, bring consolation to the sick and shrive the dying. The work was done, and it was done by Nonconforming ministers. They are the real heroes of the Plague, the men whose golden example ennobles their great profession, and condemns the political Churchmen who made them outcasts. Often in the accounts of City parishes, when churchwardens were giving their little charities or relief, I have come across entries such as " To ——, a poor Minister, 1s." and " To a poor minister's widow, 1s. 6d." [3]—it is pathetic beyond words. For these were educated, spiritually-minded men, who had sacrificed all for conscience. Dire poverty, and loss by the terror of Plague of the scholars by whose teaching they had eked out an existence, had brought some among them to find lodging in Cripplegate's pestiferous slums. Others came willingly to labour in the stricken parish, its rightful pastor having fled—unrewarded, answering the inspiring call to give service to God and humanity. They knew the risk they ran. In St. Giles

---

[1] Smyth's *Obituary* (Camden Society).
[2] Ch'wardens' Accts. 1665–6, and Burial Register, wherein " fever " is entered, but Smyth says " ex peste." The parish apparently could not admit the loss of an official by Plague.
[3] St. Anne and St. Agnes Ch'wardens' Accts. 1665–6.

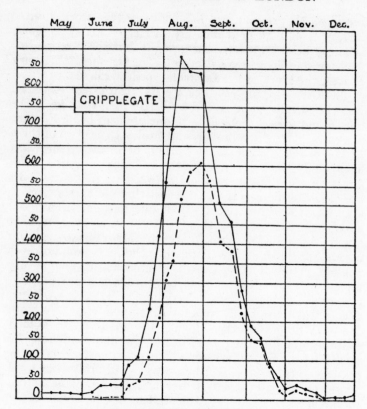

| | May | June | July | Aug. | Sept. | Oct. | Nov. | Dec. |

THE PLAGUE IN CRIPPLEGATE.
Based on the Bills of Mortality, 1665.
Solid line, all deaths.
Broken line, deaths attributed to Plague.

Cripplegate burial register you read these names, all entered at the height of the Plague—

Aug. 27.   Samuel Austin, minister, plague.[1]
Sept. 6.   John Askew, minister, plague.
  ,,   15.   Samuel Skelton, minister, plague.
  ,,   16.   Abraham Jennaway (Janeway), minister, plague.
  ,,   23.   Henry Marley, minister, plague.
  ,,   30.   John Wall, minister, plague.

[1] Not to be confused with Samuel Austen, or Austyn, Vicar of St. Mary Staining, who also perished of the Plague.

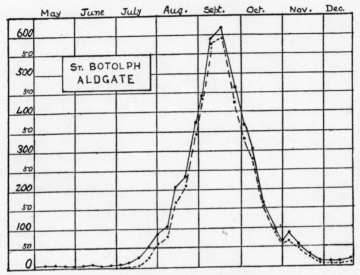

THE PLAGUE IN ALDGATE.
Based on the Bills of Mortality, 1665.
Solid line, all deaths.
Broken line, deaths attributed to Plague.

St. Botolph, Aldgate, appears to have been one of the few parishes wherein the proportion of Plague deaths was returned with rough accuracy. Note how close the Plague line keeps with the line of All Deaths, and compare with Cripplegate on opposite page, where there was wholesale concealment of Plague.

Two others, John Grimes, a well-known Nonconformist divine, and Benjamin Needham, also described as " minister," buried in Cripplegate during the Plague, one a son and the other his wife. Austin's wife perished with her husband, of Plague ; John Askew and his daughter Susan were buried together, both dead of Plague.

In the three months of July, August, and September the parish of Cripplegate lost 6,640 dead by Plague—how many more unrecorded in the Bills no one knows. Another Cripplegate surgeon who died of Plague was Thomas Fox, on September 5th ; his daughter Ann five days later followed him to the grave. There are repeated entries of deaths from Plague among servants in the dwelling of Mr. Tayler, the Cripplegate Alderman's Deputy, none among the family. Like so many others fortunate in the world's riches, the Deputy had fled, leaving to his servants the charge and risk.

In citing these few instances, taken at random, I do so because they are typical of hundreds of homes in which many members, and not infrequently the whole household, perished. It is rare to find " gent." written against names in the dreadful pages of the burial register, and as rarely the entry indicates some substantial merchant. It was the poor, in Cripplegate as elsewhere, who in the immense majority gave up men, women, and young children to the Moloch of Plague—the little-heeded, unconsidered " common people." But nothing strikes the imagination so vividly as the deaths of these many dissenting ministers, following so closely one upon another.

They were the victims of persecution within the Church, and martyrs to the duty they accepted without flinching, when the courage of others failed. Dr. Pritchett, the fugitive vicar, lived to take the Bishopric of Gloucester. So the world rewards men.

It is by comparative figures that realization best comes of Cripplegate's toll of sacrifice in the Great Plague. In September the parish had but three marriages ; there were twenty-five christenings ; and 1,957 deaths from all causes, these last filling fifty-four pages of the register— and this not, as August's record had shown, the worst. Eighty lay dead where to fill the gap in population a single child was born. The blank prospect seemed that of extermination.

From Cripplegate the Plague stretched out to Bishopsgate, there taking from the parish of St. Botolph 2,500 admitted deaths by the pestilence ; thence on to Aldgate, enfolding the City within the wall on its northern side. Aldgate fared much worse, losing 4,051 given out as the toll by the Plague, and 4,926 in all, mostly in the months of August and September. In the week ending September 19th the deaths in this single parish numbered 623. I have drawn some Plague curves, which illustrate how long a high rate of mortality lasted in these poor parishes on the outskirts, fed as they were continuously by ever new numbers of discharged workmen and servants compelled by their poverty to seek housing in the pest-ridden slums.

The place of the great Plague pit in Aldgate was with

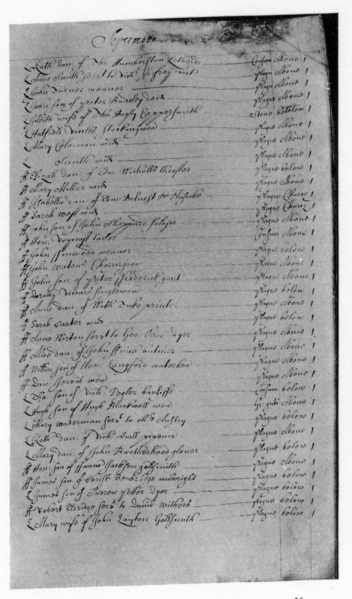

PLAGUE ENTRIES IN CRIPPLEGATE REGISTER, SEPT. 1665

much probability revealed in 1859 at the eastern end of Three Nuns Court, a little distance beyond the church. Workmen digging for foundations came upon a considerable quantity of human skulls and bones lying seven feet below the present surface.[1] Defoe's "dreadful gulf," into which he asserts that 1,114 corpses from Aldgate and Whitechapel were thrown in a fortnight, when the gorged pit had to be filled up—it could hold no more—is indicated by him at about this spot. In the churchyard itself the ground caved in during the seventies of last century, disclosing a pit.

In one parish burial register there is an entry begun and ending abruptly, the page being splashed with ink. The entry is finished in another hand, and the first penmanship is not again seen. Here, by chance, is the evidence of one of those intimate tragedies of the Plague that bring us so near to it, for the tradition lingers that the parish clerk was fatally seized and, pen in hand, fell dead over the register.[2]

The hateful blue sky, rarely crossed by cloud, the glorious sunshine—Londoners grew to loathe these, looking anxiously for dark skies and the long-deferred rain. The capital was laden with Plague; but to the stranger approaching from a distance seldom can the panorama of the city upon the Thames-side have seemed so pleasing. A hundred church towers and spires, the gables and steeply-pitched roofs of the houses massed on the rising bank, the single bridge, itself loaded with houses, that lay low upon the water, stood out with eerie distinctness in an atmosphere clear of its accustomed pollution by the closing down of the fires of the soap-boilers, the dyers, and the brewers whose chimneys had befouled it. There was unnatural quietness, as of a city asleep. It is like this so many Italian towns appear in the hot hours of afternoon, when activities are relaxed.

Trade and manufacture were carried on with increasing difficulty. Few country buyers would knowingly accept goods from so dangerous a source of origin, and the

[1] *Notes & Queries*, 2nd Ser. viii. 288–9.
[2] The particular parish among the one hundred and thirty comprised in the Bills has unfortunately escaped me. I had thought it was Shoreditch, but the register there does not contain the page.

wealthier classes having fled, London had little need itself for other than bare necessaries. Richard Baxter, the divine, who had gone into Buckinghamshire, tells that it was scarce possible to convey how fearful people were thirty, forty, or even one hundred miles from London, of anything bought from a mercer's or draper's shop, of any goods that were brought to them, or of any person that came to their houses. They shut their doors against their own friends, and if a man passed over the fields carefully avoided him.[1]

But to the stranger who risked the unseen terrors and entered the streets, neglect was at once apparent—neglect that best assisted the spread of the pestilence. No effective centralized sanitary authority existed. A freestone foot-path for pedestrians extended before the shops in the few principal highways, elsewhere being only the cobble pavement that made the road surface, with its sunken kennels. The civic rulers had inspiration to insist by repeated orders on the cleansing of the streets by house-holders and removal of refuse by the parish rakers. The Plague itself made that task impossible. The officers of a parish for health services, as to-day we should call them, might have been counted on the four fingers. Many houses being left empty, and others having their residents shut in on appearance of infection among them, it could not be effectively done, and the City's condition went from bad to worse.

The Great Plague was a tragedy of errors. It is error that confronts one in whatever direction one turns. If only those fated people could have known ! The closed dwellings were fœtid, and small wonder that any shut in them died quickly. Nothing in the burial registers is so depressing when one's eye glances down the long lists as the reappearance of names, children, father, and mother, on successive days. In many instances the entire family shut in was destroyed in a week. A common belief, widely held, and unfortunately shared by a section of the medical profession, was that the poison of Plague was in the air.[2]

[1] *Reliquiæ Baxterianæ*, pt. 3, p. 2.
[2] Dr. Thomas Mead, who wrote his well-known treatise on Plague in 1720, held this view. Dr. Nathaniel Hodges, who laboured in London throughout the Great Plague, strongly contested it. It was, of course, with the idea of burning out the Plague poison thought to be latent in the air that fires were lighted in the streets in September.

Houses received little or no ventilation. The people, anxious only to secure their safety, closed all windows and held them tight fastened, "to keep out the Plague." Fresh air, wholesomeness, the pure, life-giving oxygen— these were shut out. There were numbers who, in alarm of infection entering, even stopped up the keyholes of their doors,[1] and avoided communication with anyone. The dirt accumulated when few had liberty amid their cares to attend to cleansing. A hot sun quickly made poisonous the town refuse left about the streets and close alleys. It could not be long before houses and streets alike stank. There were quarters back of the town thoroughfares wherein the poor crowded, whose vicinity was as obvious to the nose as were the villages of New Guinea to the traveller for "the Golden Coast."

Many persons in health kept within doors, believing that thereby they would escape the gravest peril. To make the conditions of life still worse, there existed among the better informed people a firm belief in the efficacy of strong-smelling disinfectants. They had the recommendation of the College of Physicians.[2] Nitre, tar, rosin, and other like substances were burnt in the rooms, often upon clear coal fires, adding oppressive heat to that of the hot summer. Fires of woods that gave out pungent odours were deemed most effective. A popular expedient was to flash gunpowder in pans, and the fumes of saltpetre lingered in the close atmosphere. Poor folk burnt old shoes and odd scraps of leather and horn to get the smell.[3] The vapour from vinegar was inhaled. The Deanery by St. Paul's was fumed twice each week during the Plague with brimstone, hops, pepper, and frankincense.[4] James Hickes, the postmaster, made bitter complaint that the Letter Office was so fumed, morning and night, that those working in it could hardly see one another through the mists.[5]

For personal disinfection, nothing enjoyed such favour as tobacco. Boghurst held it useless against Plague, or if of service at all, then only with those who had never smoked before, or but little—but perhaps he is a prejudiced

---

[1] *Loimographia*, p. 54.   [2] *Certain Necessary Directions*, 1665.
[3] Boghurst, pp. 55, 63.   [4] Tillison to Sancroft, Aug. 15, Sept. 14.
[5] Hickes to Williamson, Aug. 14.

observer. " I never took a pipe this year," he declares, "nor ever do, nor will do. How many thousands of tobacco smokers, think you, died this year ? " [1] But belief in it was universal, and even children were compelled to light the leaf in pipes. Thomas Hearne, the antiquary, remembered an acquaintance, one Tom Rogers, telling him that when he was a scholar at Eton in the year that the Great Plague raged, all the boys smoked in school by order, and that he was never whipped so much in his life as he was one morning for not smoking.[2] It was long afterwards a tradition that none who kept tobacconists' shops in London had the Plague.

If the streets lacked their accustomed stir and animation, yet the population must live, and the capital required daily provisioning. A town's activities cannot altogether cease. The river was lifeless—the Thames that in normal times was London's most frequented highway, bearing many hundreds of wherries for hire. Pepys notes the increasing difficulty of hiring a waterman at the boat stairs. Tillison told Sancroft his doubts if it would be possible to get a stock of wood for winter firing at the Deanery brought by boat to London this summer, and he was shocked at the prices asked : " I have made it my business two days together to hire lighters, and cannot get anyone that will fetch it under 2s. the load ; heretofore the Church gave but 14d. the load." [3]

The tragedy was concealed. It must be searched for in the houses—in the desolated homes of congested courts and alleys.

It was there the people lay dying, behind the locked doors and the windows tightly closed—there the deaths piled up that, as Plague increased in violence, mounted from tens to hundreds each day that passed, and from hundreds overtopped a thousand a day before the worst was endured and left behind. The families with children were in the most pitiable plight. The children could not understand the imprisonment. Little faces peered from windows at the occasional passer-by, lost in wonderment.[4] Why was it ? Careworn mothers were unable to restrain their fretfulness, to find any substitute for their accustomed

[1] *Loimographia*, p. 55. [2] *Reliquiæ Hearnianæ*, 1720, Jan. 21.
[3] Tillison to Sancroft, Aug. 10. [4] *Golgotha*.

play, to hush them into quiet, when in the adjoining room the father or other children had fallen into the heavy slumber that ended in death.

Sleep, indeed, was peace, but there were stages in the illness when endurance gave out, and hearts were broken by the ravings of delirium and the many dreadful sights and sounds experienced. The disease made sufferers most difficult to manage. It was almost incredible, Dr. Hodges declared from his experience, how some at the height of the infection would from a very slight cause kindle into the utmost rage, and rave at one another like scolds until death parted their contentions.[1]

In their sorrow the family could not even be left alone. The unsympathetic, repellent nurse-keeper—a total stranger—was forced upon them, an unwelcome guest, and having authority too often used it with brutality that increased their misery many-fold. The dreadful old women searchers, allowed entrance by the watchman who guarded the door, tramped up the stairs to exercise their office, inquiring if any were dead. From the doctor and surgeon, their only other visitors in the long drawn-out confinement, they might expect at least humanity; but these professional men were tired and overworked, and if hasty over their functions, that was at least excusable. Hundreds of shut-in families never saw a parson—the numbers were too few—or any missioner save the parish officer who brought the stinted poor relief.

The end of all suffering came with physical appearances that frightened those who stood by. Many Plague victims slept with eyes half open, as if already dead and cold. This happened mostly to children and older people before they died. Others stretched upon beds, by some nervous disturbance kept the head continually shaking in a hideous manner. Many, dreaming, cried out in their sleep that they were all on fire, a sign that was accepted as the forerunner of destruction. At the time of release the sufferer fell into unconsciousness and quiet, but those who awakened told of frightful dreams—that they were among graves and tombs in the churchyards, and they had tumbled down from some high place and fallen among coffins.[2]

[1] *Loimologia*, p. 62.   [2] Boghurst, pp. 23, 36, 39.

Few children born in the evil time survived. Teeming women fared miserably during the Plague, when there were none to give attention, and of those who received infection it is recorded that scarce one in forty lived.[1]

None had trust in the nurses, and all feared them. Boghurst asserts that many of these attendants, by giving cooling drinks in the height of fever, destroyed their patients; others, as soon as they saw the appearance of "the tokens," of fatal omen, gave to the sufferers a little cold water, and so sent them quickly to their journey's end.[2] A common device by nurses was to wrap the newly dead in wet cloths, the effect being to drive the spots in, and the death was given out to the searcher as not having been by Plague.

Were we able by eyes and nose to fathom the horror of these Plague-stricken homes, probably we should find among the occupants a rat scurrying away to his hole, none caring. Not the rat we know to-day, the short-tailed, large, voracious brown rat, but a different creature, repellent certainly but less loathsome. The black rat was then familiar, his coat really taking a deep bluish-black hue; less heavy in bulk, longer snouted, with the larger ears spread as if to receive warning by the faintest sound. Where choice offered, his abode was by prefer-ence a human habitation, wherein he might grow fat by attacking the family's food, or failing that source forage for himself outside. An interesting little fellow.

Words cannot adequately convey the hopelessness as day succeeded day, and always the Plague enlarged. It passed unseen from one to another, a thing inscrutable, beyond human understanding.

Many of the poorest people lay ill in close and dark, unventilated cellars, for the tenements wherein the sick and the healthy were penned in together could give to some no better accommodation. Out of such places they were brought dead.[3] The constant toll of bells from one or another of a hundred church steeples, each one notifying yet another death, thrust an unbearable strain upon wracked nerves.[4] Every circumstance made for fear. No night passed but the dead-cart rumbled noisily

[1] Boghurst, p. 25.
[3] *Ibid.*, p. 27.
[2] *Loimographia*, p. 29.
[4] Pepys, July 26, 30.

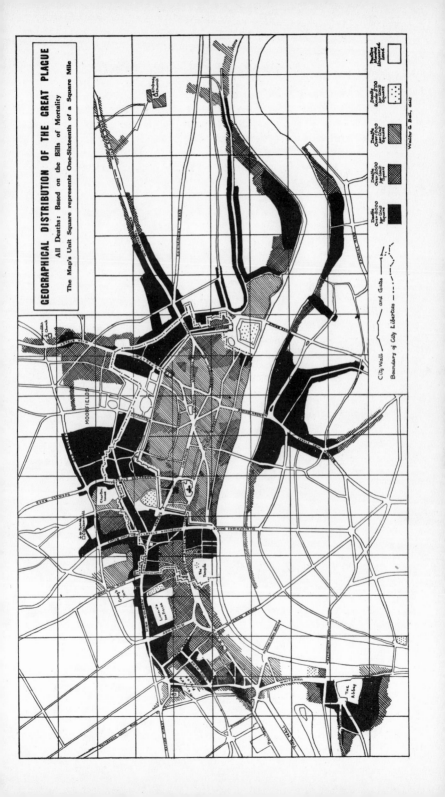

GEOGRAPHICAL DISTRIBUTION OF THE GREAT PLAGUE

All Deaths: Based on the Bills of Mortality

The Map's Unit Square represents One-Sixteenth of a Square Mile

Deaths Over 3000 per Unit Square
Deaths Over 2000 per Unit Square
Deaths Over 1000 per Unit Square
Deaths Under 1000 per Unit Square
Deaths None Unlocated Land

City Wall and Gates
Boundary of City Liberties

Walter G. Bell, del.

over the cobble stones, and the call of the bearers rang through the street, " Bring out your dead ! " The clang of a bell, and flare of links, distantly glowing, told of its approach, with many stoppages on the way.

The stricken were in terrible loneliness, a numbing dread haunting them. I find a pathetic illustration in a document that lightens with its humanity that repository of dusty dullness, the Canterbury Wills.[1] It matters nothing that it dates from an Elizabethan Plague; human nature in the last extremity is unchanging. The nuncupative will (if the term be allowed) opens with ominous words, " In the name of God, Amen," then tells its simple story. Richard Lane, of St. Margaret New Fish Street parish, being visited with Plague " and feeling himself at the beginning of his sickness weak and faint," went to the house beyond Aldersgate of the wife of Daniel Morley, his aunt—

And fynding her busye did in the presence and heering of the undernamed witnesses speake theise wordes followinge or the like in effecte, viz. Good awnte [aunt] sticke to me nowe for I am very sicke and my wife also is more sicke and I know and am persuaded myselfe that not any of my friendes or kyndred or of hers will venture to come and visit us this tyme of infection, wherefore I do request you to take the paynes to come to my house and looke unto us in this tyme of oure visitacion and sickness of the plague. And yf yt happen that I and my wyfe bothe departe this worlde then I give unto you all that I have and I make you my executrix; and whereas heretofore you have been very ernest with me to have such money and goodes as your sister Anne Burton lefte in my handes at her decease yt is my ful will mynde and intente that after my decease and my wyve's you shall have as well all the same money and goodes of your sisters as allso all and singular my goodes chattells and debts whatsoever in receyving all and paying all my debts. And further the said Richard Lane then and there in the presence of the under written witnesses delyvered unto the sayed Mildred [Morley] three two pences and prayed her to give them to some woman to dispatche her business in her absence and to go home straighte with hym and helpe to caste hym in a sweate.

The good aunt, fearless among the fearful, obtained her

[1] *P. O. C. Nevell*, 84.

little reward.   Lane's will was proved less than two months later.

A doctor's day in Plague-stricken London has been drawn for us in vignette by Nathaniel Hodges. His house was at Red Lion Yard, off Walbrook, in an area which became badly infected. There you may picture him, the tidiness in dress of the professional man—long coat, knee-breeches, and cravat—undisturbed by the horrors among which he moved; the gold-headed cane, which as he walked out-of-doors was the sign of his calling, resting in a corner. He rose betimes, first fortifying himself with a dose of the Anti-pestilential Electuary. Family and household affairs despatched, leaving his mind free for the day, he entered his consulting room. It was " a large room."

Early as was the hour, a throng of anxious patients was always waiting. What words shall express adequately the fears and hopes that these four walls contained ? Some had ulcers yet uncured, others were unnerved by fright, but without signs of infection. Commonly he spent from two to three hours among them, " as in a hospital," he tells, examining each one, prescribing for those who required treatment, advising others how to act on the first symptoms of seizure. This he did fasting, and judging it not proper to go abroad till well refreshed, he took breakfast, " as soon as this crowd could be discharged."

The interval till dinner was spent in visiting his Plague patients at their homes. On entering each threshold he had a disinfectant burnt on hot coals. He is careful to say that if hot himself, or short of breath through walking he rested, not venturing to go into the sick-room until at ease. When examining a patient he kept a lozenge in his mouth, a precaution taken by all physicians. The locked doors bearing the red cross and the supplication—there were many and many of them—opened at the doctor's call. Visits to the Plague-stricken houses occupied some hours, after which Dr. Hodges returned to Walbrook for dinner. Before the meal he drank a glass of sack, " to warm the stomach, refresh the spirits, and dissipate any beginning lodgment of the infection."

He chose generous meats, usually roasted, with pickles

or other sharp relish, condiments of all kinds being cheap and abundant during the epidemic. At dinner he drank more wine. Meantime other patients were assembling in the big consulting room, and on rising from the table he attended to these. Then, grasping his gold-headed cane, he again went abroad in the City. So many required visits at their homes, sufferers in all stages of the disease, that the hours were busily spent till eight or nine in the evening. An hour or two's rest was taken before bedtime, " drinking to cheerfulness of my old favourite liquor," and generally he slept well. He avoided smoking, holding tobacco as perdition.

In all the months while the raging Plague claimed its thousands of victims, Dr. Hodges spent the same hard-working day. He was never in serious peril, and twice only felt illness upon him. Increased draughts of sack, he declares, dissipated the effects. Grateful, with the ecstasy of the connoisseur, he sounds the praises of sack. " It is ranked among the principal antidotes, whether it be drank by itself or impregnated with wormwood, angelica, etc., for I have never yet met with anything so agreeable to the nerves and spirits in all my experience. That which is best is middle-aged, neat, fine, bright, racy, and of a walnut flavour." [1]

It is pitiful to record the last years of this stout-hearted and serviceable man. The City Corporation paid recognition of his zeal by appointing him its authorized physician, at a stipend; the College of Physicians, in acknowledgment of his work and of his book, "Loimologia," the best medical account of the Great Plague that has been written, made him a Fellow, and he held office in that learned body.[2] Many have recognized in him the "Dr. Heath " of Defoe, whose tersely drawn portrait seems founded on reminiscence. You recall how a patient of " Dr. Heath " fell a most unfortunate victim in after years to that habit of taking copious draughts of sack which in the months of epidemic he had imbibed as a preventive; and a like fate it is surmised overtook Dr. Hodges. His practice fell away, and in days of poverty he was arrested for debt. He died in the Ludgate debtors' prison in June, 1688. His tablet may be seen high on the wall of Wren's

[1] *Loimologia*, pp. 223–6.   [2] *Dict. of National Biography.*

church of St. Stephen Walbrook, bearing in Latin this inscription—

> Take heed of all thy days, O mortal man, for time steals on
> With furtive step. Death's shadow flits across the sunniest hour,
> Seeking to prey 'mong all who mortal are.
> He is behind thee ; and even though breath be in thee
> Death has marked thee as his own.
> Thou knowest not the hour when Fate shall call thee.
> E'en while this marble thou regardest, time is irrevocably passing.
>
> Here lies in his grave Nathaniel Hodges, Doctor of Medicine,
> Who while a child of Earth lived in hope of Heaven.
> He was formerly of Oxford, and was a survivor of the Plague.
> Born, September 13, A.D. 1629.
> Died 10th June, 1688.[1]

The medical hospitals of London were St. Bartholomew's, Smithfield, the oldest medical foundation in the world, and St. Thomas's across the Thames at Southwark. There was Bethlehem, already counting four centuries of vigorous age, for mental cases alone. From the " outhouses " of St. Bartholomew's in Southwark and Kingsland—actually lock-hospitals—a certain amount of work was done among the Plague-visited poor in their homes, and Plague got into the hospital at Smithfield ; there is mention of " pest wards," but nothing which shows that recognized Plague cases were accepted. What effective aid could one medical charity give, with a thousand new infections occurring each day ? The staff record bears witness of human weakness.

Two of Bart's physicians, Dr. Micklethwaite and Dr. Terne, absented themselves in the country, and a surgeon, Mr. Woodall, followed the King to Salisbury. Of two other surgeons asked to attend the cure of the Plague-stricken people one, Thomas Turpin, found " the business was too hott for him to act therein," and Henry Boone made other excuses, but Thomas Gray, a surgeon, came forward courageously as a volunteer.[2] The hospital's apothecary, Francis Bernard, did good service in attending Plague patients ; his reward came later in a Fellowship granted by the Royal College of Physicians and in enduring medical fame. The matron's tried courage the Governors attest—

---

[1] I owe this excellent translation of the Latin text on the tablet to my old friend Mr. James Macintyre.

[2] See pp. 86, *ante*, and 206, *post*.

Whereas the said Governors have a respect towards Margaret Blague, matron, for her attendance and constant great paynes about the poor in making them Broths, Caudles, and other the like Comfortable things for their accommodacon in theis late Contagious Tymes, wherein she hath adventured herselfe to the greate perell of her life

and they made her the reward that she herself desired.[1]

Faith, never strong, in the physicians and their prescriptions to repress the Plague had gone. The ignorant and often apathetic masses turned to talismans and charms to stave off the evil. Magic powers alone could drive away this Pest—

> "One with a piece of tassel'd, well tarr'd rope,
> Doth with that nosegay keep himself in hope." [2]

Such faith was not necessarily confined to the ignorant. The Plague was two and a half centuries ago. Samuel Pepys, a Fellow of the Royal Society, whose curiously inquisitive mind has given unending delight to others, trusted in a hare's foot to keep away the colic. The trouble recurring, he was puzzled, till his friend Batten solved the riddle. Pepys's hare's foot had not the joint in it ! The charm could not act. " And assures me he never had his colic since he carried it about with him ; and it is a strange thing how fancy works, for I had no sooner handled his foot but I became very well, and so continue." Pepys replaced the useless charm with one jointed. " Now I am at a loss," he jots in the " Diary " two months afterwards, " to know whether it be my hare's foot which is my preservative, for I never had a fit of colic since I wore it." [3]

The medicinal virtues of the toad won belief by so sagacious a physician as Dr. George Thomson. When after his dissection of a Plague victim he felt the symptoms upon him, he placed a dried toad on his chest to draw out the poison.[4] Perhaps because of its misshapen ugliness and remarkable appearance when shrivelled, the toad has in all ages and in many countries been held in high esteem

[1] Sir Norman Moore's *History of St. Bartholomew's Hospital*, ii. 324–7.

[2] W. P. Taylor's *Fearful Summer*, 1625. This specific held good long after the Plague visitation of 1625. See Ben Jonson's *Alchemist*, act 2, and Rowley, *Match at Midnight*, also Boghurst, p. 54.

[3] *Diary*, 1664, Dec. 31, 1665, Jan. 20, Mar. 26.

[4] *Loimotomia*, p. 86.

as a specific. It was the most common of many objects
worn as preservative against Plague in London's visitation
of 1665.[1] Dried and beaten into powder, it was carried
in quills. Other poor creatures placed their faith in
amulets. A written verse from the Psalms or the Wisdom
of Solomon, superstitious words or a cabalistic arrangement
of letters hung round the neck, they had confidence would
preserve them harmless. Others wore emeralds or sap-
phires, with the belief that the sunbeams by passing through
the gem obtained a quality to extract malignant humours
from the body. Quills filled with quicksilver or arsenic,
similarly worn, were accounted by many a true specific, or
mercury contained in a walnut shell.[2] The task would be
endless to recount all the devices and means that people
adopted—enchantments, bezoar Epithems, mystical numbers and the like—as shields against contagion.[3] Such
credulity becomes pathetic in the presence of a Plague
striking down men by tens of thousands ; but the charms
did no harm, and by keeping hope high in simple minds no
doubt did actual good.

The troops in London were in July marched out to
Hyde Park. That green pleasance was clean cut from the
town by the expanse of St. James's Park, its Royal tenant
of the Palace fled and now with every gate locked, and
meadows along the Tyburn Road (Oxford Street). London
being placed strictly out of bounds, no soldier dared enter
its infected streets for fear of the marshal. A mere handful
of troops was left to guard the empty Whitehall Palace.[4]
It was held advisable still to garrison the Tower of London,
in case riot should threaten the City's tranquillity. In
Hyde Park tents were pitched and lines drawn. But
neither in the Park nor at the Tower could Plague be kept
out. It soon appeared among the Park tents, where men
sickened and died.

An isolation camp was formed at a little distance, with
its inevitable attendant, a park burial ground. Few went
down there who returned. The troops had in their ranks
an observant, amusing fellow, who wrote his experiences
in crude verse that now has become one of the rarest of

[1] Allin, Aug. 24 ; Hodges, p. 221.
[2] Hodges, p. 220.   [3] Boghurst, p. 55.
[4] Rugge's " Diurnal," fo. 142 b.

printed tracts.[1] Like many another, he was horrified by
the treatment of the dead—

> "But that which most of all did grieve my soul
> To see poor Christians dragged into a hole.
> Tye match about them, as they had been Logs,
> And Draw them into Holes, far worse than Dogs,
> When each man did expect his turn was next."

The officers, he tells, stood amazed to see their men no
sooner sick than dead. There was no remedy. A pest-
hut was built. Still as one man died another took his
place, and as the numbers enlarged the corpses were thrown
out into the wide fields. Hyde Park even under the Commonwealth had retained some glamour, and with King
Charles II.'s Restoration had become the fashionable
parade and a centre for horse-racing and social gaiety.
It was in the Plague year wholly deserted. The soldier
noted that not a coach stirred. The Plague was virulent
in the camp. There the troops remained till October was
out.

No fewer than fifty-eight soldiers (besides others) were
received out of the Tower of London sick of the Plague,
into a pest-house that served as well for the infected
of the Tower Hamlets. Charles Wilcox was appointed
master-physician and surgeon of this East London pest-
house.

In a petition to Parliament [2] he tells a grievous tale,
somewhat typical, I fear, of the ill-usage and callous
unconcern with which many who served London well in the
Plague-time were treated by those in authority. Wilcox
represents that when he entered the pest-house in August
he found twenty-three infected persons there, no medicaments for their relief, and but 29s. in the place. As the
soldiers and others were thereafter brought in, he was at all
charges for medicines, meat, drink, washing and other
necessaries, and for the funerals of those who died. These
last, he declares with pride, " were not many." Sir John

---

[1] *Hide Park Camp. Limned out of the Life. Truly and Impartially,
for the Information of such as were not Eye-Witnesses, of the Souldiers'
sufferings. In that (never-to-be-forgotten) Year of our Lord God one thousand
six hundred and sixty five. Written by a fellow souldier and Sufferer in the
said Camp* (Brit. Museum Library).

[2] *The Petition of Charles Wilcox*, 1667 (British Museum, Pressmark
816, m. 9. No. 28).

Robinson, the Lieutenant of the Tower,[1] promised that he should be satisfied for all his pains, cares, and charges ; but he never was paid more than £33 for fifty-eight soldiers attended, nor for his civilian patients above £35.   Robinson he charges with receiving large contributions, besides the pest-rate levied in the Tower Hamlets, which he neither distributed nor satisfied Wilcox out of them.   The pest-house master claimed £403.   Finally the Lieutenant, after his fifteen months' service, without neglect or fault, put him out ; he, his wife and children were all in a perishing condition failing speedy relief.   The discreditable story rings true in its complaint.

It had been ordered that all schools should close. There were charitable foundations fitting for life the orphans of citizens, wherein the scholars could not be dispersed.   Christ's Hospital stood most dangerously situated for receiving Plague, close about its walls being the slaughter-houses of Pentecost Lane and Stinking Lane (the last renamed King Edward Street by a more fastidious generation), a neighbourhood which early in the visitation was heavily infected.   The butchers' shambles of Newgate Market were a stone's-throw distant.   Isolation was almost impossible when through the school ground ran what was practically a public thoroughfare, and there came anxious parents from all parishes of the City wanting assurance that their " Blue " children were safe.

The pay scholars being dismissed, there remained the poor children.   The masters displayed exemplary pains and trouble in their care.   " God hath given such a blessing to our endeavours," they said in a petition to the Governors after the Plague, " that all this time of sickness not more than thirty-two children of the number of 260 in the house are dead of all diseases." [2]   That death should have taken not more than one in every eight was accounted a great mercy in the terrible weeks.

[1] Pepys, although Sir John Robinson's friend, writes very contemptuously of him.   " A talking, bragging bufflehead . . . as very a coxcomb as I would have thought had been in the City, nor hath he brains to outwit any ordinary tradesman."   The diarist enjoyed " a very great noble dinner " of his mayoralty, and rewards his host with the reflection, " This Mayor is good for nothing else ! "   Elsewhere in the *Diary* he says of him, " he makes it his work to praise himself, and all he says and do, like a heavy-headed coxcomb."

[2] Bishop E. H. Pearce's *Annals of Christ's Hospital*, p. 208.

Charterhouse, too, kept "school," locking out the Plague—an adventurous course, but it succeeded. The Governors made peremptory order. No poor brother or scholar, except on call of great urgency and with permission given, should during the time of pestilence go outside the gates, under penalty of expulsion. Should the Plague so increase that such a course became necessary, powers were given to dismiss the house. With none but the manciple and the providers going in or out, the Plague was kept distant. This was well, for the community enclosed was overcrowded. A porter, being taken ill, was removed to the pest-house and there died. But it does not follow that he received infection in Charterhouse. Plague was suspected in every sickness, and no doubt the pest-house finished him.[1]

Merchant Taylors' School, at that time established in St. Laurence Pountney, had no probation in September or December, probably on account of the Plague.[2]

In the parish of St. Peter Cornhill the Plague came first to the sexton's house, and there died—

July 12.   Temperance the daughter of Walter Younge
                 Sexton plague.
  ,,   17.   Martha daughter of Walter Younge
                 Sexton plague.
  ,,   21.   Elizabeth daughter of Walter Younge
                 Sexton plague.
Aug. 1.   Mary daughter of Walter Younge
                 Sexton plague.

and thereafter most of the entries are of deaths from Plague.

In St. Olave Hart Street—Pepys's parish—were almshouses which the Drapers' Company built and maintained. The Plague in the parish first broke out there. On July 23rd Elizabeth, daughter of William Ramsay, an almsman, died of Plague; next day his child Mary; the third day a parish waif whom the family were nursing; and on August 1st the almsman himself was dead. Two other inmates of Drapers' Almshouses, a man and a woman, died of

[1] For the Governors' minute of July 3rd, 1665, here cited, and other information I am indebted to the Rev. Gerald Davies, Master of Charterhouse and its accomplished historian.

[2] H. B. Wilson, *Hist. of Merchant Taylors' School*, 1812, p. 372.

Plague in subsequent weeks.[1]   The infection spread through the parish.   St. Olave's, of no considerable area, had buried 55 parishioners in 1664.   In the month of September during the pestilence it buried 71, three weeks' mortality exceeding that of the whole of the previous year.

Thomas Vincent, the ejected rector of St. Mary Magdalen Milk Street, saw the Plague come to the City, and the end of it.[2]   His friends dwindled away.   " Of about sixteen or more whose faces I used to see every day in our house (he wrote) within a little while I could find but four or six of them alive.   Scarcely a day passed over my head for I think a month or more together but I would hear of the death of some one or more that I knew ;   the first day that they were smitten, the next day some hopes of recovery, and the third day that they were dead." [3]

The Plague entered his house.   They were eight in family all told, three men, three youths, an old woman and a maid, these having come to him on hearing of his stay in town.   Infection was contracted from neighbours. First the maid was attacked, on a Monday, and on Thursday was dead, the body being spotted with " tokens." On Friday a youth of under seventeen had a swelling on his groin, and by Sunday was dead, with Plague marks upon him.   The same day another youth sickened, and on the Wednesday following he died.   Next day his master fell sick, and Vincent tells sympathetically of this man's resignation in apprehension of death.

When the spots did appear on his body he sent for me and desired me to pray with him ; told me he was now going home, desired me to write to his friends, and let them know that he did not repent him of his stay in the City, though they had been so importunate to him to come away ;   but he had found so much of God's presence in his abode here that he had no reason to repent.   He told me where he would be buried, and desired me to preach his funeral sermon on Psalm XVI., ult—" In Thy presence there is fulness of joy ; and at Thy right hand there are pleasures for evermore." [4]

---

[1] Burial Registers. Pepys's statement (July 26) that forty in his small parish died in a night receives no confirmation from this source ; but current report tended commonly to exaggeration.

[2] Vincent, p. 25.   [3] *Ibid.*, p. 33.   [4] *Ibid.*, pp. 38–41.

Against all expectations of himself, his friends, and his physician the man recovered. The Plague had taken three of the household of eight persons, all dead within seven days. Many a home fared worse.

King Charles's stay at Hampton Court was but a stage in his progress to Salisbury. It was early decided to move the Court to that city. The growth of Plague during July in the capital, and the difficulty of preventing communication, made safety at a greater distance desirable. The resolve was hastened by the appearance of Plague at Brentford and in Thames-side villages.[1] On the eve of his departure the King wrote to the Lord Mayor expressing his concern for London's security. He recommended that no Aldermen should be permitted to withdraw from the City without his lordship's consent, to ensure that there remained a competent number of magistrates in authority. The Court of Aldermen had forestalled this request. The King further advised that the Court of Aldermen and the Common Council should assemble in the perilous times only when absolute necessity required. To the City's generosity he commended the out-parishes in their sad plight. Large charity in their relief would tend to check the growth of the contagion ; and he gave warning that failure to meet the necessities of the out-parishes might produce disorders and dangers in the City itself.[2]

It was characteristic of the age that Charles's Government felt under no obligation to assist in relieving the distress from the Plague. It was enough to enforce that duty upon others.

The Court set out upon its journey on July 27th. We can watch the departure from Hampton Court through Pepys's observant eye, the diarist mightily pleased with the sight of the cavalcade—

But it was pretty to see the young pretty ladies dressed like men, in velvet coats, caps with ribbons, and with laced bands, just like men. Only the Duchess [of York] herself it did not become. They gone, we with great content took coach again, and hungry came to Clapham about one o'clock, where a good dinner, the house having dined, and so to walk

[1] Clarendon's *Life*, ii. 403.
[2] Lambeth Palace MSS., Carthe Mis. vol. 6, fo. 14.

up and down in the gardens, mighty pleasant. By and by
comes, by promise to see me, Sir G. Cartaret, and viewed the
house above and below, and sat and drank there, and I had
a little opportunity to kiss and spend some time with the
ladies above, his [Mr Gauden's] daughter, a buxom lass, and
his sister Fissant, a serious lady, and a little daughter of hers,
that begins to sing prettily. At home met the weekly Bill,
where above 1,000 increased in the Bill; and of them, in
all about 1,700 of the plague.[1]

The Queen went direct to Salisbury, but Charles parted
from his Consort at Farnham Castle and proceeded to
Portsmouth, where he gave directions for a pest-house to be
built, lest contagion should again break out at the seaport,
as later it did.

The King reached Salisbury on the 1st August. The
Mayor, John Joyce, and his brethren had welcomed the
Queen, and bare-headed went before her to her lodgings.
In acknowledgment of the honour done to it, the city
presented a pair of silver flagons, having borrowed £100
for these and other gifts. Charles was received with more
ceremony ; the Earl of Pembroke and the county gentlemen associated themselves with the civic dignitaries, and
" a brave body of horse " escorted the Sovereign into the
city. The morrow of the King's arrival being the fast day
for the Plague, Charles attended worship at the Cathedral.
Salisbury was soon to learn that the honour of the Court's
presence was itself onerous. A horde of harpies descended
upon the city, demanding fees of homage which by custom
were due to the King's servants from the Chief Magistrate
and Sheriff of every Corporation which his Majesty first
visited, varying from £5 for the Gentleman Usher's day
waiters and £3 16s. to the Serjeant Trumpet, to 10s. given
to each Page of the Presence and a sum to the King's
Jester [2]—for the ancient office of King's Fool was so long
perpetuated.

More irksome than the money payment were the
restrictions that burdened the inhabitants. Liberty no
longer was theirs even to live in Salisbury, except with
approval. By the Sovereign's direction, a list was delivered
to the Mayor of all persons immediately attending the

[1] *Diary*, July 27.
[2] Salisbury Corporation MSS. (*Hist. MSS. Comm.*, p. 245).

Court whose presence was deemed a necessity, and for these suitable lodging was required. The Mayor had command to search out and remove all superfluous persons from the city, and a Royal Proclamation forbade the concourse of strangers, lest infection be brought in.[1]

As a timely provision for the public safety, Salisbury was ordered to build a pest-house forthwith, the City and Close being taxed to meet the cost. The new-comers paid nothing.

Despite all precautions, the Plague crept into Salisbury. The Court had not been there a week when the wife of a groom to Mr. Halsall, a Queen's Equerry, was struck down at Fisherton, a small suburb village. Mr. Halsall was bidden to keep apart.[2] Every effort was made to conceal the death, and with some success, lest the populace should take alarm that the Plague followed the Court.[3] The infected house was shut up. The danger that pestilence should spread abroad was very great in the overcrowded state of the city. Not the courtiers alone, but Ambassadors and Ministers of foreign States as well attended the King, swelling the numbers about him; the visitors and their retinues packed every house.[4] No person was allowed to stay in the city unless he possessed a certificate from the Court or the Mayor. A body of one hundred Horse Guards from York was brought to Salisbury as an additional guard.[5]

Amid these first fears, the King and Queen contemplated taking up residence at Wilton Hayes, the Earl of Pembroke's seat three miles distant. They had been favourably impressed by its magnificence. But the project was little sooner made than it was abandoned, because of the dislocation in public business that would result thereby.

The spectre of Plague was never absent, and nerves were kept taut during the eight weeks in which Charles and his Court remained the burdensome guests of the Cathedral city. An inn at Fisherton, wherein one of the King's farriers died of Plague, was shut up with all the persons in it. Worse alarm was occasioned when a servant of the

[1] Privy Ccl. Reg. 58, fo. 240.
[2] The Newsletter in Addit. MSS. 4182, which seems to have escaped the notice of Salisbury's historians, gives the fullest account of King Charles's stay in that city.
[3] Sir W. Coventry to Lord Arlington, Aug. 7.
[4] Coventry to Arlington, Aug. 14.
[5] Colonel Warden to Williamson, Aug. 14.

Spanish Ambassador fell dead in the street. A barber's tent which the man had entered to rest, feeling sick, was burnt by the Lord Chamberlain's order, and the inn where he had lodged closed so rigorously that the Ambassador's remaining servants there and his carriage and horses were shut in. The King gave his Excellency use of his own coach, otherwise he had been condemned to go on foot.

Again a move to Wilton Hayes was seriously entertained. Lord Pembroke retired to a wing of his mansion, leaving the remainder as a refuge for the Sovereign should such be needed. The long ennui of the stay was broken for the monarch by occasional visits paid to Lord Ashley at Dorchester, and to Stonehenge, Weymouth, Poole and other places, and by stag-hunting, in which sport both the King and Queen participated. The King killed a stag larger than the country usually afforded.

None was permitted to approach the King to be touched for the Evil unless presented by the Court officials. His safety was always a cause of anxiety. Riding through the city one day, Charles passed the inn wherein the farrier had died, and noticing the place shut up and the people at the windows, called out to ask if they were well. They replied " All well." He assured them they should want for nothing, and that he would consider their loss by confinement.

Visits to seaports, ostensibly to inspect their defences, gave the King opportunity of being away for most of the last fortnight of the Court's stay. Salisbury continued to be agitated by repeated shocks. In September a maid died from Plague ; there was another case at Fisherton ; two died of Plague in the city prison ; a physician was shut up sick in his own house ; there was a death in the pesthouse ; a young man who had come from London was sent out of the city Plague-stricken, and perished in a hut amid the fields.[1] " All care is taken to hinder the spreading of the infection, to which God grant success," wrote a courtier from Salisbury on September 17th. Fear alone inspired that appeal to God. With heartfelt relief all turned their backs on Salisbury in the last week of September, when the Court set out for Oxford, its carriages and waggons trailing along miles of the road.

[1] Addit. MSS. 4182, fos. 30–32b., 34, 36, 37b, 39–43.

CHAPTER VIII

THE GROWING BURDEN

IT has become a settled belief that the magistrates and parish officers were always able to cope with the Great Plague. In September, when close upon ten thousand of its victims were dying in London in a single week, even then it has been represented that the offices of the Plague service were kept filled. That, unhappily, was not the truth. Before September's emergency control had ceased to be effective, by reason of the immensity of the task. But it would mislead to portray the City as lying prostrate in helplessness, with authority broken down. Powers that once had failed could never be fully restored.

Disorders were expected. The precautionary measures taken testify to the prevailing fears.[1] A Royal Proclamation issued required all disbanded officers and soldiers who had served with the Parliamentary armies in the late Rebellion, except such as had leave to stay, immediately to depart from London and Westminster, and not to come within twenty miles thereof.[2] The Duke of York, when the Court left Hampton Court for Salisbury, travelled to York, where his presence gave authority in the North. London at the surface was orderly, in deep dejection.

The Plague, with its daily repetition of dread and its visible horror, numbed all mob instinct among the people. The spirit for violence was broken, and isolated instances were of rare occurrence. In the task of shutting up the infected houses force was at times met by force, and the majesty of the City Marshal, an officer more potent than

[1] Addit. MSS. 4182, fo. 31b.
[2] *Royal Proclamation,* June 28.

was the parish constable, was required to overawe the recalcitrants—

> May 29th [1666]—Spent on the City Marshall
>   at ye shutting up a visited house [1]   .   . 1s. 0d.

The poor remained, rooted to their Plague-infected alleys and courts. Ignorant and entirely untaught save in their different crafts, there was rarely a man or woman among them who could read or write, and they were accustomed to service. Their sheer helplessness alone made it possible for the few members of the ruling classes who were left in London so well to maintain order undisturbed. There was no excess of crime. The calendar of the first Old Bailey Sessions held after the visitation was shorter than would be expected, with eight months' accumulation of prisoners awaiting trial ; but as I shall point out, the Plague itself gave no mean assistance in the gaol delivery. Housebreaking and burglary occurred, yet such offences were not so prevalent as at the last bad Plague epidemic, when control was less efficient, and houses were openly plundered from which the inhabitants had fled. A case or two during the Great Plague may stand for all. When Richard Scarvell in October lay sick of the pestilence (from which he died) and locked in, Isabella Petty, of Whitechapel, with others broke into his house at night. Familiarity with the Plague had made most careless of infection. They wrenched off the padlock that fastened the door, then ransacked the rooms, and carried away goods valued at above £100. The woman was seized, the others escaping, and Isabella was held for trial,[2] with the prospect of the gallows always before her.

A party of thieves, having broken open the abandoned shop of a mercer, adopted an ingenious ruse to get away with their plunder. They brought in two coffins, and these they piled full with silk stockings and fine linen, then unlatched the street door from within and in a decent manner emerged, carrying the burdens on their shoulders, as if bearing away bodies of residents dead of the Plague. Coffins were too common a sight to engage much notice. By ill-fortune a watchful constable was looking on. The

---

[1] St. Botolph Bishopsgate Ch'wardens' Accts.
[2] Middlesex Sessions of the Peace Roll, 1666, Feb.

thieves went to Newgate, and the stolen goods were returned.[1]

The more common offence, more evil in its results, was that of conveying goods out of infected houses, to spread infection elsewhere. The vision of the prison and the gallows did not deter offenders [2]; it could not be stopped. With close upon a thousand persons dying of Plague to-day, a thousand others to be added to-morrow, a third thousand on the succeeding day, how should safe watch over so many houses and their contents be kept ? An army of Plague officers could not have done it. Most went abroad by theft of nurse-keepers and watchmen, and much by avarice and desperate need, surviving members of a family enclosed being willing in their want to accept the small sums offered by brokers who took the risk of handling the poisoned thing.

There goeth a tankard (wrote a contemporary pamphleteer) that shall infect the fifth cupboard ; here a set of spoons that taint the hundredth dish of broth ; this man steals a bargain of a cloak that kills ten men ; another buyeth a suit that infects Bristol ; and a third gets a fine child's coat that shall cut off a first-born son. In vain do you here object the severe laws against removal of infected goods before the forty days are past, when the careful nurse does not stay the forty hours, lest a rightful owner interpose, or cunning lawyer seize on the house and the estate.[3]

It was a great gain that the magistrates, aldermen and parish officers set over the people were those to whom they were accustomed. A spirit of revolt was seething below the apparent calm. Surly acquiescence was given when disobedience was impossible, and whenever authority could be defied, as by the processions of near relatives and friends who followed the funerals, by breaking out from the shut-up houses, and in a dozen other ways, there was no consciousness of wrong doing. The masses looked upon those charged to provide for their preservation and the public safety as tyrants and oppressors, selfishly seeking their own advantage,[4] and unwillingly submitted to

[1] Rugge's " Diurnal," fo. 143.
[2] A number of such cases were returned for trial when the sessions were reopened in Feb. 1666. Cf. *Middlesex County Records*, vol. 3.
[3] *The Shutting Up Infected Houses*, p. 10.
[4] Thomas Povey to Williamson, Sion Hill, Oct. 5, in *State Papers* (*Domestic*), 1665–6, p. 5.

restraint; till the bonds loosened as week by week the monstrous volume of Plague grew, and at length the bonds snapped.

There is a puzzling passage by Pepys. On August 12th he jotted down in his "Diary" "And the Lord Mayor commands people to be within [doors] at nine o'clock at night all, as they say, that the sick may have liberty to go abroad for air." This is but dubious authority for a Mayoral Proclamation, and Guildhall has no such proclamation or order. "As they say"—a good deal of baseless and excited rumour floated about the town. The people took license and liberty that in the circumstances of the hour none could restrain.

L'Estrange in his news-sheets attributed the rise of the Plague to the peak it reached in September to the withdrawal of those officers who were charged to guard against escapes from the shut-up houses.[1] The fact was that the Plague had outgrown the capacity to fill the appointments its growth necessitated. From a dozen sources it is made plain that the authorities were confronted with a body of Plague swollen to such monstrous size that the healthy were in insufficient numbers to give proper attendance upon the sick, and that this condition prevailed for some few weeks together.

John Tillison, a minor official of St. Paul's Cathedral, when sending to Dean Sancroft the news that the Sacrist had fled from his home, where his wife lay dead of the Plague, said—

We are in good hopes that God in his mercy will put a stop to this sad calamity of sickness. But the desolation of the City is very great; that heart is either steel or stone that will not lament for this sad visitation, and will not bleed for those unutterable sorrows. It is a time, God knows, that one woe courts another. Those that are sick are in extreme sorrow; the poor are in need; those that are in health are in fear of infection on the one side, and the wicked intentions of hellish rebellious spirits to put us in an uproar on the other side. What eye would not weep to see so many habitations uninhabited, the poor sick not visited, the hungry not fed, the grave not satisfied? Death stares us continually in the face in every infected person that passes by us, in every coffin

[1] *Newes*, Aug. 31.

which is daily and hourly carried along the streets. The bells never cease to put us in mind of our mortality.[1]

A month before, when distributing the Dean's charities, Tillison had written to him—

I am sure that the miserable condition of St. Giles Cripplegate, which is one of your peculiars,[2] is more to be pitied than any parish in or about London, where all have liberty, lest the sick and the poor should be famished within doors, the parish not being able to relieve their necessities.[3]

It made the problem immensely difficult that the sick were not gathered in some great hospital camp or group of camps, but were scattered in thousands of small houses over all parts of the town. They infected every street. Pepys roundly asserts that at the height of the pestilence in September there was no observation of the shutting up of houses infected.[4] Vincent, too, tells of the healthy being at these times mingled with the sick in the streets and houses, whom otherwise help could not have reached, " now shutting up of visited houses (there being so many) is at an end." [5]

" The poor sick are not visited, the hungry not fed, the grave not satisfied." That was the sorry truth. In the contest so strenuously waged the Plague was winning, and won—for the time. It did not spare the considerable army of workers in its service. Watchmen, nurse-keepers, bearers and buryers were struck down in performance of their perilous duties and perished, when always the call was for larger and still larger numbers as always the Plague grew in volume. Masses of the poor there were still to recruit from, but they showed increasing dislike to accepting such employment.

It would be false to represent that authority ceased. The absent Government showed little concern in London's plight, but Albemarle in the out-parishes and the Lord Mayor in the City worked untiringly to maintain the essential Plague services, not without some measure of

[1]. Tillison to Sancroft, Sept. 14.
[2] Thirteen City parishes were in the ecclesiastical jurisdiction, not of London, but of Canterbury, and these were known as the Primate's " Peculiars."
[3] Tillison to Sancroft, Aug. 15.
[4] *Diary*, Sept. 14.   [5] *God's Terrible Voice*, p. 32.

success. There was no weak abandonment of the supervision of infected houses and withdrawal of attendants from
the sick, but no longer were these measures fully effective.
The City's division into a great number of small parishes—
there were one hundred and nine in all—worked for
decentralization. The parish undertook the duty of
watching its infected houses and removing and burying
the dead, though in the emergency the Corporation seems
to have accepted responsibility for burials in the Plague
pits ; the dead-carts collected, not from one, but from
several parishes on their route. Each parish was able to
find among its needy poor some to accept the grim tasks.
I have found that the small sums due to nurses, bearers,
and watchmen continued regularly to be paid throughout
the weeks of August and September, and the same onwards.

No lapse occurs in the payments. As the tale of Plague
rose higher and higher, the sum total increased by a
thousand and more each successive week, the sole fault was
that there were not enough people who could be lured to
accept these offices.

Always there was the jar of the bells, that told only of
death. London, with its hundred and nine parish churches,
was still a city of spires ; " the ringing city " it had been
called in other times. It had forgotten the joyful wedding
bells. With every notification to the sexton, where there
were survivors to give intelligence and ask for the office, the
church bell was rung in solemn cadence, and in a city of so
many belfrys, and with so many dying, one or another was
never silent—till in September was a silence more significant
than sound. The sextons became too busy to ring the
bells. It had been made the rule to bury only at dead of
night. That served a double purpose ; the sight was
spared to the living, and there was less danger of infection
spreading from the dead-carts which carried so heavy a
load of contagion. The nights no longer sufficed for the
task ; " the people die so, that now they are fain to carry
the dead by daylight." [1] At every hour the carts, open or
hooded and always deeply burdened, came and passed.

An almost forgotten burial ground, much used in the
Great Plague, is covered by the North London Railway's
terminus of Broad Street. In excavation of a small area

[1] Pepys, Aug. 12.

adjoining in 1863, so many leather shoes were dug up with human bones as to lead to the conclusion that the dead by the pestilence largely died in their shoes and were so buried. It yielded between three and four hundred skeletons, the soil being full of them below surface level to a depth of eight or ten feet. The bones lay in disorder. Only a few of the first committals were in coffins, these being found in one corner. The corpses had been thrown indiscriminately into pits.[1]

It defeats a full understanding of London's calamity to use language of exaggeration. Hyde, the Lord Chancellor, who was with the King at Salisbury, has misstated the weekly Bills as showing that above one hundred and three score thousand persons perished, adding that " many who could compute very well concluded that there were in truth double that number who died." [2] Any idea that 160,000 persons perished in London may be at once rejected. A prevalent belief that the wide gulf left between the figures of the Bills of Mortality and the actual deaths in the Great Plague is in the mass due to the numbers of secretaries who purposely avoided notification must also be rejected.

Mention by Pepys, Craven, and their contemporaries of the Jews, Quakers, "fanatics" (Presbyterians), and Anabaptists whose burials were not reported to the parish church is so frequent that it has been taken for granted these must be counted by many thousands. The Jews formed a very small community, quite insignificant in London's population. For three and a half centuries back to their expulsion by King Edward I. the few Jews resident in England had been aliens and outcasts, with no place in the comity of the people among whom they lived, without recognition till Cromwell gave it under the Commonwealth. Dr. Joseph Jacobs has estimated their numbers in London at the Restoration not to have exceeded two hundred and eighty.[3]

A group of trading Spanish and Portuguese Jews, with

[1] Beck & Ball, *The London Friends' Meetings*, p. 329. *Notes & Queries*, 3rd Ser., iv. 85.

[2] Clarendon's *Life*, iii. 35. Actually the Bills of Mortality recorded 97,306 deaths from all causes. A mortality of double 160,000 involves that substantially every one who stayed in London died by the Plague !

[3] *Jewish Encyclopædia*, viii. 157.

Antonio Fernandez Carvajal at their head, had settled in London in King Charles I.'s reign ; and the Jew was not unfamiliar much earlier.[1] These first took disguise as Roman Catholics, many attending Mass at the Spanish Embassy Chapel.   An all-important conference which Menasseh Ben Israel had with Cromwell at Whitehall in December, 1655, though without result in itself, paved the way for conditions under which the Jews were able to worship in their faith without concealment.   The Synagogue in Creechurch Lane, a north-eastern quarter within the City wall, was openly kept from 1657.   They had liberty from Cromwell to acquire their own burial ground. It still exists in the rear of No. 253 Mile End Road, and there their dead in the Plague time were laid.[2]

The admission has unfortunately to be made that the Haham (Chief Rabbi) of the Sephardi congregation, the learned Jacob Sasportes of Amsterdam, fled before the Plague.   Nor, apparently, could he be prevailed upon to return.   Dr. Joseph Mendez Bravo, the congregation's physician, survived long afterwards.   The community by 1665 perhaps numbered four hundred, and the deaths among Jews appear to have been fewer than with others.

Moses Athias, the original Rabbi, perished of the infection,[3] as did several of his flock.   He rests in this little Jewish cemetery, wherein are five identifiable burials of the Plague year, and a sixth in January, 1666, which falls within the period.   The deaths within a few days of two sisters, Rachael and Esther, the children of Abraham de Morais, in the month of Nissan, 5425 (approximately April, 1665), certainly suggest Plague.   The others are Grace Nunes, daughter of Isaac Alverez Nunes, Moses Nunes, probably also his child, and one Samuel Viega.   Isaac Alverez Nunes was the great jeweller, whose epitaph in this same burial ground tells that his

> far gain'd knowledge in mysterious gems
> Sparkled in the European diadems.

These graves are in rows 1 and 3, and between them is space for fifteen other interments of which no record

[1] A City housewife is made to say in an old play, " You may hire a good suit at a Jew's " (*Every Woman in Her Humour*, 1609).

[2] Wilfred S. Samuel, " The first London Synagogue of the Re-settlement " in *Transactions of the Jewish Historical Society*, vol. 10.

[3] John Lightfoot's *Whole Works*, ed. Pitman, 1824, vol. 13, p. 433.

ANCIENT JEWISH BURIAL GROUND IN MILE END ROAD

Wherein the Jewish victims of The Great Plague were interred

survives. The spot contiguous to the grave last occupied was used for the next person who died, whether rich or poor, and those there lying doubtless are the Plague-stricken Jewish poor. The existing burial register, begun in 1725, has copied the names from some of the early stones.[1]

The Quaker dead in London during the year of the Great Plague totalled 1,177. That is shown by the Friends' registers, meticulously kept.[2] It may be that in the confusion of the time some were omitted. In the fœtid gaols, and where crowded on shipboard, the Friends perished in large proportion of their numbers ; but the care taken for the visitation and relief of those shut up in the infected houses probably brought their losses therein. though no doubt large, by comparison with others less fortunately placed almost low. The burial ground, once extensive, survives by Bunhill Fields, though all but a small portion, perhaps half an acre, is now covered by a school and the Memorial Buildings.

King Charles had been curious to ask if any Quakers had died of the pestilence. Learning that such was the case, he remarked that the Plague could not be regarded as evidence of Divine displeasure at the treatment they had received.[3]

The sunshine that over the wall and the trees enters the ancient Jewish burial plot at Mile End glistens upon moss

[1] For information concerning the Jews in the Great Plague I am greatly indebted to Mr. Wilfred S. Samuel, who has made considerable research into the period of the resettlement. The small number of the London community is supported by Mr. Lucien Wolf, who in his paper on " The Jewry of the Restoration " (*Trans. Jewish Hist. Soc.*, vol. 5) says that in 1660 it comprised some thirty-five heads of families, or about 150 souls. King Charles's Portuguese marriage brought about a very great change in the London Jewish community, and by the end of 1663 fifty-seven fresh names were added to the list of well-to-do Jews in London. What numbers of the poorer-class Jew had then settled in London it is difficult to say. Greenhalgh, not himself a Jew, whom curiosity led to visit the Creechurch Lane synagogue in April, 1662, counted there " over a hundred Jews," not including their wives. The estimated seating accommodation of the synagogue (based on available floor space) till its enlargement in 1674 was for 85 men and only 25 women. While the size of the congregation in 1665 is approximately known, a floating population will have added to the number of Jews in London.

[2] The original registers are at Somerset House, but complete copies are accessible at the headquarters of the Society of Friends at Devonshire House, Bishopsgate, E.C.

[3] C. Evans, *Friends in the Seventeenth Century*, p. 364.

that has gathered about the stones laid flat to earth.   No
Sephardi Jew is buried with upstanding tablet to mark his
resting-place.   The little Quaker cemetery has not even
these memorials.   Its flat, unmounded surface is not
broken by a single gravestone or any record of those name-
less dead who sleep below.   " If the visiter entering by the
Coleman Street gate," says a Quaker writer, " will turn to
the right and walk forward till he stands about 90 ft. from
the western wall, he will face a nearly square plot of ground
that may well by its associations awaken thoughts of
earnest interest.   There lie the Friends who were carried
off in the terrible year of the Great Plague.   There was
interred all that was mortal of Samuel Fisher, Richard
Hubberthorne, Edward Burrough, and about ninety
others of our martyrs who were carried to this spot on the
shoulders of their brethren from the crowded prisons in
which they expired." [1]

That is the plot left, which stands upon to-day's Roscoe
Street, E.C.   It was the first freehold property acquired
by the Society of Friends, in 1661.   The ground, being
filled by the Great Plague, was the next year extended.
It wears the aspect of a quiet private garden, with lawn
and flower beds.   A tree centrally placed gives shade,
others but partly conceal the tall houses that on three sides
surround the burial ground.   Thus the Quakers consign
their dead to Mother Earth.   " Ashes to ashes, dust to
dust."   Rich and poor have mingled here together in a
way that few London burial places can show.

The hiatus in the numbers of deaths actual and recorded
arises less from the purposeful withholding of notification
for the Bills of Mortality than from the great numbers of
dead carried direct to the Plague pits and to burial in the
fields, and the not infrequent deaths among the searchers,
clerks, and sextons of the parishes, themselves struck
down by Plague, which hindered an exact account being
kept of every week.[2]

In the terror created by Plague and the ignorance of
nurses and relatives as to sure signs of death, it is likely
that many sufferers were hastily prepared for the grave
before the faint spark of life had been extinguished.   This

---

[1] Beck & Ball, *The London Friends' Meetings*, p. 330.
[2] Cf. Clarendon's *Life*, iii. 35 ; Pepys, Hodges, and others.

QUAKER BURIAL GROUND AT ROSCOE STREET, FINSBURY

Friends who perished in The Great Plague were interred here. The solitary miniature headstone is a modern memorial to mark the spot where George Fox rests

we can never know. A news-letter writer tells that a bad
Bill of September " had numbered one more but for a
remarkable providence." A butcher in Newgate Market,
being by the searchers given out to be dead, was by
neglect of the bearers not carried away the same night.
The body was laid in an upper room. In the morning the
daughter of the house entered, whereupon the supposed
dead man beckoned to her, and complaining that he was
cold, bade her bring him clothes. The girl called up her
mother, who brought warm bed linen, and soon the man
snatched from the Plague pit was able to take a pipe of
tobacco and a meal. He quickly recovered health, and on
the following Sunday at church gave thanks to God for his
preservation.[1]

Austin, who lived and wrote while pestilence lay on the
City, recalls such a scene of revival in a Plague-stricken
home. Insufferable as a poet, he had a certain gift of
Zolaesque realism—

> " One too too weak to raise his aking head,
>   Throws off the *sheet* when friends have sold his bed.
>   Another not being us'd to *silent life*
>   Calls daughter *Doll*, maid *Sue*, and *Kate* his wife.
>   At last they come, and gape to what is said
>   Like unlearn'd clowns that hear a letter read :
>   They cry for help . . ."

And he does not stop at the sick-room. Living men
and women, by the blundering of those about them, were
carried out and thrown into the hideous Plague pits.
There is no reason to discredit this witness—

> " Wisely they leave graves open to the dead,
>   'Cause some too early are *brought to bed*.
>
>   One out of trance return'd, after much strife,
>   Among a troup of *dead*, exclaims for *life*.
>   One finding himself as some *maid* hard lace't,
>   Or as a *watch* for pocket, straightly case't,
>   Equaly terrifi'd with *pain* and *fear*,
>   Complains to those can neither speak nor hear."

That shall suffice, and details may be spared of Austin's
vision of another victim brought too early to the open pit.
" Dejected, with arms hanging," his voice lost by calling
and the sharp night cold, he whines a maddened ditty
amidst the unspeakable pollution of the dead by which he

[1] Addit. MSS. 4182, fo. 39.

is crushed.[1] If this be thought too horrible for belief, remember it is the horror of the time.

The parishes first sought to employ as bearers and buriers those who had themselves been infected by Plague and had recovered.[2] That Plague attacked none a second time was a popular belief which this visitation was to destroy. The general poverty had given the parish officers this choice. But as the numbers of a day's Plague victims rose in July and August by tens into many hundreds, then in September to a thousand in a single day, the dead-carts were not numerous enough to carry away the bodies. Additional carts had to be improvised, additional bearers employed, additional men put to work at the enlarged Plague pits which day by day were newly opened. There was no longer choice.

If evil exists in human nature, evil unhappily comes out by the too frequent contemplation of death, till it seems no longer of concern. Amid all the horrors attending a great visitation of Plague, not least was the anguish brought to those in the houses—the mournful households of the sick, the dying and the whole cooped in together—by association with the vile characters forced upon them.

They were fortunate who had not a thief for their nurse-keeper, made inhumanly callous by the sights witnessed, and little concerned to assist a lingering recovery. The watchman upon whom their dependence was absolute for food, water, and all necessaries, might be dissolute and drunken. In the last event came the dreadful old women searchers to break in upon bereavement, fulfilling their ghastly task of viewing and certifying death. Last of all came the bearers, who with rude manners and careless unconcern attached hooks and dragged away in sight of the survivors the corpse of some loved parent, sister, or child. These men mostly took care to avoid touch.

The old citizen Rugge, who survived the Great Plague, speaks of the bearers as " a foul-mouthed crew," and he adds simply—

Many of them were very idle, base-living men, and very rude they were. In the night they did affright the people

[1] Austin's *Anatomy of the Pestilence*, 1665.
[2] Rugge's " Diurnal," fo. 146.

most sadly by their swearing and cursing, either at the people [in the dwellings where they collected the bodies] or at the horses that drew away the dead.

It is not a subject one cares to linger over, and I instance a single case with the hope that it was the worst. Among those of this foul-mouthed crew was a wicked fellow named Buckingham, who made the round with his cart in the night-time. It was this ghoul's practice, when among the piled corpses of the load he carried were those of any children, to cry in the silent and deserted streets, " Faggots, faggots, five for sixpence ! " and he would take up a dead child by the leg and repeat his ribald cry, " Five for six-pence ! " Shuddering people behind the windows of the closed-up houses often heard the cry as he passed with his cart in the darkness.

This creature's inhumanity did not end there. At the lip of the yawning Plague pit he took frenzied delight in exposing the naked bodies of young women openly to view ; and his other actions were equally monstrous. Fortun-ately these matters came to the knowledge of the Earl of Craven and the magistrates, who turned the man out of his office and committed him to prison. Buckingham suffered the rough justice of the time. He was first taken to the pest-house and there soundly whipped before all the people, and afterwards whipped through several fields till his back was bloody. The lashes, one fondly hopes, were laid on with a will. Then he was imprisoned for a year, and declared incapable ever again of being employed in public service.[1]

The Great Plague destroyed many illusions. Wolsey's advice to Erasmus when he visited London a century and a half before and found it Plague-stricken, was to " get into clean air." It had been taught by early medical writers that scarcely anyone who lived upon hills in clear air took infection. Hampstead stands upon the highest ground around London. It had over 260 deaths out of one hundred houses ; a little village then called West End, but a quarter of a mile distant and lying at the bottom of the hill, had no Plague deaths out of the thirty or forty houses which comprised it. Highgate,[2] Islington, and Acton, all

[1] Rugge's " Diurnal," fos. 146–7.
[2] The church register records sixteen deaths in the small village during

on high ground, suffered severely.[1] Baxter, the divine, returning to his house in the hamlet of Acton when the Plague was spent, was shocked by the sight confronting him, " the churchyard like a plow'd field with graves, and many of my neighbours dead." [2] Bermondsey had no protection by its reeking tan pits, and there the Plague mark is black.

It is an old tradition that the Plague spreading east was stopped at Stratford, being itself destroyed at Bow Bridge by the fumes from the lime kilns kept burning there. It is not true. West Ham was infected over ten months, when there were 158 burials marked as Plague. Nicholas Reader, the parish clerk, and William Bird, churchwarden, died of the Plague. Often travellers flying from London were struck down so near, as entries in the burial register attest, " a man," " a souldier," " two children "—the identity of these was unknown to the parish clerk. The Plague spread to Plaistow in August. Hackney had 255 deaths that year, indicating the Plague's violence. No place should claim immunity from the common desolation.

London, as the hot summer advanced, with all the activities of government removed and its trade decayed, was little recognizable as the kingdom's capital. Its one concern was the Plague, and the end of the Plague the consuming interest alike of those who stayed and those who had fled. The Privy Council met in the King's presence at Salisbury. A Royal Proclamation had further adjourned Parliament from August 1st, but a constitutional question of its sufficiency arising,[3] the King directed Sir Edward Turnor, the Speaker of the House of Commons, who lived within half a day's journey of London, the Duke of Albemarle, and Lord Craven to notify members of both Houses residing nearest to London to attend that day in their places.[4] A quorum assembled, and Sheldon, the Archbishop of Canterbury, bearing the King's Commission,

the worst months of the Plague. Defoe says that Highgate had not a single death.
    [1] Boghurst, p. 57.   [2] *Reliquiæ Baxterianæ*, pt. 3, p. 15.
    [3] The judges deemed a meeting of Parliament at Westminster to receive the King's message of further adjournment to be unnecessary. See Sir W. Coventry to Lord Arlington, Aug. 7.
    [4] Clarendon's *Life*, ii. 405.

immediately prorogued the Parliament, which eventually met at Oxford on October 9th.

The Law Courts were in vacation, and did not again sit that year save for the briefest of terms at Oxford. The affairs of the Navy Office, of urgency while the war at sea with Holland raged, were conducted at Greenwich. On August 15th the Exchequer and Tally Office were opened at Nonsuch, once the favourite resort of Queen Elizabeth near Epsom, where all payments customarily made at Westminster were thereafter made.[1] The business of the Excise and Customs alone remained in London, from which it could not be diverted, and when the Plague had passed rewards were given to those high officers who had stayed " during all the time of this contagion." [2] By good fortune there was no Plague in the Custom House by the Thames, but it broke out in some poor habitations of waterside labourers built above a warehouse on the quay, wherein several died, to the great fright of shippers and merchants and the Customs officers themselves. An order came from the Royal Court to pull down the dwellings. The Lord Mayor had courage to declare that those remaining in the infected houses could not lawfully be sent away without their consent. Lawful or not, the order was repeated in peremptory terms.[3] The safeguarding of the King's revenue was of paramount concern.

The City's commerce was far scattered where not wholly destroyed. Of the Plague's numbing influence on the great trade of London, the East India Company gives an illustration. The Governor, Sir William Thomson, left the City in July and did not return till the following January. In August the Secretary obtained leave to go into the country. The clerks need attend but three days a week. It was actually decided to shut up East India House in Leadenhall Street when Plague was close about it, but that proved impracticable ; and despite drastic reductions authorized for the emergency in the size of the Courts, it proved most difficult to keep the threads of business in hand. The Company wrote to their factors in Madras in doleful mood—

[1] *Royal Proclamation*, July 26.
[2] *Cal. of Treasury Books*, 1660–7, p. 690.
[3] Privy Ccl. Reg. 58, fos. 278–9.

It hath pleased the Almightie, for the greate and multiplyed sins of our nation, to manifest His greate and feirce indignacion against us by sending and continuing amongst us the plague of pestilence, which at present hath spread itselfe in most parts of the kingdome, but more espetially rageth in and about the Citty and suburbs, wherein have dyed this weeke 7,200 persons. The God of mercy have compassion on us and withdrawe this heavy judgment from us, give us a true sight of our sins, sincere repentance for what is past, reformation and amendment for the time to come, that soe the voice of joy and gladnesse may againe bee heard amongst us and that wee may praise the name of the Lord. This greate mortallity hath caused most part of the Committee to withdrawe from the Citty, and thereby have not opertunity to meete togither to consider and direct affaires. It is our hopes that before our intended shipp will bee readie to saile toward you that the Lord will in mercy looke downe upon this poore nation and withdrawe His afflicting hand, that thereby wee may againe have the meeteing togither.

Later that month " want of a greater appearance " decided the Company not to assemble save on some urgent occasion or by the Governor's express direction, and meetings of urgency thereafter called at members' houses outside London often failed owing to the absence of the small quorum required.[1]

The Plague remained, and still each week that came and passed proved worse than the last, for always the mortality leapt up. When would the Plague cease ? The sign was not given : and instead it made new inroads to places till now exempt. Across the sunlit streets and through the deep shadows cast by the houses and into the darkness and oblivion still went on the migration from the City outwards that study of the Bills discloses and which explains so much, a hideous and repellent thing ; after the flight *en masse* and long as the Plague lasted—that continuing, persistent infiltration of the most pestilential quarters of the town's outskirts with new ranks of the poor, themselves to be struck down in turn, as master-craftsmen, shopkeepers and merchants, who had stayed out the Plague till courage forsook them or loss of trade

[1] William Foster, *The East India House*, pp. 58–62. With all its troubles the Company was able to order a dividend of 50 per cent. next March, but its sphere of trade was, of course, altogether exceptional.

made useless a longer stay in London, sought their own
safety in the country, leaving unemployed workmen and
servants destitute, to fall back into the fœtid alleys and
courts of the outer ring.

Newgate was a gate in the City wall, its prison holds
extending down Old Bailey. The Plague got in. The
Keeper, Mr. Jackson, himself died of the pestilence in
July.[1] How many of the gaol's miserable captives also
perished none can tell, but there is a rough measure. The
Conventicle Act passed the previous year [2] made itself
memorable in iniquity by punishing the third offence of
participating in prescribed forms of worship with transportation for seven years. Men and women zealous in
their faith might be sent to any plantation except Virginia
and New England.

The Quakers in London experienced the full force of
this new tyranny. It stuffed Newgate full with Friends;
but shipmasters and seamen had salutary notions of an
Englishman's birthright, and they proved so hostile to
giving passages that it was March of 1665 before the first
transportations to the Colonies took place, and till the end
of May those forcibly exiled numbered but eighteen in all.[3]
The condition of the gaol almost defied imagination.
Thomas Ellwood, the Quaker, gives a glimpse into the
common prison room that he shared. It was of stone,
"large and round," having in the middle a stout oak
pillar which upheld the chapel floor above. At night the
captives fastened their hammocks at one end to this
pillar and at the other to the wall, in three tiers, one above
the other to the ceiling, till the place was quite full. Then
on the stone floor was stretched a fourth layer of humanity,
rough beds being laid there for the sick and the weak.
A man died on one of these pallet beds. The coroner's
jury looked in at the door but could not enter; there was
no space! That was before the Plague,[4] and it may be
imagined how Plague fed fat in such quarters.

Felons lingered in the gaol while there was no delivery
and gallows to lessen the numbers. To this accumulation

---

[1] Smyth's *Obituary*, p. 64.
[2] *Statute 16th Charles II., ch.* 4.
[3] W. C. Braithwaite, *The Second Period of Quakerism*, p. 46.
[4] *Life of Thomas Ellwood.*

of the vilest characters of the town were now added large groups of captives for faith. Fifty-two Quakers in Newgate fell victims to the Plague during its rise and decline, several being women.[1]   Among them was a child, Hannah Trigg, condemned into slavery with three other girls. She was but fifteen, convicted in defiance of the law, which forbade the prosecution of Nonconformists under sixteen years of age.[2]   As these died others were passed into the Plague-stricken gaol, though to the magistrates' knowledge incarceration meant inevitably death to many.   Such was the callous brutishness of the times.   One must suppose that the mortality among the uncared-for felons packed in the reeking holds was much larger.

No London prison was closed during the Great Plague. Mr. Bastwick, the Minister of the Poultry Compter, preached to the prisoners there, and died of Plague[3]; how many incarcerated there died again one cannot tell. The Wood Street Compter also retained its prisoners while Plague raged, no attempt having been made to move them to safer lodging.[4]   This little humanity, born of the visitation, was extended to the poor debtors in the Ludgate and the Compters, that appeal was made by public advertisement to their stony-hearted creditors to come to arrangement upon " modest and reasonable composition," whereby they might be released, the Clerk of the Papers at the Poultry Compter promising his assistance.[5]

Human beings are by nature neighbourly.   The isolation among them born of this awful visitation ; the dread of contact with one's own kind, as with a leper ; the hideous selfishness of the time, self-centred wholly upon maintaining one's own existence—these were as horrible as were the ghastlier evidences of death striking down men in thousands.   " This disease making us more cruel to one

---

[1] Ellis Hookes, the Clerk to the Friends, in a letter of Nov., 1665 (see p. 117, ante), gives the names of these martyrs in Newgate.   It is noteworthy as an additional piece of evidence of the incompleteness of the Bills of Mortality that deaths in the prisons of Newgate and Ludgate and the child victims in Christ's Hospital (Bluecoat School) are not included therein (Tillison to Dean Sancroft, Sept. 14, in Harl. MSS. 3785) nor those in the Temple, Bethlehem, or Bridewell, or any institution having its private burial ground as distinct from the parochial churchyard.

[2] M. R. Brailsford, *Quaker Women*, p. 293.

[3] Symon Patrick to Mrs. Gauden, Sept. 30.

[4] " Repertory " 71, fo. 46 b.   [5] *Newes*, Sept. 7.

another than we are to dogs!" Pepys was prompted to write in his Diary.[1] In the open road Pepys talked with his friend Povy, " he himself not daring to come into the house or be seen " because his servant had fallen sick, and " most horribly he is abused by some persons hereupon, and his fortune, I believe, quite broke." [2]

Steadfastly the Plague increased its inroads upon a dwindling population. In an earlier visitation Thomas Dekker, with a poet's frenzy and a priceless imagination for horrors, had drawn a picture of London's conditions that cannot have been surpassed in the greater Plague of 1665:—

What an unmatchable torment were it for a man to be bard up every night in a vast silent Charnell-house ? hung (to make it more hideous) with lamps dimly and slowly burning, in hollow and glimmering corners ; where all the pavement should in stead of greene rushes, be strewde with blasted Rosemary : withered Hyacinthes, fatall Cipresse and Ewe, thickly mingled with heapes of dead mens bones : the bare ribbes of a father that begat him, lying there : here the Chaplesse hollow scull of a mother that bore him : round about him a thousand Coarses, some standing bolt upright in their knotted winding sheetes : others halfe mouldred in rotten coffins, that should suddenly yawne wide open, filling his nosthrils with noysome stench, and his eyes with the sight of nothing but crawling wormes. And to keepe such a poor wretch waking, he should heare no noise but of Toads croaking, Screech-Owles howling, Mandrakes shriking : were not this an infernall prison ? would not the strongest-harted man (beset with such a ghastly horror) looke wilde ? and runne madde ? and die ?

And even such a formidable shape did the diseased Citie appeare in : For he that durst (in the dead houre of gloomy midnight) have bene so valient, as to have walkt through the still and melancholy streets, what thinke you should have bene his musicke ? Surely the loude grones of raving sick men ; the strugling panges of soules departing : In every house griefe striking up an Allarum : Servants crying out for maisters : wives for husbands, parents for children, children for their mothers : here he should have met some frantickly running to knock up Sextons ; there, others fearfully sweating with Coffins, to steale forth dead bodies, least the fatall hand-writing of death should seale up their doores. And to make this dismall consort more full, round about him Bells heavily tolling

---

[1] *Diary*, Aug. 22.   [2] *Ibid.*, July 10.

in one place, and ringing out in another : The dreadfulnesse
of such an houre is inutterable : let us goe further . . .

How often hath the amazed husband waking, found the
comfort of his bedde lying breathlesse by his side ! his children
at the same instant gasping for life ! and his servants mortally
wounded at the hart by sickness ! the distracted creature,
beats at death doores, exclaimes at windowes, his cries are
sharp inough to pierce heaven, but on earth no eare is opend
to receive them.   And in this manner do the tedious minutes
of the night stretch out the sorrowes of ten thousand.

It is now day, let us looke forth and try what Consolation
rizes with the Sun : not any, not any : for before the Jewell of
the morning be fully set in silver, hundred hungry graves
stand gaping, and every one of them (as at a breakfast) hath
swallowed downe ten or eleven liveless carcases : before dinner,
in the same gulfe are twice as many more devoured :   and
before the sun takes his rest, those numbers are doubled :
Threescore that not many houres before had every one severall
lodgings very delicately furnisht, are now thrust altogether
into one close roome : a little noisome roome : not fully ten
foote square.[1]

None could go into the streets without meeting numbers
of coffins being carried.   Of the few passers-by that were
noticed, many had sores upon them.   Others limped
painfully from the effects of wounds not wholly healed.[2]
The town presented a wide and heartrending scene of
misery and desolation.   There were silent streets wherein
from end to end the red cross flamed upon doors, the few
dwellings not so marked being left tenantless and open to
the winds.   The neighbours without exception had fled.
Monstrous as the Plague over London became, families in
thousands being shut in to perish, the pest-houses that
alone served as hospitals continued in the same hopeless
inadequacy.   Had a live public spirit been existing—and
there was none—how should building keep pace with this
Plague ?   When the peak was passed in September, and
the utmost in extensions had been done, the pest-houses
of Westminster and St. Giles-in-the-Fields could still contain but sixty patients each ; and that in Soho Fields no
more than ninety, though by that time it had to suffice

---

[1] Dekker's *The Wonderfull Yeare* 1603, reprinted in the Bodley Head
Quartos, 1924.   Defoe's indebtedness to this lurid passage is plainly
apparent.
[2] Vincent, p. 32.

not only for St. Martin-in-the-Fields, but sufferers from the western parishes of St. Clement Danes, St. Paul Covent Garden and St. Mary Savoy were also brought there. It was " scarce large enough for one of these parishes." [1]

Those doctors and surgeons and apothecaries who stayed in London, much overburdened, did heroic work. No hazards to themselves were avoided.[2] It seems by a miracle that any who acted as Boghurst, the apothecary of St. Giles-in-the-Fields, tells that he acted should have escaped the pestilence alive. He commonly dressed forty Plague sores a day, and in diagnosis would test the pulse of a patient, sweating in bed, for five and six minutes. He upheld in their beds those threatened by strangling and choking, often for half an hour together, the breath frequently falling upon his face. In the haste of a busy day he would eat and drink with the Plague-stricken, sitting on the edge of the bed and talking with them, often watching the death and closing the mouth and eyes—for in death commonly the mouth was wide open and eyes staring. Help being scarce in the infected houses, he at times assisted to lay out the corpse and afterwards place it in the coffin, and as a last act of charity he would accompany it to the grave.[3]

Taking all these risks, this worthy apothecary remained in health. Like other practitioners he had his own preservatives against the Plague, a water, a lozenge, and also an Electuary Antidote at 8d. the ounce.[4] He lived for twenty years after, and was buried in his native place at Ditton, Kent, where his tablet tells that he was an honest, just man, skilful in his profession and in the Greek and Latin tongues, delighting in the study of antiquity, and an excellent player upon the lute.

When trust was given to nothing, money came under suspicion as a carrier of infection. At market, shop, and stall the more cautious tradesman provided bowls of water or vinegar, in which he required that customers should place their money, to be purified by washing before he

---

[1] Earl of Craven to the Privy Council, 1666, Feb. 19.
[2] *Loimologia*, p. 15.
[3] *Loimographia*, pp. 30, 31.
[4] Advt. in *Intelligencer*, July 31.

would touch it.[1] A filled basin was a common sight by the
house door,[2] and in country places affected with Plague,
where running water was available, the immersion of all
coins passing for purification was the usual practice.[3]
Like precautions were taken to guard against contagion by
letters, by all sorts of expedients.

A countryman delivered to Boghurst's wife at his
apothecary's shop a letter carried at the end of a long pole,
the man being too full of fears to approach near her. Of
many methods tried to ensure safety, the most foolish was
to scour the letters on the wires of a sieve, to rub away
infection ! Some would wash them in water, then dry
them before a fire. Envelopes were, of course, unknown,
and the written sheet was merely folded, sealed with wax,
and addressed on the outside. Others aired the letters at
the highest part of the house, or upon a hedge, or at
the point of a shaft, allowing two or three days to pass
before they ventured to open them. A popular practice
was to lay letters between two cold stones ; and many,
thinking heat the best disinfectant, toasted them before a
fire.[4]

The fairs were a feature of the country's life and trade.
All concourses of people being forbidden, there was an end
to them. Bartholomew Fair at Smithfield, once the great
mart for cloth, was prohibited by Royal Proclamation,
and also all fairs within fifty miles of London, for fear of
increase of the Plague.[5] Already Bartholomew Fair had
degenerated into a sort of London carnival in which persons
of every condition and degree of life mixed, the young
noble and the thief, the masked fine lady and the town
prostitute. No London citizens were to attend any fairs
whatsoever.[6] This but continued the policy inaugurated

[1] *Loimographia*, p. 54.
[2] Cf. *A Poem*, etc., printed in Appendix :—
　　　" And yet what vext us more
　Was to see water so at every door.
　　　For sure it was a shame
　That London should in anything be like to Amsterdam.
　　　All money is in water laid,
　　　And basins now are purses made."
[3] Cf. the Plague at Eyam, Derbyshire, p. 295, *post*.
[4] Boghurst's *Loimographia*, pp. 53, 54.
[5] " Cloth Fair " is the name still borne by a neighbouring street, in
which survive some few of the old houses.
[6] *Royal Proclamation*, Aug. 7.

as early as June 14th, when the great Barnwell Fair in Cambridgeshire was forbidden. As the months passed and Plague spread outwards, restriction was placed on all the principal fairs throughout the country.

A great burden fell upon London in relieving its sick. The task was done, but not by the means that to-day would first be called into operation. London had no hunger riots. The distress at times must have strained the limits of endurance. The significant line, " Starved to death," is not absent from the Bills of Mortality. In August and September many thousands fell dependent upon public relief for the bare means of maintaining life ; these apart from the large numbers who maintained a precarious existence by accepting service as watchmen, bearers, buryers, and nurse-keepers. The doles given would not receive our approval.

The Great Plague was two and a half centuries ago. A Poor-law levy was no more popular under King Charles II. than it had been under Elizabeth. Classes were sharply divided and class interests selfishly maintained ; neither those who paid nor those who received had as yet envisaged the public purse as a sort of Fortuna's box out of which every one's claims were to be met, and relief was given sparingly and only in the last resort.

It was beggarly to the utmost penuriousness. Yet the relief sufficed to keep those people who escaped the Plague alive, and that was as much as public sentiment of the time expected. Through the attenuated figures—two shillings, three shillings and the like—showing such small sums to serve so great need, we see darkly a huge mass of inevitable suffering, and privations which rendered the people more liable to receive infection and less fitted to combat disease. These evils greater generosity might have lessened.

It has passed into accepted tradition that King Charles subscribed to London's relief during the Great Plague £1,000 weekly, and this in addition to the City's own contribution of £600. It is so stated by Lingard, the historian, and by others. The cold fact is that the sums distributed in relief by the City, supplementing the poor results of the pest-rate, over the whole of its area and to the out-parishes, to which the public contribution was in part diverted, at no time reached as much as £1,000 a week. Only in nine weeks does it appear to have exceeded half that sum.[1] The burden of relief in the Great Plague, when a balance is sought, is found largely to have fallen upon charity. The maintenance of the people was made possible only by benevolence from the wealthier residents, which each parish separately received and distributed, by country donations sent to Guildhall or to the Primate at Lambeth, by private benevolences which come into no account, and collections on the fast days.

The donations of Queen Henrietta Maria, of the Duchess of York, of Prince Rupert and of members of the nobility are set out either in the City accounts or those of the out-parishes. I have searched every source likely to give the disclosure, but still await testimony that King Charles contributed anything.[2] He was magnificently careless rather than wanting in human sympathy. There is envisaged in my mind a subscription list that visitors to the Cathedral are shown, for the repairs to Old St. Paul's that were begun before the Great Fire of London, led off by the King's annual subscription promised of £1,000. " Charles " is writ large in the Royal hand, *pour encourager les autres*. But no one has succeeded in finding entry of a second annual payment.

The unstable basis of finance during the Great Plague was the special poor-rate or pest-rate that was levied in every City ward and out-parish. The amounts, in part collected weekly, appear in many of the parish accounts ; they surprise by their meanness. When City householders paid in such emergency ninepence a week, and some even fivepence and fourpence, it becomes evident that the rapacity of the modern rate-collector is not an old growth. In St. Margaret Westminster parish, where so many wealthy residents dwelt, mention has been made that of £1,652 spent in relief only £402 was from the rate. In the

---

[1] How wide of the mark was Defoe is illustrated by his reckless assertion that " many hundred thousand pounds " was contributed in relief, and that in the parish of Cripplegate alone (" which I really believe was true ") £17,800 was distributed in one week ! And this nonsense has stood as history for two centuries.

[2] In May, 1666, when the Court had returned to London and Charles at Whitehall was again a resident of Westminster, he gave for the relief of its poor £100 (St. Margaret's Ch'wardens' Accts.)—a belated contribution which is the only one I have been able to trace.

City parish of St. Alphage London Wall, the whole year's pest-rate receipt was £53 4s.; the City Cash contribution to the parish was £70.[1] St. Benet Fink, after attempting a voluntary contribution among its householders which produced only £15 7s., levied a pest-rate that brought in £41 9s.[2]

Much of the rate could not be collected. Sir Edmond Bury Godfrey, the magistrate, himself condemned the callous indifference to their responsibilities of many of the wealthier exiles from the West-end—

> The poor people cry out upon the dearness of fuel and want of employment, by reason of the King and the Court having been so long out of town, and some of the courtiers, nobility, and gentry forget their debts as well as their charity.

> To enforce payment of the Royal Aid, public notice was posted warning those who had fled from London that unless the liability was forthwith satisfied their homes would be broken open by the constables, and their household goods seized and sold, according to the Act of Parliament.

> I wish (his letter to Lord Newport goes on) we had as good power and law for levying of the pest rate and the poor's rate. We would not have undergone so much inconvenience and censure as we have done for making no better provision for the visited or poor, though I believe they were never so well relieved in any Plague time whatsoever, thanks to the Lords and other honourable persons, and our good benefactors; but I am ashamed to acquaint your honour, though nothing but the truth, that not half of our pest or poor's rate is paid by them who are charged therewith, and of right ought to pay the same, who are and have been most of them out of the town all this time of the visitation.[3]

The time was not yet ripe, nor was so till after King Charles II. had quitted the stage, for what should have been public burdens to be accepted as proper charges upon public funds. Parliament voted no money to meet the hard necessities of the Plague. Charitable benevolence at the instigation of the Sovereign, who exhorted his loyal subjects to give freely, church and house to house collections, and the begging " brief " were subterfuges most in

---

[1] Ch'wardens' Accts. [2] *Ibid.*
[3] Godfrey to Earl of Newport, Dec. 19.

vogue to avoid a call upon public funds. The attitude of the wealthier classes seems plain, and they alone governed. It was better to give voluntarily in sums left to their own discretion than to encourage a habit of public spending out of a rate in the disposal of which they could have no say.

Never were the proceeds of the rate large. On July 25th the City Chamber began to disburse money for Plague relief, its first week's contribution being £620, which apparently was wholly derived from private benevolence and the money received from the first fast-day collection, augmenting the parochial rate receipt.

Guildhall kept two detailed cash accounts.[1] The first is headed " Payments of money weekly to the parishes as followeth," and it gives the total outgoings from the City in relief each week from July 25th to December 22nd. The second bears title, " Disbursed out of the Chamber Cash for Relief of the Poor by Order of the Lord Mayor." This last begins with a contribution of £600 on September 1st to pay the sixth week's distribution to the parishes of £630, which had been passed out that week. The receipts by benevolence and the pest-rate no longer sufficed to meet the swollen expenditure. The City Cash was now drawn upon, and thereafter it bore the larger part of the burden, the charitable subscriptions by mid-September having shrunk to very little. The Plague had lasted too long. It is a strange reflection upon our humanity that the calamity of the Great Plague excited a smaller charitable response from the country than was given for the sufferers by the Great Fire of London which followed next year.[2] The material loss proved a more potent lever in unbuttoning pockets than did the loss of life.

Monthly fast-day collections yielded a generous sum towards London's relief. Unfortunately no complete account has been kept. Lambeth Palace Library has a letter by Simon Lloyd at Llanynis on March 6th, 1666, which indicates some difficulties experienced, and closes with an amusing tag—

At length Mr Draycott gives account of Caernarvonshire, nine pounds he sent me gathered in the respective parishes the

[1] Guildhall Library MSS. 270.
[2] See the writer's *The Great Fire of London*, chap. 12.

greater number of churches having made now collections. . . .
The man indeede is very honest and charitably disposed, and
I am confident has used his uttermost endeavours. But of
course ye country is miserably poore, and which is worse
growne hard hearted and senseless of other men's sufferings.
Natus es e Scopulis, etc., I know not whether those yt are
borne and bred amongst ye rocks may not p'ticipate too much
of the nature of the soile.[1]

The Plague, always most violent in the congested
Liberties and out-parishes, overspread the whole City,
till there was rarely a street wherein people were not
dying, piling up the mountain of Plague victims which the
chart most graphically illustrates, its peak thrust up to
mark six thousand—seven thousand—eight thousand—
these in each case the dead of a single week.

The river at London, its surface little disturbed,
reflected the desolation of the town. Pepys remarked in
November how amazed Sir George Cartaret was to find the
Pool still so empty of ships, and no men working at the
Custom House Quay.[2] Little trade survived beyond what
was required for provisioning the capital, and ocean-going
vessels chose any port in preference to the Thames. For
encouragement of sailing masters from Essex, a bounty was
paid by the Corporation of one farthing upon every quarter
of corn they delivered in London. Like the Coal Dues
imposed to repair the devastation caused by the Great
Fire, this payment continued long after its purpose was
forgotten. In the middle of last century there was living
an old mariner from the Rochford Hundred who remembered taking the farthing.[3]

Merchants of Bristol, petitioning the King, declared
there was no trade to carry in their bottoms with London
and other English ports.[4] Vessels that arrived down-
Thames were greatly delayed, not being suffered to unload
for fear of the infection.[5] The year brought disaster to the
port, and not alone from the restriction of trade due to the
Plague. Dutch privateers hovered about the Thames
mouth, ready to cut out sailing ships attempting to make
the river.

[1] Lambeth Palace MSS. Carthe. Mis. vol. 6, fo. 8.
[2] *Diary*, Nov. 7.   [3] *Notes & Queries*, 7th Ser., xi. 267.
[4] *State Papers (Domestic),* 1664–5, p. 577.
[5] *Ibid.,* 1665–6, p. 26.

In the bad custom of that day, the Excise was farmed among a host of speculators. They pleaded persistently for a remission of rent to save them from absolute ruin. In November a Royal Warrant discharged the Excise Farmers of London, Middlesex, and Surrey of £21,000 of their rent, in consideration of their loss by the reduced revenues collected.[1] By that time the Plague was by no means spent. When next the great lease of the Excise was issued, a clause appeared in the farmers' interests making them allowance if the Plague revived.[2]

Defoe has asserted that the East Coast ports profited by London's isolation, exporting vast quantities of goods to Holland. He overlooked the fact that the country was at war with Holland. Yarmouth even before London became badly infected with Plague, as was Colchester soon after, and Ipswich to a lesser degree. Defoe allows his Sadler to draw a wholly imaginative picture of ships in tiers lying at anchor in the Thames from the Pool away down as low as Gravesend. This cannot represent the actual scene. That keen-eyed observer Samuel Pepys, when the Navy Office had been moved to Greenwich and he lodged there and at Woolwich, spent much of the autumn on and about the Thames, and records nothing of the kind. The Plague by no means restricted its ravages to the capital, but crept down-river, infecting the villages on both banks. It was at Ratcliffe [3] and at Rotherhithe with no long delay.[4]

Plague appeared at Deptford, where a small industrial community was grouped about the naval dockyard. Evelyn was shocked to notice thirty houses in his " miserable village " of Deptford with doors locked and the red cross of Plague marked on each, one of them being that nearest his dwelling at Sayes Court. " It was only last Saturday," he wrote in September, " ere my courageous wife could be persuaded to take the alarm, but she is now fled, and most of my family. If the malignancy of this sad contagion spread no faster, before winter the calamity will be indescribable. My very blood chills within me at the contemplation of our calamity." [5]

[1] *Cal. of Treasury Books*, 1660–7, p. 695.
[2] Alton & Holland, *The King's Customs*, p. 122.
[3] Pepys, July 20.   [4] Hon. Robert Boyle to Oldenburg, July 10.
[5] Evelyn's *Memoirs*, ii. 157–60.

The Plague raged fiercely at Deptford, accounting for 374 burials ; and it became so deep-seated that in the next year these figures were largely exceeded (522 from Plague).[1] Coaling ships from the North unloaded at Deptford till the Plague crept in there, and afterwards at Blackwall and Greenwich. The coal was piled in great heaps, and brought up-stream in lighters when the vessels had left, to avoid contact between the sailors and the London bargemen.[2]

An incident with a certain element of grim humour in it may lighten the dull tragedy of these pages. With a view to encourage colliers to come to London, masters of the ships were granted special exemption of their crews from the press for the King's Navy.[3] In the urgent demand for seamen for the Dutch war, the privilege was more honoured in the breach than in the observance.

A master whose craft was in the lower Thames reaches, sighting the press gang's boat rowing out towards him, hastily wrapped three or four of his crew in sail cloths as rough grave clothes. He told the officer of the press by whom he was hailed that he had Plague in his vessel. These men were dead, and already others were at the last gasp. The " dead " lay on the deck, stiff and motionless. Making no further inquiry, the press boat pushed off, and by this manœuvre the master saved his crew intact for the return passage to Newcastle.[4]

Infection was in Greenwich and at Woolwich ; Pepys noted on August 29th that at both places " the Plague begins to grow very great." [5] The broad lower reaches of the Thames, where the flood tide surges out to the sea, were rarely without a light breeze to sing its faint music amidst the cordage and spars and reefed sails of the ships—this while London was stifling in heat. There at least health should have been found. But Barking was badly ravaged ; [6] the little village of Grays had cases ; at Gravesend Plague

---

[1] Lyson's *Environs of London*, iv. 373.
[2] Sir J. Broodbank, *History of the Port of London*, p. 378.
[3] *Royal Proclamation*, April 26. Harl. MSS. 1247, fo. 29.
[4] Rugge's " Diurnal," fo. 144.
[5] See also Pepys's *Diary*, Aug. 12. The Plague heaped up the mortality in Greenwich to more than double its accustomed figure, and, as at Deptford, raged still more disastrously in the following year.
[6] Lyson, iv. 101.

was especially virulent.[1] Everywhere the pestilence is traced, expanding down the length of the river to the sea, and hardly a place on the banks escaped it. From one or another of these, or from the stricken capital itself, ships' supplies must needs have been drawn, and it is incredible in the circumstances that shipmasters should have chosen to resort to the Thames's Plague-infested waters.

The Plague could not be kept out of the Fleet.[2] Warships at the Nore refused to take provisions from the victualling craft sent to them, some among the crews of these craft being dead of the Plague.[3] The Navy Office, transferred to Greenwich, was beset by numbers of sick seamen recovered, for whom neither pay nor refuge could be found, " they lying before our office doors all night and all day, poor wretches ! " writes Pepys. The ships' captains would not receive them again on board, fearing that they should bring contagion from the shore.[4]

There came from the King in August a belated letter— the only one—grave news of Plague spreading outwards from London having penetrated into the Councils at Salisbury. Charles commanded the magistrates to stop all goods being carried up and down the Thames from London, lest infection be taken by them. They were to be diligent and circumspect in preventing the removal of goods and persons from the capital to other towns and villages. They must be strict in seeing that the houses shut up be sealed against the possibility of escape of their occupants, committing offenders to Newgate, there to be severely proceeded against at the next sessions.[5]

---

[1] Pepys, Aug. 12, Oct. 2.

[2] Evelyn's *Diary*, Aug. 7 : " I went to the Duke of Albemarle for a pest-ship, to wait on our infected men, who were not a few." Also Pepys, Aug. 12. Many references in State Papers, Charles II.

[3] Denis Gauden to Pepys.

[4] Pepys, Sept. 30.

[5] *State Papers (Domestic)*, 1664–5, p. 513.

CHAPTER IX

LONDON DESOLATED

IN the very height of the Plague several doctors lay dead of the pestilence. The fact is plain enough, but it is difficult to arrive at the truth. John Allin, priest, alchemist and student of medicine,[1] and John Tillison, then a minor official of St. Paul's, both report in their letters an appalling medical tragedy. Tillison, writing to Dean Sancroft from London on September 14th, passes on this news then going about the town, but with reservation, accepting no responsibility for it—

Dr Burnet, Dr Glover and one or two more of the College of Physicians, with Dr O'Dowd, which was licensed by my Lord's Grace of Canterbury, some surgeons, apothecaries, and Johnson the chemist, died all very suddenly. Some say (but God forbid that I should report it for truth) that these in a consultation together, if not all yet the greatest part of them, attempted to open a dead corpse which was full of the tokens, and being in hand with the dissected body, some fell down dead immediately and others did not outlive the next day at noon.[2]

Allin on the same day sends the intelligence to his friend Fryth, the Rye solicitor, as something not to be delayed. Dr. George Starkey he names as one of those dead, with about six more unnamed. They gave money for the most infected body they could hear of to dissect. On opening the corpse to search for the seat of the disease, " a stench ascended from the body and infected them every one, and it is said they are all dead since, most of them distractedly mad, whereof G. Starkey is one." Mad, quickly thereafter dead.

[1] See Chapter XI., *post*. [2] Harl. MSS. 3785, fo. 35.

Allin, himself a Galenist, could not grasp the heroism of the deed he recorded. These were chemical practitioners, and the war between Galenists and Paracelcists, waged with fierce and most unreasoning animosity, clouded his reason. A martyr to science and healing was not in his mind ; these were, he says almost with insult, " chemical practitioners who, in an insulting way over other Galenists, and in a sort over this visitation sickness, which is more a judgment than a disease, because they could not resist it by their Galenical medicines, which they were too confident that their chemical medicines would do "— they in their arrogance sought a triumph over their professional adversaries, and this was the award. His only comment is : " God is resolved to stain the pride of all glory ; there is no boasting before him, and much less against him." [1]

Tillison, at St. Paul's, was best situated to get news authoritatively. He seems affected quite unnecessarily with a sense of shame in forwarding it. Allin, keeping to his house in Southwark, would hear only current reports. Circumstantial as this account of the joint post-mortem and its terrible results would seem to be, there is much reason for doubting if it actually took place. Dr. George Thomson, as already recorded, did dissect a Plague corpse, and has left an account of his work.[2] Attending in August a patient named Pick in Petticoat Lane, Whitechapel (to-day's Middlesex Street), he preserved the man's life by chemical remedies, but Pick's servant, a youth of about fifteen years, became infected, developed raving madness, and died. Dr. Thomson obtained the master's permission to open the body, and ten hours after death performed the dissection, the only person watching being the master's other man-servant.

A few hours passed, and Dr. Thomson felt the Plague symptoms upon him ; he had taken a terrible risk. But more to the point is that the same evening Thomson visited Dr. Day, relating to him the incidents of his dissection. A fortnight earlier Dr. Day had himself developed the Plague smart. The danger seemed past and he went about, but the worst symptoms revived, and relating his death Thomson says of him that he would have been safe had he not been too venturesome to save others rather than secure his own life.

He was a learned scholar in deed as well as in word, a pious, modest, charitable, humble man, so far free from ostentation and vainglory that he hid his excellent parts, when other of his brethren, far inferior to him, made ten times the glittering show. He took such laborious pains night and day in his faculty that I am certain he exhausted his spirits, and thereby disenabled the Archeaus to resist the contagion. *Carendo non fruendo agnoscimus ;* he hath his exit with applause, and is wanted by many that better value him now than when they enjoyed him.

Dr. Starkey, whom Thomson also saw after his own dissection, had the Plague then upon him, and his intellect was affected. His rapid death thereafter, with the fatal " tokens " evident, Thomson attributes to his having drunk too much small beer when suffering the raging thirst of fever.

Both had been his close friends. Both, he clearly infers, became infected with Plague in their practice. He expressly denies " a confident report (the broachers of which it is not difficult to conjecture) that Dr. Day and Dr. Starkey were present at the dissection of this pestilential body " by Thomson. " It is an absolute untruth," he declares, " contrived on purpose to represent them as presumptuous rash persons, in undertaking such a desperate business, which cost them both their lives, as they would have it, that thereby the good estimation and fame of chemical preparations may be eclipsed." (The meaning seems to be " exalted.") No word is given or suggestion made by Thomson of any dissection of a Plague corpse having taken place other than his own. It is incredible that in the warm tribute he pays to his friends he would have omitted mention of the dissection in consultation and its tragic result had it, in fact, occurred. I have dealt with the matter in some detail because it is of interest in historical medicine, and Munk, in his " Roll of the Royal College of Physicians," and the medical writers in the " Dictionary of National Biography " have accepted the unchecked report by Tillison and Allin.

It is, I think, plain how that " confident report "

arose. There had been this dissection by Thomson ; there had been deaths of eminent doctors in the worst weeks of the Plague in August and early September, when the pestilence had become too vast to be bound and confined, and the sick and the healthy wandered together about the streets ; and public rumour related them as cause and effect.

Let Starkey's sacrifice leave for him only the kindliest remembrance. Dr. Thomson has testified that he had an extraordinary gift of curing others. He had no collegiate associations with healing. He had dabbled much in alchemy. To-day men would call him a " quack," and his pugnacious, assertive character is made plain by his claim to be " a Professor of that Medicine that is real, not Historical," and " a Philosopher made by fire." Trimming to catch the breeze of Royal favour, he had advocated to King Charles II. retaliation upon the Puritans.[1] His death ennobles him.

The medical roll of honour is large when taken from the few physicians who remained in London to combat the Plague. Hodges says that eight or nine fell in the danger-ous work, but this understates the sacrifice.[2] Among them was Dr. William Conyers, whose goodness and humanity claimed an honourable remembrance with all who survived him.[3] Edward Harman and Thomas Gray I have mentioned in an earlier chapter as having been appointed by the City authorities to receive £40 apiece at Christmas, should they " be then living and continuing in the service." Money was paid to their widows, for both before then had perished of the Plague.[4] Dr. Parker, another of the City's appointed physicians, also succumbed in the visitation.[5] Johnson was the Apothecary of the Royal College of Physicians, appointed to distribute their remedies to the afflicted poor, and himself, with many

[1] *Dictionary of National Biography.*
[2] Allin wrote to his friends at Rye on Sept. 14 : " I hear also that above seven score doctors, apothecaries and surgeons are dead of this distemper in and about the City since this visitation "—a good example of the wild reports that gained currency in the excitement and distraction of the Great Plague. Those of these professions who remained in London probably little exceeded this number, if at all.
[3] *Loimologia,* p. 15.
[4] " Journal." Also see C'ippendale, *Medical Roll of Honour.*
[5] " Repertory " 76, fo. 272b. See also p. 87, *ante.*

DR. GEORGE THOMSON

Author of " Loimotomia," who practised in London during the Plague

another unknown, died of the contagion. The death of Dr. Burnet, who was Samuel Pepys's physician, has already had mention.

No tribute to them all can be finer than that of their co-worker, Dr. Hodges : " Their memory will doubtless survive time, who died in the discharge of their duty, and their reputation flourish who (by God's providence) escaped." [1]

The Plague sign came to be marked on almost every alternate door of the inhabited streets ; from some, and those the better-class streets, substantially every one had fled, leaving a caretaker or two, or else shuttered windows and emptiness within. As the Bill was issued, always it showed that the Plague had spread wider to enfold a yet larger tale of victims. Always the week's return was worse than the last, as summer's heat increased in the stifling town. Overhead was the blue sky, with but seldom a cloud to cross it or yield a shower to cool the atmosphere and cleanse the streets of their poisonous accumulations, giving the first faint promise of relief. Once only rain came throughout the fateful month of August, when for a day or two it was very wet,[2] and in the closing days of the month the temperature fell.[3] The calm and serenity of the weather were ominous. Dr. Baynard wrote that it seemed as if rain and wind had been banished together. He observed that for weeks on end that summer there was not breeze enough to stir a vane. There fell abundance of mildews. The very birds would pant for breath, and were observed to fly more heavily than at other times.[4]

In the first week of August (1st to 8th) the mortality in London had leapt up to 4,030, and out of these numbers 2,817 were credited to the Plague. Its victims, acknowledged or misreported, were being borne away in the proportion of 550 a day. It was a grievous toll, but before the month expired London was to witness upwards of a thousand corpses being carried through its silent streets to the burial grounds and the pits between one sunset and the next—visible evidences that indicated how vast was

---

[1] *Letter to a Person of Quality.*
[2] Pepys, Aug. 13.
[3] Pepys to Lady Cartaret, Sept. 4.
[4] Cited by Echard, *History of England*, p. 823. This conforms with indications of the weather given by others, but see Hodges, p. 252, *post.*

the mass of suffering that the desolated houses in every street concealed. Even then still the curve shot up.

The alarm in the first week of July had caused the Court incontinently to fly from London. The first Bill for August was three times as large as that with which July had opened. It showed that the Plague had carried off an additional 1,016 human lives in the seven days it covered over the numbers of the previous week. Save for a single week out of the four in August, not the total figures alone, but the proportion of increase each successive week, climbed higher up to the climax reached in September.

The Bill greatly shocked Pepys; but he was to experience worse than this. He had anticipations of death. He drew out a new will, " which I had bound myself by oath to despatch by to-morrow night, the town growing so unhealthy that a man cannot depend upon living two days." The next night he jotted down, " Settling my house and all things in the best order I can, lest it should please God to take me away, or force me to leave my house." [1]

In the " Diary " many glimpses are given of the stricken town, although no ordered picture; the Clerk of the Acts was too busy a man for that.

Aug. 2. Up, it being a public fast, as being the first Wednesday of the month, for the Plague.

Aug. 8. The streets empty all the way now, even in London, which is a sad sight. And to Westminster Hall, where talking, hearing very sad stories from Mrs. Mumford; among others of Michell's son's family. And poor Will, that used to sell us ale at the Hall door, his wife and three children dead, all I think in a day. So home, through the City again, wishing I may have taken no ill in going; but I will go, I think, no more thither.

Aug. 15. It was dark before I could get home, and so land at Churchyard Stairs [by London Bridge] where, to my great trouble, I met a dead corpse of the Plague, in the narrow alley just bringing down a little pair of stairs. But I thank God I was not much disturbed by it. However, I shall beware of being late abroad again.

The growing emptiness of the streets most impressed those who were compelled to move about London.

[1] *Diary*, Aug. 10 and 11.

Aug. 16. To the Exchange, where I have not been a great while. But Lord! how sad a sight it is to see the streets empty of people, and few upon the 'Change. Jealous of every door that one sees shut up, lest it should be the Plague; and about us two shops in three, if not more, generally shut up.

Aug. 19. I by water to Charing Cross, to the post-house, and there the people tell me they are shut up [Plague being within the house] and so I went to the new post-house, and there got a guide and horses to Hounslow.

Aug. 20. [at Brentford] Told my bad news, and hear the Plague is round about them there. And to church, where a dull sermon and many Londoners. After church to my inn, and ate and drank, and so about seven o'clock by water, and got between nine and ten to Queenhithe, very dark; and I could not get my waterman to go elsewhere for fear of the Plague. Thence with a lantern, in great fear of meeting dead corpses, carrying to be buried; but, blessed be God! met none, but did see now and then a link, which is the mark of them, at a distance.

Aug. 22. Walked to Redcliffe, troubled to go through the little lane, where the Plague is, but did.

Aug. 28. To Mr. Colvill, the goldsmith's, having not for some days been in the streets; but now how few people I see, and those looking like people that had taken leave of the world. To the Exchange, and there not fifty people upon it, and but few more like to be, as they told me. I think to take adieu to-day of the London streets.

Aug. 30. I went forth, and walked towards Moorfields to see (God forgive my presumption!) whether I could see any dead corpse going to the grave; but as God would have it did not. But, Lord! how everybody's looks, and discourse in the streets, is of death and nothing else; and few people going up and down that the town is like a place distressed and forsaken.

Aug. 31. Thus this month ends with great sadness upon the public, through the greatness of the Plague everywhere through the kingdom almost. Every day sadder and sadder news of its increase. In the city [area of the Bills of Mortality] died this week 7,496, and of them 6,102 of the Plague. But it is feared that the true number of the dead this week is near 10,000; partly from the poor that cannot be taken notice of, through the greatness of the number, and partly from the Quakers and others that will not have any bell ring for them. As to myself, I am very well, only in fear of the Plague, and as much of an ague, by being forced to go early and late to Woolwich, and my family to be there continually.

The town was dirty, the paved streets dirty. Quiet and dirt and glorious sunshine were together. Garbage thrown from windows or swept out of doors lay strewn about, awaiting such time as the parish rakers were free to clear the kennels. Abandoned houses were left in utter neglect, with none to care for them. In those wherein Plague was shut up, and others where people lived in daily dread of the Plague's appearance in their midst, all energies were bent to the single task of maintaining life. With the wealthy classes and most of the richer citizens fled, the public services inadequate, and all individual initiative crushed out of existence, London presented a thoroughly bedraggled appearance. The sunrays penetrated into obscure alleys, close and stagnant, lighting up places where putrifying refuse heaped in corners invited the Plague death.

Then a new horror grew up. There arose in the desolate town a stench as of a pestilential miasma. Its origin was all too plain. The condition of the churchyards had become almost past belief. Full as were the Plague pits, these had not taken all, and the ground around the parish churches continued in use till it was so choked that in most instances the surface had been raised high by the numerous burials. The covering was but the slightest. In the carelessness born of the time and haste, not alone were human bones left lying above ground, but the cemeteries were littered with fragments of broken coffins thrown up in later burials. At night fires lighted in the midst of the churchyards sent up flame and smoke, and any passers by shuddered and hurried away. These relics of mortality by order of the Aldermen were collected and so burnt, to stop infection spreading from them.[1]

Direction was given to the churchwardens of all City parishes to lay mould thickly over the graves.

Repeated complaints were made of the new churchyard adjacent to Bethlehem Hospital, now covered by Liverpool Street Station. The Plague corpses were cast into pits, and the Court of Aldermen were informed of " noisome stenches arising from the great numbers of dead bodies buried therein during this mortality." This place was a charity by Sir Thomas Rowe, Lord Mayor and Merchant Taylor,

[1] "Repertory" 70, fo. 153b.

who in 1569 had given an acre in Moorfields for burial
ease to such parishes in London as wanted convenient
ground. It was especially intended for St. Botolph
Bishopsgate, and the dead from the mad-house and others
dying in St. Thomas's Hospital in Southwark were also
brought there.[1] The ground became the resort of every
parish in difficulties in disposing of its dead. The Corporation opened additional burial places beyond the City's
northern wall, in Finsbury Fields and on land adjoining
Bunhill Fields, the last being surrounded by a brick wall,
and the keeper expressly forbidden to dig pits therein.[2]
By common error a Plague pit is often accredited as the
origin of Bunhill Fields Cemetery, where John Bunyan
lies entombed with so many eminent Dissenters gathered
around him. It was not used during the Great Plague.

From any window an onlooker peered down streets
wherein were few save groups of people paying to the dead
the last offices. George Wither, then an aged poet, his
inspiration gone, described the dread aspect of London in
one of the last verses from his pen—

> " Before us and behind,
>   And likewise on each side,
>   We empty dwellings find
>   Where thousands liv'd and dy'de.
>   In every street,
>   Both night and day, in sad array,
>   The mourners meet.
>   He that did rise
>   At morning well, ere noon his knell
>   Tells us he dies." [3]

Hardly any traffic stirred. The accustomed sounds of a
city, the pleasant hum of human voices—these were
stilled. People heard with a distinctness that was arresting
the water of the rapids tumbling through the arches
of Old London Bridge. The Plague's cruelty was performed in stealth and in silence—a silence enveloping the
stricken city that was broken only by the throat cries of
its distracted victims, without the noise and the tumult,
the unthinking exhilaration, the flashes and explosions
that in war would accompany the achievement of a
hundred thousand dead.

[1] Mrs. Basil Holmes, *Burial Grounds of London*, p. 176.
[2] " Repertory " 70, fos. 153, 155b.
[3] George Wither's " Poems " at the end of his *Meditation on the Lord's
Prayer*, published 1665[–6].

The sights in the streets would have appalled the stoutest heart. Coffins were seen everywhere. They were brought out from the houses at all hours, now the nights no longer sufficed for such large numbers of burials. Many corpses wrapped only in rough shrouds knotted were carried away to the graveyards and the pits. The coffin-maker's craft was the one flourishing trade that remained.[1] Vincent records as very affecting among the sad spectacles he witnessed, that of a poor woman coming alone and weeping by the door where he lived—he was himself in the midst of the infection, near Aldgate—with a little coffin borne under her arm, carrying it to the church-yard. "I did judge that it was the mother of the child, and that all the family besides was dead, and she was forced to coffin up and bury with her own hands this her last dead child."

Another day might have been seen, at the corner of the wall enclosing the Artillery Ground, a Plague victim who in his agony and frenzy had dashed his head against the wall. There he lay huddled up, with his face hanging over the rails, blood streaming down it and upon the ground. Compassionate onlookers moved the man into Moorfields, where they placed him beneath a tree upon his back. "I went and spoke to him," says Vincent; "he could make me no answer, but rattled in the throat, and as I was informed within half an hour died in the place."[2]

The dread of receiving infection was such that those compelled to pass through the streets moved in corkscrew fashion, crossing from side to side to avoid contact with other pedestrians. Many would hold their noses when hastening past a door marked with the Plague cross, or on meeting a searcher, or a corpse being carried to burial.[3] It was very dismal, wrote one who stayed, to behold the red crosses and read in great letters "Lord have mercy upon us!" on the doors, and watchmen standing before them with halberds, and such a solitude about those places, and people passing by them so gingerly, as if they had been lined with enemies in ambush, that waited to destroy them.[4] A sharp cry of pain from sufferers in the

---

[1] Austin's *Anatomy of the Pestilence.*
[2] Vincent, p. 32.   [3] Boghurst, p. 29.   [4] Vincent, p. 27.

upper stories of the shut-up houses not infrequently broke the prevailing silence, some in their frenzy rising out of their beds, and leaping about the room, others roaring and crying at the windows. At times a door would burst open and a demented man, almost naked, dash out into the streets, running about till he fell. A Plague-stricken victim, left alone and frantic in his agony, burnt himself to death in his bed.[1] None should take comfort that recovery after infection gave him protection against renewed attack and death. The Plague was inscrutable. "I have known many infected," Dr. Hodges wrote after the Plague, "who although all things succeeded well the first and second time, and each cure was perfected, yet the third seizure, upon the account of a new infection and not a relapse, hath proved fatal to them ; some this year fell the fifth, others the sixth time, being before very well recovered."[2]

Often the sick, in the frenzy born of acute pain which attended the breaking of the Plague sores, if not restrained by main force were ready to commit any violence upon those near them, whether wife, mother, or child. A sad instance occurred in a miserable house in Fleet Lane, a narrow way—still surviving though unrecognizable amid the railway arches—that ran up from the uncovered Fleet River to the Old Bailey. The man of the house had a great swelling, the breaking of which might have brought ultimate relief, when in an uncontrollable fury he rose out of his bed, in spite of his wife's efforts to restrain him, and grasping a knife savagely attacked her with it. She seized a bed-sheet to enfold the man, and thereby saved her life, though she received several stabs. Her screams of "Murder ! " brought in a neighbour, himself shut up, who burst open his own door and forced a way into the house. A few hours later the stricken sufferer was a corpse.[3]

A young girl being dead of Plague, the bearers came in the night and removed the body, and in the dim light mistaking an elderly woman in the same house for a corpse, they talked of taking her away next. The poor wretch, shivering with horror, cried out that she was not dead ;

---

[1] Vincent, p. 33.   [2] *Letter to a Person of Quality.*
[3] *The Shutting Up Infected Houses*, p. 19.

but after another sunset she was duly passed out to the night-cart.[1]

A man collapsed at Alderman Sir William Browne's door near by St. Peter Cheap Church, and there died.[2] Bethlehem Hospital's inhospitable wards, wherein madness received the rough and brutal handling of an age that knew no better treatment for the insane, sheltered growing numbers whom the insufferable horrors daily witnessed had left distraught—

> Paid to Mrs Berris housekeeper at her going to
> Bedlam [3]   .   .   .   .   .   .   11s.

and there are other like entries.

Assuredly there were many instances of willing help given by neighbour to neighbour, despite the known risk, but unfortunately few can be recalled. I gladly recover two from the most unlikely of places—from the criminal rolls. When Plague was violently raging in Cripplegate, Edward Smallie took three children out of a house in Whitecross Street wherein a death had occurred (the parent most likely) but four days before, and gave them shelter in his dwelling at Hoxton. The magistrate came, fearing further infection in the village, and ordered him to return them. This he bluntly refused to do, and he was committed to stand trial at the next sessions. It was the basis of accusation against a charitable labourer, William Francis, that he received into his house at Hackney several children brought out of a place in London heavily infected with Plague, thus endangering the health of the whole parish.[4]

In Crooked Lane a poor mother, distracted by the scenes and the suffering that she daily witnessed, murdered her child ; the same week of July there was a like case at Stepney ; two mothers destroyed their infants in Cripplegate and St. Clement Danes, two of the most heavily infected parishes, in another week. The Thames was always close at hand for the city built upon its banks. Its depths were the last refuge of some, and there is a suspicious rise in the returns of " Drowned " in the Bills of Mortality,

---

[1] Hodges, p. 130.   [2] St. Peter Westcheap Ch'wardens' Accts.
[3] Allhallows the Great Ch'wardens' Accts.
[4] *Middlesex County Records*, iii. 375.

recurring for the first time week by week when the Plague raged its worst. In July " Found dead in the streets " began to appear as an entry, but was soon dropped ; a full count could not be kept.[1]

The poor it was who gave their lives in thousands to the Plague. Looking among the names of the dead it is rare to find any of note ; but some few there were. Sir Martin Noel, a farmer of the Additional Aid and a wealthy financier engaged in large transactions, perished in London of the Plague in September, after eight days' sickness.[2] He had been M.P. for Stafford in the last Commonwealth Parliament, was knighted by King Charles two years after the Restoration, and became Alderman of Aldersgate Ward for a day, paying the heavy fine by which the City profited rather than serve the office.[3] His wife expired of grief very shortly after. Peter Llewellyn, a Clerk of the Council and Pepys's pretty constant companion at the theatre and the tavern in happier days, returning to London, died at his house in St. Martin's Lane of the Plague.[4] John Bide, who had been Alderman of Vintry Ward for four years under the Commonwealth, and a Master of the Brewers Company, died at his house at Haggerston of the pest. The Goldsmiths Company lost its Prime Warden, Mr. Charles Everard, dead in Lombard Street of the pestilence ; and Mr. Hyett, the Clerk of the Vintners Company, was one of the earliest of September's victims, the Plague having entered Vintners' Hall.[5]

The City Companies with the greatest difficulty carried out their duties. Mr. Millet, elected Upper Warden of the Pewterers Company, begged to forego service from the Court on September 5th, his house being visited with Plague. The Master, Mr. Seeling, attended the Court held on October 12th, and four days later died of Plague ; Ralph Marsh, elected his successor on October 19th, died and was buried the next night.[6] Nathaniel Whitfield, a time-expired apprentice, came to Carpenters' Hall to take up his freedom of the Company, bringing his indentures,

[1] *Bills of Mortality*, 1665.
[2] Pepys's *Diary*, Sept. 29, Oct. 8.
[3] Beaven, *Aldermen of the City of London*, ii. 87.
[4] Pepys, Nov. 20.
[5] Smyth's *Obituary*, Sept. 14, Oct. 28, Sept. 2.
[6] Welch, *Pewterers Company*, ii. 132.

and a letter from his master telling that he was shut up with Plague in his house and himself sick, and he did not know what would become of him. The Carpenters' beadle, lodged by the Hall, died of Plague, causing such fright that for the next Court only two or three persons arrived ; the records say " some of the Assistants are fearful to meet at the Hall in regard to the Plague," the audit was postponed, and fires were lighted and fumes burnt in the Hall, apartments, and passages. The books show that several Assistants fell victims to the Plague.[1] The election of master and wardens by the Saddlers Company, fixed for August, took place next January, it having been found impossible to assemble a Court meanwhile by reason of the pestilence.[2]

Roger L'Estrange, the Licenser of the Press, and the owner-editor of the only newspaper published, had the courage to stay in London, though the infection came into his family. The printing press was kept severely under restraint by the new monarchical power in England, and of the diminished body of workmen to whom it gave employment eighty fell victims to the pestilence.[3]

A true return of the numbers of the dead became increasingly difficult, as parish clerks, sextons and searchers, whose callings exposed them to especial risks, were cut down by the Plague. The Bills are necessarily short. Robert Foster, parish clerk of St. Mary Aldermary, died of Plague in August, and his wife and son a few days after—Lewis Butler, parish clerk of Allhallows Bread Street, died of Plague—John Nicholls, parish clerk of St. Mary-le-Bow, Cheapside, died, probably of Plague— Nicholas Pyne, parish clerk of St. Giles Cripplegate, died of Plague—Mr. Osbaldston, parish clerk of St. Botolph Aldersgate, died of Plague—Hurlock, the parish clerk of St. Michael Bassishaw, died of Plague—Nicholas Reader, parish clerk of West Ham, died of Plague.[4] How amid so many changes, and death the cause of all, should a proper account be kept ?

A Plague-laden ship lay out in the Thames, the

---

[1] Jupp & Pocock, *Carpenters Company*, pp. 130-1.
[2] J. W. Sherwell, *Guild of Saddlers*, pp. 105-6.
[3] L'Estrange to Lord Arlington, Oct. 19.
[4] Parish Burial Registers.

Black Eagle, afloat below Greenwich at Bugsby's Hole.
Its story is a particularly revolting one. The magistrates
had become embarrassed by their own rigorous enforce-
ment of the Conventicle Act. It had been proposed to
make a clearance of Quakers and Nonconformists who
overcrowded the gaols by sending out those under sentence
of transportation in a King's prize ship taken from the
Dutch. The Sheriffs at length found a man to their purpose
in one Fudge, nicknamed " lying Fudge." He was master
of the Black Eagle. Fifty-five Quakers were taken out of
infected Newgate on July 20th and carried down in barges
to Fudge's ship. The Quakers refused to embark, no
sailor would give a hand, and four only were put on board,
the turnkeys returning the rest to Newgate.

Later, in August, some soldiers from the Tower of
London finished the sorry business. With rope and tackle
the captives were hauled aboard by legs and arms, others
dragged, punched and kicked till the full company was
stowed away, thirty-seven men and eighteen women.
The men were confined below deck, in a space too low for
them to stand upright. The ship remained in the Thames
for seven weeks, getting no farther than Gravesend,[1]
through the sweltering months of August and September,
when the Plague ashore reached its height. It could not
be kept from a vessel close packed with human freight as
this was. George Whitehead, with the devotion and fear-
lessness borne by all Quakers in the terrible time, went on
board and conducted a meeting of the Friends.

Fudge, the master, was arrested for debt, the crew
became mutinous. At length the Black Eagle reached the
Downs, where she was still lying in January, 1666. By
October's end nineteen of the Quaker prisoners had died of
Plague in the crowded holds, four being women,[2] and many
of the sailors had perished from the contagion.[3] It was
late in the February before the Black Eagle reached
Plymouth, where the shore authorities refused permission
to any to land from " the Plague ship," [4] or to have contact

[1] W. C. Braithwaite, *The Second Period of Quakerism*, pp. 46–7.
[2] Swarthmore MSS. at Devonshire House, Bishopsgate, vol. iv., p. 121.
[3] Fox's *Journal*, ii. 91.
[4] The Plague on land is terrible ; it is yet more dreadful on the sea.
In a later Plague in the Near East than that which last visited London,
news came to Southampton of a Dutch ship cruising from port to port in

with it. The day after she left that port for the West
Indies the Black Eagle was captured by a Dutch privateer,
and the Quakers were speedily thereafter liberated in
Holland. But twenty-seven of their number—the full
half—had succumbed to the Plague on board, most of the
bodies having been buried in the water marshes below
Gravesend.

A gift of science is entire preoccupation. The Royal
Society abandoned its meetings while Plague held the
town in close grip, but wherever two or three Fellows
could foregather the problems of chemistry and mechanics
engrossed attention. Evelyn draws a thumb-nail sketch
of such a coterie who took asylum at The Durdans, Epsom
—Lord Rosebery's seat has the same site—where on
August 4th he " found Dr Wilkins, Sir William Petty,
and Mr Hooke contriving chariots, new rigging for ships,
a wheel for one to run races in (surely a prevision of the
bicycle) and other mechanical inventions ; perhaps three
such persons together were not to be found elsewhere in
Europe, for parts and ingenuity." [1] The Plague, then
killing its thousands, did not distract the philosopher's
calm.

The acknowledged toll of Plague victims taken in the
second week of August (8th to 15th) was 3,880. Fever,
spotted fever, and " Purples " added 543 deaths to these,
most, no doubt, being cases of Plague concealed or mis-
understood. Mortality in London that week reached 5,319.
The curve had climbed higher to mark an additional
1,289 deaths over the stage reached in the previous Bill.
The shut-up houses gave these results, wherein in the

the Mediterranean. She had put into Malta with her master and fourteen
sailors dead of Plague, and only twenty-three survivors. The Grand
Master of the island had her towed out to sea. She tried to enter
Tunis, but the Bey refused to admit her. She entered Naples, and was
driven out to sea again, and the Italian Officers of health placed sentries
along the coast to prevent those of her crew still surviving from landing.
Every man's hand was against them. The British sloops and men-of-war
were apprised, and directed to keep the ship out if she appeared off the
British coast (Alton and Holland, The King's Customs, p. 342). What
became of the Plague-stricken craft in the end none can tell, whether left
floating derelict, her decks strewn with the rotting corpses of men, or in her
unmanageable state sunk by a storm. Vanderdecken's ghostly ship had
no cruise comparable with this in horror.

[1] Evelyn's Diary, Aug. 4.

reeking, unwholesome atmospheres, with destitution ever attendant upon care, and often entire neglect, the calamity growing too vast to be encompassed, whole families perished. Dr. Mead, a famous physician, half a century later admitted that he could not understand how the Plague should have been more enforced than by such treatment.[1]

A curious device to appease the public fears was the posting on the walls in prominent places of a broadside printed by Peter Cole in Cornhill. It bore in big type the heading, "The Four Great Years of the Plague, viz. 1593, 1603, 1625 and 1636," and gave the figures from the Bills

FROM "LONDONS LORD HAVE MERCY ON US."
A broadside in possession of Dr. David Moses.

of Mortality, "by which its increase and decrease is plainly discerned in all those years," the largest toll being 35,417 deaths from Plague in 1625.[2] All other Plagues had, then, decreased, and that was reassuring. The sheet was rather frightening, with its grim ornamentation of skull and crossbones.[3] Cole, the printer, having survived the worst months of Plague, became distracted and hanged himself in his warehouse.[4]

[1] *Short Discourse on the Plague*, 1720, p. 34.
[2] The London Bill did not then comprise certain out-parishes.
[3] A print of this broadside is in the Pepys Collection at Magdalene College, Cambridge.   [4] Smyth's *Obituary*, Dec. 4.

There was another broadsheet which had a popular vogue, bearing the title " Londons Lord Have Mercy On Us," with a crude illustration seen overleaf, the figures from the Bills of the last seven Plagues in London, and some simple medical prescriptions.   It was repeatedly printed during the Great Plague, each reprint bringing the weekly figures up to date.   The harassed people found occupation in filling in the columns with the totals from the Bills as they were published, and many families treasured these simple but pathetic records.   In the copy I have used the mortality is penned by a contemporary hand up to the autumn of 1666.   It has some admonitory verse—

> " The *Red Crosse* still is us'd, as it hath bin,
> To shew they Christians are that are within :
> And *Lord have mercy on us* on the door,
> Puts thee in mind, to pray for them therefore.
> The *Watchman* that attends the house of sorrow,
> He may attend upon thy house to-morrow.
> Oh where's the vows we to our God have made !
> When death and sickness came with axe and spade,
> And hurl'd our Brethren up in heaps apace,
> Even forty thousand in a little space ;
> The Plague among us is not yet removed,
> Because that sin of us is still beloved.
> Each spectacle of Death and Funerall,
> Puts thee and I in mind, We must die all."

There grew up a gruesome trade.   There were " brokers " of the dead—or more correctly of their effects. Often it happened that none survived who could make claim to these.   The parish, in the absence of other claimants, seized the property left in the infected houses or rooms, and this it sold to recoup itself in part for the burden borne in paying watchmen, relieving the inmates' wants, and giving the last office of burial.   In many a City parish buildings had specially to be rented to store the quantities of such derelict possessions.[1]

The brokers, dealing in goods which it was perilous even to handle, be sure paid little for what they gained. I have seen many of their accounts.   A typical one is that of John Taylor and John Boldnesse.   At the height of the Plague in St. Bride's parish they " bought the poore peoples goods that dyed of the visitation (vitz.) for ye goods of "—then follow eleven names, with the prices paid

[1] St. Olave Silver Street Ch'wardens' Accts., and others.

against each. A Plague victim of comparatively easy circumstances was one Hunt, of Whitefriars Dock, whose chattels were judged worth £10, one-third of the sum total paid for the deal complete. Widow Horne's household treasures produced only £2 10s., one Badger's goods a poor 10s., and for others ten and fifteen shillings sufficed.[1]

The chapel wardens of the hamlet of Wapping had chargeable the orphans of several Plague victims. They held the dead men's effects, and before selling these took precaution to obtain indemnity by the inhabitants in vestry assembled.[2] The "little lumber" left in the rooms of Thomas Pritty, Clement Bynny and Mary Waller, all dead of the Plague in St. Benet Paul's Wharf, was given to the parish clerk "for his great pains taken for ye parish in the time of the contagion." [3]

In the despair occasioned, when no man's life was safe for a day and always the outlook grew darker, the people turned eagerly to the consolations of religion. They gave the last, the only hope. Locked doors and desolate altars of City churches were deplorable witnesses of forsaken duty ; but others were open, and the people remaining at liberty crowded into them for worship. The problem confronting the churches was of perplexing difficulty. Every congregation was a peril, threatening to scatter yet wider and to increase the Plague, yet to debar worship at such a time was impossible. Not infrequently the services were few, as at St. Christopher-le-Stocks (by the Mansion House) where a weekly service was held on Sunday afternoons alone, there having been a great concourse of people to the church on week-day afternoons, many of whom were known or believed to resort there from places infected.[4]

The Benchers of Lincoln's Inn locked all gates giving access to their private Chapel save one, itself jealously guarded to ensure that "none but persons of quality" be admitted.[5] At St. Dunstan-in-the-East two men were paid to watch at the church doors and keep out all persons suspected to be infected.[6]

[1] St. Bride's Ch'wardens' Accts., 1665.
[2] St. John Wapping Vestry Book, March, 1665[-6].
[3] St. Benet's Vest. Mins., vol. 1, fo. 238.
[4] Vest. Mins., July 27.
[5] W. Paley Baildon, *Records of Lincoln's Inn*, p. 46.
[6] Vest. Mins., Sept. 25.

No open church went short of worshippers. "Those heard them oft one day who were sick the next, and quickly died," Baxter has observed. Words of comfort one would expect at such a time, but human nature is a strange complex. The violence of the sermons delivered from the pulpits it is difficult to understand. Take this single excerpt—

Are not many of your gentry more debauched, more full of blasphemous oaths, more enemies to holiness, sobriety and civility, than they were before ? Assure yourselves both one and another, God will fulfil his word upon you, even utterly to root you out except you repent.

As to the common sort who have been encouraged by your example, are they not wretchedly polluted ? Nothing but swearing, cursing and drunkenness, and among them Hell is broke loose, and the very reins of Modesty and Humanity are relaxed, so that God may justly spread your carkases as dung upon the face of the Earth, and make room (by your destruction) for a more righteous and sober generation.

Now, therefore, to conclude,—You that have any tenderness left, that have not quite transformed yourselves to Beasts and Devils, you that would escape Hell, you that can with any remorse behold the dying pale-face of this Nation, stabb'd at the heart by these sins of yours, oh ! tremble at the fierce wrath of God that is gone forth against you, and abhor yourselves for all your abominations, there is yet some encouragement left for you to turn and be saved.[1]

The Rev. Thomas Vincent, preaching in Aldermanbury Church at the funeral of Abraham Janeway, frightened his listeners, let us hope to repentance, by a vision of Hell from beneath moved by the numbers of guests received into its chambers.[2]

The divines were more insistent upon the sins of London than on the good qualities of its citizens in adversity. The Plague was God's judgment. It would misrepresent to show the capital as converted to religion by the vast calamity. This is an eye-witness's description : " In one house you might hear them roaring under the pangs of death, in the next tippling, whoring and

---

[1] *A Voice to the City ; Or a Loud Cry from Heaven to London, setting before her her Sins, her Sickness, her Remedies,* 1665.

[2] *A Sermon preached at the Funeral of Mr. Abraham Janeway,* Lond. printed in 1667.

belching out blasphemies against God ; one house shut up
with a red cross and ' Lord have mercy upon us ! ' the
next open to all uncleanness and impiety, as if altogether
insensible of the vengeance of Heaven." [1]

Not all the horrors of Plague could purge humanity of
its grossness, or destroy the vice and profligacy and crime
inseparable from a large town. That is the dark side of
the picture. In the reverse, Church and Nonconformity
alike are agreed that ministrations were eagerly received.
The ever present uncertainty of life and near prospect of
death awakened in men's fears a new consciousness. [2]

In St. Paul's Cathedral, its Dean absent, prayer and
divine service were conducted three times each day
throughout the Plague months, although as August opened
but three Petty Canons, Stephen Bing, James Clifford and
Masters, and two Vicars Choral, Simpson and Morrice,
remained in London to serve the altar. Mr. Portlington,
who was to have preached the first Sunday, lay at the
point of death. The Cathedral did not fill, but there was
" a comely congregation, considering the times." [3]

The angry contempt with which the populace regarded
the emigrant clergy and the fugitive Government found
expression in many ways ; at St. Paul's service was
interrupted by religious zealots who, in what the good
Stephen Bing characterized as " the fury of monstrous
spirits," openly declared in the face of the congregation
that the calamities under which London suffered were
caused by the government in Church and State. [4] Pamph-
lets were flung about the streets that in ribald language
announced "Pulpits to let !" [5] As each week in August
the Plague grew more virulent, Nonconforming Ministers
ejected from their livings took courage openly to resume
their ministries. They resolved in their consciences that
no obedience to laws of man could justify them in neglecting
men's souls and bodies in such extremity. They went into
the forsaken pulpits to preach to the people who thronged

---

[1] Cited by Echard, *History of England*. Echard dated his preface
forty years after the Great Plague, and he wrote within the period when
there would be vivid memories of it.
[2] *Reliquiæ Baxterianæ*, pt. 3, p. 2.
[3] Bing to Dean Sancroft, Aug. 3.
[4] *Ibid*., Aug. 10.
[5] Vincent, p. 42.

about them, they visited the sick, they entered, taking relief, the shut-up houses which few others dared to enter.[1]

Truth of the Church's part in the Great Plague is not pleasant to tell.   The fault lay with the parochial clergy. Archbishop and Bishop are without blame.   Sheldon stayed at Lambeth Palace throughout the months of greatest danger.   The influence of his courage, his work, and his example was invaluable.   His constant effort to maintain spiritual provision in this time of test met with but partial success, the obstacles to be overcome being too great ;   the effort was not wanting.   Not alone did his diffuse charity preserve numbers alive who otherwise must have perished, but his affecting letters to all the Bishops throughout the wide province of Canterbury procured large contributions for the relief of London's distress.[2]

Humphrey Henchman, Bishop of London, the son of a London merchant, also set a worthy example by remaining firmly at his post.

Less can justly be said of William Sancroft, Dean of St. Paul's.   In a censorious age his absence did not escape censure, as his close friend Dr. Barwick in a letter from London to him discreetly hints—

It will be no news to tell you (for you can easily imagine it) that the mouths of a slanderous generation are wide open enough against those that are withdrawn, both of your profession and ours ;   but one of my neighbours told me (who I indeed think wishes well both to you and the Church) that it was wondered that you would go and not leave anything that they had heard of behind you for the poor neighbours.   I told him that in what cases it was lawful to go was not in the skill of everyone to determine ;   but as for your going to the Wells, you had resolved it, and by my advice, long before any Plague was heard of, and as for your charity to the poor, I knew you had given a considerable sum (to a parish that a little money would not relieve) before you went.[3]

Sancroft had left London in July to take the waters at Tunbridge Wells, and he remained at the Spa, and afterwards at Durham, not returning while the pestilence raged.

[1] *Reliquiæ Baxterianæ*, pt. 3, p. 2.
[2] Le Neve's *Lives of the Bishops since the Reformation*, p. 183.
[3] Barwick to Sancroft, Aug. 5, in Harl. MSS. 3785, fo. 19.

His whole life rebuts the charge of any want of practical charity. From time to time he sent sums of money, which Stephen Bing, the Petty Canon, acting as almoner, distributed in relief chiefly in the close and crowded streets immediately about St. Paul's, in St. Gregory, St. Augustine, and St. Faith parishes, which became heavily infected.[1]

Bishop Henchman, a plain-spoken man, declared to Lord Arlington that most of his own officers had deserted him, but that the sober clergy remained. Attendance at public worship had greatly increased, Nonconformists had not occupied vacant pulpits—that was true when he wrote —and he was busily "making collections and taking counsel as to the best distribution of the money among the poor." [2] He gave frank warning to the emigrant divines, that if they did not speedily return others would be put in their places.[3] The threat brought none back. The City incumbents as a body failed in their mission, their moral fervour was at its lowest ebb ; and little wonder. At the Great Ejectment of 1662, fifty-five of the clergy of City parishes alone surrendered their offices rather than submit in matters of conscience. These men had been among the most earnest and devout in the Church's ministry. Pluralists and placemen crowded to accept the vacant livings,[4] and they absented themselves from London with the first when Plague invaded its streets.

The courage and sacrifice of those who stayed lighten a dark story, but the admission is forced that the proportion among the clergy serving the City's one hundred and seven parishes is small, discreditably small. In the roll of honour the martyrs come first. John Pechell, curate of St. Mary Aldermanbury (it had neither rector nor vicar), died at his post, on June 21st.[5] Samuel Austen, rector of St. Mary Staining, followed.[6] Timothy Long, rector of St. Alphage London Wall, was a third ; Francis Raworth, vicar of St. Leonard Shoreditch, a fourth [7] (" ex-peste " is against their names); Dr. Randolph Harrison, rector of St.

[1] Letters from Bing to Sancroft in Harl. MSS. 3784–5.
[2] *State Papers (Domestic)*, 1665, pp. 497, 524.
[3] Bing to Sancroft, Aug. 3.
[4] See the writer's *The Great Fire of London*, pp. 307–8.
[5] Hennessy, *Novum Reportorum*, p. 299.
[6] *Lond. & Midd. Arch. Soc., New Ser.*, i. 277.
[7] Smyth's *Obituary of Persons that he knew* (Camden Society), p. 67.

Christopher-le-Stocks, a fifth.[1]   These died in the height of
the Plague in September and October.   Edward Wakeman,
rector of St. Matthew Friday Street, expired in November
of Plague.[2]   Heavy as was the toll, that is not all.

One Mandrill, lecturer at the parish church of St. Benet
Fink, died of Plague.   Mr. Bastwick, who preached to the
caged prisoners in the Poultry Compter, the Sheriff's
prison, succumbed.   The roll included Mr. Throckmorton,
curate of St. George's Southwark ; Mr. Knightley, curate
of St. Saviour's Southwark (perhaps not from Plague), and
a priest who supplied the absent rector's place at St.
Michael Bassishaw, named Phillips.   The circumstances
were peculiarly tragic of the death of the last named.
He preached at Bassishaw on Sunday, September 3rd, and
he, his wife, and their three children, all they had, were
dead of Plague by next Thursday night.[3]   That makes
eleven priests of the Established Church dead, a number
desperately high when taken from the greatly diminished
band who remained in London.   In these the Church may
find justifiable pride.   They had been faithful unto death.

Of others of high courage who survived, honourable
mention is due of Dr. Outram, rector of St. Mary Woolnoth [4] ; John Meriton, rector of St. Michael Cornhill [5] ;
Dr. Thomas Horton, who had been silenced in 1662 but
afterwards conformed ; and Peter Lane, rector of St. Benet
Paul's Wharf.[6]   Symon Patrick, the vicar of St. Paul
Covent Garden, figures elsewhere in these pages.   Richard
Pierson, curate of St. Bride's, signs every page of the
Plague burials.   William Clark, vicar of the much-suffering
parish of Stepney, stayed.   They, at least, with others
unnamed, are absolved from the reproaches of Vincent
against priests " leaving the greatest part of their flock
without food or physic, in the time of their greatest need."

Richard Edwards, rector of St. Anne and St. Agnes,
held also the living of Chislehurst, and was broad-minded
enough not to refuse the help in London of William Dyer,
the Nonconformist and Quaker sympathizer.   Edwards

[1] Smyth's *Obituary*, p. 69.   Patrick to Mrs. Gauden, Sept. 30.
[2] Smyth's *Obituary*, p. 70.
[3] Symon Patrick to Mrs. Gauden, Sept. 30.
[4] Addit. MSS. 5810, fo. 290.
[5] Dunn's *Divines*, p. 210.
[6] Vest. Mins., 1665.

can be acquitted of neglect of his City parish, for he and his minor churchwarden contracted the Plague, and both recovered ; the parish clerk died of the pestilence.[1]

The Nonconforming clergy, too, had their martyrs. Cripplegate's long outstanding roll I have already given. One Grunman, a silenced Nonconformist, was too poor to remove his family from London, and perished ; and two others who sought the country took infection with them, a Mr. Cross dying with his wife and some children as soon as they reached a hospitable refuge. Mr. Roberts, a Welsh minister, less fortunate, lay stretched upon a little straw and expired, with none to tend him.[2] In recalling some who stayed to labour in the city, the tribute goes unspoken to those others whose names have escaped notice. The fine record of Nonconformity is brightened by the example of James Janeway, who amid the horrors and sufferings of the Plague in London first felt the call to preach [3]; of one Walker, a minister serving at St. Katherine Coleman in the rector's absence [4]; of Robert Franklin, who but the year before had come to London in dire straits, having resigned his living at Westhall, Suffolk, "rather than defile my conscience by the then conformity " [5]; and of the Rev. Edward Turner, ejected from Sudbury, Suffolk, who preached at the conventicle that afterwards became, and is to-day, the Moravian Chapel in Fetter Lane,[6] John Grimes, and Edward Chester.

The Great Plague had one effect made permanent in our history, of momentous significance. We must not overlook it, for it has vastly influenced English life and thought in all subsequent generations.

The Great Plague established English Nonconformity. Till Plague visited London in 1665 and spread into many country places, the silenced ministers had worked in seclusion among their small flocks. Rarely were they

[1] W. McMurray, *A City Church Chronicle*, p. 42. Dyer's *Christ's Voice in London*, printed in 1666, consists of a couple of sermons delivered in St. Anne and St. Agnes Church, and dedicated to the parishioners.

[2] *Reliquiæ Baxterianæ*, pt. 3, p. 1.

[3] *Dict. of National Biography*.

[4] Vest. Mins. Possibly this was Dr. Anthony Walker, who for a time had held the living of St. Mary Aldermanbury (Calamy's *Nonconformist Memorial*).

[5] *Nonconformist Memorial*, iii. 291.

[6] W. G. Bell, *Fleet Street in Seven Centuries*, pp. 527–31.

able to preach under the persecution.   They found courage
in that testing time.   From their secret meetings they
went out into the public places.   Freedom openly to
preach the Gospel that these men wrested and won, when
none dared to suppress them, took such deep lodgment in
the public conscience that thereafter neither by guards of
soldiers nor the imprisonment of congregations could it be
restrained.[1]

None did nobler work than the Rev. Thomas Vincent.
Ejected for nonconformity from the City church of St.
Mary Magdalen Milk Street, he had taken service with
Mr. Doolittle at Islington in teaching young scholars, and
in the tumult of the Plague was inspired to carry spiritual
aid to the dying people.   Friends warned him of the peril.
He declared that his whole life could have no prospect of
service equal to that which offered ; and daily he went
about his self-imposed work, preaching each Sunday from
the pulpit left vacant of a parish church, one day at
St. Botolph Aldgate, another at St. Helen Bishopsgate,
another at Allhallows-the-Great.[2]   " His subjects," said
one who heard him, "were the most moving and important;
his management of them most pathetic and searching.   It
was a general inquiry through the preceding week where
he was to preach.   Multitudes followed him wherever he
went.   He visited without the least dismay every one that
sent for him, doing the best offices he could for them in
their last extremities." [3]   Vincent escaped the Plague,
though, as I have already told, it came into his household
and some died.   His book, " God's Terrible Voice in the
City," has passed through many editions, and has been the
most widely read of the religious treatise that the Great
Plague inspired.

It is unpleasant to record the sequel to such heroic
work.   It is found in the Five Mile Act passed by the
Parliament sitting at Oxford that autumn, as monstrous a
piece of persecution as ever disgraced the Statute book.
Alarmed by the revived popularity of the Nonconformists
in their old stronghold, the Church by its own ministers,

---

[1] Cf. Richard Baxter in *Reliquiæ Baxterianæ*, pt. 3, p. 2.

[2] John Blemell, rector of Allhallows-the-Great, died on New Year's
Day, 1666.   From the fact that his pulpit was occupied by a Nonconforming preacher I imagine that he, too, fled from the Plague.

[3] Rev. John Evans' intro. to *God's Terrible Voice*, ed. 1722.

and laymen in Parliament more clerical than the Church itself, sought only to sharpen the instruments that should reduce the religious life of the country to a dull and uninspired conformity. Conventicles had sprung into existence. Many of the Nonconforming preachers, embittered by their ill-usage and taking license when there was none to restrain them, reflected openly in their sermons on the sins of the Court and the selfish negligence of the well-to-do classes, not omitting to ventilate their own wrongs.

This was represented very odiously at Oxford,[1] where the faint-hearts forgathered. The Commons were so hot for persecution that only by a majority of six votes were they restrained from imposing the test upon the entire nation. The silenced ministers, who had already lost everything by refusal of the Act of Uniformity, were required to take oath that resistance on any pretence was unlawful, and that they would at no time seek an alteration in the government of Church or State. Those refusing were forbidden, under penalty of £40 and six months' imprisonment, to come within five miles' distance of any city or Parliamentary borough, or of any church wherein they had ministered. They were no longer allowed to teach the young, and thereby the last means of livelihood of the majority was denied them. The cup of their humiliation was filled. Such was the Five Mile Act, and its effect was to crowd the gaols. Permanent exclusion from the Church, the public exercise of their worship prescribed, and themselves placed under intolerable restrictions—that was the State's reward for their labours.

Not one merchant in a hundred was left in the City, where nothing but the Plague mattered. Debts could not be collected or goods sold.[2] The toll as recorded in the Bills advanced from 5,319 deaths in the second week of August to 5,568 in the third (4,237 of Plague, but Allin asserts " rather in verity 5,000, though not so many in ye bill of the Plague "[3]).

Formerly the hope of recovery might have been indulged

---

[1] Burnet's *History of His Own Times.*
[2] R. Fuller to Mrs. Play, Aug. 17.
[3] Allin, Aug. 24.

in ; but at this time infection became the almost certain
harbinger of death, and killed rapidly after seizure.[1]

Then at one stride the figures moved up to 7,496 dead in
the fourth week.　I should hesitate to attempt a description
of London in these sorrowful days, but there is a letter by
Pepys, poignant in its concentration and brevity, which
suggests enough.　He wrote to Lady Cartaret on September
4th—

I have stayed in the city till above 7,400 died in one week,
and of them above six-thousand of the Plague, and little noise
heard day or night but tolling of bells ; till I could walk
Lumber [Lombard] Street and not meet twenty persons from
one end to the other, and not above fifty upon the Exchange ;
till whole families, ten or twelve together, have been swept
away ; till my very physician, Dr. Burnett, who undertook
to secure me against the infection, having survived the month
of his own house being shut up, died himself of the Plague ;
till the nights though much lengthened, are grown too short to
conceal the burials of those that died the day before, people
being thereby constrained to borrow daylight for that service ;
lastly till I could find neither meat nor drink safe, the butcheries
being everywhere visited, my brewer's house shut up, and my
baker with his whole family dead of the Plague.　Yet, Madam,
through God's blessing, your poor servant is in a perfect state
of health.[2]

The Rev. Thomas Vincent allowed himself no freedom
from his self-denying labours.　He gives a pen-picture of
the town, flamboyant in style and therefore less convincing
than the diarist's cold and matter-of-fact recital.　His
sentences fall like a cascade—

Now death rides triumphantly on his pale horse through
our streets, and breaks into every house almost where any
inhabitants are to be found.　Now people fall as thick as
leaves from the trees in autumn, when they are shaked by
a mighty wind.　Now there is a dismal solitude in the London
streets : every day looks with the face of a Sabbath Day,
observed with greater solemnity than it used to be in the city.
Now shops are shut up, people rare and few to walk about,
insomuch that the grass begins to spring up in some places,
and a deep silence almost in every place, especially within
the walls ; no rattling coaches, no prancing horses, no calling

[1] *Loimologia*, p. 12.
[2] Pepys's *Diary*, Lord Braybrooke's ed., vol. 4.

in customers nor offering wares ; no London cries sounding in
the ears ; if any voice be heard it is the groans of dying persons
breathing forth their last, and the funeral knells of them that
are ready to be carried to their graves.

Now in some places where the people generally did stay,
not one house in a hundred but is infected ; and in many
houses half the family is swept away ; in some the whole, from
the oldest to the youngest. Few escape with the death of but
one or two ; never did so many husbands and wives die
together ; never did so many parents carry their children
with them to the grave, and go together into the same house
under earth, who had lived together in the same house upon it.
Now the nights are too short to bury the dead ; the whole day
though at so great a length, is hardly sufficient to light the dead
that fall therein into their beds.[1]

The Bill returned for this last week in August 6,103
deaths from Plague. If to that count be added the numbers
of concealed cases and the burials in the Quakers' and
Jews' cemeteries, and the many bodies hastily consigned
to the pits that did not come into the official record, it is
certain that never did the sun set over the city but in the
night and the day Plague had claimed its thousand victims
and more.

In the streets where few in health ventured to linger
might have been seen some pale ghost muffled up at the
throat, one of those who had come out of the sickness alive,
if little more. The proportion of such was not large ; the
doctors are agreed that the Plague obtained such malignancy in August and September that few who were attacked
recovered. Another man would pass dragging his legs
after him by reason of a tumour in the groin. None needed
to look far among the miserable creatures about, flushed
with fever or shivering despite the summer warmth, to
find one spotted with "the tokens" which foretold
rapidly approaching death. In the City and out-parishes
were the frequent alarms of death. Little sound was
heard save groaning, and crying, and dying.[2] Even the
funeral bells in time ceased their clatter, when none could
be spared from more pressing duties for their ringing.
Coffins being carried, or the dead roughly tied head and foot

---

[1] *God's Terrible Voice*, pp. 30, 31.
[2] John Sturgeon to Sir Robert Harley, Aug. 16 (Portland MSS.,
Hist. MSS. Comm., iii. 292).

in their shrouds and hurried away to burial, were the most common sights in all the public ways.

The madness of people seems extravagant beyond belief. They would follow bodies to the graves in groups, despite the repeated prohibitions. The devout sought the churches, undismayed by the unseen terror ready to pass from one to another, that even struck down the parson in the pulpit.[1] In the days of gravest peril the most moving preachers attracted such large followings that often they could not get near their pulpit doors for the press of people, but were forced to climb over the pews to them.[2] Many who in mortal fear attended to hear a sermon should never hear another. London, in part depopulated, suffered that month of August 20,030 deaths admitted to be from Plague. The mass of such a loss from a fell disease in what was still a small city is not easily grasped ; and its bulk was to be yet larger (26,522 dead from Plague) in September.

Along the Strand one morning when the Plague was at its height, on September 4th, might have been witnessed an astonishing spectacle. The doctor of a pest-house, clad in his College robes, there walked at the head of a procession, with a woman riding on horseback and upholding on a stick a paper flag, across which the words " Laus Deo " had been written. Following on foot were thirty persons with white staves in their hands. They were patients from the pest-house who had recovered from the Plague, poor people sent to the justices to make appeal for relief. The doctor appeared much content with the stately march, and the evidence it gave to all onlookers of his successful cures.[3] Probably none gave a second thought to the folly of it.

Incidents in the Great Plague there were that it would be best to dismiss untouched—by far best, were they not unhappily too well authenticated. Liberty is not given to the historian to chose and to reject. Nature at times reacts terribly in human beings upon whom has been thrown an intolerable strain. What war has there been in which some atrocities have not horrified those who sit safely at home, away from the peril and the nerve strain, the wrack and the noise that undo certain men ?

[1] *Loimologia*, p. 18.   *A Poem* (printed in Appendix).
[2] Vincent, p. 43.   [3] Symon Patrick to Mrs. Gauden, Sept. 8.

It is not good to be too familiar with death. It can conceivably be to no person's advantage to spread Plague.[1] Pepys has left on record what would seem incredible, that " in spite " people in London sick with Plague would out of their windows breathe into the faces of uninfected passers-by, to carry contagion to them.[2]

Then a letter I have read, not indeed from London, but from Portsmouth, which suffered the Plague visitation very severely, tells of the same class of act. Commander Thomas Middleton, of the Royal Navy, from the dockyard wrote this to Pepys : " The people are so wicked in this town, that it is reported they take their foul plasters from their sores, and in the night throw them into the windows in fresh houses." [3]

Dr. Hodges has borne witness to this " delirious pleasure " in the infected, even at the point of death, in communicating death to others, which he saw in his practice.[4] And if such evidence is not enough, there is his testimony that the most callous nurse-keepers in the shut-up houses of London, anxious only to hasten a clearance of the living that they might be left free to ransack the

[1] The most lamentable results of frenzied imagination during a Plague occurred in the fearful epidemic which devastated northern Italy in the years 1631–2. In the state of Milan above 600,000 were reported to have died ; in the city and lazarettes alone 140,000. Cremona had one-third, and Pavia and the other cities one-half of the population dead. The towns and cities of Lombardy were almost dispeopled. The Duke of Palma gave houses, cattle, and land free to bring back settlers. The people, maddened by their sufferings, got the belief that certain men had wilfully started and spread the Plague by powders and waters, and " confessions " wrung from individuals under acute torture gave some sort of semblance to the fable. A Mons. Daimont, writing to Lord Feilding from Augsburg on Feb. 10, 1632, concerning these " damnable spirits," for whom there was close search, says : " Divers have byn executed with cruel torments, having confest to have byn agents, amongst which a surgent (surgeon) that at the place of exsecution confest to have aplied the said untion upon the garments of many hundred, whose operation houlds so great antipati with man's nature that non which are touched escape except the actours which have the counterpoison. This seems a fable : your honour ought to believe it for certaine, for I have spake with divers of qualite that have bynn present at the exsecution of many of them. Ther remaine yet many imprison'd for the sayd fact, and som great ones, whos names I wil not trust the paper with." (Earl of Denbigh's MSS., *Hist. MSS. Comm.*, part 5, p. 6).

[2] *Diary*, Feb. 12, 1666.
[3] *State Papers (Domestic)*, 1665–6, p. 389.
[4] *Loimologia*, p. 10. A case cited by Hodges of the importunities of a married woman stricken by Plague is particularly horrible.

rooms of their poor contents, would secretly convey the pestilential taint from the sores of the infected to those who were in full health.[1] Murder seems of less account when death is everywhere. I do not seek to explain the perversion of mind that prompted such actions ; it is sufficient to record them, and hasten from the subject.

This Plague spared no order, age or sex. The divine was taken in the very exercise of his priestly office. Some physicians could not find assistance in their own antidotes, but died in the administration of them to others. Although the soldiery had withdrawn from the city and encamped outside, the pestilence followed them and slew them. Many persons in their old age, others in their prime, sunk under its weight. Of the women infected most died, and hardly any children escaped. It was nothing uncommon to see an inheritance pass to three or four heirs in as many days. The numbers of sextons were not sufficient to bury the dead. The church bells seemed hoarse with continual tolling, until at last the knells ceased.

In some houses carcases lay waiting for burial, and in others persons suffering their last agonies. In one room might have been heard dying groans, in another the ravings of delirium, and not far off relations and friends bewailing both their loss and the dismal prospect of their own sudden departure. Death was the sure midwife of all children, and infants passed immediately from the womb to the grave. " Who would not burst with grief," says a compassionate spectator of this misery, " to see the stock for a future generation hanging upon the breasts of a dead mother ? Or the marriage bed changed into a sepulchre, and the unhappy pair meet with death in their first embraces ? "

Some of the infected ran about staggering like drunken men, and fell and expired in the streets. Others lay half dead and comatose, never to be awakened in this life. Some lay vomiting as if they had drunk poison. Others again fell dead in the market, while they were buying necessaries for the support of life.

The burying places would not hold the dead. They were thrown into large pits dug in waste grounds, in heaps, thirty and forty together. Often it happened that those

[1] *Loimologia*, p. 8.

who attended the funerals of their friends one evening were themselves carried the next to their own long home. Still the worst was not certain, for although London was nearly drained by her funerals, the disease as yet had no relaxation. Grim as such a recital is, lest it be thought that I make use of language of exaggeration let me explain that these passages are not mine. Sentence by sentence in ordered progression, altering nothing, I have but repeated Dr. Nathaniel Hodges, who in unforced words tells this,[1] when the sights were fresh in his eyes and the sounds in his ears ; and he knew.

[1] *Loimologia*, pp. 16–19.

CHAPTER X

THE PEAK OF THE CURVE

IT was as a last desperate resort, that nothing which might possibly check the Plague's increase and give relief should be left untried, that fires were lighted in the London streets in early September. The Bill issued, made up to the fifth day of the month, showed that for the first time a week's deaths had overtopped eight thousand—in all, 8,252 dead, and of these numbers 6,988 were credited to the Plague.

All other effort had failed. There had been expectation aroused when a personage of distinction, going to France on affairs of State, learnt that some Frenchmen had discovered the anti-pestilential remedy. He made haste to send over to London some doses. By command of the absent Government the physicians were directed to test it upon patients with due caution, and this they did, expecting an uncommon success. It proved no better than the nostrums hawked by quacks about the streets; in fact, much worse, for the medicine, which was a mineral preparation, quickly brought death.[1]

It was a remedy old as the Plagues of classic Greece to light fires to destroy the infection thought to be present in the air. This practice had been resorted to at previous London visitations. There was that for it which the authorities greatly over-valued, namely precedent. In the first great Elizabethan pestilence of 1563 every house-holder in London had been ordered to lay out wood for making bonfires in the streets on three days of each week.[2] Pitch and faggots were burnt in the streets by the Lord Mayor's command in the epidemic of 1603 ;[3] and various

[1] *Loimologia*, p. 20.
[2] Lambeth Palace MSS. (Stow's *Memoranda*, Camden Society, p. 123).
[3] St. Benet Gracechurch Ch'wardens' Accts.

combustibles, having no common property save that they were strong-smelling—charcoal, "stare," pitch, "franconsense" and incense—had been ignited in earthen pans at the Plague that attended King Charles I. to the Throne.[1]

The College of Physicians had mentioned fires made in the streets and stink pots, and good fires kept in and about the visited houses, as well as the frequent discharge of guns, as means of correcting "the infectious air." [2] Hippocrates cured a Plague-laden city by setting fire to a wood encircling it. That might be (or not). Few men believed in the efficacy of fires at this day. Physicians generally were incredulous, many holding such a showy and expensive project to be more than superfluous, and actually harmful,[3] but in the fact that the recorded deaths from Plague fell by 444 in that week of September some people affected to find advantage from the fires.[4] Albemarle's approval assured observance in the out-parishes. The Court of Aldermen for the City gave their assent. There was yet this means to put to the test.

A stranger entering London would have found what might have been a city of the dead, with its funeral pyres still burning. Night and day their smoke and stench gave added foulness to so much else that was foul. After dark, the coal glowed red and flames flickered in a city wherein few people were seen. So night and day, till on the last of the three appointed days the fires were extinguished, with choking smoke and steam, by a deluge of rain.[5]

The fires were lighted on the night of September 5th, at eight o'clock, every twelve houses in a street—six a side —bearing the charge of one great blaze before the door of the middlemost inhabitant. Each parish provided the fuel and collected the cost. Coal was recommended, but so scarce was it in London that quantities of wood and faggots, and even tar barrels,[6] fed the flames. The cost of maintaining the separate fires three nights and days proved burdensome, the charges borne by the numerous small City parishes varying from 70s. to £5 6s. Watchmen

---

[1] J. Charles Cox, *Churchwardens' Accounts*, p. 317.
[2] *Certain Necessary Directions*, 1665.
[3] Hodges, p. 19.
[4] Addit. MSS. 4182, fo. 43.
[5] Austin's *Anatomy of the Pestilence*. Hodges, p. 20.
[6] St. Margaret New Fish Street Ch'wardens' Accts.

gave attention to keep the fires burning. No traffic stirred, and rarely a passer-by was seen. The Lord Mayor's Proclamation forbade during the time all concourses of people and the use of vehicles in the obstructed streets, and enjoined that in narrow places particular care be taken against the danger of igniting the overhanging timber houses.[1] Where dwellings had been made dry as chips by the heat of summer, and so many opportunities offered for lodgment of sparks, there was actual peril of stifling the Plague in the destruction of London by fire.

From every pulpit the stricken city's appeal went up to Heaven ; the clergy exhorted the people " to be forward in so hopeful a means, if God shall please to grant His blessing thereupon."

Pepys, back in London for a few anxious days to pack up more of his goods, saw from the Navy Office windows in Seething Lane the fires burning in the street, and going by water to Westminster to consult the Duke of Albemarle, he noticed all the way fires on each side of the Thames.[2] They were placed and kept fed with fuel in every street within the walled City, in the Liberties, and in Westminster,[3] one before each group of twelve houses. It was, as most had foreseen, of no avail. Dr. Hodges, who held from the first that good could not result, declares that as the fires burnt the most fatal night of all the visitation occurred, in which, with lowered vitality by the suffocating heat or the wet condition of the air that immediately followed, more than four thousand victims of the Plague perished [4]—the numbers seem exaggerated.

Nothing was wanting in the picture of the town's desolation when, refreshed by the rain, the grass grew up between the cobble stones the length of Whitehall Court. None save a few soldiers keeping guard occupied the deserted Palace of Whitehall, wherein had been so much of the gaiety of life that distinguished King Charles II.'s

[1] *Mayoral Proclamation*, Sept. 2 (Brit. Museum, Pressmark 21. 4. 5. No. 35).

[2] *Diary*, Sept. 6.

[3] Rugge's " Diurnal," Sept. 5. Rugge asserts that the fires were lighted by order of the King in Council, but no such order is contained in the Privy Council papers, nor does the Mayoral Proclamation mention it.

[4] *Loimologia*, p. 20.

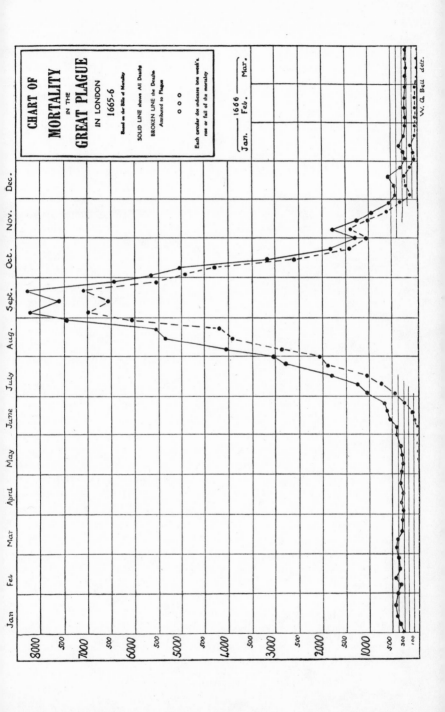

CHART OF
MORTALITY
IN THE
GREAT PLAGUE
IN LONDON
1665-6

Based on the Bills of Mortality

SOLID LINE shows All Deaths

BROKEN LINE the Deaths
Attributed to Plague

o o o

Each circular dot indicates one week's
rise or fall of the mortality

——— 1666 ———
Jan.   Feb.   Mar.

W. G. Bell   delt.

Court. Silence brooded in its empty chambers. The Royal Palace but reflected the state of the City. No boats plied upon the Thames ; none but poor wretches were seen in the streets.[1] John Evelyn, still sorely troubled by the care of sick prisoners of the wars in increasing numbers left on his hands, stayed on alone at Sayes Court, Deptford, in this perilous time " trusting in the providence and goodness of God." He made one of his rare visits to London on September 7th. Approaching by the Old Kent Road, he found the streets on the Thames' south bank and through the length of the City to St. James's, " a dismal passage, and dangerous to see so many coffins exposed in the streets, now thin of people. The shops shut up, and all in mournful silence, not knowing whose turn might be next." [2]

The Rev. Symon Patrick, the courageous vicar of St. Paul Covent Garden, had after a brief country visit returned in July to London and the care of his Plague-stricken parish. Friends now urged him to seek safety in flight. He wrote in reply—

What am I better than another ? Somebody must stay here ; and is it fit that I should set such a value upon myself as my going away and leaving another will signify ? For it will, in effect, be to say that I am too good to be lost, but it is no matter if another be. Truly I do not consider myself so considerable to the world. I must let reason prevail and stay with my charge, which I take hitherto to be my duty, whatever come. I cannot tell what good we do their souls, though I preach to those who are well, and write to those who are ill (I mean print little papers for them, which are yet too big to send by the post) ; but I am sure while I stay here I shall do good to their bodies, and perhaps save some from perishing ; which I look upon as a considerable end of my continuing. I will not grow bold, and confident by being safe so long, nor would I grow timerous, as such ease as you require I doubt will make me.[3]

In his daily vigilance he went into the infected houses, distributing charitable relief. He was in constant peril of contagion by receiving persons coming out of them. The autumn wind chilled him when standing at the graveside, burying corpses at night, " a thing I have often found

---

[1] Pepys, Sept. 20. [2] Evelyn's *Diary*, Sept. 7.
[3] Patrick to Mrs. Gauden, Sept. 8.

prejudicial (he wrote) but there is nobody else to do it
now." He thought that none of his neighbours was so
burdened as himself, but with undaunted fortitude worked
on. Early in September his brother became very ill,
vomiting forty or fifty times. His servant's face swelled ;
he had himself a pain in the leg that gave sleepless nights,
and made him suspect Plague, " which was now come to
its height, there dying ten thousand in one week." [1]

That was London's pitiful state in September. The
month brought news that in other circumstances would
have aroused the capital to patriotic enthusiasm. Lord
Sandwich, in command of an English fleet, had attacked
the Dutch ships in the harbour of Bergen. He did not
wait before committing this breach of neutrality for communication of the consent secretly given by the Danish
King, and being fired on by the shore forts was compelled
to beat an ignominious retreat ; but later, when the Dutch
ships sailed, he picked up at sea twenty-one prizes. Pepys
hastened with the intelligence to the Exchange, through
heavily infected streets, " the Plague being all thereabouts." He was surprised to find so good an attendance,
the rumour having brought out about two hundred people
to the Exchange, " but not a man or merchant of any
fashion, but plain men all."

The carrier of glad tidings found himself much sought
after, and his news highly welcome ; but he was wary.

" Lord ! to see how I did endeavour all I could to talk
with as few as I could . . . that to be sure we do converse
and meet with people that have the Plague upon them."
The victory in the second place, the finding that his money
and plate and all else in London were safe in the first place,
raised great content in Pepys, but could not drive out of
mind the deadly reality of the horrors surrounding him—

My meeting dead corpses of the Plague, carried to be buried
close to me at noonday through the City in Fenchurch Street.
To see a person sick of the sores carried close by me by
Gracechurch in a hackney coach. My finding the Angel Tavern
at the lower end of Tower Hill, shut up ; and more than that,
the alehouse at the Tower Stairs ; and more than that, the
person was then dying of the Plague when I was last there,

---

[1] *Autobiography of Symon Patrick.* Letters to Mrs. Gauden in Addit.
MSS. 5,810.

a little while ago at night, to write a short letter there, and I overheard the mistress of the house sadly saying to her husband somebody was very ill, but did not think it was of the Plague. To hear that poor Payne, my waiter, hath buried a child, and is dying himself. To hear that a labourer I sent but the other day to Dagenhams, to know how they did there, is dead of the Plague; and that one of my water-men, that carried me daily, fell sick as soon as he had landed me on Friday morning last, when I had been all night upon the water, and I believe he did get his infection that day at Brainford [Brentford] and is now dead of the Plague. To hear that Mr. Sidney Montagu is sick of a desperate fever at my Lady Cartaret's at Scott's Hall. To hear that Mr. Lewes hath another daughter sick. And, lastly, that both my servants, W. Hewer and Tom Edwards, have lost their fathers, both in St. Sepulchre's parish, of the Plague this week, do put me into great apprehensions of melancholy, and with good reason. But I put off my thoughts of sadness as much as I can, and the rather to keep my wife in good heart and family also.[1]

To every citizen of London there came daily some similar experiences and tale of loss. The Rev. Anselm Harford stayed to labour in the capital, lodging in the Dean's rents in the badly infected area about St. Paul's, and there saw every member of the household swept away by the Plague.[2] Bing, writing to Sancroft, admitted that he had "outrun the bank"—the money left with hin for distribution—in extending the Dean's charity to meet the many calls that were made upon it.

In that week when the fires burnt in the streets the recorded mortality fell to 7,690, a drop of 562 on the full Bill, and of the total 6,544 were returned as Plague—a decrease in the Plague cases, as already said, of 444. Perhaps the heavy rainfall, washing the streets and ditches after such long drought, and a few cool days accompanying it, were factors in bringing this about. It was human nature to give some credit to the efficacy of the fires. It should be of interest to recall the parishes that made the greatest contributions to the toll. Into such small areas is the City within the wall parochially divided, that the largest mortality therein was that at St. Ann Blackfriars, and there only sixty-four.

[1] *Diary*, Sept. 14.
[2] Harford to Dean Sancroft, Dec. 9.

MORTALITY IN THE WEEK SEPT. 5 TO 12.

City Liberties.	Total number of deaths.	Attributed to Plague.
St. Andrew Holborn [1] . .	255	235
St. Botolph Aldgate . .	584	570
St. Sepulchre . . .	284	206
St. Giles Cripplegate . .	504	401
St. Botolph Bishopsgate .	354	298
Southwark.		
St. Saviour Southwark . .	419	394
St. Olave Southwark . .	478	307
West.		
St. Margaret Westminster .	349	331
St. Martin-in-the-Fields .	277	214
East.		
St. Mary Whitechapel . .	428	400
Stepney Parish . . .	742	685
St. Leonard Shoreditch .	235	210

The worst of the Plague had already passed in St. Giles-in-the-Fields, in St. Martin-in-the-Fields, and some other western parishes that earliest received infection, and at Cripplegate, otherwise in the chart the peak of the curve would have had to be raised yet higher.

I have given but few figures, realizing their inadequacy, but notice here that while St. Botolph Aldgate, returning 584 deaths, credits all but fourteen of these to the devastating Plague, St. Giles Cripplegate, with less mortality, returns 103 deaths from causes other than Plague. Stepney parish, with the highest death roll of all that week of September, namely 742, gives 57 only as not from Plague. Yet the parish clerk of St. Olave Southwark, a waterside parish with a poor population, heavily infected, has the temerity to represent that of a roll of less than five hundred, 171 deaths—a proportion of over one-third— were from other accustomed diseases ! St. Olave's average weekly mortality till the Plague came had been sixteen. The dishonesty of the Bills could not be more flagrantly illustrated.

[1] St. Andrew Holborn and St. Sepulchre's are parishes part within the City Liberties and part within Middlesex.

That week in which the fires burnt gave the first decrease that the figures had shown since the Plague began. The town was deeply stirred thereby. The fall was but small, yet it meant everything to the living survivors who had seen the populace by tens of thousands committed to the grave and the pits. They had waited with growing despair for that first sign of relief—waited through all those weeks and months when epidemic Plague had been piling up an ever-increasing tale of dead back to distant days of May, when first it came into the Bills. An awful toll, that 6,544 dead from Plague in a single week, almost a thousand a day—yet the Plague was itself dying! Eager hopes were entertained that the next Bill would indicate a greater decline in the mortality.[1] Every one was heartened, though within the City wall residents learnt that among them there had been actual increase.

The summer's heat was spent. A noticeable coolness in the air following the rain, and coincident with the advance of autumn, served to raise expectations still higher.[2]

Next week eager hopes were turned to black dismay when again the Plague leapt up, and in the seven days, September 12th to 19th, the recorded mortality in the Bills reached the ghastly figure of 8,297. Of these, 7,165 deaths were accredited to the pestilence in a capital that flight and death had depopulated by one-third. The spectre of imminent death stared each man nakedly in the face. Never before throughout the visitation had the Plague been so fierce and violent. Hardly a person attacked now escaped with life. The patients quickly were afflicted with a raging madness. Where at other times they might have been expected to linger for four or five days, they now lived not forty-eight hours. The doctors were amazed. The Plague had taken the masses of its victims from the close courts and alleys. Now it dominated the open streets, and those few of the better classes left in London, more careful of their conditions of living amidst the danger, bore their share in the common calamity.[3] Mr. Edward Morton, the London Coroner, died on September 9th[4];

[1] Pepys, Sept. 14.
[2] Ibid., Sept. 20.
[3] Tillison to Sancroft, Sept. 14.
[4] St. Mary Aldermary Burial Register. Smyth (*Obituary*) enters his death under date the 20th.

George Dalton, the Lord Mayor's Remembrancer, perished in St. Mary Axe a fortnight later, having had Plague among his family ;[1] against both names is written " ex-peste."

The Plague that had spared its victims on their first taking infection, now after their recovery attacked again and ruthlessly destroyed.[2] For days together the deaths were so many that burial on the same day could not always be secured.[3] The dead-cart rumbled by ; it could receive no more. The streets and fields presented some fearful sights to any wayfarer who chanced to pass. Corpses lay piled in heaps above ground, lightly covered and often naked, for some hours together before either time could be found for their removal or place to bury them in,[4] and the dreadful spectacle decently hidden under earth.

The figures given fell far short of the truth—at least, that each man knew well. Albemarle told Count Cominges, the French Ambassador, that the deaths were 14,000, without including the many Quakers who were buried " in their gardens," and of whom no official count was made.[5] Dr. Hodges roughly computed the deaths that week in September to have been more than 12,000.[6]

None can tell actually how many died that week, and none will ever know. No hand could keep the tally. The spotted corpses lay about in streets and in the houses, the visible evidence of the dread calamity that now had overspread all London, to be committed directly to their rough burial without return made to the overworked parish clerks, without notification of any kind—these in hundreds daily.

The weather had been for a few days broken, the skies overcast, the air chilled after the rain—conditions which, suddenly oncoming, the physicians noticed brought about the most violent manifestations of Plague[7] ; and now

[1] Smyth's *Obituary*, Sept. 25.
[2] Hodges' *Letter to a Person of Quality*.
[3] Austin's *Anatomy of the Pestilence*.
[4] Tillison to Dean Sancroft, Sept. 14.
[5] Bibliothèque Nationale MSS. Fr. 15,889, " Relation de l'Angleterre en l'annee 1666," by Count Cominges. The Quakers were laid in their burial ground by Bunhill Fields (see p. 182, *ante*) and as it bore no gravestones or any indication of those who slept below, it may well have retained the appearance of a garden, which it bears to-day.
[6] *Loimologia*, p. 19.
[7] Boghurst, p. 24.

again the sun flared, and overhead was the hopelessness of the same unchanging blue sky.

" The biggest Bill yet," says Pepys, " which is very grievous to us all." The Plague was universal. It had overspread everywhere that London spread out. In all the wide area included in the Bills of Mortality, all the 113 separate parishes returning in the City and Liberties, in Westminster and the out-parishes stretching away to Islington, Knightsbridge, Stepney, and Newington—in all were but four parishes that gave nothing to the Plague toll. And these were four of the smallest City parishes, Allhallows Honey Lane, St. Benet Fink, St. Benet Sherehog, and St. John the Evangelist Walbrook, wherein few people had stayed once the alarm had instigated flight.

The Plague attained its supreme height. The worst, although London could not then know it, had passed. The five weeks' Bill of Mortality, from August 22nd to September 26th, was fated to show a record of 38,195 human lives swept away, of which 32,332 were attributed to Plague [1]— not then the true numbers, but as many of them as the authorities could count. " Multitudes ! multitudes ! in the valley of the shadow of death," said Vincent, " thronging daily into eternity. The churchyards are now stuffed so full with dead corpses that they are in many places swelled two or three feet higher than they were before, and new ground is broken up to bury the dead." [2]

The loss was in fearful proportion, yet in dark days the people would not deny themselves hope. Human reasoning in the distress of a vast calamity is an unaccountable thing. The clapper had fallen out of the Great Bell of Westminster. The news went round the town, and the populace recalled that the same thing had happened when the last severe Plague was about to end. It was a sign. Others spoke of daws returning in greater numbers to the Palace and Abbey of Westminster, a hopeful portent, for

[1] It has been commonly asserted that the Plague was more fatal to women than to men. The reverse seems to have been the case. It is fair to assume, as vital statistics have shown since they have been carefully kept, that females were in a small excess in the population, though not in the birth rate, and taking the figures of the Bills of Mortality, in these five worst weeks of the Great Plague in London the larger proportion of females over males (19,017 males, 19,178 females) among those who perished is but one-third of one per cent.

[2] *God's Terrible Voice*, p. 34.

the departure of birds by popular tradition was a fore-runner of Plague.[1] At such poor straws the desperate people clutched.

Not in the months of its growth and decline, or the return of any individual week, but in the accumulated mass of its victims in those five weeks of its full fruition, we have the measure of the immensity of the Great Plague in London. The population after the flight into the country can little have exceeded 350,000. The real story of the Plague is contained in those weeks, wherein at the peak four and twenty men and women perished in a day—and had we the true numbers, probably thirty—when one alone had died in times of normal health. Long as the epidemic lingered, it could not have lasted had the mortality always been on the same level. The Plague would have taken all.

The Great Plague was, perhaps, inevitable in that fated year 1665 in the conditions prepared for its rise and pro-gress, yet should not have occurred. The traditional belief of its origin, to which Defoe has largely contributed, is that it was brought to England in a parcel of infected goods from Holland. Dr. Hodges says the Plague came by this means from Smyrna to Holland, and thence passed into England,[2] and no doubt he reflects the opinion of his own time, which could account for Plague in no other way save than by contact.

The belief is not to be dismissed as impossible. East Coast shipping ports, which handled most of the trade with the Continent, had for generations received persistent infection. Yarmouth had epidemic Plague in 1664, before London (as had Portsmouth) and there is significance in that fact. But no actual evidence is forthcoming that this last Great Plague in England came as a foreign immigrant to our shores. That explanation is not necessary.

Were that the fact, there should have been some definite result by contact, some date at which a healthy community received infection. There is no such date. There had been Plague in Holland in 1663, and it raged its worst at Amster-dam in 1664, before war shut out Dutch trade from England. No epidemic Plague desolated England in either year. None can tell when the Plague began ; we

[1] Patrick to Mrs. Gauden, Sept. 30.   [2] *Letter to a Person of Quality.*

know only how it swelled in summer into the vast mass of
disease that justified the name—the Great Plague. The
bulk of medical opinion of King Charles II.'s time, so far
as it had expression, seems to have been that infection
originating by contact remained in the air, and entered by
pores of the skin. The Plague made the air foul. Boghurst,
the apothecary, disputed this theory, believing the Plague
to be of local origin, and that the virus was harboured in
the soil. Long after the Restoration era medical science
groped in blind bewilderment.

In this twentieth century, after Plague has for ages
afflicted Asia and Europe, destroying untold millions of the
human race, we know at last the source of Plague, thanks
chiefly to the labours of the Indian Plague Research
Commission. Plague is an animal disease, passing from
animal to animal, with the capacity to spread to man.
It is a disease of rats. The communicating agents are the
fleas of infected rats, the germ, *B. pestis*, the cause of all
the trouble, being conveyed by the infected flea direct from
rat to man by innoculation by flea-bites through the skin.

It was only in 1894 that the bacillus of Plague was discovered during the Hong Kong epidemic by the Japanese
doctor Kitasato. Not until some years later was the con-
nection between rat fleas and Plague ascertained. The
bacillus is a rod-like structure, short in proportion to
girth, and where elongated is sometimes contracted in the
middle. Each bacillus repeatedly elongates and divides
across, thus increasing the total number at a rapid rate.
Always in places which harbour infected rats there is the
latent possibility of Plague spreading to man. The rat
flea, in this country most commonly the *Ceratophyllus
fasciatus*, readily feeds upon man when hungry and the
natural host is not available. The flea leaves the Plague-
killed host when the dead rat is cold. Risk of infection
of man consequently may be regarded as likely to be proportional to the extent to which house or workplace is
infested by Plague-infected fleas.

There is a curious fact in natural history, in the migrations and characteristics of rodents, that has bearing upon
the Plague in England. The English rat, itself a migrant
from the East, the ancestral home of Plague, was for
centuries the black rat (*Mus rattus*), and this variety was

prevalent in the towns in the Great Plague. It was not till the early eighteenth century that the brown rat (*Mus decumanus*)—the miscalled Norwegian rat—began to invade England, brought by the shipping. Large and powerful, and when driven by hunger almost without fear, the brown rat soon almost entirely replaced its smaller and weaker rival in this country, a result usually credited to its fierceness and cannibalism, though changed environment and social habits among the English people probably had much to do with it. The habitats of the two rodents widely differ. The brown rat in towns is found chiefly in sewers, docks, slaughter-houses, granaries, and like places which provide it most readily with food. In the country it lives in burrows in the hedgerows and in ditches and ricks. It is a shy animal and avoids man, but rarely taking up abode in human habitations. The black rat, the original English rat, now rarely found in this country but still the most common rat in India, there lives and breeds in the houses and huts of the natives, in close proximity to man.

With the knowledge of the source and origin of Plague, wrested after long and as it had seemed for generations hopeless inquiry, we can survey the Great Plague in London better equipped than were the doctors of the Restoration, to whom nothing of this was known. By popular intuition, dogs were regarded with suspicion as carriers of infection and were destroyed by thousands, and cats largely shared the same suspicion and fate. No attention appears to have been paid to rats. The Plague Orders say nothing, unless, indeed, they be comprised within the phrase, " dogs, cats and other vermin." Medical writers of the day, floundering wildly, have no mention of the rat. No campaign of rat extermination during Plague was attempted. The rat seems to have been regarded as little harmful, though destructive and a never welcome guest in the house. Truly it may be said of the Restoration citizens that they entertained the Devil unawares.

Yet the classical ages seem to have had some glimmering of the truth. The figure of Apollo Smintheus, the sender of Plague, is represented with his foot upon a rat.[1]

[1] In Biblical literature, 1st Samuel, ch. 6, is a reference that is very curious in the light of knowledge so recently gained. The Philistines having defeated the Israelites in battle, they carried off the Ark of the

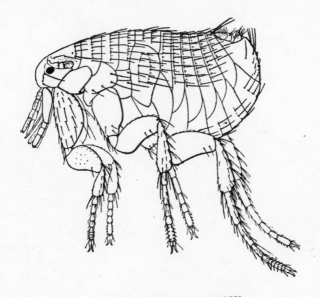

RAT FLEA, XONOPSYLLA CHEOPIS
A carrier of Plague
Magnified 36 times

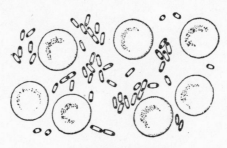

THE BACILLUS OF PLAGUE
Magnified 1,500 times
*The bacilli of Plague occur in the fluid part (plasma) of
the blood, and not in the corpuscles, which under the
microscope appear as flat circular globulæ*

*Illustrations by permission of the Trustees of the
British Museum*

The English black rat by choice lived with man. Now, as we look back over two and a half centuries to the Great Plague, much that was then puzzling beyond human understanding is made plain. The rat had his liberty, not greatly disturbed. London's timber-built houses, with boarded floors of cellars or ground storeys almost or actually touching the undisturbed earth, and lath and plaster walls easily penetrated for runs, invited his presence. The uncollected garbage left about in dwellings and streets, and laystalls heaped high with refuse on the outskirts of the habitable quarters, providing food, the cesspools and open sewers and ditches, gave all the rats' needs—and food the more plentifully because in Plague time other natural scavengers were destroyed. There, unheeded, was the originating cause of all the terrible suffering and mortality of which these pages have borne witness.

Plague is sometimes described as a dirt disease, which is not accurate; but it is, as Colonel Glen Liston, I.M.S., an original member of the Indian Plague Research Commission, has declared in a happy phrase, "a disease of primitive civilizations." [1] In Bombay the brown sewer rat is now displacing the black house rat in the new and more Europeanized parts of the city, while the black rat remains supreme in the still Easternized suburbs. Had those who lived through London's Great Plague thought it worthy of mention, probably we should have learnt of mortality amongst rats. Curiously, various writers mention birds falling to the ground dead, killed by " the infected air " (this is illustrated in the broadside picture reproduced facing p. 104, *ante*), but not the rat.

Covenant to their city of Ashdod, where thereafter pestilence broke out. " And he smote the men of the city, both small and great, and they had emerods [buboes] in their secret parts." The afflicted Philistines consulted their priests and diviners, who advised that the Ark should be returned to Canaan, and not empty. " 4. Then said they, What shall be the trespass offering which we shall return to him ? They answered, Five golden emerods, and five golden mice, according to the number of the lords of the Philistines : for one plague was on you all, and on your lords. 5. Wherefore ye shall make images of your emerods, and images of your mice that mar the land ; and ye shall give glory unto the God of Israel ; peradventure he will lighten his hand from off you." The Indian *Bhagavata Parana* warns men to leave their houses when rats die, for plague is at hand.

[1] Milroy Lectures on Plague, reported in *British Medical Journal*, 1924, May 24, 31, and June 7. These lectures are particularly valuable as a survey of the most recent knowledge acquired of the Plague.

Infection thus having come about, the course of the disease may be followed.[1] In bubonic Plague infection from man to man—infection by actual contact—rarely happens, and it was bubonic Plague that desolated London in 1665. The masses of the poor, sharing a measure of Eastern fatalism, were careless in going among Plague sufferers. But some observations by medical writers of exceptional cases, entirely beyond their understanding, do indicate a certain amount of pneumonic Plague, and pneumonic Plague is highly infectious. The bacillus is ejected in expectoration, and possibly also in the droplets by coughing. The rare pneumonic Plague, however, may be disregarded for our purpose.

In the conditions prepared for the spread of bubonic Plague is found sufficient to account for London's Bills of Mortality. In old Cairo, once a notorious Plague centre, as many as 33,000 persons have perished in a single visitation within the past century, but since Western ideas of sanitation and house cleanliness have been enforced in the city it has not known epidemic Plague, though outbursts still occur in neglected villages of Egypt ; and Stuart London, in squalid, overcrowded quarters where the poor herded together, was not unlike old Cairo. Rat infested, filthy and unventilated, the locked houses in which families were shut up grew necessarily only filthier as the days progressed. Fleas left the dead, the fouled bedding, the fouler floors and refuse and dirt and dust lying about to find nourishment from the living, who unwittingly acted as distributors. Each dwelling became a focus for the accumulation and dissemination of poison, and clothing and goods taken away, always dangerous harbourage, were agents for carrying the sources of infection afar.

Why look abroad for the origin of the Great Plague ? The Plague was seated in London, and for generations and for centuries past had been seated in London. Only habit of mind and long immunity from Plague have pre-

[1] The conclusions of the Indian Plague Research Commission are fully verified by the inquiry carried out in Upper Egypt in 1911–13 by Dr. G. F. Petrie, of the Lister Institute, and Major Ronald Todd, R.A.M.C., assisted by Dr. Riad Skander and Dr. Fouad Hilmy. Their *Report on Plague Investigations in Egypt*, issued by the Government Press, Cairo, in 1923 (delayed by the war) contains some striking evidence of immunity obtained in old quarters of Plague infection when rats have been destroyed and elementary hygiene enforced among the native population.

vented us from realizing that till the middle seventeenth century London and the Plague-smitten East had much in common. The influences that worked to create out of endemic Plague, apparently of a mild type, the violent outbursts with great loss of life of which the Bills of Mortality bear repeated testimony, we still do not grasp. There was need of certain conditions favourable to epidemic before it should spring up with violence as if from the ground.

Plague was not absent. Every inducement prevailed for concealment. I have shown in these pages how false is the record that the Bills of Mortality give of the Great Plague of 1665. No reason exists for belief that the earlier Bills were more truthful. Why should they have been? But some truth will out, "even in an affidavit," as a distinguished Judge once remarked, or in an official print; and a truth these Bills tell—not the whole truth—is that out of the long series of sixty-three years from 1603 to 1665, in not more than four years was London immune from Plague mortality, and doubtfully so in those. The many references to Plague, often of a violent type, in documents of the reigns of Elizabeth and Henry VIII. carry the story of continuous Plague in London back much farther.

There were sequences of years when the manifestation of Plague was kept down; epidemics rising in recurrent waves. It was so in England, and so on the Continent. The conditions of bad housing, bad sanitation, bad water, stinking open ditches and sewers, and laystalls heaped with rotting refuse in the immediate vicinity of dwellings, that had so well served the growth of Plague at the most violent epidemics remained to work the same ill after those epidemics had passed.

The climatic circumstances most favourable to violent outbursts of Plague remain obscure. The spring and summer of the Great Plague were dry. The summer of the previous worst visitation, that of 1625, is recorded as having been remarkably wet; earlier few persons troubled to chronicle weather. We are confronted there, as elsewhere, by flagrant contradictions. It would be rash to dogmatize. Many hot summers had passed without a grievous epidemic.

But the conditions of 1665 were more than abnormal; they were phenomenal. There was drought over a long period of months that was almost unprecedented. Frost held the land in its grip from December till the end of March, and but a sprinkling of showers came in April. Thereafter was no rain in London to relieve the parched land till the fall in August, followed by the downpour on September 7th that put out the fires lighted in the streets. In an earlier chapter I have recalled how meadows on the town's outskirts that were accustomed to bear forty loads of hay produced that season only four loads, and the land was burnt hard like the highways. Dr. Bayard's testimony of the general calm and serenity of the weather, with so little wind that rarely a church vane was stirred, I have already cited. There was little cloud. It has been assumed from these conditions that the summer was exceptionally hot throughout; there are Pepys's occasional references: "the hottest day (June 7th) that ever I felt in my life"; "it was (July 16th) most extraordinary hot that ever I knew." I cannot tell. It is curious that contemporary writers nowhere indicate a summer of exceptionally violent heat, and Dr. Hodges among them asserts that the whole summer was refreshed with moderate breezes.[1] The fact well established is that four months passed in the hot period of the year without rain.

It was an old, undrained City of London, of timber-built houses, the picture of which I have but dimly suggested in these pages, and have described with more detail in another work.[2] Its outskirts, where the poor crowded together in close alleys as none to-day would herd cattle, were habitually pestiferous. Given this place, the evils of the dirty streets and the dwellings, the last rat-infested and sealed tight till the atmosphere within reeked, the fœtid open sewers and ditches and pollution to be found on every hand, in summer months under the prolonged drought, when the town was unwashed by rains and left to increasing neglect, and can it be wondered that Plague, constant in London for centuries past, should that year have raged with violence probably unknown since the Black Death in the Middle Ages ?

The Great Fire of the following year destroyed five-sixths of the City of London within the wall, and a considerable area outside the wall. It burnt nothing of St. Giles-in-the-Fields, nothing of St. Martin's, St. Margaret

[1] *Loimologia*, p. 13.   [2] *The Great Fire of London in* 1666.

Westminster and the Strand parishes in which the Plague first developed ; the flames never reached the parish of Stepney, which had the largest mortality of all in the Great Plague, nor Cripplegate. These were untouched by fire, and for the time, at any rate, were left unimproved. Yet we know that epidemic Plague never thereafter occurred in London—or, indeed, once it had died down, in England. There seems an obvious weakness in the argument, popularly expressed in the epigram that the Fire of London burnt out the Plague. It made but a partial clearance of the ancient, insanitary, dirty town. Only in the flame-swept area was that promptly replaced by something better.

Epidemic Plague disappeared not alone from England, but within fifteen years of the Great Plague in London it disappeared from Europe, till a partial revival in the next century, of which the terrible visitation of Marseilles in 1720–2 was the chief explosion. The shadow of Plague had been over England for many centuries, as darkness over Earth during eclipse, and at length the shadow moved away.

Some cause for the withdrawal of the pestilence there must have been which we do not grasp, but which I suspect lies in the better conditions that slowly raised the masses of our poor out of the thraldom of " primitive civilizations." It looks, too, to be more than mere coincidence that the disappearance of Plague in Europe in the seventeenth and early eighteenth centuries was in the main, in point of time, coincident with the arrival of the brown sewer rat and the disappearance of the black house rat.[1] None the less, I hold that the events of 1666 and 1665 cannot be dis-associated. The Fire, with all its fearful destruction, was providential. The Fire did save London from further Plague. It is popular belief that infection ended with the year of the Great Plague, but it did not. In the following year—that of the Great Fire—the deaths from Plague in London numbered no fewer than 1,780, and these figures,[2] taken from the printed Bills of Mortality, no doubt under-state the mortality from the pest. Plague continued *in London,* it is true on the smallest scale, until so late as the year 1679. In that interval of fourteen years the burnt

[1] Colonel Glen Liston, M.D., *The Milroy Lectures on Plague.*
[2] See footnote on p. 321, *post.*

area of the City had been rebuilt with better houses of brick, and its most noxious alleys swept away.

That alone was not enough to account for the subsequent immunity from epidemic Plague. We grope in the dark for any explanation that satisfies. But what was more important than the flames for its health, London City after the Fire had for the first time an established central sanitary authority, it had drainage of a kind, its streets were by comparison well kept, and the pure water supply from the New River was extended to a larger area. London City set an example of building better, of better regulations, from which the outskirts as time went on by needs profited. Both in the Parliamentary and civic legislation after the Fire [1] may be detected great strides towards what became in a later day the science of sanitation. Before, in what curiously seems to have been a cycle of weather, another such phenomenal year as 1665 came round, London had made big advances towards reform, and was no longer the same pestilential city that for generations had invited violent outbursts of Plague.

The Great Plague was not in itself an isolated occurrence, but linked back with the long series of epidemics that through the centuries had occurred in England. " The poore's Plague " was not a misnomer. There is significance in the circumstances in which it fell upon England to which it would be idle to shut one's eyes ; in its frightful ravages among the poorest people, themselves poorly nourished, and herded together in the most squalid conditions of life that can be conceived ; and in the very large measure of immunity of those living in better conditions and with more care for elementary hygiene, themselves better nourished, which it is my endeavour to bring out in these pages.

The Great Plague had no foreign source. It was of home birth. It rose out of the same evil conditions that had made Plague endemic in London through successive ages, and with London improved the Plague has been unknown for two and a half centuries past, and with much probability has gone from our midst for ever. An isolated case or two even now occasionally reported at the shipping ports only gives reminder of the need for watchfulness.

[1] See the writer's *The Great Fire of London in* 1666, wherein these matters are dealt with in detail.

CHAPTER XI

JOHN ALLIN'S LETTERS [1]

THE Great Plague inspired no great literature from those who lived through the time. It has left no outstanding prose, no verse that had merit to survive. Dryden, who in his "Annus Mirabilis" of the following year devoted ninety-six quatrains to describing the Fire of London, has no more than six lines to give to the Plague—

> "O let it be enough what Thou hast done,
>> When spotted death ran arm'd through every street,
> With poison'd darts, which not the good could shun,
>> The speedy could out-fly, or valient meet.
>
> The living few, and frequent funerals then,
>> Proclam'd Thy wrath on this forsaken place."

He put London behind him before the pestilence became severe, and passed the months with Lord Berkshire, his father-in-law, at Charlton, Wilts. The calamity and suffering might have moved John Milton to colossal imagery, but Milton stayed throughout the visitation at Chalfont St. Giles, and is mute. The playwrights, so numerous for the Restoration stage, have no concern with it. George Wither was a poet whose muse flowered early, and he lived to bury his fame beneath a mass of indifferent and tiresome rhyme. It was his tragic experience to be in London throughout the Plague of 1625, of which he gave a long account in "Britain's Remembrancer," and in old age also that of 1665. The last entered his house, and during the sorrowful months he prepared in prose his "Meditations upon the Lord's Prayer," containing one short hymn.

[1] Much of this chapter I have previously published in *Unknown London*, in a paper entitled "Letters from London during the Great Plague."

Austin's "Anatomy of the Pestilence," though insufferable as verse, has value as a picture of the time.

Even the theological and medical books that sprang from the Great Plague are few in number and poor in quality, although the latter give proof of some patient observation. The Plague's morbid horror seems to have numbed those activities which find an outlet in the written word. Few letters from London recording experiences were sent abroad, judging by the paucity of such that survive, but there is a single packet of them to which I have eagerly turned, for one man at least wrote frequently, and his letters reveal the thoughts and emotions of an intelligent observer cooped up in London while the town lay sick and dying of the Great Plague. John Allin, minister of the Gospel and student of medicine, wrote these letters. All of present concern are addressed from his lodging at Southwark, in the river-side parish of St. Olave by London Bridge. In the summer's heat that parish became heavily infected, and the Plague, seated in every poor street about him, took from it 2,785 lives.

Allin had mentioned in his letters—they deal with many topics—that severe winter frost, starting about Christmas, 1664, had continued almost without a break till April. Then on the 27th April he gives casually in a sentence, as if of little consequence, the first indication of all that was to follow: "I heard yesterday there are 2 houses shut up in Drury Lane for the sickness."

He wrote much; the letters number in all one hundred and ninety, extending over ten years. Something impelled him to write, and frequently, while the Plague was raging at its worst, probably a longing for human intercourse and sympathy, even though he knew—for people are brutally frank at such times—that his letters were received with dread lest infection should be carried by the written sheet. That fear was so general that Dr. Barwick, at Angel Court, in the Plague's early days made his apologies to Dean Sancroft. "I hope you will pardon me for writing to you, which I would not have done but that I have not been in any house that I could so much as suspect of contagion since I saw you." [1]

John Allin was a parson, ministering at the quaint old

[1] Barwick to Sancroft, July 9.

Cinque Port town of Rye, till in 1662 the Conformity
Act put the problem of conscience nakedly before him.
Could he serve God and do also what man required ?
He decided that he could not, and his name has honourable
place on the roll of those many hundreds of devout and
brave Churchmen who went out into the wilderness at the
Great Ejectment. His journeyings brought him to London,
and there he took up the study of medicine. He addressed
his letters to two friends he had left behind at Rye, Philip
Fryth, a solicitor, and Samuel Jeake, the historian of the
Cinque Ports ; and they reveal a somewhat surprising
personality—surprising that is to ourselves at this day,
though no doubt common enough two and a half centuries
ago. For John Allin, priest of the Anglican Church, a man
of education, probably trained at college—a lettered man—
held strange beliefs. At night he looked out upon the
stars, intent on divining from them the decisions of Fate ;
he dabbled in alchemy, with something of the unbeaten
faith of the old searchers after the secret of the transmu-
tation of metals ; and his astrology and alchemy mixed
together in a curious pottage with those medical studies by
which he hoped to give benefit to suffering humanity.

He writes no connected narrative of the Plague. In
certain letters, especially when the infection came nearest
to his home, the absorbing topic occupied all his thoughts,
but at times the mention is most casual, merely the
number of deaths in London for the week recorded in the
published Bills of Mortality. The reader is often annoyed
at omissions of what might be told ; but there is enough to
hold attention, remembering that these are authentic
letters by a man who lived through the Plague. Defoe's
" Journal " did not deceive its author, who gave it to the
world as fiction. Allin is fact. The original letters are
preserved in a private collection.[1]

" MAY 26.—Ye sicknesse is said to encrease in Holland,
as it also doth here ; ye bill mentioned 3 last weeke, and
14 this weeke, but its rather beleived to bee treble the
number. At ye upper end of the towne persons high and
low are very fearfull of it, and many removed ; one house

---

[1] Many of these letters have been printed in *Archæologia*, vol. 37,
pp. 1–22, in a paper by Mr. Durrant Cooper.

if not two, are lately shut up in Chancery Lane, and one about Cripplegate."

"JULY 26.—I confesse the sicknes doth encrease and spread, though none very neere mee yet ; thanks bee to God. I heare ye generall bill this weeke wilbee about 2,500, and the particular of ye Plague neere 2,000, but I know not the certainety till the morning. I thanke God I goe about my business without any slavish fears of it ; yet my body too apt for such a disease, which proves very mortal where it comes : many whole familyes of 7, 8, 9, 10, 18 in a family totally swept away. I thinke there is no fleeing from God's hand, and truely this sicknes so highly pestilential in some places speakes it to be more of a judgment than any thing else, and true repentance is the best antidote, and pardon of sin the best cordiall."

"AUG. 5.—Through mercy I am yet well, and the sicknes not very neere me, though in the parish. This last weakes bill of mortality, through mercy, did not increase like the former weekes, beeing but 229 in all increase, and ye sicknes in some places then decreased ; through this wee feare (as wee then also did) an higher increase."

Allin had but casually mentioned, in a letter of July 1st, that the increasing Bill made many fly from town. Apparently his friends had suggested that he should himself seek safety, for on August 11th he wrote to Fryth—

" I shall not thinke myselfe safer there [at Rye] then here, whilest my call is to stay here ; yet I am troubled at the approach of the sicknesse neerer every weeke, and at a new burying place which they have made neere us, and with some piece of indiscretion used in not shutting up, but rather makeing greate funeralls for such as dye of the distemper ; which yet I thinke God will not putt an end to till sin be left and suppressed more then it is : but God seemes to pursue a designe which doubtlesse Hee will efect before Hee hath done. 4,030 in all ; 2,817 Plague. 142 in all, 64 Plague, in our parish."

"AUG. 18.—Through mercy I am hitherto well, and all our next neighbours, but the sickness increaseth : 5,319 this weekes bill in generall, and 3,880 in the bill of the Plague, of which disease Mr Symond Porter, Mr Miller's

brother-in-law, dyed last Tuesday : I am afrayd to write
to Mr Miller of it, least hee should bee afrayd of my letter ;
but pray let him know of his brother's death."

"Aug. 24.—I am, through mercy, yet well in the
middest of death, and that, too, approaching neerer and
neerer ; not many doores off, and the pitt open dayly
within view of my chamber window. The Lord fitt me and
all of us for our last end ! The sicknes yet increaseth :
this bill is 249 more than ye last, viz—of all diseases,
5,568 ; of the Plague, 4,237 : but rather in verity 5,000,
though not so many in the bill of ye Plague. Here are
many who weare amulets made of the poison of the toad,
which, if there be no infection, workes nothing, but upon
any infection invadeing from time to time, raise a blister,
which a plaister heales, and so they are well : perhaps I
may by ye next get the true preparation of it, and send
you. I saw this day some *prima materia* in our streetes."

Let us not, presuming on the fuller knowledge that now
is common property, call the honest man " quack." He
promised the true preparation. The ex-Vicar of Rye, a
scoffer, as above made plain, at simple folk who placed
their faith in the toad amulet, was himself an earnest
seeker after the elixir that should conquer the Plague.
On the essential merit of cleanliness, sanitation, fresh air,
purity in food and water he, in common with medical men
of his age, had small enlightenment. His mind confused
with alchemy and astrology, he believed the cure would be
found in an extract from the little plant growth best known
as *Coelifolium*. That it fell from heaven in the night was
once the popular belief. The plant, which is indicated
so often in these letters by the general term " Materia
Prima," was the *Tremella Nostock* (Linn.). It appears in
the summer after rain on sandy and parched soils, is
agitated with a tremulous motion when fresh, and is so
frail that gatherers must be out before sunrise. The
warmth of the sun's rays quickly leaves it dry and
shrivelled, and nothing remains except some membranes
brownish in colour. Distilled, the plant yields a dark
fœtid oil, which was believed by alchemists to contain the
universal spirit that, when extracted pure, would be the
solvent of gold so long sought after.

Allin employed a man to gather the plant for him, and moreover pestered his correspondents for supplies. In the true spirit of the scientific inquirer, he asked also for " the moss that grows on dead men's skulls and bones," instancing a certain churchyard in Winchilsea where it might be found. That churchyard can have been kept with little reverence.

He resumes the story of a stricken London in his weekly letters, when the Plague was climbing rapidly to the peak of its curve—

" Aug. 29.—Ye sicknes here is very much increased : this weeke I feere ye bill wilbee neere double the former ; and truely I know not how to think it should lessen, when as the greatest thing done to stoppe it, viz. takeing ye phanatickes out of their owne houses, and sometimes caught meeting and carrying them to infected prisons, of which wee have none free, wilbee found in the end to heighten it, though its said one major of ye soldjers hath threatned by that meanes quickly to drive that plague away :—remember that there wilbee little *prima materia* found after a rainy, but most in a dry night after a rainy day or weather, the wind south-west."

Four days later he made a harrowing report. A thousand dying daily did not give the measure of this calamity.

" Sept. 2.—Ye sicknesse encreased very much last bill, viz. 1,928 increase ; ye totall, 7,496 ; of ye Plague, 6,102. Since that bill I have not particularly heard anything whither still increasing or not, but feare, by the dolefull and almost universall and continuall ringing and tolling of bells, it doth increase. I am sure it approacheth to mee, I meane my concernment : for it hath pleased God to take from mee the best friend I have in ye world, and one wherein my children [he had three] stood as much concerned as in myself with reference to what they should have expected from the relations of my wife : it is my brother, Peter Smith, who was abroad on Lord's day last, in the morning ; towards evening a little ill, then tooke something to sweate, which that night brought forth a stiffness under his eare, where he had a swelling that could not be brought to rise and breake, but choacked him ; he dyed Thursday night last. I blesse God I am well ; was not with my brother after wee see what it would be, as little else upon any distemper here can be expected : it is a greate mercy now counted to dye of another disease."

"Sept. 7 (to Fryth).—The increasing sickenes hath now drawne very nigh mee, and God knoweth whither I may write ony more or no : it is at the next doore on both hands of mee, and under the same roofe . . . but I have no place of retireing, neither in the city nor country ; none in heaven nor earth to go unto but God onely ; the Lord lodge mee in the bosom of his love, and then I shall be safe whatever betides. . . . There is in my deske a little booke new written, I intituled it ' Liber Veritatis ' : it is the true use of the elixer magnum for physicke, profitt, or delight, given by a true master of the arte to a friend, whence I transcribed it. I would have Mr Jeake to have that, and you to transcribe it ; but bee sure to keepe it both of you as a secrett. If I live I hope to have some *materia prima* from you ; if you could inclose a little dust in a letter I shall be glad to receive it. This weekes bill is increased 756 : the whole is 8,252 ; of the Pl. 6,978 ; and in our parish 439, about 120 increase in our parish, and it is truly still increasing. These 3 dayes hath bene sea cole fires made in the streetes about every 12th doore, but that will not do ye work of stopping God's hand : nothing but repentance will do that, of which no signe yett, but oppressions, etc. yet increasing."

The spectre was at his door, a Fury beating down men ; thousands were dying around him ; and his one consuming care was lest his book revealing the true use of the Elixer of Life should be lost to humanity ! Such are the contradictions of over-wrought minds. The letter discloses the first presentiment of death coming to him that the correspondence gives. Hitherto he had been buoyed with hope. Allin was a devout man. This Plague was God's judgment, and as now he saw it stalking onwards to what seemed the goal of a universal death, it was almost blasphemy to expect that he should escape. Still the mortality rose. Too sick at heart to dwell upon it, Allin found distraction by telling the gossip of a medical tragedy consequent upon a Plague post-mortem, the accuracy of which I have had reason to doubt ; by reporting those ministers of his cloth who had perished in faithful discharge of their duties ; and by writing for his friends' information a long and intricate description of Plague symptoms and the progress of the malady. The observation is at times shrewd, but the deductions therefrom are muddled, and Allin is more profitable reading when apart from his pseudo-learned manner.

" SEPT. 20 (to Jeake).—It is some refreshing to mee to thinke you are yet willing to receive a line from mee. It was an afliction to mee that I knew not to whom I might send a letter with acceptance (except Mr. Fryth only). I am afrayd that some of my friends there are this day too much afrayd where no feare need to bee, for were my pen infectious my hand would soone let it drop . . . Gracious Mr Cobb (one whom God sometimes imployed in the worke of comforteing and supporting others in this darke and gloomy day of the Lord) who yet fell by this sicknes, and last Lord's day entered into his father's bosome . . . Clouds are gathering thicker and thicker, and I thinke veryly the day of the Lord will yet prove more blacke. Whether the Lord will make good that word spoken by a child here concerning the increase of ye Plague, till 18,317 dye in a weeke (which all indeavours are used to conceale) though still goeth on in reality to increase it : and that word too of a yeares time of greate and sad persecution spoken by ye same mouth after death had once cooled it in this visitation, time will show."

Did ever the brain of Edgar Allan Poe yield anything quite so gruesome as this story, badly phrased as it is, of the child, struck down by the Plague, yet after death prophesying by word of mouth another year of great and sad persecution before the Plague should be lifted from the city ? The dead lips had spoken this. Distraught minds give willing belief to the most incredible things. The water cistern of Mr Secretary Morice's house had in a night changed its contents into blood. It was a sign, the red portending yet greater evil as many interpreted.

The next letter, after two days' interval, contains the figures of the culminating week of all the months of the

Plague, 8,297 dead in London, and of the Plague, 7,165 ; and on the 27th September Allin writes—

" I am where ye Lord hath hitherto, amidst 100 dyeing weekely, preserved me, and yet through mercy am in health, the Lord be praysed. The Lord hath decreased this weekes bill 1,837 ; there dyeing this week but 6,400 ; Pl. 5,533 ; and in our parish there was 50 decreased ; but it is still very hot near me : I fear it will increase with you. If you send any *prima materia* in a glasse I pray cover it with paper, and double seale it that nothing of it bee seene."

These later letters had added interest for his correspondents, for Plague, spreading through Kent, had in August broken out at Rye. Safe himself, Allin imparted to Fryth the precautionary measure to which, in part at least, he attributed his own immunity. " Freind, get a piece of angell gold, if you can of Eliz. coine (that is ye best) which is phylosophicall gold, and keepe it allways in your mouth when you walke out or any sicke persons come to you : you will find strange effects of it for good in freedome of breathing, &c, as I have done ; if you lye with it in your mouth without your teeth, as I doe, viz. in one side betweene your cheke and gumms, and so turning it sometimes on one side, sometimes on ye other." There it was, surviving in 1665 and Allin shared it—that old, persistent, ineradicable belief in the efficacy of gold to cure all human ills, if only it could be obtained really pure ! Thereafter the references to the Plague become shorter and more casual.

" OCT. 7.—The sicknes is now very hot at the next house to us one way, but hath beene neerer, though none of our family hath been ill at all yet, through mercy. What with some imployment on Lord's dayes, at other dayes sometimes, in this scarcity of ministers (many being dead, though more fled) I am streightened in time."

" OCT. 19.—Wee have had this weeke, God be praysed ! a very mercifull abatement of ye bill of mortality, viz. 1,849 decreased this weeke ; ye whole bill being 3,219, whereof ye Plague 2,665, but yet it doth creepe into fresh houses still. Ye Lord fitt me for what his good will and pleasure is."

The long trial had told upon Allin. The Plague mortality in general declined with winter's approach, but an increase in Southwark reawakened alarm. "My head aketh at ye present," he writes in his first letter of November. Again he repeats the prayer, "Ye Lord fitt me for what hee intends towards me."

He looked at night into the vault of the heavens to read his fate. The portents boded ill. It is pitiable to realize from the next letter that the man who had lived so long in daily and intimate contact with the facts of life and death, preaching the Gospel of Christ in public and taking the consolations of religion to many a sorrowing family, in extreme peril himself, at the end of his trial found no peace, but must needs worry his wracked nerves with vain imaginings about the malign influences of the stars. His mind remained simple. Allin clearly was a fatalist, but with faith undiminished—the faith he held while thousands were dying around him, and weary months passed in his unfruitful researches, in the efficacy of the little plant *Coelofolium* if only its secret should be vouchsafed to him.

"Nov. 8.—Through mercy I am yet very well, though never without dayly feares, and truly not without cause, if I either consider the will of myne owne hearte, or yet if there bee any truth in ye language of the starrs ; for Mars is comeing to my ascendant in my nativity, which was there lord of the eighth ; and in my revolution for this yeare Lord of the Asc. ; and in the course of progresse and regradation hee will continue within the compasse of my ascendant in my nativity till 1st July next. I had thought to send Mr Jeakes the scheames, with ye directions and perfections for this yeare for his judgment, but I have not time now . . . Send as much *prima materia* as you can get gathered in Scorpio, by itself; if in Virgo, by itself."

"Nov. 16.—You will see a little decrease in this' bill, but truly God seemes now in divers familys to visit us the 2nd time, after they have beene all well 6 or 8 weekes ; and fresh houses in divers places, besides some whole familys, swept away that have returned to ye City allready."

A new trouble threatened in his harassed life, that he must again be a wanderer upon the earth. On Nov. 23

Allin tells Fryth: "The cold pincheth soarely here, seeing that coales are above 40s. per chaldron; but ere long I must bee forced (if I live so long) to a country climate; I thinke it must be Sussex ward, but where I doe not know. If you can learne some place for me, somewhat about five miles from you, with honest people, you may doe well to let mee know of it, where I may practise physicke." The iniquitous Five Mile Act, but a few weeks since passed by the Oxford Parliament, forbade that he, an ejected parson, should reside within five miles of Rye, in which town he had ministered, or live in London, or within the distance named of any corporate town.

"Dec. 7.—Some fresh houses in divers parishes are still visited besides more of them that come to towne, or are imployed in the aireing of other's houses."

"Dec. 12.—Divers persons and familyes at their returne home to the City have mett with what they fled from, in so much that I feare and heare this weekes bill hath an increase. I heere there is a new blazing starr seene last weeke, 4 or 5 nights together, about north-east."

"Dec. 14.—Ye sicknes is now agayne increaseing, as by ye totalls doth appeare, but yet is increased in the sickness 33, and wholly in the City; divers fresh houses since the returne of fresh persons hither visited and swept [of all inhabitants]."

"Dec. 26.—The totall of the generall bill this yeare is, of all diseases, 97,306, whereof the Plague, 68,596. The sicknesse, wee feare, is still increasing this weeke agayne."

Allin survived the Great Plague certainly for some years, for his letters date to 1674. He failed to obtain a license to practise medicine, his scruples forbidding a denial of the Covenant that was required of him. He practised unlicensed, for a time at Woolwich, where again in 1666 he had Plague for neighbour in the streets. Then, the world having "gone very hard" with him, he came back to London, living at Moorfields, and there the exhaustive researches of the late Mr. Durrant Cooper (*Archæologia*, vol. 37) which have been my authority for the facts of his life, lose trace and touch. John Allin was not the type of man, suffering injustice, to thrive in such times, and his chief memorial is these letters from London concerning the Plague.

CHAPTER XII

DECLINE OF THE PLAGUE

THE fall of the Plague was more rapid than had been its rise. The virus seemed to have exhausted its strength in those terrible weeks of August-September, in each of which the admitted loss from Plague in London had exceeded six thousand lives, and for thirty days on end the actual loss undoubtedly had been over a thousand each day. From the 7,165 Plague deaths returned in the week Sept. 12th to 19th, when the mortality reached the peak of its curve, the figures fell in the next seven days to 5,533; a week after were down to 4,929; and in the succeeding week to 4,327.

Then in the Bill from October 10th to 17th, completing the fourth week after the worst of the Plague was experienced, there was a great drop to 2,665 fatal cases. The next Bill showed 1,421 cases. In five weeks the deaths had become fewer than one-fifth of those that made September's tragic record. The check certainly was not due to want of subjects to act upon, despite the summer's death roll. Its malignity, Dr. Hodges said of the Plague, began to relax, insomuch that few died, and those chiefly such as were ill-managed.

"Blessed be God! being the first considerable decrease we have had," Pepys wrote in his Diary of the first of these diminishing Bills. He notes regularly the continuing "good news" as the returns of epidemic Plague fell. But no confidence had yet revived after the shock that had brought the town to despair, no relief was given from distressing sights that had become all too familiar. The Plague had shifted towards the eastern skirts of London, and there persisted. Still the night-cart went its round. The cry of the bearers, "Bring out your dead!" came nearer and louder as the loaded cart approached and stayed by one or another of the shadowed houses—a dreadful variant of the musical street cries that had enlivened London in happier days. On thousands of doors the red cross of Plague flamed for all to see. Others displayed a white cross, welcomed as a sign of modified quarantine after deadly infection had left the dwelling.

Abandoned shops and houses in utter neglect, the occupants being either dead or fled, the decay of trade, the few people in health astir, and tufts of grass, refreshed by the rains, springing up amidst the pavements [1]—all these appearances in what had been a busy and populous capital emphasized the desolation. On shuttered dwellings and closed windows the town's grime accumulated. A wheeled vehicle, rarely passing, awakened echoes in the silent streets as it rattled over the cobble stones. The paralysis of effort was apparent by a hundred signs.

London, when cool days succeeded the autumnal heat, was the same stricken town, looking yet worse than when the Plague enlarged from the accumulated mass of misery, the evidences of which steadily multiplied. In the weeks when the peak had been passed people with Plague sores still upon them swarmed out of the houses to beg. It should have been a first duty for the city's health to relieve and remove them. Not infrequently sores broke out after recovery.[2] Evelyn, coming to London after a month's absence and having occasion to alight from his coach at several places, was environed with multitudes of poor pestiferous creatures, begging alms. " The shops universally shut up, a dreadful prospect ! " [3] Pepys noted the same sight : " Melancholy to see so many poor sick people in the streets full of sores " ; and passing with Captain Cocke in his coach upon London Bridge, he watched at its Southwark approach people sitting sick and with plasters about them in the street, making mute appeal to the whole man's charity. " A sad place through the Plague."

In the highway at Woolwich, where still his wife stayed, he overtook two women crying, who were carrying a man's coffin between them, " I suppose the husband of one of them, which, methinks, is a sad thing." [4]

---

[1] Vincent, p. 31.   [2] Boghurst.   [3] Evelyn's *Diary*, Oct. 11.
[4] Pepys's *Diary*, Oct. 16, Nov. 14, Oct. 29.

Harrowing stories of the Plague were upon every man's lips—

Oct. 3 [Tuesday].   This night I hear that two of our water-men that used to carry our letters, and were well on Saturday last, one is dead and the other dying, sick of the Plague; the Plague, though decreasing elsewhere, yet being greater about the Tower and thereabouts.

Oct. 7.   Talking with him (a constable) in the highway, came close by the bearers with a dead corpse of the Plague; but Lord ! to see what custom is, that I am come almost to think nothing of it.

Oct. 16.   Upon the Exchange, which is very empty, God knows ! and but mean people there.   I walked to the Tower; but Lord ! how empty the streets are ; and so many sad stories overheard as I walk, everybody talking of this dead, and that man sick, and so many in this place, and so many in that.   And they tell me that in Westminster there is never a physician and but one apothecary left, all being dead : but that there are great hopes of a great decrease this week ; God send it !   To the Steelyard, which place, however, is now shut up of the Plague ; but I was there, and we now make no bones of it.[1]

Long before the Plague had climbed to its peak the western out-parishes in which infection first appeared had seen its towering shadow move away.   The sound in health had paid their toll, if there be truth in Diemer-broeck's testimony that Plague left the rotten bodies and took the sound.[2]   In the dreadful week of Sept. 12th to 19th the deaths in St. Giles-in-the-Fields attributed to Plague had fallen to 125, little more than one-third of a week's Bill in July ; in St. Andrew Holborn they were 270, a considerable fall from the record of 380 of August's most calamitous week ; in St. Martin-in-the-Fields a week later were down to 171, after having been as high as 287.   They are the figures of the Bills.

The Plague crept steadfastly from west to east, and with two extended arms, as of pincers, enclosed the City in its grip ; first passing north by Holborn, engulfing Clerken-well, and outside the City wall to Cripplegate, Bishopsgate, and Aldgate.   A little later it overspread Southwark across the river and the City parishes.   The old row of

[1] Pepys's *Diary*.
[2] *Tractatus de Peste*, 2nd ed., Amsterdam, 1665.

butchers' houses and shops in Aldgate stands to-day, leaning in picturesque age, a typical relic of London of the time of the Great Plague. Already the built town massed thickly about and beyond Houndsditch into Spitalfields and Whitechapel, as crowded, insanitary and unwholesome as were the outskirts elsewhere, and a sparse line of houses extending outwards marked the great highways into Essex. It is curious how persistently East London has maintained its character. John Stow wrote in Queen Elizabeth's last years in hot indignation at the encroachments upon the fair open country.

Without the [Aldgate] Bars both sides of the street be pestered with cottages and alleys, even up to Whitechapel Church and almost half a mile beyond it, into the common field : all of which ought to be open and free for all men.

His wrath rises at the desecration—

But this common field, I say, being sometime the beauty of this city on that part, is so encroached upon by building of filthy cottages, and with other purprestures, enclosures and laystalls (notwithstanding all proclamations and Acts of Parliament to the contrary) that in some cases it scarce remaineth a sufficient highway for the meeting of carriages and droves of cattle, much less is there any fair, pleasant or wholesome way for people to walk on foot, which is no small blemish to so famous a city, to have so unsavoury and unseemly an entry or passage thereunto.[1]

This, then, was East London of Elizabeth ; it was more populous, with more filthy cottages, more " purprestures," yet more unsavoury under King Charles II. The crowding into these skirts of the town of large additional numbers of the poorer classes, ready victims of the Plague, had made it so. In the shambles of Aldgate much of the meat of London's supply was killed. It is ghastly to know that at the Newgate Shambles within the City wall and at this extra-mural market, about the slaughter houses the Plague was deeply seated. When the Great Plague had passed, a woman, the widow Harborough, figures as the parish sexton of St. Mary's Whitechapel, and she was directed to dig all graves above a yard deep, and not to lay one corpse upon another [2]—an indication of the shallow

[1] Stow's *Surveigh of London*, 1598.
[2] Vestry Minutes, 1665[-6], Mar. 7.

burials that in the haste had been customary. There had
been complaints when the Plague was at its height that
in some of the gorged burial-places bodies were piled even
to the level of the ground, poisoning the whole neighbourhood.[1] Whitechapel in its worst week in September had
given 540 Plague victims to the toll.

East London, apart from one or two smaller parishes
that made contact with the City boundaries—Shoreditch,
Whitechapel, and St. Katherine by the Tower—was
Stepney, which spread far out to Blackwall. It had the
largest mortality, 8,598 dead, of any single parish in the
Great Plague. Stepney had returned but a solitary case
in June and 170 during the whole month of July. The
Plague was late in arriving east ; but having become deeply
seated there amidst the dirt-infested habitations of the
poor, the mortality rose rapidly in August to 1,698, and in
September showed a startling upleap. The weekly burials
in Stepney's large parish in normal times had been about
thirty.

Plague Deaths in Stepney in September.

(From the Bills of Mortality.)

Week ending Sept.	5	.	.	.	666
,, ,, ,,	12	.	.	.	685
,, ,, ,,	19	.	.	.	686
,, ,, ,,	26	.	.	.	579
,, ,, Oct.	3	.	.	.	631

Stepney Church stood in the country, aloof from the
road into Essex, as it is to-day, surrounded by its capacious
churchyard, and the little High Street twisting by. A
mound in that " God's acre " still has the tradition that
it was first heaped high by Plague burials in a pit. When
the place could take no more, a burial ground was opened
on the north side of the Mile End Road.[2] In the hamlet
around the church a labouring population made their
homes in tenements and weather-boarded cottages, but
the greater accumulation, and the greater death roll, was
about Ratcliffe Highway and by the waterside, where a

[1] *Newes*, Aug. 29.
[2] Its site is shown in a plan by Sir Christopher Wren printed in Lyson's
Environs of London, iii. 477.

fringe of poor dwellings ended in fields, and more especially
in the densely populated slum areas that elbowed the town.
There, as in the western out-parishes, the darkest Plague
spots are found. The weavers of Spitalfields gave many
victims to the Plague. An epitaph summed up a simple
life-story—

> Here lies the body of Daniel Saul,
> Spittle-fields weaver, and that's all.[1]

It told all there was to tell of so many toiling lives of the
poor. The nurse-keeper's aid, seldom welcomed, was not
always available. A man and his wife at Spitalfields, in
needy circumstances, had Plague in their house, and the
man being first seized, was so near death that his wife fully
expected she must deliver up the corpse that night when
the cry of the bearers, " Bring out your dead ! " was
heard in the dark street. He mended before the hour
arrived, and recovered. The wife was herself seized
immediately afterwards, and the husband assisted in like
manner till she made the same unexpected recovery.
They lived to become wealthy.[2]

Stepney's chief concern was with the sea. Often, when
glancing down the terrible pages of the burial register, my
eye caught the word " Mariner "—these perished in
hundreds. Ashore while the dwindling trade laid idle
many ships, they spent their last leave in the Plague-
infested alleys. Lord Clarendon emphasized the difficulty
in obtaining seamen for the Royal Navy in the following
year, Stepney and the places adjacent where they mostly
resided having been almost depopulated. No record bears
out Defoe's assertion that Stepney employed in all one-
hundred and sixteen sextons, gravediggers, and bearers,
but deaths in these callings must almost of necessity have
been high. In East London a large mortality continued
into the winter months when elsewhere the Plague was
itself dying.

The most surprising experience of mortality in any area
was, perhaps, that of Clerkenwell, a scattered parish, not
thickly populated save about the highway, where poor

---

[1] So given in *The Spectator*, No. 518, but the stone in Stepney churchyard is no longer to be found.

[2] Oldmixon (*History of London*, i. 522), to whom the experience was
told forty years after the Great Plague.

tenements sheltered many industrial workers. The infection, travelling west to east, struck Clerkenwell early and stayed long. I give from the Bills, by way of contrast, the

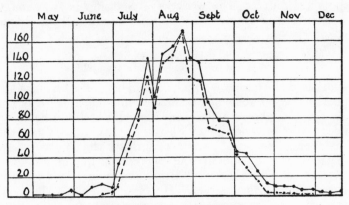

THE PLAGUE IN CLERKENWELL.
Based on the Bills of Mortality, 1665.
Solid line, all deaths.
Broken line, deaths attributed to Plague.

normal weeks' returns and the deaths from Plague alone when at its height—

PARISH OF ST. JAMES CLERKENWELL.

1665—All Burials.				1665—Deaths from Plague alone.			
Week ending Feb. 7	.	5		Week ending Aug. 8	.	136	
,,	,,	,, 14	.	6	,,	,,	,, 15	.	145
,,	,,	,, 21	.	5	,,	,,	,, 22	.	172
,,	,,	,, 28	.	10	,,	,,	,, 29	.	122
,,	,,	Mar. 8	.	8	,,	,,	Sept. 5	.	119

These are startling figures. In the month of February Clerkenwell buried twenty-six of its parishioners; in four weeks of August 575 were dead of the Plague alone. The Plague was fed, as at Cripplegate, by constant accessions of poor people to Clerkenwell's squalid slums, largely journeymen, servants, labourers, and others thrown out of employment when the well-to-do fled and trade decayed. Otherwise the parish population could not have borne the full Bill for 1665. It was the out-parishes and Liberties that heaped up the huge figures. If it be charged against

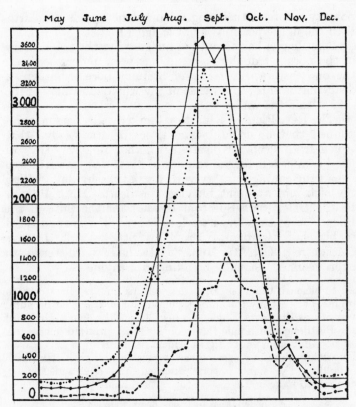

CHART ILLUSTRATING THE GREAT EXCESS OF MORTALITY IN THE
LIBERTIES AND OUT-PARISHES OVER THAT WITHIN THE CITY WALLS.

Based on the Bills of Mortality, 1665.

Solid line shows all deaths in the Liberties.
Dotted line, all deaths in the Out-parishes.
Broken line, all deaths within City Walls.

me that in this book I have concentrated almost wholly
upon the outer ring of London, in seeming neglect of the
City within the wall—the central area that in history and
wealth, in public buildings and in civic pride, is London—
the reason should be apparent; the Plague was not there.
Dr. Sydenham has said that two-thirds of the citizens left,
and if thereby he means those within the City wall, counting
together the merchants and tradesmen who sought the
country and those thousands of the workless poor whose

T

poverty enforced their migration to the town's outskirts, then the figure possibly is not exaggerated.

The Plague has compelled me to write the tragic story of the poor. I doubt if ever it has been understood that the one eastern out-parish of Stepney bore a burden of dead that is three-fifths that of the whole mortality of the City within the wall.[1]

The Rev. Richard Kingston, Clerkenwell's parson, complained that he could find no time for study, save that stolen from sleep. Kingston—whether rightly " Dr." or not I cannot tell, for the validity of his Orders was attacked —had the courage to stay with his people, by day visiting the sick and at night burying the dead. His " Pillulae Pestilentiales, or a Spiritual Receipt for the Cure of the Plague "—as tiresome a work as others like—he addressed to his churchwardens, " From my Study at St. James's Clerkenwell, Oct. 18, 1665." He had weird terms of expression, occasionally breaking into rhyme—

It pleased the wise Dispenser of all things (he wrote in preface) to cast my lot among you in one of the most dreadful visitations that ever England knew, when the black Horse of the Pestilence, with pale Death on his back, pranced our streets at noonday and midnight, at which dreadful (and never to be forgotten) time our sense of seeing was well nigh glutted with beholding the sight of our diseased and deceased friends, enough to have extinguished the optical faculty.

> No papers then over our doors were set
> With chambers ready furnished to be let ;
> But a sad " Lord have mercy upon us ! " and
> A bloody Cross, as fatal marks did stand,
> Presaging the noisome pestilence within,
> Was come to take revenge on us for sin.

And as our eyes might well be dimmed, so might our ears be deafed with the doleful cries of the poor for food to keep them from starving, of the sick for physic to keep them from dying, and for them that were marked for spiritual helps to preserve them from perishing.

[1] The mortality in the year's return is : Ninety-seven parishes of the City within the wall, All Deaths, 15,207, of Plague, 9,887 ; Stepney parish, All Deaths, 8,598, of Plague, 6,583. Moreover, the unrecorded burials in Stepney are likely to have been in much larger proportion than within the walled City, where the division of the work among so many parish officers would have enabled a closer count to be kept. On a single day Sept. 11th, the register gives the burials of 154 persons in Stepney parish.

> We well might hear of Death there was such plenty,
> One bell at once was fain to ring for twenty ;
> No clocks were heard to strike upon their bells,
> 'Cause nothing rung but death-lamenting knells.

Which dreadful noises so terrified some, and affrighted all, that men knew not what course to steer to preserve themselves from the wounding shaft.

> Some by their fear to go to church debarred,
> Anon are carried dead into the yard ;
> And churches now with too much burial fed,
> Fear'd they should have no meeting but of dead.

He tells of men lying down to rest in the evening, who made their sleep true kin to death by dying before morning, so rapidly did death follow the first signs of Plague in very many cases.

The open Fleet River, receiving every possible pollution, flowed by, skirting Clerkenwell, and in every parish along its banks the Plague stayed and destroyed. Mortality was high in St. Andrew Holborn ; it was high in St. Sepulchre's, where in one August week 447 died. Through St. Bride's parish the Fleet discharged its foulness into the Thames where now Blackfriars Bridge gives a crossing to Surrey. St. Bride's suffered as severely as any City parish of equal area. The register, unlike those of Cripplegate, Stepney, and so many more, does not distinguish the Plague deaths ; their presence is obvious enough on the crowded pages. I take a few entries at random out of hundreds, some showing that father, mother, and children all perished together :—

Aug. 17.   Elizabeth Temple (doubtless a foundling of the Inns of Court).

18.   Mr Wolpools servant ; a woman in Rackett Court ; a woman att Mr Dadfords in new street.

28.   Benjamin Bayley, Frances Bayley. On the 29th Benjamin Bayley again (doubtless father and son). Mary Burton. On the 29th Elizabeth Burton.

Sept. 4.   John Smith. John Smith his sonne. On the 5th Thomas Smith and Bartholomew Smith.

6.   William Browne, Margaret Browne, Hannah Browne. On the 9th Hannah Browne again. On the 11th Sarah Browne.

Sept. 8.   John Millar, Elizabeth Millar. On the 11th Hugh
            Millar and Ann Millar.
   11.   Johnson Watts. Rebecca Watts.
   13.   Mr Choralls man. Mary Johnson. Elizabeth
            Johnson. On the 14th William Johnson.

When Plague was most virulent in August and September, twenty persons had died each day where normally one alone was the toll. If allowance be made for unrecorded burials, perhaps the truth was five-and-twenty. Over five successive weeks' span that was the record. It was so in St. Bride's—in Stepney—in St. Giles-in-the-Fields—in Cripplegate ; and the proportion fell little short in others of London's poorest outskirts that gave the big toll to the Plague. It was not as if Plague had leapt up for one fearful week, and then as rapidly diminished. The long continuance of epidemic in parts heavily infected, sweeping away almost the entire populace, does much to explain the excessive proportion of loss among the town's population after the flight which I have found when setting out the full Bill.

In dirty alleyways and festering courts about the Fleet River and the debtors' prison, horrible for their mixed poverty and dissoluteness, the Plague found lodgment. As August opened St. Bride's Churchyard and the outlying burial ground were becoming choked, and the vestry sought to appoint two persons who should give orders for digging Plague pits and pay the gravemaker and labourers. They were to see that the space " be well husbanded "—the land made ready for the harvest. None could be found to undertake the duty.[1] John Tanner, the second Churchwarden of St. Bride's, had already fled. He was selfishly wise. Henry Clarke, his fellow churchwarden, alone stayed and worked, and he died of Plague in September. A Mr. William Clarke, chosen to act in the vacancy, after fourteen days' service took the Plague and died.

At the first onset St. Bride's had relieved the necessity of the neighbour parish of St. Dunstan's in Fleet Street by receiving some of its dead in the outer burial ground, and had also lent its bearers.[2]

[1] Vest. Mins., Aug. 12.
[2] Vest. Mins. and Ch'wardens' Accts.

The Plague immensely increased the work and risks of all London churchwardens, whose office was at no time a sinecure. That Cripplegate lost three of these officers by Plague already has been recalled. Others who made the sacrifice of life were Mr. Wyborne, churchwarden of St. Dunstan-in-the-East [1]; John Collyer, of St. Margaret New Fish Street [2]; Thomas Champney, of Allhallows the Less [3]; Thomas Rawlins, of St. Botolph Bishopsgate; and John Phillips, of St. Olave Silver Street.[4] The parish of St. Clement Danes had to replace both overseers during the visitation, one being dead from the Plague and the other sick.[5] William Wiley, collector for the poor in St. Thomas Apostle parish, was a victim, struck down while performing his duties.[6] At St. Katherine Cree, so many of the parishioners appointed for the audit were dead that the task was cast upon the whole vestry.[7]

Sir John Lawrence, the Lord Mayor, laid down his burdensome office at the close of October. Never, one imagines, was duty relinquished with greater relief. The Plague had come into his family. His parish of St. Helen's Bishopsgate had been loaded with the sickness. "And less than what I am about to say," wrote Roger L'Estrange in the *Newes*, "cannot in justice be spoken of Sir John Lawrence, the late Lord Mayor, which is, that throughout this dreadful visitation he has, in spite of all hazards and mistakes, persisted in his duty."

London owed much to its Lord Mayor. Pepys dined with Lawrence, but records only that " My Lord Mayor treated me with great respect." [8] One could wish his vanity away, this once, to have such a rapid sketch as the diarist draws of Sir Thomas Bludworth, Lawrence's successor in the civic chair—so vivid, albeit so unflattering. Of Lawrence all men spoke well. Albemarle in the west, and Lawrence in the City, were the two pillars upon whom the governance of London had rested. Each had loyal assistants, in the justices and Aldermen respectively. Fortune was kind in that in both cases authority was confided to men of character. It was no small thing that in all the months of trial, amid all the despair—the

---

[1] Vest. Mins., Sept. 25. [2] Ch'wardens' Accts. [3] *Ibid.*
[4] *Ibid.* [5] *Ibid.* [6] Vest. Mins., July 26.
[7] Vest. Mins., 1666, April 1. [8] *Diary*, June 5.

imprisonment of a population—no riots had disturbed public order.

Lawrence had the courage to stand alone. When, owing to the swelling volume of Plague, the Court of Aldermen and the Common Council met but seldom, and could not be brought together on emergency, he accepted the responsibility of filling public offices made vacant by sickness or death.[1] He shirked no duties, though their performance daily brought risk of infection. He worked without flinching, with the trust that Providence would protect him which was ingrained in the Puritan character. The Lord Mayor had been accessible to all ; none was turned away from his door ; his advice was freely given. John Bell dedicated to Lawrence his "London's Remembrancer," the valuable collection of Bills of Mortality during successive Plagues, " as a person to whose care and piety it seems but a fair respect and duty." Pope in a later day eulogized him.[2]

A week before his term expired Sir John Lawrence held his last Common Council, and to pay him honour and testify their respect Aldermen and Common Councilmen assembled at Guildhall in numbers unusually large for that stricken time.

The presentation of the new Lord Mayor at Westminster was, of course, out of the question. The Exchequer had been removed into the country, the Judges were scattered. Sir John Robinson, Lieutenant of the Tower, acting as the King's representative, received Sir Thomas Bludworth, with whom came the new Sheriffs of the City, Robert Hanson and William Hooker, the retiring Lord Mayor, and five or six Aldermen. Near the Bulwark Gate of the fortress a barber's shop had been hanged with draperies and fitted up for the purpose. Robinson, himself an Alderman of London and two years before its Lord Mayor, gave to the occasion such small state as was within his

[1] "Repertory " 70, fo. 150b.

[2] Erasmus Darwin, the Georgian poet, has characterized Sir John Lawrence as one who—

"When Contagion, with mephitic breath
And withered Famine urged the work of Death,
  With food and faith, with medicine and with prayer,
Raised the weak head, and stayed the parting sigh,
  Or with new life relumed the swimming eye."
                                    . *Loves of the Plants*, Canto II.

power. He was surrounded by officials, the Steward of the Tower, the Comptroller of the Mint and a few more, a guard from the garrison being mounted, " the soldiery all new clothed for the better grace of the ceremony." Afterwards the new Lord Mayor entertained the small company at dinner at his house [1] in Gracechurch Street, and no others—as quiet a Mayoral Feast as the City has known. The times were sadly changed.

The new Sheriffs, whom custom brought into office before the Lord Mayor, come little into this narrative ; but Hooker cannot escape the lively portraiture by Pepys, who says of him during his shrievalty that " he keeps the poorest, mean, dirty table in a dirty house that ever I did see any Sheriff of London, and a plain, ordinary, silly man I think he is, but rich." [2] A thumbnail portrait could not suggest more. The City's high officials did their duty manfully. I have but rarely found a gap in their ranks by the Plague. The City Coroner and the City Remembrancer, as already stated, died of it during the explosive outburst of September. The Court of Aldermen, placing on record the Sword Bearer's constant attendance upon the Lord Mayor, " at extraordinary peril and hazard of life," made him a gift of £100. [3]

The Plague dragged on to winter's approach, with its thousand and more weekly of dead, more fearful still than when the first fright of it sent people hurrying out to the country. October was near its close before the town gave the first indications of reawakening life, encouraged by the continuous fall of the mortality. The Exchange, reopened a month before, when few attended, became " pretty full." Shopkeepers and merchants were the first to venture back, long before the world of fashion was willing again to trust itself in the infected town. As yet the streets remained significantly empty, and most of the shops were shut. [4]

---

[1] *Newes*, Nov. 2. Rugge's " Diurnal," fo. 147.

[2] *Diary*, Dec. 13.

[3] " Repertory " 70, fo. 157. Dr. Creighton is wrong in his *History of Epidemics in Britain*, in saying that two of the London Aldermen died of the Plague. Sir Martin Noel had been but nominally Alderman for a day in 1657, that his fine for refusing to serve the office might be imposed and paid, and Bide had resigned his Aldermanic chair during the Commonwealth (see p. 215, *ante*). No one of the Aldermen who stayed in the City to perform their duties during the Great Plague succumbed to it.

[4] Pepys, Oct. 26.

November brought disconcerting news; the Bill for the first complete week told of a rise in the Plague mortality of 383 deaths, to 1,414 in all, the increase being pretty generally distributed over the City and the eastward out-parishes. The Plague took men of better condition than had fallen before. " The sickness," a news-letter writer expressed his fears, " will this week increase, at least in London, where 'tis observed that many merchants and eminent citizens have within these four or five days been taken away by that disease." [1] In over-weening confidence the returned refugees, who for months while in retreat had been afraid of the sight of friends and relatives, ventured into houses and rooms where the Plague-stricken had but a little time before breathed their last.[2] That the mortality should again rise none could wonder.

In a fortnight the Bill (Nov. 14th to 21st) fell to show a new low record, 652 in all dead of the Plague, and the alarm passed. In the resurgence of grave fears the Governors of the New River Company had leave to forego their annual meeting, the officers acting for another year; they could not, they said, meet without imminent danger to themselves and others.[3]

The worst sights had been withdrawn when the first of the home-coming citizens appeared, and there was little that should convey the picture of the full horror of London at the height of the epidemic. The dead-cart had been thrust back into the nights. No longer were corpses to be seen littering the streets and lying in the fields awaiting opportunity for burial. The authorities, as the contagion diminished, regained full control. But the watchmen posted outside the shut-up houses while the forty days' quarantine was being observed were familiar everywhere, and always there were the beggars, both men and women, multiplied a hundredfold—the victims in health and pocket of the Plague, limping about the streets from the unhealed wounds of their sores. The well-to-do classes, finding safety in flight, had known nothing of these ; they were the first disturbing evidences confronting them on their long-delayed return.

[1] Addit. MSS. 4182, fo. 42.   Clarendon's *Life*, iii. 33.
[2] Hodges, p. 27.
[3] Privy Ccl. Reg. 58, fo. 289.

And to the least observant eye the raised height of the City churchyards, choked with the dead, was a constant reminder. It made a new feature in London, that should have permanence after the Plague had passed ; indeed, down into this twentieth century the City churchyards stand high, mute witnesses to every passer-by of the sorrows and loss of the Great Plague. Few stones were raised ; the time allowed little thought of this commemoration. Snow fell in winter, and those who ventured into the narrow, tortuous City streets, darkened by the overhanging houses, were startled at every turn by the sight of these great mounds under their mantle of white, an entire burial ground fashioned to the shape of a single gorged grave. They had a haunting dread. Pepys has described the horror it gave him when first passing through a churchyard : " It frighted me more than I thought it could have done, to see so many graves lie so high upon the churchyards where people have been buried of the Plague." [1]

On the skirts of the town, most marked beyond the City's northern and eastern wall, were more livid scars where had been the Plague pits. Loose brown earth was piled upon them, with loads of lime for disinfectant—hillocks rising here and there above the surface level of the ground, whereon nothing grew, each one a place of horror. The bounty of spring next year covered them with a coarse vegetation.

The sites of the larger number of Plague pits we can never know. They were made in fields, and at the height of the epidemic each successive one dug was used for but a few days, at most a week or two, and then was filled in. No Plague pit was marked as such by any memorial stone, no single gravestone was raised at any to perpetuate a lost relative or friend. It is uncertain that in all cases the owners were paid for the public service to which on emergency the land was put, and the Plague having passed, the land reverted to them and its former use. Inevitably the sites were forgotten.

London has built for itself houses and streets over the field pits wherein uncoffined victims of the Plague by tens of thousands have crumbled to dust. Chance alone may have left a few not so covered, in squares and public

[1] *Diary*, 1666, Jan. 30.

gardens. Mrs. Basil Holmes has sought to identify the
Plague burial grounds mentioned by Defoe [1]; they will
have been well known in his early manhood. One so
indicated was " near Mount Mill " beyond Goswell Street.
Mount Mill stood on the north side of Seward Street.
That at Shoreditch is doubtless the Holywell Mount
burial ground, behind the church of St. James's, Curtain
Road, which continued in use long after the Great Plague.
A fraction of it, about one-quarter acre, survives. Another
plot Defoe describes was " at the upper end of Hand Alley
in Bishopsgate Street," then a green field, used particularly
for Bishopsgate parish, though many carts out of the City
brought their dead there, notably from Allhallows London
Wall. He writes also of two thousand corpses being cast
into pits railed round in an adjoining passage. New Street,
Bishopsgate, to-day overruns Hand Alley. Defoe's other
" piece of ground in Moorfields " may have been the
Bethlehem burial ground.

Stepney's wide fields were used as pest-grounds. A
plot originally lying south-west of Stepney churchyard, and
now incorporated, contained human remains when in 1886
the public garden was laid out. These were without
coffins and very close to the surface, suggesting Plague
burials. Defoe indicates the churchyards of St. Paul's
Shadwell, to-day a public garden, and the detached and
still closed yard of St. John Wapping as other pest-fields.
Mrs. Holmes adds to them possibly Gower's Walk, Whitechapel, where in excavations in 1893 for Messrs. Kinloch's
buildings human remains without coffins were brought up.

It is likely that Marylebone dug a great Plague pit in
the ancient churchyard of St. John the Evangelist. Apart
from quantities of human bones found when the old Marylebone Courthouse was built on the reputed site in 1727,
and the new Courthouse in 1822, I am told by Mr. Arthur
Ashbridge, a former district surveyor of St. Marylebone,
that when a bookshop in Oxford Street adjoining the
Courthouse was rebuilt a few years ago, numbers of human
bones were disturbed about eight feet down. They were
not in rows, but lying as if the bodies had been thrown in
indiscriminately.

Southwark's Plague victims, when the churchyards

[1] Mrs. Basil Holmes, *The London Burial Grounds*.

could hold no more, were buried in thousands in fields at Deadman's Place. This site is undoubtedly historical. Long afterwards it continued to be used as a cemetery,[1] and an Independent Chapel became attached to it, around which many eminent Dissenters were interred. Messrs. Barclay & Perkins's great Southwark brewery has spread over the old burial ground, which to-day is enclosed in one of their paved yards. In the west there were Plague pits in Soho Fields, but no sites can with certainty be identified. At Fulham, Lintaine Grove and a row of houses in Lillie Road cover part of a Plague burial ground.[2] Cartloads of human bones found at the rear of No. 41 Beak Street, Golden Square, when the houses now standing were erected, suggested a Plague pit there.[3]

Tradition lingers in many neighbourhoods that certain spots were pits. It cannot be summarily rejected, for the memory is likely to have been handed down. A natural horror of such places, and men's fear of soil that only awaited disturbance for Plague to spring out from it anew, delayed building in great numbers of cases. There are green wastes undisturbed to this day all about Greater London to which this origin is given. The curious triangle of ground railed in opposite Tattersall's Gate in Kensington is one of these.[4]

In the City Road, at the corner of Windsor Terrace (of " Mr. Micawber's " residence) is a large open space now flagged over, where less than half a century ago was a complete circular plot of grass contained within an iron railing. That was said to have been a Plague pit; the ground before the junction of the Brompton and Kensington Roads, to-day thrown into the roadway, another; and more could be recalled. A triangular plot in front of St. John's Church, St. John's Wood, has the same legend. But evidence is in all cases lacking.

[1] The Plot is indicated in Rocque's Map of 1746.
[2] Mrs. Basil Holmes's *The London Burial Grounds*.
[3] *Notes & Queries*, 12th Ser., ix. 35.
[4] Mr. Percy Armstrong says in *Notes & Queries*, 12th ser., ix. 12, that the plot in front of Tattersall's is all that remains of a village green that had its maypole down to the end of the eighteenth century. A portion of this green was set apart as a burial ground to a lazar house that had existed at Knightsbridge from mediæval times, and there is a tradition that the old lazar house was used as a hospital for victims of the Great Plague, and those who then died were buried at this spot. But it does not necessarily follow that there was a Plague pit at the green.

It is singular that nowhere in London is the Great Plague memorialized on gravestones or by epitaphs. The writers of these last allowed themselves such wide range that it was to be expected some would have made the allusion, but obviously the families bereaved desired neither to identify themselves with the Plague nor to recall it. Alexander Davies's stone in St. Margaret Westminster churchyard, mentioned in an earlier chapter, gives no indication that he died of the Great Plague. The tablet of Dr. Nathaniel Hodges in St. Stephen Walbrook Church says only that he survived the visitation. At Sutton, Surrey, is a ledger stone in the churchyard, with arms and crests of the Pistor family, two of whose members are recorded to have " dyed young in the great sickness, A.D. 1665." [1] I know of no other.

The oncoming of a severe winter frost brought the trading classes hurrying back in increased numbers, believing that now they might find safety. The month of November had been cold ; on the 22nd hard frost held the ground in its grip. Four days later Pepys called it " a horrible cold frost," and having escaped Plague he was in no mood to risk his life with a chill caught on the water, so made a journey to Erith by land. These rigours remained till the month was out. December had a few warm days,[2] then was marked by frosts almost without intermission. Again the Thames was full of floating ice.[3] Nothing could have served better for clearing London of the Plague.

The frozen highways revived with life ; the stir of people returning was as great as it had been in early summer, in the excitement of the panic flight. Loaded full with passengers, the country coaches and carriers' waggons, which for months had been off the roads, again were seen journeying to London.[4] They brought quantities of manufactured goods, large stocks having been accumulated by the cloth weavers and others when trade decayed and consumption fell very low ; and high hopes of revived

[1] *Notes & Queries*, 12th Ser., iv. 220. A marble monument in All Saints' Church, Huntingdon, to William Fullwood, physician and mayor of the town in 1680, records that he " prescribed and administered Physic to the people gratis in the time of their sickness "—meaning the Great Plague.
[2] Pepys, Dec. 13.   [3] *Ibid.*, Dec. 18.   [4] *Ibid.*, Nov. 30.

prosperity were fed by a popular belief that the war must
end in the winter.[1] It did not end, but spirits that so long
had been depressed were again buoyant. Houses which a
little time back had been full of dead were again inhabited
by the living, and shuttered shops that for half the year
had been locked were re-opened for trade.[2] The arrival
of a New Year found the City peopled and normal conditions fast recovering; the West-end alone continued
empty.

A first inquiry was as to who was alive and who dead.
Pepys, making a purchase of oysters in Gracechurch
Street, naïvely expresses delight at finding " my fine woman
of the shop " alive after the Plague. The oysters he
judged " good, though come from Colchester, where the
Plague hath been so much." He was " mighty glad to see
the 'Change so full." Venturesome, he took a hackney
coach, " the first I have durst to go in many a day, and
with great pain now for fear." His more intimate concern
was for his new fashionable periwig, " bought a good
while since, but durst not wear, because the Plague was in
Westminster when I bought it ; and it is a wonder what
will be the fashion after the Plague is done, as to periwigs,
for nobody will dare to buy any hair, for fear of infection,
that it had been cut off the heads of people dead of the
Plague." [3]

All past experience had been that cold drove the Plague
out, and the popular instinct was right. The authorities
realized the danger in any great concourse of people unused
to the hygienic restrictions that an epidemic of Plague
required, and stringent orders were issued by the Lord
Mayor that none should occupy houses wherein infection
had been until the rooms and their contents were
thoroughly fumed and aired.[4] Sulphur, brimstone, and
lime were the common disinfectants, burnt in a chafing
dish. " People come to town," Sir George Downing wrote
from London in December, " and tumble over the goods
and household stuff in infected houses during this sickness,
which occasions the lengthening out of the malady." [5]

[1] Burnet's *History of His Own Times.*
[2] Hodges, p. 27. [3] *Diary*, Sept. 3.
[4] Mayoral Proclamation, Dec. 7.
[5] Downing to Williamson, Dec. 14.

The Plague was wonderfully abated, the Lord Mayor declared in a cheering Proclamation to the Aldermen, but it still became the City rulers to observe all means to its cessation. Public feasting and all forms of hospitality should continue suspended. The Aldermen were directed to omit the customary dinner and entertainment given by them to the inhabitants of each ward after the holding of the wardmote on St. Thomas's Day (Dec. 21st), and the wardmote inquest was also to abandon its annual dinner.[1]

Fools are produced by every crisis, who are as dangerous to others as to themselves. The Plague's aftermath found them in plenty. Lack of elementary precautions among the home-comers had its inevitable sequel. Many, wholly careless, Dr. Hodges has asserted, went into beds wherein persons had died before they were cold, or even cleansed.[2] The Plague mortality fluctuated, rising at times ominously, and some among those who had been first to fly fell victims immediately upon their return to London, whole families perishing as a result of reckless indifference in contact with possible causes of infection.[3]

The pest-rate and public charity had proved insufficient before the epidemic reached its height, and the City Cash continued to give the chief financial supply during the remaining months of the year. This source provided an additional £1,600 for relief in September; in October the weekly contribution fell to £300, and figures only on three separate weeks; in November there were two payments each of £200, and that ended the demands for public relief made upon the City Cash. The total sum so borne was but £3,500.[4]

In addition, payments for Plague services during the year of the visitation charged to City funds totalled £2,026.[5] These fell chiefly under the following heads :—

[1] Mayoral Proclamation, Dec. 7.
[2] *Loimologia*, p. 27.
[3] Boghurst, p. 70. Allin, Nov. 16, Dec. 7, 12.
[4] Guildhall Library MSS. 270. The City Corporation at that time lacked the large heart to make the gesture of a gift. The whole of the City Cash disbursements were regarded as a recoverable loan, and there were repeated demands for the levy and collection in the parishes of additional pest-rate from which the City's outgoings might be reimbursed (" Journal " 46, fo. 197b; "Repertory" 70, fo. 156).
[5] Sickness and Pest-house Bills, Guildhall Library MSS. 359. " Repertory " 70, fo. 154.

	£	s.
To Apothecaries and Chyrurgeons in the Plague time	1,300.	0
Additional to Dr Peck for his care in the Plague time	50.	0
To Edward Higgs, Chyrurgeon, for dressing the poor visited of the Plague	30.	0
For medicines for the poor in Plague time . .	93.	11
For fitting up the pest-house with necessaries .	222.	15
More for the Pest-house	12.	0
For fitting up of a churchyard in the sickness time	209.	0
Paid the Comon Hunt for killing of Dogges in the beginning of the Plague	36.	10

Nothing is available to explain the £209 paid " for fitting up of a churchyard." Bunhill Fields is not a Plague ground, and I assume that the payment was made for burial lands outside the walls in which the City's dead were largely consigned to pits. The bill above set out does not represent all. The City was as coy as are private patients to-day in settling its doctors' bills ; the City Cash continued to bear payments to doctors and apothecaries for services given in the stricken months years after epidemic Plague had ceased.[1] It is characteristic of the finance of the time that the City finally satisfied its accounts owing to apothecaries and for medicines from the fines imposed upon substantial merchants for refusing to serve the life office of Alderman,[2] a calculated extortion. On the day in May, 1667, when the Court of Aldermen so decreed, they discharged one John Jermyn, a wealthy citizen and Salter, then lately elected Alderman for Chepe, on payment by him of a fine of £1,000 and £20 more to the maintenance of the ministers of the City prisons—a promising start in getting together revenue ! Aldermen's fines ranged not infrequently from £200 to as much as £800.

Late as July, 1670, a committee of Common Council was set up to clear off medical claims that were still outstanding.[3]

Valued relief came to London by the liberality of other cities and towns. A separate Guildhall account [4] appar-

---

[1] City Accounts, 1666–7–8.
[2] " Repertory " 72, fo. 986.
[3] " Journal " 47, fol. 55.
[4] Guildhall Library MSS. 270, fo. 54, *passim*.

ently represents the benevolences of private citizens; this certainly is the case in several instances where the common form used is, " By the hand of Mr ——, who has recently returned " from a place named. London citizens who were " faire-keepers " in Bristol in August—no doubt attending a country fair that had escaped prohibition because of the Plague—made a collection for the capital's visited poor, which brought in £61. Five and twenty citizens were engaged in the charitable work.[1] Subscriptions of note in September were : Taunton, £100; Bristol, £205; Wakefield, £59; Plymouth, £69; Dartmouth, £25; Totnes, £32; and Exeter, £170. All this money went out in relief as fast as it was received, the ravages by Plague being then at their height.

From Minchinhampton and Woodchester, Gloucestershire, six inhabitants sent in October £35 collected by them; Warrington, Lancashire, gave £70 " for ye visited poore in London "; Manchester, £60; with second donations from Exeter, £52, " by a private hand," and Taunton, £15.

There came a further £31 from Manchester in November; from Chester, £190; Preston, Lancashire, £60; Swansea, £25; with smaller sums such as North Allerton's £4 12s. and many gifts by individuals. The total sum of the country gifts so received to February, 1666, was £1,397, raised ultimately to £1,522.

The City of London played a compassionate part in lightening the miseries of its neighbours. London within the bars that at Whitechapel, Holborn, Temple Bar and elsewhere marked the outward frontiers of the City and the limits of the Lord Mayor's jurisdiction, lived as a separate entity, with its own privileges, customs, courts of justice and ancient institutions, clean cut apart from the people outside. Large as were the City's own needs, it was decided at Guildhall that only money raised in the City should be spent there; it should forego all advantage from the country's benevolence. The sums above mentioned received from provincial towns, and also the country fast-day collections that by Royal Command were forwarded to London, were devoted to relieving the sufferers by Plague in the out-parishes.

[1] *Newes*, Aug. 24.

This fine determination, well worthy of the pride and greatness of the City, is a milestone down the centuries ; for in the agony of the Great Plague the essential unity of Greater London was thus for the first time recognized. The City's paternal care should extend beyond its frontiers. That King Charles had advised a large charity and given nothing matters little. The decision meant much to the stricken out-parishes. They were situated in Middlesex and Surrey. They had no funds save those locally amassed on which to draw, no commercial centre of eminence, and except in Westminster and others of the nearer western out-parishes they could count but few wealthy residents whose charity should substantially relieve the urgent need. The poverty of waterside East London especially was severe. Sir John Robinson, the Lieutenant of the Tower, in this matter acted as almoner, the actual distribution among the parishes being undertaken by the magistrates of the two counties.[1]

Many other contributions swelled the sum-total spent in relief. Derby town sent £94, which I do not find included in the Guildhall accounts, supplemented by £57 10s. contributed by London citizens at the time resident there, and this was devoted by Sir Thomas Player, the City Chamberlain, wholly to the out-parishes.[2] By the hand of John Hackett, Bishop of Lichfield and Coventry, came £150 collected in his diocese, and an additional sum for the needs of St. Andrew Holborn,[3] which he had served as rector for forty years. The nobility resident in Westminster sent their donations direct to the churchwardens of St. Margaret's, in whose accounts they appear, and other parish books record contributions not entered elsewhere, totalling many hundreds of pounds.

Such benevolences as those of Dean Sancroft, which Stephen Bing, the Petty Canon, distributed among the Plague-stricken poor immediately about St. Paul's Cathedral,[4] do not appear in any writing. A good deal was done by unorganized private effort.

It is, in fact, impossible to arrive at a close estimate of the cost borne in relieving public distress in the Great Plague. The measures have entirely altered. The £30

---

[1] *Intelligencer*, Oct. 16.   [2] *Ibid.*, Oct. 30.   [3] *Newes*, Oct. 19.
[4] Bing to Sancroft in Harleian MSS. 3785.

paid to Edward Higgs, the surgeon, for the extremely perilous work over successive months of " dressing the poor visited of the Plague," would not now suffice for a single operation, and the £50 to Dr. Peck (additional to £75 before received) " for his care in the Plague time " appears equally inadequate. To most of those attacked by Plague death came swiftly, and that saved expense. After all allowances made, the few thousands of pounds which covered relief during the Great Plague must seem incomprehensible to-day, with our more humane and enlarged ideas of public responsibility. The people were kept from actual starvation ; that alone was the object, successfully accomplished.

It would do less than justice to the doctors to leave only a memory of those who fled and those who died. A devoted band, if few in numbers, stayed to work unselfishly among the poor, and these stand out in honour in their great profession. Dr. Peter Barwick, the devout brother of the former Dean of St. Paul's, kept his house by St. Paul's Churchyard, in a district heavily infected, " consecrating the beginning of every day to God, as he always dedicated the next part of it to the poor, prescribing to them in their sickness gratis, furnishing them with medicines at his own expense, and charitably relieving their wants." [1] The City itself made lasting record of the especial services of Dr. Samuel Peck in visiting and prescribing for the infected poor.[2] Of others who escaped the martyr's crown, I recall Dr. Francis Glisson, Regius Professor at Cambridge, a founder of the Royal Society and thrice President of the Royal College of Physicians ; [3] Dr. Nathan Paget, Milton's intimate friend, practising in Coleman Street ; Lawrence Arbilleur, a foreign Doctor of Surgery resident in London, of whom Lord Craven testified that he was ready to venture his person and to apply his medicines and plasters to all who desired his assistance ; [4] Dr. Jeremy Astell and Mr. Slade, an apothecary, to each of whom, in recognition of services during the Plague, the

[1] Intro. to Peter Barwick's *Life of the Rev. John Barwick*, 1724.
[2] Guildhall Library MSS. 295, " Services of Dr. Pecke."
[3] He lived in New Street, by Shoe Lane, and is buried in St. Bride's Church.
[4] *State Papers (Domestic) Addenda*, 1660–70, p. 55.

King gave a piece of inscribed silver plate ; [1] and mention must include Sir John Baker, Dr. Thomas Allen, Dr Elisha Coysh, and Mr. John Fife [2]—these in addition to others who have figured in earlier pages.

Dr. Thomas Wharton was physician of St. Thomas's Hospital. The long inscription on his tablet from the now destroyed church of St. Michael Bassishaw tells that when Plague mortality had become excessive his resolution never wavered, and that he kept his post, ministering to the sick poor and his own patients. The Guards from Hyde Park as they fell ill were sent to St. Thomas's, and there, faithful to his undertaking with the Government, Dr. Wharton attended them. King Charles's promise to appoint him Physician in Ordinary was never fulfilled, and his sole reward was a grant of augmentation of his paternal arms, for which empty honour the College of Heralds exacted from him a stiff fee. [3]

Nicholas Butler, who held license from the Archbishop of Canterbury, was given his Cambridge M.D. at the King's request. He practised at St. Helen's Bishopsgate throughout the Plague, giving medicine and advice gratis to some two hundred of the poor daily, few of whom are said to have miscarried in his hands. [4]

The ominous year ended on a Sunday, with all the people at the churches, devoutly praying that never might they experience such another ; and Pepys in his lodging at Greenwich wrote up his *Diary*. The faithful servant had won his reward :

Thus ends this year, to my great joy, in this manner. I have raised my estate from £1,300 in this year to £4,000. I have got myself great interest, I think, by my diligence, and my employments increased by that of Treasurer of Tangier and Surveyor of the Victuals. It is true we have gone through great melancholy because of the Great Plague, and I put to great charges by it, by keeping my family long at Woolwich, and myself and another part of my family, my clerks, at my charge at Greenwich, and a maid at London.

[1] Privy Ccl. Reg. 59, fo. 22.
[2] See Dr. Clippendale's list in *British Medical Journal*, Feb. 5, 1909, to which I have added many names.
[3] Munk, *Roll of the College of Physicians*, i. 256–7.
[4] *State Papers (Domestic) Addenda*, 1660–70, pp. 78–9, 117, 307.

The poor servant girl had been left alone in the house in Seething Lane to face the Plague !

But I hope the King will give us some satisfaction for that. But now the Plague is abated almost to nothing, and I intending to get to London as fast as I can.   The Dutch war goes on very ill, by reason of lack of money ; having none to hope for, all being put into disorder by a new Act that is made as an experiment to bring credit to the Exchequer. . . . My whole family hath been well all this while, and all my friends I know of, saving my aunt Bell, who is dead, and some children of my cousin Sarah's, of the Plague.   But many of such as I know very well, dead ; yet, to our great joy, the town fills apace, and shops begin to open again.   Pray God continue the Plague's decrease ! for that keeps the Court away from the place of business, and so all goes to wrack as to public matters, they at this distance not thinking of it.

He made his own return to London in the New Year, riding with Lord Brouncker in his four-horsed coach to that nobleman's town house in Covent Garden.

But Lord ! what staring to see a nobleman's coach come to town !   And porters everywhere bow to us ; and such begging of beggars! And a delightful thing it is to see the town full of people again as now it is ; and shops begin to open, though in many places seven or eight together, and more, all shut ; but yet the town is full, compared with what it used to be.   I mean the City end ; for Covent Garden and Westminster are yet very empty of people, no Court nor gentry being there.

A fortnight later he again noticed how " infinitely naked " were Covent Garden and other resorts of fashion, the City then being almost as full of people as ever it was.[1] The world of fashion awaited the King's example.   The doctors and divines at last began to return.   Pepys does not conceal his contempt.   Gresham College held its first meeting since the Plague on January 22nd, when " Dr Goddard [2] did fill us with talk in defence of his and his fellow physicians going out of town in the Plague time ; saying their particular patients were most gone out of town, and they left at liberty ; and a good deal more." Pepys was at his parish church of St. Olave Hart Street

[1] Pepys, Jan. 19.
[2] Jonathan Goddard, M.D., the Gresham Professor of Physic, whose permanent residence was at Gresham College in Bishopsgate.

on January 30th, making his first attendance since he
had left London on account of the Plague, and next
Sunday worshipped again there—

My wife and I the first time together at church since the
Plague, and now only because of Mr Mills his coming home to
preach his first sermon; expecting a great excuse for his leaving
the parish before anybody went, and now staying till all are
come home; but he made but a very poor and short excuse,
and a bad sermon. It was a frost, and had snowed last night,
which covered the graves in the churchyard, so as I was the
less afraid for going through.

The saddest story of the Great Plague is that of Eyam—
sad enough in all conscience, but brightened by the revela-
tion it gives of nobility of character and steadfastness till
death in a group of simple villagers. Here are all the
elements of an epic tragedy. It is out of time and place.
Back in classic days and in ancient Greece, the tale of
heroism would have gone ringing round the world. It
happened in Restoration England, and they are few whose
hearing it has reached.

The village is in Derbyshire, in a hollow of the hills.
It is, and was, an agricultural country, but there are lead
workings, though whether these were exploited so late as
King Charles II.'s age I do not know. The little community numbered together some three hundred and sixty
souls. There had been no Plague up to September, 1665,
and no thought of any. How should there be? The
winds of heaven that sweep over the fresh clean lands of
the Peak—what happenings should they have with pestilence?

It is a sheltered, remote place. But the Plague did
come to Eyam.[1] If confident report can be trusted, it
came from London, in a box of tailors' samples and—of
more deadly significance—some old clothing, received by
Edward Cooper, a village trader.

The box was opened by George Vicars, a servant.
Finding the contents damp, he placed them before a fire.
Quickly sickness seized him. The third day the character-

---

[1] The fuller narrative is in William Wood's *History and Antiquities
of Eyam*, 1847, reprinted in many subsequent editions. See also Dr.
R. Mead's *Short Discourse on the Plague*, 1720.

istic Plague spot appeared on his breast. A day after, the 6th of September, he was dead. Edward Cooper, the next to succumb, was buried on September 22nd. Later that month four more were laid in the churchyard. The Plague had taken all, and in October it claimed twenty-two others. Eyam thereafter was never free from Plague. A hard winter in the Peak kept it down, the deaths fluctuating between four and nine each month ; and by the time of the return of midsummer's heat as many as 76 villagers had succumbed. That was more than one-fifth of the whole population, a ghastly sacrifice.

Eyam had no doctor, but by good fortune there dwelt in the village two ministers. The elder, Thomas Stanley, had been its rector in the Commonwealth. Ejected by the Conformity Act, he stayed on, and of him we know little. The rector, the Rev. William Mompesson, had taken the living the year before the Plague appeared, a young man of twenty-seven, having a wife and two children. He had been chaplain to Sir George Savile. In the portrait of him at Southwell Deanery he looks a frail, slight figure, not a man of action and of heroism, but rather the typical embodiment of the poor scholar. The end seemed at hand, but unhappily in June, 1666, the Plague again broke out with reinvigorated fury. That month among the dwindling numbers it claimed nineteen victims.

In alarm, some few of the inhabitants fled to the moor or farther distant, as the most timorous had fled when first the Plague created alarm.

Mompesson played an heroic part. He refused to leave his flock, and his wife refused to leave him. They sent their children away. As July's death-roll piled up, to reach in the village the appalling total of 56, the terror-stricken people seemed likely to fly *en masse*. Mompesson, like a man inspired, roused in them a sense of man's duty to his neighbour. They could not escape infection. Many unknowingly were already infected ; the peril lurked in themselves and everything they might take away. The safety of the surrounding country was in their keeping. He would await death with them, as God should please.

He wrote to the Earl of Devonshire at Chatsworth, confident that he could prevail upon his stricken and rapidly

WILLIAM MOMPESSON, RECTOR OF EYAM
From the Portrait in Southwell Deanery

diminishing parishioners to confine themselves within the village, whereby the pestilence should be prevented from spreading out, if provisions and necessaries could be secured. These supplies the Earl provided.

The decision being taken, a circle was drawn around Eyam of about a half-mile radius, marked by well-known stones and hills. With superhuman courage, the inhabitants solemnly agreed that none should go beyond that limit, whether infected or not. They shut out the world, and shut themselves out of the world. The pledge was faithfully kept. Helpless and alone, self-immured, they perished. To two or three places on the boundary provisions were brought and left before dawn by messengers from the nearest villages, there being no personal contact. A rivulet where it fills a shallow stone-lined well is one of these places, and is called to this day " Mompesson's Well." Any money passing was thrown into the running water for purification. There, too, Mompesson left accounts of the Plague's progress, the numbers of deaths, and other information.

August's torrid days made a frightful record—78 added to the death-roll, and Catherine Mompesson, the rector's wife, was among them. The Plague was hemmed in in that desolating struggle, and destroyed and finally buried with its own victims.

The gates closed on a churchyard already choked full. Each Sabbath day service was held in the open air, in a dingle that still is known as Cucklett Church. There, standing where rock makes a natural arch, ivy-clad, Mompesson appealed to the God of Mercy to stay the deadly pestilence, attempting consolation, strengthening hope where hope was small. The congregation kept apart from one another, avoiding contamination. He was himself prepared for death, daily expecting it,[1] but was fated to live. So many were dying that burial rites became impossible. The rattle was but a moment out of the throat, when the corpse was hastily dragged into field or garden around the cottages, and laid uncoffined in a shallow grave.

[1] See the pathetic letter from Mompesson to Sir George Savile, Sept. 1, 1666, written as a dying man and bidding his patron " hearty farewell for ever," printed by Wood, pp. 74, 75.

Fear forbade the ready help and friendly hand. None would touch, or even look upon, a corpse of another family. One woman endured the agony of digging the graves of, and herself burying, her husband and six children. Still in desolated houses lay stretched out the last sufferer, for whom someone must do the office, and a villager of herculean build, Marshall Howe, gave to his neighbours this little charity, burying among others his own wife and son. Tales of this man have lingered at Eyam—of his strength—how on returning from an interment he would say, " Ah ! I saw Old Nick grinning on the ivied rock as I dragged such a one along the dell." They tell there, too, that for a generation and more after the Plague parents would bring their children to rule and obedience by threatening to send for Marshall Howe.

Few were left in September, but of these 24 were taken, leaving but 47 in the village alive. Out of that small number 14 more succumbed in the early days of October. The last Plague burial was on the 11th October. Mompesson wrote after the calamity—

The condition of this place has been so sad, that I persuade myself it did exceed all history and example. Our town has become a Golgotha, the place of a skull. My ears have never heard such doleful lamentations—my nose never smelled such horrid smells, and my eyes never beheld such ghastly spectacles. Here have been 76 families visited within my parish, out of which 259 persons died. Now (blessed be God) all our fears are over, for none have died of the plague since the eleventh of October, and the pest houses have been long empty. During this dreadful visitation I have not had the least symptom of disease, nor had I ever better health. My man had the distemper, and upon the appearance of a tumour I gave him some chemical antidotes, which operated, and after the rising broke he was very well. My maid continued in health, which was a blessing ; for had she quailed, I should have been ill set to have washt and gotten my provisions.[1]

The church registers give 267 as the total mortality. Eight out of every nine who had remained at Eyam village perished.

Catherine Mompesson's monument is in the church, but of Mompesson nothing. There is that sad-faced

[1] Mompesson to John Beilby, Eyam, 1666, Nov. 20.

RILEY GRAVES

MOMPESSON'S WELL

MEMORIALS OF THE PLAGUE AT EYAM

portrait at the Southwell Deanery, here reproduced. " Peace hath her victories no less renowned than war," but we make little of her heroes.

Eyam's tragic story, the fortitude till death of these Derbyshire villagers under the influence of one inspired man, even after the lapse of two and a half centuries it is impossible to read unmoved. Was the sacrifice necessary ? In the light of present medical knowledge—No. It seems now assured that had the inhabitants *en masse* quitted the village soon after the appearance of Plague, leaving everything possible behind them, and submitted to isolation for a period till all fear of disseminating infection had passed, the death-roll need not have bulked one-tenth as large. Eyam paid toll in hundreds, and London, by the shutting up of infected houses, by tens of thousands, for medical ignorance. There is nothing more terrible in its consequences than medical ignorance.

CHAPTER XIII

THE OXFORD PARLIAMENT

THE King was at Oxford on September 27th, having posted from Salisbury with speed, and arrived so late at night that only the Dean of Christ Church and the Canons were present to receive him, arrayed in their scarlet gowns. The Queen travelled with greater comfort in two days; the Duke of York, fresh come from York, was awaiting them, his children being already lodged at Oriel.[1] Charles made Christ Church his headquarters, little anticipating that his stay in the University City would drag out over four months. Merton College accommodated the Queen and her Court; and there, too, Charles had the execrable bad taste to lodge the Lady Castlemaine, then daily expecting to be brought to bed of that child of his who became the Duke of Northumberland. The manners of the time hardly allow print.

The Public Orator attended next day at Christ Church to welcome their Majesties; the Colleges by their members expressed thankfulness for the great honour of the visit.[2] The Public Orator's harangue is lost. No doubt its sentiment was akin to that of the anonymous loyal poet who found only sacrifice in Charles's flight with the Court from London—

> " Thus does our King, and is once more content
> To suffer 'midst his subjects banishment."

He broke into heroics when singing Oxford's welcome to Charles—

> " Amidst the troubled world, we must confess,
> Great Britain's misery our great happiness.
> While others blame malignant heaven, we'll say
> To us the planets wander the right way.

[1] Addit. MSS. 4182, fo. 40. [2] *Ibid.*, fos. 44b, 46.

And while Your Majesty (great Sir) shines here
None shall a second Plague of Athens fear.
The tyrant fiend that chief command does bear,
And sways the sceptre of infected air,
Shall find the utmost of his power too weak
Into the circle of your Crown to break :
While to You, Sir, our laurels' shade shall be,
(We hope) as friendly as the Royal Tree,
And like that Tree, which a thick swarm of ants
Converted once into inhabitants ;
And with stout myrmidons Ægina fill'd,
Whose natures a quick Plague had lately kill'd,
Our laurels shall (proving the fable true)
Re-people England in preserving You." [1]

The Mayor, Aldermen and leading citizens also waited upon the King, bringing gifts ; the city's greeting and loyalty were expressed by the Recorder. Charles in reply, admitted a warm affection for Oxford, acknowledging its singular fidelity manifested at all times to his martyred father and to the Crown.[2] It was wayward fate that no sooner had the Court settled down in its new place of refuge than alarm spread because of suspicious sickness in a tailor's house near St. Abb's Church,[3] but Oxford was, and remained all that year, in health. It enjoyed complete immunity from Plague. An excellent system of surface drainage carried out by Bishop Richard Foxe during a time of floods and pestilence a century and a half before, and the rigour of the measures adopted, lawless for the most part and undertaken on the Royal Prerogative, to secure the safety of the King and those about him, no doubt contributed to this end.

As a measure of precaution against infection the King's correspondence was forwarded via Towcaster or Newbury, avoiding the capital. James Hickes, the acting postmaster, asked appealingly if other letters to and fro were so to be dealt with ? It meant ruin for the London Letter Office.[4]

Little news of the Plague filtered into Oxford, where the Court idlers were anxious only to forget it. To Hyde, the Lord Chancellor, to Lord Arlington, the Earl of Manchester, and the few other serious men of affairs about the King, it gave cause for grave anxiety, but was not a subject to be

[1] Anonymous, *Upon the Present Plague at London and his Majesties leaving the City*, 1665 (Guildhall Library, Pressmark L. P. 12. 31).
[2] *Intelligencer*, Oct. 2.
[3] Addit. MSS. 4182, fo. 47.
[4] Hickes to Williamson, Oct. 4.

introduced in that unreceptive atmosphere.   L'Estrange's
bi-weekly sheets, *The Newes* and *The Intelligencer*, left
any curiosity there might be unsatisfied, printing little
beyond a summary of the weekly Bills of Mortality—three
or four lines indicating how the Plague's virulence rose or
fell.   Visitors from the infected capital were few in number,
and found themselves objects of distrust.   But rarely one
of these succeeded in passing the close cordon drawn
around the city and the Court.   The statesmen were as
atoms adrift in a whirl of enforced gaiety and irresponsible
light-heartedness.   The talk at Oxford was not about
London's many thousands of Plague victims, but of the
impending birth in its midst.   Nimble wits passed the
day's news of Lady Castlemaine, and the gossip and scandal
from many another half-sealed chamber.

Such were the matters of moment, not London's
plight.   A volatile Frenchman, one Denis de Repas, did
enter Oxford with much difficulty (unable to find stabling
in the overcrowded city, he let his horse lie out in an alley)
and his letter to Sir Robert Harley admits a whole flood of
light.   Were I to paraphrase it, the picture so drawn might
seem incredible.

For news from Court (he wrote on Oct. 16th) I shall tell
you that one cannot possibly know a woman from a man,
unlesse one hath the eyes of a lynx who can see through a wall,
for by the face and garbe they are like men.[1]   They do not
wear any hood, but only perwick (periwig) hatts and coats.
There's no othere plague here but the infection of love ;   no
other discourse but of ballets, danse and fine clouse ;   no other
emulation but who shall look the handsomere, and whose
vermillion and Spanish white is the best ;   none other fight than
for " I am yours."   In a word, there is nothing here but mirth,
and there is talk that there shall be a proclamacon made that
any melancoly man or woman coming in this towne shall be
turned out and put to the pillary ;   and there to be whep till
he has learned the way to be mery a la mode.[2]

This was Oxford ;   and this the contrast with the
desolated, Plague-stricken capital wherein Albemarle,
almost alone, was supporting the burden of government.
With balls and entertainments and scandal the exiles from
Whitehall made life bearable, out of place as they felt

---

[1] See Pepys on p. 169, *ante.*
[2] Portland MSS (*Hist. MSS. Comm.,* iii. 293).

themselves in the University city. After all, what should they do ? They lived—if others died, it was the will of Providence. Impending events disturbed their complacency. The Parliament was summoned to Oxford for October 9th [1] and nothing could prevent its meeting. No further prorogation was possible. The war with the Dutch dragged along, and the grant made to Charles of £2,500,000, intended for three years' needs, already was mostly spent within a twelvemonth. Failing an additional Supply to carry through the winter, hopeless confusion lay ahead. The Michaelmas Law Term had been adjourned to Oxford in November.[2] Greater than the peril of Parliament was that of Plague being brought in by the lawyers and suitors and their shabby retinue.

In anticipation of the unwelcome incursion the Privy Council, reciting Charles's princely care for " the preventing (by God's blessing) as much as may be any growth of the infection so dreadfully spread from this his City of Oxford," directed the Mayor and Vice-Chancellor of the University to make a general search and inquiry in every parish within the city and suburbs. They took the names of all inhabitants and record of their quality, and of lodgers in every house. Lists so compiled were submitted to the Lord Chancellor and the Chancellor of the University, who after scanning them arbitrarily made a clearance from Oxford of all persons whose presence was judged to be unnecessary. These were summarily ejected, without further consideration and without appeal.

Members of Parliament arriving found that they were required to produce certificates of health of themselves and their servants to the Vice-Chancellor or his officers ; those attached to the Court or pleading any business therewith submitted their certificates to the Knight Marshal or officers of the Board of Green Cloth ; and others coming out of the country or bringing commodities for sale were examined by the Mayor.[3] The host of the King's Head Inn at Oxford had sharp reminder of the privileges of Parliament. He detained a waggon of De Vere, Earl of Oxford, and was brought to the Bar of the House to answer for his misdemeanour.

---

[1] *Royal Proclamation*, Aug. 30.   [2] *Ibid.*, Sept. 26.
[3] Privy Ccl. Reg. 58, fo. 257.

The Commons fixed upon Convocation House as their place of meeting, and the Lords chose the Astronomy School, after which the two Houses of Parliament attended the King at Christ Church on Oct. 10th. A Throne had been raised at one end of the great hall. The scene reflected the unusual circumstances of the assembly. The King dispensed with his Royal robes and ornaments. The Peers also were unrobed, his Majesty having made this concession in view of the Plague. " I am confident you all believe," Charles said in his Speech from the Throne, " that if it had not been absolutely necessary to consult with you I would not have called you together at this time, when the contagion hath so spread itself over so many parts of the Kingdom. I take it for a good omen to see so good an appearance this day ; and I doubt not every day will add to your number." That was the sole reference to the Plague. The King at once plunged into the topic of the Dutch war, as did the Lord Chancellor who followed him.[1] There was, in fact, but a sparse attendance, the Commons numbering less than two hundred.[2] The bishops from their sees swelled the small body of the Lords.

The City of London's interest in the Parliament was chiefly concerned, in its impoverishment by the Plague, in securing from the Ministers an abatement of the assessment and the grant for Additional Aid. Sir John Frederick and the three other Members for the City were hurried off to Oxford, charged to use all possible influence to obtain these concessions.[3]

The Parliament at Oxford performed the business which was the sole purpose for its being called together, granting the King a new Supply of £1,250,000 for carrying on the war. A clause in the Subsidy Bill restricted the expenditure from this sum to the war alone. There were reasons for belief that many thousands sterling of public money had disappeared with no proper authorization, in meeting the personal extravagances of the King and his profligate Court. Charles, more far-seeing than the counsellors about him, accepted the limitation ; Hyde denounced it as " an introduction to a Commonwealth, and not fit for a Monarchy." The short Oxford Parliament

---

[1] *Lords' Journal*, xi. 684–7.   [2] Addit. MSS. 4182, fo. 48b.
[3] " Repertory " 70, fo. 156.

gains constitutional importance by having introduced a principle of responsibility in national finance that ever since has ruled.[1]

It passed the persecuting Five Mile Act. Incidentally, the Oxford Parliament gave some attention to the Plague.

The Lords by resolution declared that with the sad and fresh experience which most persons now had throughout the Kingdom, it was evident that the increase and spread of the pestilence were in part due to defect of the law. The Attorney-General was directed to bring in a Bill.[2]

No sooner had the Commons assembled for business than the House appointed a committee to inspect the Statute 1st James I., ch. 31, concerning Plague. They were charged to frame a Bill making good the defects of that antiquated measure, and at the same time to provide remedies that should prevent contagion spreading.[3] Rarely had a Parliament confronted a more necessary task.

The Commons were first ready with their Bill, and the Lords, having received it, made two additions and some amendments. A Conference with the Commons became thereafter necessary.

In their effort to combat a great public evil, the House of Commons had acted wisely. After second reading, they sent the Plague Bill to a large and representative committee, which included not alone members of their own House, but as well three doctors, presumably medical— Arras, Burwell, and Quarterman—and Christopher Wren, at that time Savilian Professor of Astronomy at Oxford. It was expressly provided that all members of the committee " are to have voices," [4] and by appropriate choice the place of meeting was the Physick School. The Lords at the conference of the two Houses agreed to omit an amendment they had inserted against the harbouring of inmates, the Commons having rejected it as destructive of trade.[5] They had also introduced a proviso inhibiting the

---

[1] " It drew with it (remarks Hallam) the necessity of Estimates regularly laid before the House of Commons ; and by exposing the management of the public revenues, has given Parliament not only a real and effective control over an essential branch of executive administration, but in some measure rendered them partakers in it " (*Constitutional History*).

[2] *Lords' Journal*, xi. 698.

[3] *Commons' Journals*, viii. 614.

[4] *Ibid.*, 617.

[5] *State Papers (Domestic)*, 1665–6, p. 351.

building of pest-houses and the opening of burial grounds near the houses of peers and persons of note and quality.

The spirit of concession was abroad. The Lords allowed that " persons of note and quality " in this regard should be jettisoned from the Bill. But the Lords made and obstinately adhered to a demand that their own residences should be exempt from search and shutting up at the direction of constables, and that peers should be free from the annoyance of pest-houses erected in their neighbourhood.[1] A free conference was held the same day, but without reaching agreement. It is right to say that the bishops had mostly returned to their sees.

On this claim for a purely class distinction and privilege negotiations broke down. Andrew Marvel, then Member for Hull, attended the Oxford Parliament. " The Bill for better preventing the Plague could not pass, because the Lords would not agree with us that their houses, if infected, should be shut up," he wrote to the Mayor.[2] To the Lords' obstinacy the designed " Additional Act for making further provision for such as are infected with Plague " was sacrificed. The highest incidence of the Plague in London had occurred little more than a month before ; there was no assurance that the mortality, fallen it is true, but still computed by a thousand and more weekly, might not climb higher. Parliament was prorogued the day after the last fruitless conference, November 1st, having passed no Act for dealing with the Plague, having contributed nothing.

Nigh upon one hundred thousand human souls had already perished in London alone, but there was some compensation—a score or two of peers' residences had been saved from enforced visitation by parochial officers, and their noble owners spared the offence of possible pest-houses erected in their vicinity. The historian stands staggered and speechless.

---

[1] *Lords' Journal*, xi. 698 ; *Commons' Journals*, viii. 624.
[2] Marvel to Robert Bloom, Mayor of Hull, Oxford, Nov. 2.

CHAPTER XIV

THE FULL BILL

IN November the King had it in mind to employ
Albemarle at sea. The Lord-General begged that
his acceptance, reluctantly given, might for a
while remain a secret, " for if his wife should come
to know of it before he had by degrees prepared her for it,
she would break out into such passions as would be very
uneasy for him." The great man had in Nan Clarges,
the Strand blacksmith's daughter, a termagant for wife.
Pepys has recorded her " cursed words " at the news ;
that had her lord been a coward he had gone to sea no
more, but might have been excused and made an
Ambassador.[1] The insult was aimed at Montagu Earl of
Sandwich, who after the undignified departure of the
fleet from Bergen had been given an Embassy to Spain.
Pepys dismisses the virago as " a damned ill-looked
woman."

Albemarle had, in fact, hesitated much. He had said
that he stood in greater peril in London than if in action
against the Dutch. He believed himself to be more
necessary there than at sea, and that he had done the
King better service by staying in London than he could
have given in any other place.[2] There he was right.

A coward Government, skulking into cover from the
Plague, should have at least credit for its prescience in
leaving sole trust in the capital to one of such well-tried

---

[1] Pepys's *Diary*, Dec. 7. A letter dated Oxford, Dec. 15, from Patrick
Vans to Henry Slingsby, says of the Duchess that the decision to send
Albemarle to sea " occasions his Lady to give all the Court to a bad keeper
to keep them "—in plain words, the angry Duchess consigned the entire
Royal Court, King Charles included, to the devil in hell (*Hist. MSS.
Comm.*, 6th Rep., p. 336b).

[2] Clarendon's *Life*.

courage, in whom public confidence rested as in no other. London has never made enough recognition—or indeed, any recognition—of Albemarle. Although lacking her birthright, he was one of London's most devoted sons. His part in holding the capital quiet and in the hollow of his hand at the King's Restoration ; his manly decision to stay among the people throughout the Great Plague ; and finally his example in London after the Great Fire had left so much in ashes, mark him out as one to whom London, in quite exceptional degree, stands a debtor.

" The Duke of Albemarle never over-valued the services of George Monck," said the cynical King Charles, who might have taken the same truth to himself.   Albemarle was buried among Kings, but his grave in Henry VII.'s Chapel of Westminster Abbey is without even his name to mark it.   Fifty years after a family bequest bore the cost of a monument, which still gives no indication of the hero commemorated.   His funeral wax effigy among the Abbey's " ragged regiment " is to-day too mutilated to be shown ;   his cap, taken from the same figure, long served the vergers as a collecting bag for pence. George Monck, Duke of Albemarle, shares London's gift of contemptuous indifference which the great city so gracefully extends to every man without exception who has served her well.

Once only in all the Plague-stricken year 1665 did Albemarle absent himself from London.   The King and the Court could not assist him, and were well content that he should do his work at a distance.   He set out on November 28th to meet Charles at Oxford ; the first interview between the Sovereign and his most powerful counsellor since in early days of July the Court had fled from the Plague.   He committed to Lord Craven, in his absence, the direction of affairs in the capital.[1]   A Royal coach was sent to Wycombe to convey Albemarle on the last stage of his journey, and high officers of the King's suite to greet him.   Charles received him with marked honour and respect.[2]   On the night of December 5th the Lord-General was back at the Cock Pit at St. James's.

In that first week of December, under influence of the continued frost, the recorded Plague mortality in London

[1] *Intelligencer*, Dec. 4.   [2] *Newes*, Dec. 7.

fell from 333 cases to 210. It had been in the first week
of November as high as 1,414, and the rapid fall gave
promise that the month would see epidemic Plague stamped
out. It is human nature to minimize the peril that seems
passed. The town, so recently roused out of despair,
indulged an exaggerated confidence. The Court's return
to London was openly discussed. Hopes were high that
Whitehall Palace would again shelter the King, or that,
if not there, Charles might spend his Christmas as near
London as Windsor or Hampton Court.[1] The people
reckoned without the Plague. Not only did it persistently
continue in London, but it actually enlarged, the mortality
rising higher each week in December from the figures with
which a month of unfulfilled promise opened. Ten days
before Christmas the King made it known that he would
stay at Oxford for the festival and for the New Year.[2]

A last glimpse of Oxford we may take. Parliament
had gone. The life of pleasure, ennui, and restless desire
that the Plague should end, so that all might safely get
back to the greater distractions of the capital, continued
for the Court. As privileged spectators, we may stand at
a door, onlookers of a ball which the Duke of Monmouth
is giving to the Queen and the ladies of her train. Many
others are at the door waiting, a fashionable, vivacious
throng, numbering four or five hundred, but none may
enter. It is a very exclusive ball. Not a dozen persons
are in the ball-room besides the dancers, these being the
pick of the nobility and the beauties. Charles's Queen,
coming at half-past eight, " danced all the while she was
there with an extraordinary great modesty." She stayed
till eleven to grace the ball.

Modesty went out with the Queen. Others came who
stayed till two in the morning. In the country dances
(we have the word of a French onlooker) " they did jumpe
and leape as those creatures who live upon your moun-
taines "—eleven or twelve Court ladies and as many
courtiers. Rosy Mrs. Stuart was there, the latest
favourite and object of scandal among Charles's curious
menage, " extraordinarily merry," attracting all attention.
After dancing she sang four or five French songs, " as

---

[1] Addit. MSS. 4182, fo. 54b; *State Papers (Domestic)*, 1665–6, p. 47.
[2] *Oxford Gazette*, Dec. 14–18.

well as I ever heard any woman sing." The Plague was sixty miles away.

The courtiers found a new butt for their wit in the lawyers, the Michaelmas term having been adjourned from Westminster to meet at Oxford on November 18th. The same lively foreigner tells—

> The towne is so full of lawyers that hardly one can goe in the streets. They are the jest of the Court and the hate of all the people. Their cloase are as much out of date as their speech, which none can understand but when they ask their fees. Wee do hope in God they shall all goe out of the towne on Tuesday next, and all will blesse them with the saying of your good wife of Bath. They generally all curse this town by reason that they cannot gett any lodgin. They did lay sixty last night in a barne full of haye, not far from my lodgin.[1]

The law term was a mere semblance, with everything curtailed to reduce the risk of infection being brought to Oxford, and to hasten the lawyers' departure. Even to get the poor accommodation of sleeping sixty together in a hay barn, they were required first to submit certificates of health to the Mayor and his officers.[2] No Chancery or Exchequer causes were taken ; no juries sat in any case whatever unless of some special importance in the King's service, all other jury trials being postponed ; no litigant might be compelled or needed to appear save by attorney.[3] A few days sufficed for as short a term as is on record.

It was April before Albemarle put to sea. At Christmas he wrote from London that Naval matters required his personal communication with the King. But this was his dilemma, that he could by no means advise his Majesty to leave Oxford, yet found many objections to absenting himself from the Plague-stricken capital.[4] Not until January 27th, 1666, was the practical difficulty of audience overcome. Charles and his brother, the Duke of York, then came specially from Oxford to Hampton Court,[5] setting themselves in motion in order to meet Albemarle, who for seven perilous months in the Court's absence, with death constantly about him and Plague's victims swept

---

[1] Denis de Repas to Sir Edward Harley, Oxford, Nov. 24, in Portland MSS (*Hist. MSS. Comm.*, iii. 294).
[2] Privy Ccl. Reg. 58, fo. 257.
[3] *Royal Proclamation*, Oct. 11.
[4] Clarendon's *Life*, iii. 33.
[5] *Oxford Gazette*, Jan. 25–29.

into the pits by thousands, had unflinchingly performed duties which brought him into contact with all conditions of people, and consequently dangerous exposure.[1]

The Court had left London hurriedly in distant July ; its return had as little pre-arrangement as its departure. As events fell out, the King did not return to Oxford. He was accompanied to Hampton Court by several of his principal Ministers, and left behind the Queen, the Duchess of York, and the courtiers generally, his intention being to stay only a few days for discussion of urgent public affairs with Albemarle, then make a quick journey back to Oxford.[2] Yet the hope was not absent, as expressed in the new official sheet then published, *The Oxford Gazette,* that the Plague might so rapidly die down " that his Majesty may with safety to his Royal person and the public immediately return to Whitehall, which he is pleased to express a very longing desire to do."

The villages about Hampton Court were free from infection ; the Bill of Mortality, auspiciously issued at this moment, conveyed the heartening intelligence of a further decrease in the week's deaths from Plague in London, now as low as 56 ; and Charles learnt that there was a strange and universal joy in the capital from his being so near.[3] Moreover, the weather had become most favourable for the rapid disappearance of Plague. Hard frost, returning, held the country in its grip, and everywhere deep snow covered the landscape.

Albemarle came to Hampton Court by day, returning to London at night, and so for the few days. Public business proving burdensome, and the Plague still decreasing, the King made the resolve to return himself to Whitehall.[4] The tedious exile should end. That this step would not be long delayed had been foreseen when the Exchequer was transferred back to Westminster on January 20th. The Hilary Law Term had been adjourned from Oxford to Westminster, but fear being entertained of a spread of the infection by the too early resort of lawyers and suitors to the capital, order was made in January that the term be kept at Windsor Castle.[5] Should the Plague

---

[1] *Intelligencer,* Oct. 23.   [2] *Hist. MSS. Comm.,* 6th Rep., 366.
[3] Pepys, Jan. 31.   [4] Clarendon's *Life.*
[5] Privy Ccl. Reg. 58, fo. 317.

be gone, it need be but a morning's work to bring the courts again to London.[1]

Charles was back at Whitehall Palace on February 1st, to the whole-hearted content and relief of his subjects. He was alone. It was a furtive home-coming, as that of most other refugees from the Plague. What thoughts were behind that strangely immobile Stuart face it would be interesting to read, as in his approach to the capital that he had so long forsaken the King was noisily acclaimed. Along the roads villagers and townsmen in thousands turned out to witness his passing. From a hundred church towers the bells clanged a merry welcome—a change indeed ; they were the same bells that over months had rung out nothing but the funeral knell. That night bonfires were lighted in many streets of London and Westminster.[2] He had played no kingly part. It was only in keeping with Charles's well-known temperament to thrust cares aside, that in his absence from London and his indifference, he and his Government had displayed hardly an atom of practical concern for the fate to which they had abandoned London. They had trusted wholly in Albemarle's initiative.

The welcome to the King no doubt was sincere, only it may be questioned how far it was personal. The return of Charles to London, as his departure from London, marked a stage in the tragedy so long drawn out. With the flight of the Royal Court, the leisured class and the wealthy merchants, the capital had lapsed into the deepest misery, its trade and normal activities gone. Their return was the breaking of a new dawn. By tens of thousands the people they had left behind had perished in these streets now ringing a welcome. If those who survived felt in their hearts no admiration for the King who had deserted them in their need, and only contempt for the moneyed and professional families who now ventured back,[3] thinking themselves safe at last, yet they did not fail to realize that only could London's prosperity be revived and the City be itself again when the

---

[1] Hyde to Sir H. Grimston, Oxford, Jan. 15 (Verulam MSS. *Hist. MSS. Comm.*, pp. 59–60).

[2] Rugge's " Diurnal," fo. 152.

[3] Cf. Pepys, Jan. 22, 30, Feb. 4, 10.

A Bill of Mortality (viz) of all Persons Buried within the Town and Parish of Great Yarmouth, from Friday ~~ffob~~: 16~~4~~ to Friday ~~ffob~~: 23 Anno Dom. 16~~~~

Aged		Impostum	
Ague		Infants	
Appoplexie		Kingsevil	
Bruised		Meagrome	
Cancer		Plurisie	
Childbed		Plague.	
Consumption		Rickets	
Convulsion		Rising of the Lights	
Cough		Scurvy	
Distracted		Sore legge	
Dropsie		Spotted fever	
Drowned		Suddenly	
Feaver		Surfet	
Small-pox		Teeth	
Flux		Thrush	
Gowt		Tissick	
Grief		Ulcer	
Griping in the Guts		Wind	
Jaundies		Wormes	

3 psons wherof there are not one of the Plague the Lords Name be praise for life & Health —

John Johnson Parish Clarke

A YARMOUTH BILL OF MORTALITY, 1665

John Johnson, the parish clerk, has written on the Bill: " Three persons, whereof there are not one of the plague, the Lord's name be praised for our life and health "

King and these others again sought London. These were the harbingers of better times, after unparalleled suffering.

Next day after King Charles's arrival at Whitehall Palace the Lord Mayor and Sheriffs waited upon him, with the City's greeting. Their reception was most gracious, and Charles knighted the Sheriffs, Aldermen Robert Hanson and William Hooker.[1] The departure of the Queen and her entourage from Oxford was delayed for several days. Charles met his Consort at Sion, and they passed by water in the Royal Barge to Whitehall.[2] London, deserted for so long by all in supreme authority save Albemarle, in the period of a few days reconstituted herself as the capital of the Kingdom and State, with speed and thoroughness which testified how eager was the desire of all to put the Plague behind them and restore normal conditions. As early as February 9th the Judges of the High Court again sat at Westminster Hall.[3] No courts of law had sat there since the previous June. The adjournment of the legal term to Windsor Castle could be dispensed with.

Ten days later sessions for the gaol delivery of Newgate were opened, with the immediate result that sixteen felons placed on trial met their fate on the gallows, and one, a highwayman standing mute, chose to undergo the fearful death by *peine forte et dure*.[4] For none capitally sentenced was there the mercy of reprieve. The Plague itself had delivered the gaol of many more.

The long calendar of this remarkable assize contained the names of ninety-two prisoners, four for murder or attempted murder, others for housebreaking, pocket-picking and felony of various kinds. A wretched woman, Mary Gifford, had been in Newgate awaiting her trial since the previous July 11th, amid the constant perils of confinement, Plague and gaol-fever, for a felony valued at fourpence. In curious contrast, Anne Allen had been "uppon baile," committed for murder. There were but six survivors of those committed in July, three from August, five from September, while the month of January, closing less than three weeks before the gaol delivery,

---

[1] *London Gazette*, Feb. 1–5.   [2] *Ibid.*, Feb. 15–19.
[3] *Ibid.*, Feb. 8–12.   [4] *Middlesex County Records*, iii. 372.

produced seventeen.[1] These figures indicate with what results the Plague had swept through the gaol.

The King having found courage to return, none need now fear. The laggards who still had kept their country seats hastened back to share in the restored gaieties of the capital. Each day the fashionable ends of the town filled marvellously, and little time passed before the London streets were as full, the Exchange as crowded, and the people who mattered in all places apparently as numerous as before the visitation. The nobility and wealthier classes had found the best antidote against Plague in flight, and in the reunion at Court and in the great houses there were few who missed those of their acquaintance.[2] "The town," a gossip wrote to the Earl of Ogle on the 15th of February, "is very full of people after this great mortality, there being no miss of any, and very few shops shut up." [3]

The Great Plague passed ; and with much reason one may doubt if the English people have ever really understood its character. A line or two given to it in our books has been enough. The most conservative estimate admits that year a hundred thousand dead (the Bills of Mortality, unquestionably short, admit 97,306), and I believe full statistics would give many thousands more ; and the course of English history by this devastation in the capital is wholly unaffected. No single gap was made by the Plague in the ranks of statesmen ; no member of Lords or Commons is returned dead by Plague ; no Judge, dying by the infection, left a vacancy on the Judicial Bench ; even among the better-known names in Restoration medicine and in the higher ranks of the clergy there is none found missing. The City Aldermen for the greater part stayed in London, bearing their burden, and no vacancy was created in the Court of Aldermen ; the magistrates in the out-parishes whom King Charles by name directed to stay in London all survived the furious epidemic—no one was struck down.[4] I have not found that a magistrate succumbed

---

[1] Guildhall Sessions Papers, Feb. 1665[-6]. For clearances from Newgate of Quaker prisoners see pp. 190, 217, *ante.*

[2] Clarendon's *Life*, iii. 35–6.

[3] Portland MSS. (*Hist. MSS. Comm.*, iv. 146).

[4] All their signatures I have found attached to one or another of the parochial accounts of expenditure which the justices were required to audit after the Plague.

to the Plague. The Court and professional classes, the big financiers, Vyner, Backwell, Meynell and others, who assisted King Charles in his often desperate need for money, the wealthier London merchants and tradesmen— all returned to London to take up the broken thread of their affairs. Yet there were one hundred thousand dead. To these others the Plague had been an inconvenience, a monetary loss, no more. The social interests, even the business interests, of the capital underwent no lasting disturbance.

With unerring instinct the masses of the people who suffered had given to this visitation the name that should keep it in remembrance for all time. It had been " the poore's Plague."

The City shared the public intoxication of spirit, lifted out of despair to heights of hopefulness which the time did not justify. The Plague was not actually extinguished. On January 23rd the Lord Mayor had dismissed the physicians employed in attendance on the infected poor ; the great abatement of the sickness was judged sufficient reason. That same day a Mayoral Proclamation directed the reassembly of the Lord Mayor's and Sheriffs' Courts for the trial of actions.[1] The new dawn in the New Year was signalized by a very necessary effort to clear the City of the rogues, vagabonds and sturdy beggars who were declared exceedingly to swarm in and about it,[2] and by yet another attempt to rid the houses of " inmates," pursued with re-invigorated zeal. Constables, churchwardens, and overseers, with others specially employed, made search in every parish for their discovery, warning all householders not to fail to turn them out by an appointed date. Thereafter the officers were directed to make a second visitation, and bring before the magistrates all offenders.[3] What the poor lodgers should do for shelter was their affair.

The mantle which Albemarle so long and well had worn fell from his shoulders on the Court's return. There was not wanting enthusiasm for their new task in those who grasped it. A cynic must needs smile at the long series of directions for stifling the Plague which emanated from the Privy Council after the date of February 1st, remembering

---

[1] "Repertory " 71, fo. 17. [2] "Journal " 46, fo. 98.
[3] *Ibid.*, fo. 97b.

the emptiness of their lordships' effort ever since the
previous July.   At Oxford the King and Court had been
safe ; in London Plague was about, taking some fifty
victims weekly, and still lurked, with enfeebled strength,
in hundreds of poor houses marked with a red cross.
There was yet a certain peril that was in its novelty disturbing to the returned exiles.

So many surgeons had died by Plague, not alone in
London but at the shipping ports, that the Royal Navy
could not be staffed—that was always a difficult task.
The Corporation of Surgeons were required not to stand
strictly upon their charter when admitting men of whose
sufficiency and experience they had proof.[1]   That done,
the Council, the King being present, devised restrictive
Plague measures, and issued on February 14th a long letter
to the Lord Mayor and Aldermen of the City of London,
the justices of Westminster and the home counties, and
others concerned.   Charles's " deep sense of the sad contagion," his " utmost care for the preservation of his
people," his pious intentions for their welfare and the like
passages may be read for what they are worth—nothing.

The document illuminates the ignorance of the Council
as to the practice in London.   Albemarle, perhaps contemptuous, had worked alone ; no reports of his survive,
or anything that suggests he took trouble to write them.
The Council prohibited further burials in City churches
and churchyards, for fear that disturbance of the Plague-
laden earth would scatter infection.   Such burials had
been stopped already by the choked state of the ground.
All churchyards were required to be covered with twelve
inches of unslaked lime, laid over with a like quantity of
gravel or fresh earth.   Lime was unobtainable in such
large quantities.   Parish wardens or beadles were charged
continually to walk the streets and apprehend all rogues,
beggars and vagabonds, the constables being held responsible that these be punished.[2]   " Inmates " were to be
ejected ; and the King wrote to the Lord Chief Justice
emphasizing the peril both to the health and good order of
the town and danger of fire, by the sufferance of so many
cellars and " bulks " in the houses having doors opening
upon the streets.   The families inhabiting them, said his

[1] Privy Ccl. Reg. 58, fo. 333.   [2] Ibid., fos. 345–7.

Majesty, had by sad experience proved a means of spreading Plague. Further, these places were used for tippling houses and receptacles of loose and debauched persons.[1] Let them be emptied.

Lord Craven called the magistrates together, and after several consultations he addressed to the Lords of the Council on February 19th a letter that admirably summarizes what had been done—

The Lord Bishop of London was consulted withal concerning burial places, who could not consecrate any ground unless a perpetuity of the same might first be obtained. Nevertheless, the justices have directed that such persons who die of the sickness shall be buried in the late usual places assigned for that purpose.

Such infected who were removable were sent to the pesthouses, and others who could not have been shut up; their doors were marked with a Red Cross and " Lord have Mercy upon us ! " in capital letters, for forty days, wardens appointed to guard them within as well as hinder the approach of any company from without, etc., with a White Cross afterwards for the same time ; there have been no complaints brought to the justices of any neglect herein, but do believe that due execution hath been generally made of this order, having themselves made a particular observation in several places.

The churchyards have not been so generally covered with lime, in regard to the dearness and scarcity thereof, there not being sufficient quantity to be had for that end and purpose, but much fresh earth and lime has been laid in many churchyards, and those bodies which have been there buried so deep that we hope no inconvenience can from thence arise. Besides, special care is taken not to open the same graves again.

The streets are daily cleansed and the filth carried away by the raker, who brings his carts every morning, and giving notice thereof to the inhabitants by the sound of his bell, to the end that every particular house also may be cleared of its filth. As to the laystalls too near the streets and passages, much care has been taken for to remove them, many difficulties having arisen therein. Notwithstanding, by the industry and diligence of the justices, some are already quite removed, and the rest we hope in a very short time will be removed, to the great advantage of the inhabitants, as well as to the satisfaction of the Lords of the Council's order.

Beggars have been and are daily removed and punished, and provision made for the poor of each parish, according to law.

[1] Privy Ccl. Reg. 58, fo. 353.

As to the state of the pest-houses, the justices have frequently and very lately considered of it, and do conceive it highly convenient for the preservation of the adjacent parishes that they were enlarged, that in Westminster being able to contain but 60 persons, and that other in the Soho but 90 persons, which now serves for St. Martin's, St. Clement's, St. Paul's Covent Garden, and St. Mary Savoy—scarce large enough for one of the said parishes. That in St. Giles's will contain but 60 persons, which considering the multitudes of poor in that parish, cannot be of any considerable use if the sickness break out amongst them. Now, how these may be enlarged, or indeed continued as they are for the public use of the above-mentioned parishes—the ordinary taxes and parochial duties being so numerous, the middling sort of persons so much impoverished by the late calamity of the Plague, so few, or rather none, of the nobility and gentry likely to continue here in case it should please God that the Plague break out again—is submitted to the wisdom of the Board, whose aid and assistance is, with all humility and speed, begged herein, it being the most probable means of hindering the spreading of the contagion amongst us.

The business of inmates and inhabitants in cellars has been very often debated and advised upon by the justices ; and although many difficulties have appeared to them, by reason of particular leases and contracts between the respective householders and inmates for a certain term of years yet to come, and that in regard that several of the said inmates, most of which are poor necessitous persons, and if once removed would prove excessively chargeable to the parishes (which at the time are least able to bear it) notwithstanding the justices have made a progress herein, having convened before them all the respective landlords within the adjacent parishes, and taken an account of each particular case, to the end that this affair might be put in such a method that in a short time they doubt not but to give a good account thereof, very many being removed already and are daily removing.[1]

The " inmate " or lodger triumphed first, second and always, by the very necessities of his situation. Every effort to eject him had provoked great discontent. Householders represented that if the magistrates persevered it would be their second undoing after the pestilence, and worse to them than the Plague ; and the magistrates rightly hesitated. Landlords said it would be their ruin ; manufacturers foresaw enhanced prices by scarcity of

[1] *State Papers Charles II*, vol. 149, no. 88.

labour ; mechanics and seamen protested against measures
that would leave them homeless, their wage being insufficient for rental of an entire house.[1] The Privy Council
displayed no wisdom in attempting to enforce a course
that, if ever practicable, must have driven substantially
the whole body of labour away from the chief centre of
manufacture and trade.

The Plague still lingered. It is a popular miscon-
ception that London was clear of the infection in the
calamitous year. In this second year 1666, there were in
January no fewer than 334 deaths in London attributed to
Plague by the Bills, and no doubt many others concealed ;
and in February 222, in March 107, in April 118—close
upon four hundred and fifty dead of Plague in the three
months that followed the Court's return. There was sharp
alarm in Whitehall Palace that month of April. Tom
Chiffinch, the King's closet keeper, who had been playing
backgammon there one night, apparently as well as ever,
and was not very ill by six o'clock next morning, yet was dead
before seven. " It looks fearfully among people nowadays,
the Plague, as we hear, increasing everywhere again,"
wrote Pepys.[2] In May grave fears were entertained of a
recrudescence of Plague with the arrival of the hot weather,
as bad as the visitation of the previous year. The Committee of Privy Council appointed on the outbreak of
Plague a twelvemonth before was again called together on
May 11th, to consider the best means of preventing the
pestilence from spreading.

Lord Craven was added to that body [3] ; his long experience will have proved valuable. He gave frank advice
that the old policy for meeting the Plague had failed—that
disastrous course of the imprisonment of whole families in
the infected houses, the terrible results of which I have
endeavoured to make plain in these pages. Short of
adequate pest-houses for isolation being erected in convenient places both for the City and suburbs, any measures
taken, Lord Craven declared, would signify but little.
Had that been done, the Plague would have been stifled

---

[1] *State Papers (Domestic)*, 1665–6, p. 351.
[2] *Diary*, 1666, April 8. Chiffinch lies buried in the centre of the
South Transept of Westminster Abbey.
[3] Privy Ccl. Reg. 59, fo. 13.

much earlier, "the infection," he said, "not proceeding from the air, but from want of conveniency and care for the timely removal of infected persons in the beginning, whereby to have hindered the spreading of it."[1] His letter, before cited, does but emphasize the alarming insufficiency of the pest-houses already provided. To Lord Craven, as to every one who had stayed in London and had witnessed its suffering, the frightful lesson had been borne home.

That same month of May, 1666, the Privy Council caused to be printed and distributed a code of "Rules and Orders" to be observed by justices of the peace, mayors, bailiffs and other officers of cities and places infected, or should infection occur therein.[2] I have given them in extenso in Appendix I., and they show by the proposals for effective segregation of the sick from the whole that at last the Council itself was alive to the folly, as well as the evil, of cooping in the infected households till Plague destroyed them. Each city and town was commanded to allocate forthwith some convenient place remote from itself, where an adequate pest-house, huts or sheds should be erected in readiness should Plague break out. In that event able and faithful searchers and examiners were forthwith to be appointed. The Plague-stricken were at once to be removed to the pest-house or huts so provided, "for the preservation of the rest of the family," the house thereafter being marked, locked, and guarded in the accustomed way. If any under ward developed Plague, these would in like manner be taken to the pest-house. Otherwise the family in health won liberation after forty days, but for a further twenty days their house was to bear a white cross, being meanwhile aired and fumed. No lodger till thereafter should take up residence in that house. Relief of the visited poor must be adequate, "want and nastiness being great occasions of the infection."

The "Rules and Orders" of May, 1666, are a revocation of the vital things that had been done, by inference a frank condemnation of them, a tardy admission that the whole policy by which for a century past Plague had been met

[1] Lord Craven's Recommendations, Brit. Museum Stowe MSS. 152, fo. 113.

[2] Privy Ccl. Reg. 59, fo. 13. The "Rules and Orders" are preserved in State Papers Charles II., vol. 155, fo. 102.

in England had been a fatal mistake—how fatal a mistake it has been the object of this book to show. It has, I indulge a hope, been made quite plain. The Great Plague in London, with its upwards of one hundred thousand dead, was a tragedy of errors.

The " Rules and Orders " were not, in fact, acted upon, but were disobeyed. If operative at all, it was only in a few towns like Colchester, Ipswich, Gravesend, Chatham and others which received infection from London in 1665, and suffered the Plague with much greater virulence in 1666. None in that careless age troubled about Plague when the spectre was itself absent. No general visitation recurred. The peril past, the authorities became as supine as before, and they avoided the large expense of acquiring additional lands and buildings for a contingency of Plague that, as the years went by, seemed ever more remote. There was not a town in England that had escaped severe impoverishment by the cessation of trade. The City of London spent a small sum, £44 only, in the year 1669 in putting its pest-house in repair.[1] Salisbury demolished its pest-house in 1668 as being no longer of utility, and sold the materials [2] ; the Cambridge pest-house lingered till its destruction in 1703.[3] The old Westminster pest-house in Tothill Fields, much rebuilt and patched, served in its last stage as an almshouse for twenty-four poor people, till dismantled early in the nineteenth century.

Lord Craven had longer vision than his contemporaries. In the year 1687 that public-spirited nobleman acquired three acres of land in St. Martin-in-the-Fields, and this he gave in trust that the land should be used by the Westminster out-parishes for pest-houses should Plague again break out in London. The plot figures in early eighteenth-century maps as " Pest House Field," and for this reason has been identified as the site of the St. Martin's pest-house, which it was not. London had grown out so far by 1732 that Lord Craven's heirs then obtained an Act of Parliament (Statute 7th George II., ch. 11) whereby three acres of meadow at Bayswater, now known as Craven Hill Gardens, was substituted for the original site, which

---

[1] " Repertory " 74, fo. 315.
[2] Salisbury Corporation MSS. (*Hist. MSS. Comm.*, p. 245).
[3] *Notes & Queries*, 3rd Ser., vi. 299.

thereafter was built over, and became Carnaby Market and neighbouring streets.

London's expansion a century later had incorporated Bayswater. There was a lawsuit to determine whether the Craven family had rights over the substituted land. They had then let it for building, protecting the parochial interests and themselves by covenants from the lessees to deliver up the land (and consequently houses standing upon it) if and when, on Plague recurring, it should be required for purposes of a pest-house. The risk of disturbance seemed small. A judgment delivered by Sir John Romilly, Master of the Rolls, in 1866 held that the family interests had been satisfied and were extinguished by the transfer, and that the land at Bayswater belongs wholly to the five Westminster parishes.

The annual rent goes to-day, under the Charity Commissioners' approved scheme, to the hospitals serving the parishes of St. Martin, St. Clement Danes, St. Paul Covent Garden, St. James Westminster and St. George Hanover Square, these undertaking to relieve the sick poor sent to them, infectious or otherwise (save cases of small-pox). Now a few hundreds sterling only, the income, when the leases fall in twenty years hence of thirteen houses in Craven Hill Gardens and coach-houses in the mews, will be as many thousands—a benefit to twentieth-century London arising out of the Great Plague and men's fears of its recurrence.

Few people know that the gift is still operative. This ground, and the height of the City churchyards raised above the street levels, obvious to any observant eye, are reminders borne in London to-day of the terrible epidemic of the Great Plague.

The very cold weather of the early winter did not last, and the Plague fluctuated a good deal in the first months of the New Year, yet was never absent. The Bill for January 2nd recorded 253 deaths in all in the week past, 70 being from Plague—there had been as many as 8,297 admitted deaths in a single week when the Plague raged its worst. This mortality was the lowest that had been experienced for twenty years, but was less an indication of the City's health than of its depopulated state.[1]

[1] Pepys, 1666, Jan. 3.

A generall Bill for this present year,
ending the 19 of December 1665, according to the Report made to the KINGS most Excellent Majesty.

By the Company of Parish Clerks of London, &c.

Parish	Buried	Pla.	Parish	Buried	Pla.	Parish	Buried	Pla.	Parish	Buried	Pla.
St Albans Woodstreet	200	121	St Clements Eastcheab	38	20	St Margaret Moses	38	25	St Michael Cornehill	104	52
St Alhallows Barking	514	330	St Dionis Back-church	78	27	St Margar. New Fishst.	114	66	St Michael Crookedla.	179	133
St Alhallows Breadst	35	16	St Dunstans East	265	150	St Margaret Pattons	49	24	St Michael Queenehi.	203	122
St Alhallows Great	455	426	St Edmunds Lumbard.	70	36	St Mary Abchurch	99	54	St Michael Querne	44	18
St Alhallowes Honila	10	5	St Ethelborough	195	106	St Mary Aldermanbury	181	109	St Michael Royall	152	116
St Alhallowes Lesse	239	175	St Faiths	104	70	St Mary Aldermary	105	75	St Michael Woodstreet	122	62
St Alhall. Lumbardstr	90	62	St Fosters	144	105	St Mary le Bow	64	36	St Mildred Breadstreet	59	26
St Alhallowes Staining	185	112	St Gabriel Fen-church	69	39	St Mary Bothaw	55	30	St Mildred Poultrey	68	46
St Alhall. wes the Wall	520	356	St George Botolphlane	41	27	St Mary Colechurch	17	9	St Nicholas Acons	46	18
St Alphage	271	115	St Gregories by Pauls	376	232	St Mary Hill	94	64	St Nicholas Coleabby	125	91
St Andrew Hubbard	71	25	St Hellens	108	75	St Mary Mounthaw	56	37	St Nicholas Olaues	90	62
St Andrew Vndershaft	274	189	St James Dukes place	262	190	St Mary Summerset	342	262	St Olaves Hart-streete	237	15c
St Andrew Wardrobe	476	308	St James Garlickhithe	189	118	St Mary Stainings	05	22	St Olaves Iewry	54	32
St Anne Aldersgate	282	197	St John Baptist	138	83	St Mary Woolchurch	65	33	St Olaves Siluerstreet	250	132
St Anne Blacke-Friers	652	467	St John Euangelist	9		St Mary Woolnoth	75	38	St Pancras Soperlane	30	13
St Antholins Parish	58	33	St John Zacharie	85	54	St Martins Iremonger.	21	11	St Peters Cheape	61	35
St Austins Parish	43	20	St Katherine Coleman	299	213	St Martins Ludgate	196	128	St Peters Corne-hill	136	76
St Barthol. Exchange	73	51	St Katherine Cree-chu.	335	231	St Martins Orgars	110	71	St Peters Pauls Wharse	114	86
St Bennet Fynch	27	23	St Lawrence Iewrie	94	48	St Martins Outwitch	60	34	St Peters Poore	79	47
St Bennet Grace chur.	43	27	St Lawrence Pountney	214	127	St Martins Vintrey	417	349	St Stevens Colemanst	560	391
St Bennet Pauls Wharf	355	172	St Leonard Eastcheape	42	27	St Matthew Fridayst.	24	22	St Stevens Walbrooke	34	17
St Bennet Sherehog	11	5	St Leonard Fosterlane	335	255	St Maudlins Milkstreet	44	22	St Swithins	93	56
St Botolph Billingsgate	83	50	St Magnus Parish	103	60	St Maudlins Oldfishstr.	176	121	St Thomas Apostle	163	110
Christs Church	653	467	St Margaret Lothbury	100	66	St Michael Bassishaw	253	164	Trinitie Parish	115	79
St Christophers	60	47									

Buried in the 97 Parishes within the walls,——15207 VVhereof, of the Plague——9887

Parish	Buried	Pla.	Parish	Buried	Pla.	Parish	Buried	Pla.
St Andrew Holborne	3958	3103	Bridewell Precinct	230	179	St Dunstans West	958	665	St Saviours Southwark	4235	3446
St Bartholmew Great	493	344	St Botolph Aldersgate	997	755	St George Southwark	1613	1260	St Sepulchres Parish	4509	2746
St Batholmew Lesse	193	139	St Botolph Algate	4926	4051	St Giles Cripplegate	8069	4838	St Thomas Southwark	475	371
St Brigdes	2111	1427	St Botolph Bishopsgate	3464	2500	St Olaves Southwark	4793	2785	Trinity Minories	168	123
									At the Pesthouse	159	156

Buried in the 16 Parishes without the VValls——41351 VVhereof of the Plague——28888

Parish	Buried	Pla.	Parish	Buried	Pla.	Parish	Buried	Pla.
St Giles in the Fields	4457	3216	St Katherines Tower	956	601	St Magdalens Bermon.	1943	1362	St Mary Whitechap.	4766	3855
Hackney Parish	232	132	Lambeth Parish	798	537	St Mary Newington	1272	1004	Redrisse Parish	304	210
St James Clarkenwell	1803	1377	St Leonards Shordtich	2669	1949	St Mary Islington	696	593	Stepney Parish	8598	6583

Buried in the 12 out-Parishes, in Middlesex and Surrey 28554 VVhereof of the Plague——21420

Parish	Buried	Pla.	Parish	Buried	Pla.		
St Clement Danes	1969	1319	St Mary Sauoy	303	198	The Total of all the Christnings——	9967
St Paul Couent Garden	408	261	St Margaret Westmin.	4710	3742	The Total of all the Burials this year——	97306
St Martins in the Field	4804	2883	thereof at the Pesthouse		156	Whereof, of the Plague——	68596

Buried in the 9 Parishes in the City and Liberties of Westminster—— 12194
Whereof, of the Plague—— 8403

Diseases and Casualties this year.

Abortive and Stilborne	617	Executed	21	Palsie	30
Aged	1545	Flox and Smal Pox	655	Plague	68596
Ague and Feaver	5257	Found dead in streets, fields, &c.	20	Plannet	6
Appoplex and Suddenly	116	French Pox	86	Plurisie	15
Bedrid	10	Frighted	23	Poysoned	1
Blasted	5	Gout and Sciatica	27	Quinsie	35
Bleeding	16	Grief	46	Rickets	557
Bloudy Flux, Scowring & Flux	185	Griping in the Guts	1288	Rising of the Lights	397
Burnt and Scalded	8	Hangd & made away themselves	7	Rupture	34
Calenture	3	Headmouldshot & Mouldfallen	14	Scurvy	105
Cancer, Gangrene and Fistula	56	Jaundies	110	Shingles and Swine pox	2
Canker, and Thrush	111	Impostume	227	Sores, Ulcers, broken and bruised Limbes	82
Childbed	625	Kild by several accidents	46	
Chrisomes and Infants	1258	Kings Evill	86	Spleen	14
Cold and Cough	68	Leprosie	2	Spotted Feaver and Purples	1929
Collick and Winde	134	Lethargy	14	Stopping of the Stomach	332
Consumption and Tissick	4808	Livergrowne	20	Stone and Strangury	98
Convulsion and Mother	2036	Meagrom and Headach	12	Surfet	1251
Distracted	5	Measles	7	Teeth and Worms	2614
Dropsie and Timpany	1478	Murthered, and Shot	9	Vomiting	51
Drowned	50	Overlaid and Starved	45	VVenn	1

Christned { Males 5114, Females 4853, In all 9967 }   Buried { Males 48569, Females 48737, In all 97306 }   Of the Plague 68596

Increased in the Burials in the 130 Parishes and at the Pest-house this year—— 79009

Increased of the Plague in the 130 Parishes and at the Pest-house this year—— 68590

Pepys, going to Bennett's, the mercer's in Paternoster Row, found that few of the shops there had yet been reopened.[1] The deaths from Plague rose next week to 89, and after another seven days' lapse the Bill for January 16th showed a week's Plague deaths to have been 110— the highest return for several weeks, of bad omen.

The returned refugees took new alarm, convinced that they had been too venturesome ; there were fearful forebodings of the fate awaiting London when summer's heat again came round.[2]   But the rise in mortality was happily followed by an equally rapid fall.   On January 23rd the town received the good news that the Plague deaths were down to 79, and on January 30th to 56, with a new low record of 227 dead in all.   This was the Bill which induced King Charles's rapid decision to trust himself again at Whitehall Palace.   The incidence of Plague mortality continued to fluctuate thereafter, always keeping below 50, till in May came a week's record of 58, a total of Plague deaths that London, after its calamitous experience, was destined never again to know.

The Plague was not eliminated when what we call the Great Plague had passed.   It struck here and there, and before completely exhausted had taken 1,780 lives in London in the second year, 1666.[3]   As spring developed after the hard winter, the infection left London save for a few isolated cases each week, but other towns and villages in England thereafter were terribly visited.   The fate of some of these was worse than that of the capital.   London's vast death-roll has by sheer weight of numbers monopolized all attention for two and a half centuries ; the towns afterwards infected, lacking such figures, have received scant notice.   Eyam's tragic story has been recalled. Deal in 1666 was said with small exaggeration of language to have been depopulated.[4]   Colchester had but a small community ; no fewer than 3,500 of its inhabitants were carried off by Plague in a few months ; the Mayor sent a

[1] Pepys, 1666, Jan. 8.
[2] *Ibid.*, Jan. 16.   Finch MSS. (*Hist. MSS. Comm.*, p. 404).
[3] Bills of Mortality.   The printed return gives 1,998, but the year is so divided as to include the last twelve days of December, 1665, wherein the deaths from Plague exceeded two hundred.   I have given the corrected figures as from January 1st, 1666.
[4] Pepys, 1666, Aug. 9, so told by John Evelyn.

pitiful petition to the Privy Council for relief, representing
the Plague as dispersed in all parts, the town being brought
thereby to extreme poverty.[1] Colchester was a chief
source from which came the supply of cloth for the great
market at Blackwell Hall, by Guildhall. The Lord
Mayor and Aldermen, fearful that London would be
reinfected if clothiers and cloth from Colchester were
permitted free access to the market, petitioned that both
men and goods should be held for a month in quarantine
at Stratford-atte-Bow, beyond the City's eastern border.
The justices at Stratford were directed by the Privy Council
to lodge and keep, for such time as they should think fit,
all merchandise from Colchester, taking care that it be well
aired with brimstone and other fumes before being brought
into London.[2]

Colchester, during the time the Plague lasted from
August, 1665, till its disappearance in the December of the
following year, was almost denuded of inhabitants, there
being 4,731 deaths among them.[3] For the town's relief
a sum of £1,311 was raised by collections made in all the
churches within the London diocese.[4]

London, the richer classes being now back, contributed
freely to the relief of towns suffering in this second year
the aftermath of its own visitation. Winchester was so
badly infected that quarter sessions were removed to
Basingstoke ; [5] the school was closed, and did not reopen
till December, when " in all human appearance the sickness
in that city and suburbs was extinguished." [6] There was
little Plague in Salisbury in 1665 (though enough to
expedite the Court's departure for Oxford), but next year
it raged with violence between June and December.
Royal License was given to elect the Mayor at an assembly
held in the Cathedral Close, as a place of greater safety on
account of the pestilence.[7] Plague was in Bristol from the
middle of April, 1666, to September, when seventy-two
persons died of it.[8] The infection was in Rochester,
Chatham, Maidstone, and Canterbury.

[1] Privy Ccl. Reg. 59, fo. 5.   [2] *Ibid.* 58, fo. 394.
[3] Morant's *Essex*, i. 74.
[4] Privy Ccl. Reg. 59, fo. 5.   Cromwell's *Colchester*, p. 163.
[5] Privy Ccl. Reg. 58, fo. 397.   [6] *London Gazette.*
[7] Salisbury Corporation MSS. (*Hist. MSS. Comm.*, p. 245).
[8] *Cal. of Treasury Books*, 1660–7, p. 731.

The North of England generally, save for a mild outbreak in Durham and Northumberland, escaped Plague. Lancashire was wholly free, and it is scarcely traceable in Yorkshire. The town of Derby suffered severely in 1666. The residents, with Eyam's example before them, mostly fled. Those who remained erected at Nun's Green, outside the town, a market stone, or headless cross, whereon market people from the country, coming with their mouths primed with tobacco as a disinfectant, left provisions.[1] The stone is preserved in the Derby Arboretum.

Cambridge became infected when the Plague curve in London was at its peak, cases lasted into the winter, and the town was fated to undergo a much more severe outbreak in the following year, when there were 797 burials in the churchyards. A letter from Clare Hall, soon after the Plague's onset, affords a glimpse of the alarm—

Alderman Mywell the Brewer and one of his children dyed of the plague this last Munday ; he hath had 4 children in all dead of it. Clayton, the Barber in Petty Cury and one of his children dyed last Satturday of the sickness. It is newly broken out sadly by Christs (though they are all fled from that Colledge upon Mr Bunchly, their manciple's dying of the plague) where Nickolson the smith, his wife and 2 children are dead within these 3 days, his other children being deadly sick in the house. But it most rageth in St. Clements parish, where seldome a day passeth without one dead of the sickness. Poore Mr Brown the old man that is one of the University Musitians and Mr Saunders that sings the deep base are shut up in Mr Saunders house in Green Street, whose child dyed last week suspected. 2 houses at Barton are infected by 2 of Alderman Mywells children that are dead there. Ditton is broke out just by the Butcher from whom we had our meat which made us hastily remove to Grandchester. H. Glenton the Carrier fled from this town to Shelford, where he dyed within 2 or 3 days suspected. Thus is our town unhappy not onely to its self but to its neighbours. Royston is sadly in 2 or 3 places the last of which is just in the middle of the town, the infection they say was brought thither by a Cambridge man, whom they caught and shut him up but he hath since made an escape.[2]

[1] *Archæologia*, vol. 37, p. 20.
[2] Letter of Oct. 19, 1665, in Clare College Library. J. R. Wardale, *Clare College Letters and Documents*, pp. 69, 70.

Mr. Thomas Warren, apothecary at the Golden Hart and Anchor in Basing Lane, was appointed by Cambridge University to receive such moneys as should be contributed by the London citizens for relief of the sufferers.[1] It was January, 1667, before the Vice-Chancellor and the Heads of Houses notified that the scholars might return to the colleges.[2]

The Plague's worst effects when, its strength in London spent, it spread outwards, were in East Anglia and the South of England. Norwich suffered most severely in the second year ; in the twelve months ending October 3rd, 1666, the town had 2,251 deaths attributed to Plague, which in a single week in August claimed 203 victims.[3] Its trade and manufactures ceased, the poor were brought to great extremities, and a subscription for relief was opened in London.[4] A general collection for Norwich was taken in all London churches on August 14th, a day of public thanksgiving for victory over the Dutch at sea.[5]

Ipswich Fair in September, 1666, was prohibited because of the continuing pestilence, and so many inhabitants fled from the town that the rates could not be collected.[6] In King's Lynn Plague was epidemic in both years, the gates were shut, and no markets were held.[7] Peterborough received the Plague in September, 1665, it being brought by a woman travelling from London, if local report is true. After a mild visitation that autumn and winter, it reappeared in May, 1666, taking 377 victims in four months. Many corpses were buried in the gardens. It was March, 1667, before Peterborough was clear of infection.[8] A proclamation of October, 1666, stated that the Plague was much spread about the Sussex town of Battle.[9] Pepys tells of a curious experience at Petersfield, that " one side of the street had every house almost infected through the town, and the other not one shut up." [10] For many of these stricken towns a weekly collection in aid was made in the London churches, the Lord Mayor and the Bishop

[1] *London Gazette*, No. 72.
[2] *Ibid.*, 1667, Jan. 21–4.
[3] Blomefield's *Norwich*, i. 410.
[4] *London Gazette*.
[5] Privy Ccl. Regs. 59, fo. 116.
[6] Clarke's *Ipswich*, p. 50.
[7] Richards' *Lynn*, p. 1203.
[8] *Archæologia*, vol. 37, p. 21.
[9] *London Gazette*, 1666, No. 98.
[10] *Diary*, 1667, April 4.

NORWICH.

From the 8 of August to the 15 1666

	Bapt.		Bur.	Pla.
St Peters at the Gates			3	3
St Audries			3	2
St Julians			19	18
St Peter per Mounter-gate			26	25
St John Sepulchre			26	24
St Michael Thorne			4	4
St John Timber-hill			4	4
All-Saints			8	7
St Stephens			18	10
St Peters Mancroft			62	62
St Giles			2	2
Haigham	2		2	2
St Bennets			2	2
St Swithin			2	4
St Margaret			8	5
St Lawrence			26	5
St Gregories				5
St John Madre-market				
St Andrews				
St Michael the Plea				
St Peter-Hungate			1	1
St Georges Tomland			2	2
St Symonds			2	1
St Martins Pallace			1	
St Hellers			5	5
St Michael Costany			3	3
St George Colgate			3	1
St Clements	1		3	1
St Edmonds	1		1	1
St Maries				1
St Martins at the Oak			18	12
St Augustins			2	5
St Saviours			2	3
St Pauls			24	14
St James				

Baptized		Buried		Pla.
Males	3	Males		
Females	1	Females		
In all	4	In all	196	137

And at the Pesthouse — 4
The total of the Burials — Whereof plague

A NORWICH BILL OF MORTALITY
ONE WEEK'S DEATHS IN PLAGUE OF 1666
Actual Size.

of London apportioning the contribution amongst the most necessitous places.[1]

Nottingham has the distinction of having been the last place visited by epidemic Plague. In 1667 the pestilence appeared in the higher part of the town, but must have been of an unusually mild type, for the burials that year are only 55 above the average numbers of uninfected years,[2] and the identification with bubonic Plague is not quite convincing. Curious that after centuries of Plague's ravages, evidenced in hundreds of thousands of deaths, we should be in this uncertainty as to its last appearance in epidemic.

London by its mass dominates all our conceptions, and must necessarily do so. It was London's experience that gave to the visitation of 1665 the name of the Great Plague. There remains an epitome to be made—the epitome of all the tragic story that I have endeavoured to tell in these pages. What was the loss? The Bills of Mortality for the fated year record deaths from all causes numbering 97,306, and of these 68,596 were attributed to the Plague. It is unlikely to exaggerate if the actual deaths be put down at 110,000, to comprise the Nonconforming sects who refused notification to the parish church, and—more important because more numerous—the loads taken by the dead-carts to the pits, of which no full record was or could be kept. Of those left behind in the capital when the more prosperous classes fled, in proportion almost of one out of every three London's populace had perished. This loss is, I am aware, higher than has before been conceded, or even thought possible. I have not stated it without much searching of mind; but after giving full consideration to the best available estimates of population, I am convinced that it is the truth.

In the next year, when London's habitants had returned and accessions from the countryside filled many gaps— from December 19th, 1665 to December 18th, 1666—there was a decrease of no fewer than 84,568 in the number of burials recorded in the Bills of Mortality. These are significant figures, for it will be noticed that the reduction is in excess by 17,000 of the Plague deaths which the Bills had grudgingly allowed in the year of visitation.

[1] Privy Ccl. Reg. 59, fos. 83–4. [2] *Archæologia*, vol. 37, p. 22.

That summer and autumn of 1666 there still were cases in London.   Sheldon, the Archbishop of Canterbury, absented himself from the Court and the Council in July, his chaplain's servant having died at the pest-house of the Plague.[1] The Mermaid Tavern in Cornhill was shut, marked with the red cross, locked and guarded, a drawer there having fallen sick and been taken to the City pest-house.[2] The experience that earlier had been that of many of the returned exiles so late as August, 1666, overtook Daniel Rawlinson, a London wine-merchant and father of a future Lord Mayor ; [3] his man died of Plague, his wife and a maid were sick, and his house in Fenchurch Street was shut up—this after he and his family had found safety in the country in the previous year in all the months that the Great Plague raged.[4] That month of August the pest entered Chelsea Hospital, and ten Dutch and French prisoners of war lodged there perished of the Plague.[5] Proclamation was again made prohibiting Bartholomew Fair in Smithfield, " for fear of increasing the contagion in this city by the resort thereto," the great fair at Gravesend, and also all other fairs for the year at or near any place visited by Plague.[6]

The ruling authorities still held their fears ; so far were they from considering the menace passed, that observation of the day of solemn fasting and humiliation " for the continuing pestilence " went on into this second winter. When Dr. Hall, Bishop of Chester, preached the monthly fast sermon on October 3rd before the House of Lords, the sorely tried Londoners had other causes for distraction. The Great Fire had broken out on September 2nd and destroyed the larger part of the City ; and the Bishop derived a moral lesson from God's judgment in the double calamity.[7]   Anxious in the presence of this new cause of woe to put the pestilence behind them, the public again

---

[1] *State Papers (Domestic)*, 1665–6, p. 581.
[2] Privy Ccl. Reg. 59, fos. 44–5.
[3] Sir Thomas Rawlinson, President of Bridewell Hospital and Lord Mayor in 1706.
[4] Pepys's *Diary*, 1666, Aug. 6.
[5] Privy Ccl. Reg. 59, fo. 132.
[6] *Royal Proclamations*, 1666, Aug. 7, Sept. 26.
[7] *A Fast Sermon Preached to the Lords . . . on the Day of Solemn Humiliation for the continuing Pestilence, October 3, 1666, by George Lord Bishop of Chester*.   Lond. 1666.

filled the churches in the following month, November 20th having been appointed a thanksgiving day for the cessation of the Plague.[1]

Pepys, worldly minded, saw a worldly purpose in this undue scurry : "But Lord ! how the town do say that it is hastened before the Plague is quite over, there dying some people still, but only to get ground for plays to be publicly acted, which the bishops would not suffer till the Plague was over." [2]

That ends this narrative of the Great Plague in London. A single desire has impelled me, to tell the plain truth, and I am oppressed by the conviction that the whole truth is not told. Its best is omitted. In the shut-up houses, where anguished parents witnessed their offspring passed out at night to the dead-cart, till their own turn should come to die ; in the flight to the country, when every man was an object of suspicious enmity to his fellow men ; within the shadowed shelter of those tragic pest-houses— there must have been acts of high courage and self-denial, many and many and many in number. Of these this book tells nothing. They have escaped preservation in letter and memoir, and after two and a half centuries' lapse are not likely now to be recovered.

So throughout, the story of the Plague has been one in which the dark seams of life stand out conspicuous, and those more humane aspects of the time upon which I would wish most to dwell have suffered eclipse. The sympathy that links the human race in one great family, the kindly help given at times of gravest peril in the service of fellow men, at known risk and without expectation of reward, the charity (and none are more charitable) of the poor— these must have been evidenced in plenty in a catastrophe that swept away one hundred thousand men, women, and children. So many of them children ! Our forefathers of Restoration London would have been less than men had it been otherwise. I have shown little of human nature except at its darkest. Thus far I have failed.

[1] Lincoln's Inn Library (Brydall 32, No. 19) has *A Form of Common Prayer with Thanksgiving to God, for assuaging the late contagion and Pestilence*, 1666, used on this occasion.
[2] *Diary*, 1666, Nov. 20.

It is the penalty that inevitably awaits any historian of the Plague. The material is not there. The masses of the poor were swept into the graveyards and the pits. As these men and women perished, unlettered themselves and little regarded, mere names in those terrible columns of the burial registers, so long and attenuated, page following page in almost endless succession—and thousands without even that little memorial—the remembrance perished with them of many a golden deed that I should have longed to tell. A novelist with license that is not mine, to create and to picture in warm colours that which I have been able only dimly to suggest, would in this case, perhaps, have been the truer historian. But long before these last pages are reached the fact will, I have confidence, have been borne in upon the reader, that something is missing. He will have had intuition to detect the hiatus, and while reading all that I have felt compelled to write down, reading so much that has been depressing and gruesome, and often repellent, he will not have been without a sense of the reality of those more honourable qualities in which, in destiny's darkest hours, Englishmen have never been lacking—qualities that I feel assured were exercised in this time of calamity and suffering, though I have been unable adequately to recall them.

The acts of almost all public bodies in the crisis of the Plague are open to just censure. That becomes monotonous. Yet it has been worth while to make this record, extenuating nothing and minimizing nothing, and one may derive satisfaction from the greater care and concern for human life that now is extended over the meanest and the poorest. No man dies but his death is of some concern. That corporate sense of the sanctity of human life, wherever found, has developed but slowly over the centuries, and it is the strongest testimony of the uplifting tendency of civilization. It was less evident two and a half centuries ago.

The Parliament at Oxford, the absent Government, the profligate Court, pleasure-seeking and careless while tens of thousands died—how difficult it is to avoid contempt for them ! The Church failed to achieve its great mission ; the College of healing won no glory and but small credit by its practitioners. It would seem that but five years after the Restoration the fibre of the ruling classes was at its feeblest. The magistrates who stayed among the people by King Charles's direction, and the fathers of the City, are fortunate exceptions. It is to individual men and their fine example that credit is due for all that was done in great emergency, and some of these I have recalled. Monck, Lawrence, Hodges, Vincent, Whitehead, Mompesson—they did fearless work during the Great Plague, and their names derive from it added lustre. Such names are few. If but rarely has a golden shaft lightened the gloom of my narrative, it is not necessarily that it was absent, but that the historian is not privileged to catch the light. I have, too, written of London and for the most part omitted the capital city that is its heart; a curious omission from a London book. Not under the Cathedral's shadow or at the centre of great commerce, but in squalid quarters of the outskirts wherein the poor were crowded thickest the story of the Plague is found.

The Great Plague passed, to become a memory. Still Plague lingered in London years after the Great Fire that followed, though never again was it to return in epidemic form. In the year 1667, thirty-five cases recorded as Plague occur, and fourteen and three in the succeeding years, and only in 1670 was the capital reported entirely free from it. Thenceforward one traces in the Bills of Mortality its rare appearance and slow extinction, till in the year 1679 the last case (at Rotherhithe) figures therein.

We had done with Plague, after centuries of tragic experience which curiously our historians have little regarded. Lady Mary Montagu, writing long after the Great Plague in London, in her letters from the East remarked that, " asking the Turkish ladies how they expected to provide for their numerous stock of children (many had twenty) they answered, ' The Plague would certainly kill one half of them.' This indeed," she adds, " generally happens, without much concern to the parents." The Oriental saw in it only the working of Fate. The London mother was not bereaved by Plague to such extent; but certainly after the early years of Elizabeth's reign—before, the records are sparse—rarely did the London child live to adult life without passing through one,

or possibly more, grave epidemics, and always there were
the isolated cases. Plague was a settled habitant.

And when the Great Plague had passed, and after 1679,
still the line for Plague is found in the printed Bills of
Mortality, always filled up by an " 0 " marked opposite.
So long had that desolating malady been known in their
midst that the Londoners could not believe in its permanent
absence. For more than twenty years thereafter they
retained this place for its shadow, like the chair set at
Macbeth's banquet to be filled by a spectre guest.

The Bills record a death-roll of 97,306. A gap was
made in London's population that in fact far exceeded
100,000. Yet the Great Plague left no lasting effects, so
surprisingly does Nature work in providing compensations
—in maintaining the average. Its influence on the
statistical returns was quickly wiped out. London refilled
its ranks from the countryside. Births not alone rose to
the old figure in two years, but surpassed it. Dr. Creighton
has pointed out that there were many years before 1665,
in the intervals of the greater explosions of Plague, when
the baptisms in London exceeded the burials by various
fractions up to twenty-five per cent.

Inversely, freedom from Plague brought no uprush in
vital statistics. It is curious to observe, after what has
just been said, that in no year after the extinction of
Plague until the last decennium of the eighteenth century
do the London Bills of the parish clerks show an excess of
baptisms over burials. The shortage is too great to be
accounted for by some negligence in registration. The
Plague took adult life in large proportion. Infant mortality thereafter kept down the population, much as Plague
had done. So vast was the sacrifice of infant life in London
from the Restoration until late in the eighteenth century,
that the deaths under the age of two years amounted in
some years to two-fifths of the deaths at all ages.[1]

Like the Turkish woman, the London mother could
expect the survival of but one-half, or little more than one-
half, of the family to which she gave birth. Still there was
this human sacrifice, not indeed to the Moloch of Plague,
but to another of the vexed gods. To man's ignorance
Nature is inexorable in extracting the penalty.

[1] Dr. Charles Creighton, *Social England*, iv. 646.

Many times Plague recurred on the Continent. Its appearance in the Baltic in early years of the eighteenth century invoked a stringent Quarantine Act.[1] The outbreak in Marseilles in 1720–2 revived the worst fears, inspiring Defoe to write his "Journal of the Plague Year." In panic Parliament passed legislation which condemned all persons infected to be taken to lazaret or pest-house, by violence if necessary, and any escaping therefrom to suffer a felon's death. London fortunately was spared these rigours. The Act further empowered the Crown to draw lines or cast trenches around any infected city, that night and day should be guarded, and breaking out from the place so isolated involved penalty of death.[2] A year or two later, when alarm had subsided, the City of London petitioned Parliament for the withdrawal of these clauses. Lord Harcourt then observed that to guard entrenched London and Westminster would require over 200,000 men, and as such a force could not be raised, it mattered nothing whether the powers survived or not. They were soon after expunged.

In July, 1760, a false report of Plague in St. Thomas's Hospital, then situated in Southwark, spread consternation throughout London. Next morning the demand made for rue and wormwood in Covent Garden advanced prices 40 per cent. Gardeners were employed all the day in taking those commodities to market.[3] The Governors of the Hospital deemed it necessary to advertise a denial in the *London Gazette*.

Fear of Plague born of the great visitation lingered to the very end of the seventeenth century. Late as 1698 this item of account in a fashionable lady's housekeeping book appears :

June 19. Ingredients had by Mistress Monroe for Plague Water, 1s. 1d.[4]

---

[1] *Statute 9th Anne, ch.* 2.
[2] *Statute 7th George I., ch.* 3.
[3] *London Magazine*, 1760, p. 434.
[4] Verulam MSS. (*Hist. MSS. Comm.*, p. 214).

APPENDICES

I. PRIVY COUNCIL RULES AND ORDERS.

Issued in May, 1666.

In State Papers Chas. II:, vol. 155, No. 102.

RULES AND ORDERS

To be observed by all Justices of the Peace, Mayors, Bayliffs, and other officers, for prevention of the spreading of the infection of the Plague.

PUBLISHED BY HIS MAJESTY'S SPECIAL COMMAND.

1. You are to take care, That no stranger be permitted to lodge or abide in any City, Town, or Village without a sufficient Certificate of health, and the consent of the next Justice of the Peace, or chief Magistrate (if within a Corporation) which said Certificate to be made by the Minister and Churchwardens of the Parish from whence such person came, and confirmed under the Hand and Seal of the next Justice of the Peace to the said parish.

2. That no old Household-Goods whatsoever be received into any City, Burrough, Town, Village or Hamlet, coming from any place suspected to be infected with the Plague, without sufficient Certificate.

3. That all publique Meetings and Concourses of people, as much as may be (especially to Funerals, Wakes, or Revels) be Prohibited, where there is any suspicion of the Plague.

4. That no Vagabonds nor Beggars be permitted to go and wander about the Countrey, or in any other City or place; and That you appoint Watching and Warding for that end; and that all publique places (especially Streets and Passages) be kept sweet and clean; and that all Laystalls, Dunghills and Slaughter-houses near any Dwellings be removed to places more remote.

5. That Order be given to all householders to keep their

Dwelling houses sweet and clean, and to keep shut all windows opening towards Infected Houses.

6. That Fires in movable Pans, or otherwise, be made in all necessary publique Meetings in Churches &c., and the convenient Fumes to correct the Air be burnt thereon.

7. That care be taken that no unwholsome Meats, Stinking Fish, Flesh, musty Corn, or any other unwholsome Food be exposed to Sale in Shops or Markets.

8. That no Swine, Dogs, Cats or tame Pigeons be permitted to pass up and down in Streets, or from house to house, in places Infected.

9. That the laws against Inn-Mates be forthwith put in strict execution, and that no more Alehouses be Licensed than are absolutely necessary in any City or place, especially during the continuance of this present contagion.

10. That each City and Town forthwith provide some convenient place remote from the same, where a Pest-house, Huts, or Sheds may be Erected, to be in readiness in case any Infection should break out ; which if it shall happen to do, That able and faithful Searchers and Examiners be forthwith provided and Sworn to Search all suspected bodies, for the usual signs of the Plague, viz, Swellings or Risings under the Ears or Arm-pits, or upon the Groynes ; Blains, Carbuncles, or little Spots, either on the Breast or back, commonly called Tokens.

11. That if any house be Infected, the sick person or persons be forthwith removed to the said Pest-house, Sheds, or Huts, for the preservation of the rest of the Family : And that such house (though none be dead therein) be shut up for Fourty days, and have a *Red Cross* and *Lord have mercy upon us*, in Capital Letters affixed on the door, and Warders appointed, as well to find them necessaries, as to keep them from conversing with the sound.

12. That at the opening of each infected house (after the expiration of the said Fourty days) a *White Cross* be affixed on the said door, there to remain Twenty days more ; during which time, or at least before any stranger be suffered to lodge therein, That the said house be well Fumed, Washed, and Whited all over within with Lime ; And that no Clothes, or Household stuff be removed out of the said house into any other house, for at least Three months after, unless the persons so Infected have occasion to change their habitation.

13. That none dying of the Plague be buried in Churches, or Churchyards (unless they be large and then to have a place assigned for that use where other bodies are not usually buried Boarded or Paled in Ten foot high) but in some other con venient places, and that a good quantity of unslackt Lime be

put into the graves with such bodies, and that such Graves be not after opened within the space of a year or more, lest they infect others.

14. That in case any City, Burrough, Town or Village be so Visited and Infected, that it is not able to maintain its own poor, That then a Rate be forthwith made by the adjoyning Justices of the Peace, and confirmed at the very next Quarter-Sessions, for that use, upon the neighbouring Parishes, according to the Statute 1st *Jacobi*, so that such Visited Poor may have sufficient Relief; want and nastiness being great occasions of the Infection.

15. That you yourselves use your endeavours, not only to see these Directions punctually observed, and be in a readiness to render an Accompt as often as you shall be required, but that you strictly enjoyn all High Constables, Petty Constables, Headburroughs and other Officers, to execute their respective duties according to their places, and if any shall fail herein, to use the utmost severity against them according to Law.

What relates to Physitians, Chyurgeons, and such other persons as are necessary for the preservation and help of such who shall be Infected, the same is left to your particular care and discretion.

Lastly, That you take special care, that not onely the Monethly Fasts, but that the publique Prayers on *Wednesdays* and *Fridays* also, be strictly and constantly observed according to His Majesties Proclamation; And that such Collections as shall be then made, be strictly applied to the relief and necessities of the poor in Infected places, by which means God may be inclined to remove his severe hand both from amongst you and us.

LONDON

Printed by *John Bill* and *Christopher Barker*, Printers to the King's most Excellent Majesty, 1666.

II. POST-MORTEM ON A PLAGUE VICTIM.

From Dr. George Thomson's *Loimotomia: or the Pes Anatomized.* Lond. 1666.

[Dr. George Thomson's post-mortem examination of a Plague victim appears to be the only one made during the epidemic of 1665 of which record was kept and survives. The passages printed below contain all that he gives; afterwards he goes on to explain symptoms present in

himself from which he diagnosed infection by Plague
during the examination, but the attack did not develop
to grave risk.]

In the year 1665, a most ruefull lamentable time as ever
London suffered in this Kinde, when the Sickness swept away
many thousands in a week in the Moneth of *August*, I visited
a lusty proper man, by name M^r. *Wil: Pick*, living in *Peticoat-
lane*, grievously wounded by one of those poisonous Arrows
that flew thick about poor Mortalls : so that his condition
seemed to be almost desperate, and finding no relief at all
from those frivilous and vain preparations a *Galenist* had ex-
hibited to him *usquo ad nauseam* : was in some short space
preserved by Chimical Remedies : the poison being therewith
excluded, and the Archeus of the Stomack redeemed from
captivity.   At the same time there lay a servant of M^r. *Picks*,
a youth about 15 yeares of age, labouring under most horrid
symptomes, raving as it were extimulated by some Fury ;
which Tragical Interlude was quickly terminated by a mortal
Catastrophe.   Upon this, I took occasion to request my then
recovering Patient his Master, to grant me liberty to open this
defunct body ; for my own instruction, and the satisfaction
of all inquisitive Persons, to which, having given him some
perswasive reasons to that purpose, he strait condescended,
yet not without some jealousie and kind fear least I should
do my self injury ; upon his concession I being much exhilarated
in my spirits, having obtained that desire which was often
denyed me by those who pretended several slight excuses, I
girt up my self with all expedition, getting in readiness what
Instruments were fitting, with a porringer containing Sulphur
to burn under the Corps, which was at that time placed in the
open air in a yard there adjacent, which for several respects
was very convenient ; and for my better accommodation a
Servant by the permission of the foresaid Master was ready
to afford me his service, in opening the Coffin nailed up, and
administering some other things necessary for my design.

The head of the Coffin being taken off, and the linnen
cleared away, I could not but admire, to behold a skin so
beset with spots black and blew, more remarkable for multitude
and magnitude than any I have yet seen ; some of which
being opened, contained a congealed matter, in one more
shallow, and in another more deep.   Here I conceived something more than of ordinary Rarity might be discovered; wherefore perforating the Membrane that involves all the rest, I
made entrance into the lowest venter or Region, where appeared
a virulent Ichor, or thin liquor variously coloured, as yellow,

greenish, &c. the small guts being much distended with a venemous flatus, did contain a great quantity of a foul scoria or dross in them, but they were not, as some apprehended, outwardly spotted as the skin, only some obscure large markes were made in their inward part, as likewise in the stomach, arising from the poisonous liquamen therein lodged. The *Vena Porta* and *Arteria Cœliaca* being divided, afforded only a serous liquor, no rubified juice at all, that which was inclosed in these vessels, was a firmly congealed substance of a very dark colour, the Parenchyma of the Liver being separated was very palid, and did straight weep and send out a thin yellowish excrament. The Spleen dissected, appeared more than ordinary obscure, a livid Ichorous matter following the Incision : the Kidneys laid open abounded with a Citrine water, but altogether exanguine, as likewise the other *viscera ;* at length I came to that most excellent usefull part, the Stomack, whose tender membranes when I had divided, a black matter like Ink did shew it self, to the quantity (as nigh as I could guess) of a wine pint, somewhat tenacious and flimsy : the inward membrane of the Ventricle was much discoloured, but the bottom thereof not perforated, as *Helmont* found in the like case : in such a manner (sayes he) as if a potential cautery had been applied thereto.

Having sufficiently lustrated and viewed the lower venter, I ascended to the middle, and making a divulsion of the sterne from the *Mediastinum*, I intentively beheld the superficies of the Lungs, stigmatized with several large ill favoured marks much tumified and distended : the inward part of which being pertunded with my knife, a sanious dreggy corruption issued forth, and a pale Ichor destitute of any blood, for which I searched by cutting this Organ of respiration into various particles, but could finde none but a dirty coagulation in the branches of the *Vena* and *Arteria Pulmonica*. After this I disparted the descending Trunck of the *Cava*, and the Artery called *Aorta*, expecting some considerable emanation of blood there, if any where, that might make a little inundation, but no such thing succeeded, for only some very few spoonfulls of a thin liquor of a pale hew came forth, which might easily be licked up by a small handkerchief. Dissecting these pipes *secundum rectitudinem*, I found them stuffed with a thick curdled blackish substance, which once laid hold on might be drawn out to some length.

Next I separated the Pericardium, that robust coat that circumvolves the Heart, replenished with a deeply tinged yellow liquor : Then having opened the right cavity of the Heart, I therein found a white congealed matter, extracting

z

which with my fingers, and narrowly viewing it, I could not
compare it to anything more like, than a Lamb-stone cut in
twain, which the Servant beholding, standing nigh, easily
assented to in his Judgement.   To render a sound reason of
this albified coagulation in this right Ventricle of the Heart,
may perhaps puzzle a good Physiologist.   For in all those
cadavers I ever saw dissected, this hollow receptacle did still
contain a blackish blood condensed, arising from a stopping
of the Circulation of it first in that place.   Now the most
probable cause (as I conceive, with submission) of this unwonted
white substance, may come from a sumption of meer crude
milk, which an indiscreet Nurse had given this youth not long
before he died, part of which passing out of the stomach little
altered, might be conveyed, upon a pinch and stress to preserve life, through the *Venæ lacteæ* in the Mesenterie, or some
shorter passage, into the subclavian vessels, and there entring
the right cavity of the Heart, be changed according to the
capacity of the Matter by a virulent preternatural ferment,
into this seeming glandulous flesh.   'Twas strange to behold
instead of candid, a black fuliginous matter, fitting only for the
infernal stomach of the Dogg *Cerberus* inclosed in one ventricle,
that publike shop and treasury of life, that ought to be furnished
with all manner of utensils requisite for the sustentation of this
little world : and in another a white innocent lamb-like juice
lodged, instead of a duskie concreted clot of gore, and all this
proceeding from the deletery ferment of this Heteroclite
poison ; which, that I may give you a further account, had so
altered the substance, texture, consistence, and colour of that
Solar Nectar contained in those curiously contrived Pipes,
veins, and arteries, that I may truly say not one spoonfull of
that ruddy liquor properly called blood could be obtained in
this Pestilential body, being partly congealed, and partly
colliquated into a *Tabum* or filthy matter : Which I have
experimentally found to be the usual effects of those poisons
I have given to some Creatures, whose carcasses I have afterwards dissected.

III. A POEM ON THE GREAT PLAGUE.

[When engaged upon this book I was able to acquire
this manuscript poem upon the Great Plague in London,
which so far as can be ascertained has never been printed,
and is unknown.   It is apparently a clean copy, the author-
ship not being disclosed, and is written in a neat contemporary hand.   Internal evidence suggests that it was
completed at the time of King Charles's arrival at Oxford,

in the last days of September. It has little merit as
verse, but is of interest as a rather clumsy delineation of
the effects of the calamity by one who lived through it. I
have rejected many lines which do no more than indicate
the writer's acquaintance with the classics, a matter
unimportant to others.]

THE PLAGUE OF LONDON AN⁰ D^NI 1665.

1.

Our land being blest so long wth health & ease
We now thought health a tedious thing, as if
　　We had beene weary of our life ;
　　As if that health itselfe were a disease.
　　　We now began to bragge
We had both got & crown'd A King w^thout A plague [1]
A plague which had we, we should have thought
Even at y^t rate Charles had been cheaply bought.
　　The people were so healthfull then
　　And did increase so every where
And in such mighty stormes in every place appear,
That we almost began to feare a plague of living men.
　　Scarce A sick body was thene known
　　Or in ye Country or in ye Towne :
　　Diseases all were fled as though
Even ye diseases had beene cured too
　　And yet this is not all, but we
　　As well As health had victory.
　　Our forraigne foes we did oercome
And slew as fast abroad as we increas'd at home.
　　But now as on y^t wretched Towne
　　The Morning sun shin'd very bright
　　Shedding his gentler flames & milder light
　　Where hotter fires did reigne ere Noon.
　So on our nation after all
　Its happinesse a storme doth fall.
　A plague by whose hot flames we burned are
　Almost as bad as they wth fire & brimstone were.
An army of destroying Angells downe
From heav'n there came, & rag'd in every Towne
　　Slew all they met, & wth as much
Ease did destroy & conquer us, as we ye Dutch.

---

[1] The accession to the Throne of Queen Elizabeth, King James I. &
King Charles I. had each been coincident with violent epidemics of Plague
in London. No Plague occurred when Cromwell became Lord Protector
of the Realm, an exception claimed as of Divine grace of which his sup-
porters made much.

2.

London ye stately Palase is
A desert growne
When on yᵉ Israelites yᵉ plague did size
It found yᵐ in a Willderness
Here it makes one.
England was clear'd of salvage beasts in vain
They are all return'd againe.
The people up & downe
Mad & distracted runne.
The people is a tyger, woolfe & beare
And now yᵉ men themselves yᵉ wild beasts are.
Our multitudes are grown
From numberless to none
And what perhaps might bring a 2ⁿᵈ pestilence still
We though agᵗ our will
Doe easily count yᵉ little number yᵗ remaine
And feare another plague for yᵗ againe.

3.

In feilds yᵉ mixed corps ly up & downe
Upon yᵉ Master are yᵉ servants thrown ;
As in A storme th' inferior ships doe fall
Foule on their Admirall.
How A rich Lᵈ, whose land knows no bound
Lyes now contented wᵗʰ two yards of ground.
There lyes A gallant Lady dead
At whose deformity we wonder more
Then at her beauty wⁿ she liv'd before,
Those Roses on her cheek are withered
And blasted are all through.
They lye in th' open feild where flowers use to grow
Thus doe yᵉ bodyes all lye bare
And have no other sepulchre but Aire.
The Aire, wᶜʰ was their death, wᵗʰ an intent
To make amends is now become their monument.

4.

*   *   *   *   *   *

5.

Into yᵉ vallies are yᵉ bodyes throwne
Vallyes no more but now dead mountains grown.
Thick grass & moss begins to growe
Out of ye Putrified corps and now
The Cattell did yᵉ men devoure
As greedily as men did them before.

The Countryman is made A feast
      To his own beast
      And now alas !
All men w^{th}out a metaphor are grass
W^n as ye age to come shall 'plore this ground
      And all theire carcasses be found
      Surely they'll startle back & feare
And think ye Cadmus hath been sowing there.

6.

The Sun, whose fire hath oftimes plagues begot
      Behind A cloud doth trembling lye ,
      And dares not trust his beames so nigh ;
But feares ye Plague he did himselfe create.
How falsely doe old Poets speake when they
      The Sun ye God of Physick call
When as we see y^t by his burning ray
      He cures not any, but doth murther all
      His scorching fire doth peirce our hearts
And his beames wound us more y^n doe his darts.
      The glorious starres admire,
      And trembling at ye dreadfull sight
At ye dead corps doe loose their trembling light.
The dogstar strait put forth his head
        Yet could not long look on
But blushing wth A more y^n nat'rall red
Retired, as if asham'd of w^t he had done.
But yet thou angry Star, we learne a way
By kiling dogs thy cruelty to repay
      And sure tis just to be revenged thus
      And kill his dogs as fast as he kills us.
      Yet they as well infected are
      And howl & cry & groan
And bark no longer at ye moone.
      But their own starre.

7.

Mars looks upon ye dead from out his spheare
Wonders w^t bloudy Conq'roar hath been there.
      And angry is to see
      Himself outdone in cruelty
      The palefac't moone
Grew paler than ye very ghosts she lookd upon,
And though she's fixt in heaven she still doth feare
And hardly thinkes herselfe secure e'en there.
      Nay some men through their optick glass
      Closely beholding her bright face,
      When her black spots they view
They allmost think y^t even she's infected too.

8.

Ah greedy plague must Brittaines be thy food ?
And must thy thirst be quench't wth English bloud ?
    Unto ye Dutch base glutton fly
There fatter corps will better feed thy luxury.
Carry to them thy Carbuncles, they'll thinke
They're onely ye effects of their strong drink,
They'll nere mistrust those botches to be thine
But think they came by their own brandy wine.

9.

In vaine we bid her goe, she still doth stay
    And does destroy us, whilst we pray
Our holy'st sighes are tainted wth ye Aire,
And wee are murther'd by our very prayer.
    The Priest comes not to Church, for if he come
He's sure to dye, & have his pulpit for a Tomb.
    He feares, whilst others he doth teach
He should fall downe, & his own Funerall sermon preach.
    Now he, who by his prayers & teares
Many a dying man did use to save
Is not secure, but for himselfe he feares
And wants ye life wch he to others gave.
    How a Priest ready just to reade
    In his white Robes doth fall down dead
        As if he thought it meet
To turn his surplice to A winding sheet.
Th' infected people out of Church doe fly
Cursing their very prayers & Piety :
    And of their godliness doe more
Repent, then of their very sinnes before.
    The antient custome's alter'd, soo
    ffor life run to ye Sanctuary
    And now not to serve God, nor goe
To Church is wisdome both & piety too.

10.

*   *   *   *   *   *

11.

Organs are dumb, instead of their sweet voice
    Nothing but y^t dreadfull noise
        Of dolefull knells
        And tolling bells ;
Bells, y^t doe strike ye trembling heavens too
Almost as dead as they for whom they goe.

Away ye singers all are flowne
And though before they wisht & would be glad
Yet now they are afraid.
The Churches empty stand & bare
As silent as ye graves wth in ym are.
Here A man brings his shovell & his spade,
In ye churchyard he digs A pit,
But dyes as soone as he has finisht it.
And falls into ye grave he for another made.
One for A dead man goes to toll ye Bell
Scarce had he toll'd 3 tolls but downe he fell
Rings his owne death & toll'd his owne knell
And now we may too truly all
England ye ringing Island call.

12.

Loe ! how ye wretched mothers come
Over their children to lament
Now of their fruitfullness they doe repent
And curse ye very blessings of their womb.
Some tender mothers taking care
To save their babes, y{m}selves infected are :
Death from their chilldren they receive
Their chilldren, unto whom they life did give.
How doth A little son
To ask his fathers blessing run
And breathe forth poysnous aire
Grows murth'rer by his duty & his prayer,
Turnes Parricide & doth infect his Father
Nor gets his blessing but his curses rather.
How women big wth childe doe dye,
They slay ye infant wch is not,
Murth'ring their offspring ere it be begot.
There doth A mother sit
With swollen cheeks & drowned eyes,
Over her burning babe shee weeps & cryes
Hopeing wth tears t'allay ye scorching heat.

13.

Yonder a lover lifting up his hands
By his dead Mistress stands ;
And now he beats his breast as if he meant
The pest'lence to prevent,
And doe himself wt was ye plagues intent.
Then looking on his Deare he cryes,
Yee Gods why teare yee not away these eyes
I've nothing now to looke upon
Since yt my faire one is gone.

Tell me, Curst plague, tell me
How could her breath infected be :
Breath, y^t doth sweeten all where e'er it comes,
Breath ! y^t was able to have cur'd e'en Thee,
And turne thy poysons to p'fumes.

14.

The people now to cheat & steal grow mad,
A sin wch to ye plague new plagues did adde :
One breaks into a house & by & by
With his full coffin home doth hie ;
Wherein a little afterwards himself doth lye,
No fitter judgm^t could ye Gods invent
Then to make w^{t's} his sin his punishment.
Another wⁿ ye plague had clear'd ye house
At midnight into it he goes
And stealing all he there could finde
Doth take away w^{te}'er ye plague had left behind.
Unhappy surely is y^t nations doome
Wⁿe'er ye men unto y^mselves A plague become.
Strange kind of people sure are they
For whilst ye plague all other men doth slay,
They by ye pestilence doe thrive
And by ye very plague doe live
Nothing can satisfye their greedy pelf
They stripe & rob ye dead, & seize
On ye infected carcases :
As if they meant to steale away ye plague itselfe.

15.

The Major [Mayor] wthin ye City stayes,
And is imprison'd where he wieldes & swayes.
He hates ye glory of his sword & mace,
Curses his very honour & his place.
He feares to keep his numerous guards least he
Should e'en by them infected be.
He feares their throng will annoy,
And, wⁿ they should protect, destroy.
He strives to get away in vaine ;
Alas ! he's fetter'd wth his golden chaine.
Oft did he think upon ye Roman, who
Did make his horse A Consul once, & now
Wishes that he might doe so too ;
Wishes y^t he might out o'th' city goe
To take a little country aire
And leave behind him his great horse to be ye Major.
Sad & disconsolate he sits alone,
Nor will he have too many waiters on :
Nothing he cares for watch & ward,
But thinks he's safest now wthout A guard.

16.

But y^n as if ye plague destroy'd too slow
    And murther'd not enough,
Behold a cursed traitors band
Prepar'd to lend ye plague their helping hand.
        A plot those Rebells had begun,
A plot, wch is high treason but to think upon.
    They thought ye plague had been too tame
And therefore doe invent A hotter flame.
        They mines of sulphur get
To adde unto ye burning flame a fiercer heat.
        Fools y^t they were
The very powder which they did prepare
        Was ye best thing to cleane ye Aire.
They had been kind had they been cruell thus
And wth their powder they had not murther'd but cur'd us.
    Such dull Ridiculous souldiers sure as these
        Would never knowe, who choose
        Weapons y^t may not hurt their foes
That fight not to destroy but save their enemyes.
    There was A valiant Troup indeed
Of living souldiers, now there was no need,
We could have overcome y^m with our dead.
    A mighty Army sure, where one
Dead infant might have made y^m all to run :

17.

  *   *   *   *   *   *

18.

Here's one wth such thinne hollow cheek, we may
Thinke y^t his teeth had eat his cheeks away.
        Yonder's another nought but bone
        A walking skeleton
    Here's one with legs so thinne & bare
    That e'en ye naked bones appeare,
So y^t you'd think they not his legs but crutches were.
    Painters there art now needless finde
    To paint A Lady with grim death behind
        She takes her looking glasse
    Startles to see her hollow eyes and face ;
        And her selfe now
        Is both ye Lady & death too.

19.

People no more frequent yᵉ Theatre
Since this new Tragedy began to rage,
  A Tragedy nere heard of, where
  All yᵉ people Actors are,
  And all yᵉ City is the stage.
  We act awhile & then we have
  Our exit, & retire into ye grave.
  Onely in this our far worse doome
  From players is distinguished
    For we, alas ! are dead
Both on yᵉ stage & i' th' retireing Room.
  The gallants are affraid to goe
    Unto yᵉ Playhouse now.
  Lest they should there infected be,
And Act yᵉ Tragick part they onely came to see.

20.

  But now behold A cursed crew
Wᶜʰ did more mischief yⁿ yᵉ plague could doe
Nurses ! who slew so fast as if they meant
  To make yᵉ Pestilence innocent
  People for want of help begin
To perish, yet dare let no body in.
  Hopeless they choose alone to lye,
And rather yⁿ with two they will wᵗʰ one plague dye.
  The milder plague compar'd to them
  Doth mercifull & gentle seeme.
  That onely takes ye men away,
  But these their land & houses slay ;
Destroy their riches & their wealth, & doe
Infect & murther men in their estates too.
Nay ye plague seeing how they made such wast
And how they did infect whole familyes at last
  For her owne selfe began to feare
And wⁿ a house was dead & all was clear
    Away shee flew
For fear at last they would infect her too.

21.

  Some for their safety doe begin
To shut themselves in houses, yet e'en there
Perish, because they cannot take ye Aire,
Aire, wᶜʰ should they take, would murther yᵐ agen.
  Death's writt in bloud on every doore,
Red characters upon our posts are signs of life no more.

In vaine where e're ye plague hath been
Before ye house we set a ward
Tis just like keeping an outguard
When as ye Enemy is got within.
The liveing, w^n they heare bells toll so fast
Think y^t ye Aire will cleansed be at last.
Wish y^t they'd sound againe & were e'en glad
To heare them, though they sounded for ye dead.
Yonder a numerous company prepare
With their loud cryes & shouts to cleanse ye Aire
But by their very breath infect it more
And make it worse than 't was before.
Allmost at every doore are bonefires made
As if they meant (as once of old) to burne ye dead
Here one to carry faggots out doth goe
W^{ch} on ye bonefires he doth throw ;
Then strait falls in & is himselfe a faggot too.
Here one runnes out & just ag^t his Doore
He stands, & wth his burning heat doth roar ;
No, no, he cryes, they need no more
Bonefires desire
Here will I stand before my house & be myself ye fire.
Strange way methinks is this
With fire to cure ye hot disease
We dare not bonefires make least we
Should be destroy'd by ye Remedy,
Least th' Antidotes y^mselves should poysons be,
Was ever sicknes like to this endur'd ?
W^{ch} can by nothing but it selfe be cur'd.
How can we thinke ye smoak will clear
W^{ch} is ye onely thing y^t clouds ye Aire.

22.

Strange conqu'rour sure is y^t wch wth more ease
Doth overcome his strong y^n his weak Enemyes
Yet such a one is this disease.
Old men doe live secure & safe
And they who nearest are, are farthest from ye grave.
Should but ye plague begin
With its hot fire & burning paines
To heat their chill old blood & warme their veins
They would rejoyce, & think they're growing young againe.
Like souldiers scorning an old ruin'd wall
Doe onely shoot at Castles high & strong,
So deales ye plague with old men & doth fall
Upon ye lusty & ye young.
The young men dye at their best time
When health & life are in ye Prime.

23.

The Drunkard felt ye plague begin
To burne, & swore he'd put it out with wine,
He for Physitians doth not care at all,
And 'stead of Doctors doth for Tapsters call,
And makes ye wine-seller his Hospitall.
He drinks till he can't stand (just like ye vine
Wth wch he's drunk) unless ag^t A wall.
  But just as drinke to fev'rish men
The sack at 1st increast the burning paine ;
   And finding now ye wine so hot,
   He doth beleive, Alas !
   That his God Bacchus was
   With lightning & wth fire begot.
But w^n anon perceiving ye disease
   Within him to decrease
  He thinks no more upon ye sin,
Rejoyseth in it & doth strait begin
To thank ye heavens for his drunkenness.
Wine, wch had often made him sick before
   Doth now his health & life restore :
   The sack revives him in a trice,
And he like Bacchus is begotten twice.
   And now being cur'd he goes away
   Burneing the sheets in wch he lay.

24.

The gamesters view'd y^{m}selves & were dismay'd
For all their faces & their bodyes o're
  They now black spots & patches were.
And look just like ye dice wth wch they played
In vaine they meet at ordinaires, when
     Amongst them in ye Room
A strange unheard of gamester there was seen
W^{ch} did not play for money but for men.
Small comfort now ye winner had to boast
That he won gold, w^n strait himself he lost
Yet still ye loosers quarrell, curse & rave
Wishing ye plague might have y^m wch they have
A wish so needless y^t they might as well
Curse and damne those allready are in Hell.
The miser under ground his money layd,
   Hoping to find it w^n he's dead :
   But ah ! he dare not thither goe,
   Finding his house infected so.
He feares his very ghost will be infected too.
   The lustfull man who burnes wth hot desire
   Felt a new flame burne hotter y^n his lust
     And surely heavens now just
To send ye plague on him & punish fire with fire.

25.

Here an old man his son his heir doth make
W^n strait ye childe out into tears doth burst,
As though before he would his portion take
He meant wth teares to wash it first
No money durst ye people now have seen.
W^{ch} had not in ye water been.
Nay some too were affraid to looke upon
That glorious coine of heav'n ye golden sun.
The Merchants gold doth from ye Indies come
W^{ch} he into ye water strait doth cast.
The shipwrack wch is past
At sea, it meets at home
Now ye only way to save his gold he found
Was to cast 'it away & drown 't.
And yet w^t vext us more
Was to see water so at every doore.
For sure it was A shame
That London should in anything be like to Amsterdam
All money is in water layd
And basons now are purses made,
And yet ye very water wch made clean
All other things, it selfe began
To be polluted now
And was infected so
That we had need to wash ye very water too.

26.

We laught at all diseases else, for they
Like small guns but one a time doe slay
This like A Canon teares whole Troups away.
Here one doth in a fever burne
And is himselfe both fire & wine.
He nothing feares ye plague, for he alass !
Hath fires, wch doth ye plague surpasse
As well might all our flaming Martyrs feare
To scorch their finger or to singe their haire :
Those who in quiv'ring & cold agues lye
Would leap to see ye plague come nigh.
Yonder's another in A dropsy
Both his own ship and sea
Who is both Tantalus & ye water too :
He at ye burning plague doth laugh
And thing[k]s y^t by his water he is safe :
The dropsie, though in time it selfe be sure
To kill him, keeps him from ye plague secure
Is both his lifeguard & his Murtherer.

27.

*　　*　　*　　*　　*　　*

28.

In their owne wine-cellars some bury'd be
   And happy surely they
   If like their wine
By being bury'd under ground they could have quick'd againe.
  Some w^tout Coffins they in gardens throw
  Makeing ye Earth their greater Coffin too.
  Upon ye Corps grew flowers all along
   Decking ye Bodyes whence they sprung.
Flowers as fading as ye corps on wch they grow.
  Here Roses start from out their beds
  But finding all their smell was fled
They blush't y^mselves into A double red,
  And strait drew in their heads.
The Roses did before infect ye men,
And they infect ye Roses too againe.
  The Violets peep'd from out their Azure cell
And none indeed too truly like ye plague did smell
Here flowers made their swelling banks their grave
And their own banks for coffins have.
   Nay & ye fruit it self so much
   With ye Contagious heat did burne
We fear'd to gather, least that wth A touch
They should like Sodom's apples into Ashes turne.
  Where ere ye dead did lye, as though
The Fairyes had been there, no grass would grow.
   Thus did they hide ye dead,
And every garden a churchyard was made.

29.

Spots in their bodyes did appear, as though
   The angry sun
Had not on y^m sent forth his beams alone
   But his spotts too.
Ladyes, who wore black patches out of pride
  Now weare y^m their plague sores to hide :
  And are ashamed more
Of those black spots yⁿ they were proud before.
They need not jewells buy to make y^m fine
Their bodyes doe wth nature's jewells shine.
  To India they need not come
Rubies & carbuncles they have at home :
  They put on patches not to grace
  But to hide their blushing face.

Their beauty in these sable weeds adorn'd
Did looke as if for its own death it mourn'd.
Their cheeks wch lately painted were wth red
          In a black mask now are clad.
The peoples whiter skins are speckled 'ore
And all ye common rout ye Royall Ermine b[ear].

30.

And yet ye Londoners make no such moane
That thus they dye, as y^t y^r King is gone.
          The plague they would not feare
          If that their CHARLES were there.
          Cursed disease what hast thou done ?
Drawne Charles from his Imperiall seat & Throne
          As if 't were thine intent
To make him undergo A 2nd banishment.
          He wanders up and downe for feare of Thee
          And is an Exile though at home he be
          Yet still, curst plague, he scapes thy spite
          And like A Parthian conquers Thee by flight.
Then wellcome, mighty S^r, to Oxford now
W^{ch} keepes it selfe clear from ye Plague . . .
Yet were it not, y^r presence, S^r, would make it so
          Thus wheresoever
          The Sun appeare
          It needs must there be day ;
          Onely in this
          Twixt these two suns ye diff'rence is
One breeds ye Plague, you drive it, S^r, away.
          [The bells in L]ondon shall not ring
          [Save but to W]ellcome Home our King
          For since it falls out thus
          Great S^r, y^t comeing thence
               You doe repaire to us,
We cannot choose but thank ye very Pestilence
          No noisome plague, great S^r, you see
          Hath reach't our University,
And Athens is ye place y^t now alone is free.

FINIS.

AUTHORITIES

I HAVE attempted no more than a working bibliography, aiming to give those printed and manuscript sources that are most useful. For official action during the epidemic of Plague, the chief authorities are the Privy Council Register, not yet printed to the Restoration, and the State Papers of the reign of King Charles II., for which calendars are available, supplemented by various documents in private collections. Many of these last are printed, in part or whole, by the Historical Manuscripts Commission. The civic records are chiefly comprised in the Journal of the Common Council and the Repertory of the Court of Aldermen, kept in manuscript in Guildhall. They are less full than I had hoped. Also at Guildhall are the Accounts of the City Chamberlain and the books of City receipts and payments during the Plague. The original letters at Guildhall are richer for the earlier Plagues than for that of 1665. Information concerning the out-parishes has to be sought chiefly in the vestry minutes and churchwardens' accounts of the various parishes, which are now stored in the different Borough Council offices, and the burial registers kept in the churches. These intimate parish records are also of great value for the City area ; large numbers of the books are collected together in the Guildhall Library.

Of contemporary printed historical sources, there is an informative introductory chapter in Dr. Nathaniel Hodges' " Loimologia," and a description of the Plague visitation, written in somewhat florid style, in the Rev. Thomas Vincent's " God's Terrible Voice in the City." Clarendon (with many inaccuracies), Burnet and Echard among historians of or near the time should also be consulted. Pepys is most valuable, and the memoirs or other writings of Evelyn, Reresby, Baxter the divine, and George Whitehead the Quaker, are valuable in a lesser degree. The respective Journals of the Lords and Commons contain most that is known concerning the action of the Oxford Parliament towards the Plague. The Harleian MSS. 3,784 and 3,785 in the British Museum contain many letters from London, mostly addressed to Sancroft, the absentee

Dean of St. Paul's. The Rev. Symon Patrick's correspondence in Addit. MSS. 5,810, and what appears to be a copy of a Newsletter, extending over many months, in Addit. MSS. 4,182, are also of great service. Lambeth Palace Library has documents, including a letter to the Lord Mayor, which are not accessible elsewhere.

The Bills of Mortality for the year are available in two printed books by John Bell and by the Company of Parish Clerks.

Defoe's " Journal of the Plague Year " cannot be omitted from any bibliography. I have already expressed an opinion concerning its strength and its weakness. Any printed work published after the year 1722, when Defoe's " Journal " appeared, must only be used with extreme caution. It is remarkable how Defoe has influenced every subsequent writer. Certain publications with alluring titles, such, for instance, as " A Short Account of the Plague which prevailed in the City of London in the year 1665 : Extracted from the memoirs of a person who resided there during the whole time of the infection," published in 1793, and " The Dreadful Visitation," making similar claims, which appeared four years earlier, when examined are found to be merely Defoe's stories reprinted without acknowledgment. The so-called " Historical Narrative of the Great Plague at London in 1665," published in the year 1769, is in bulk Defoe. The " City Remembrancer " version, 1769, is doubtfully ascribed to collections made by Dr. Gideon Harvey, and is much filled out with matter from Defoe's pages and excerpts from Hodges, Vincent, the *Gazette* and other sources. In none among them all can reliance be placed.

The medical literature of the Great Plague is small. At the time the Plague fell upon London the standard work consulted by physicians and surgeons was Diemerbroeck's " Tractatus de Peste." Careful observations of the Plague in 1665 are recorded by Dr. Nathaniel Hodges in " Loimologia," by Dr. George Thomson in " Loimotomia," and by the apothecary William Boghurst in " Loimographia." The last named existed only in manuscript in the British Museum until it was edited by Dr. Joseph Frank Payne for the Epidemiological Society of London in 1894. Dr. Sydenham had no personal observation of the Plague for the treatise that he subsequently wrote, having left London when it broke out ; and Dr. Richard Mead's " Short Discourse," which enjoyed extraordinary popularity in the alarm of 1720–22, could do no more than discuss the observations of others, upon which the author built up a theory and proposals for treatment.

There is a not inconsiderable theological literature born of the Great Plague. Its use for historical purposes is necessarily very restricted, as is my space, and the omission will be forgiven.

PRINTED.

† *A Collection of Very Valuable and Scarce Pieces* relating to the last Plague in the year 1665. Lond. 1721. Contains the " Orders Conceived and Published " ; " Certain Necessary Directions " by the College of Physicians ; Dr. Hodges' " Letter to a Person of Quality " ; John Graunt's " Reflections on the Bills of Mortality."

Archæologia, vol. 37. Contains digest of John Allin's letters.

Austin, William. *Anatomy of the Pestilence.* 1665.

Baxter, Richard. *Reliquiæ Baxterianæ.* 1696.

Bell, John. *Londons Remembrancer :* Or, A true Accompt of every particular Weeks Christenings and Mortality, in all the Years of Pestilence, etc. 1665[–6].

Bell, Walter George. *The Great Fire of London in* 1666. 3rd Ed. 1923.

Boghurst, William. *Loimographia :* Or an Experimentall Relation of the Plague, of what hath happened Remarkable in the last Plague in the City of London. 1666. Ed. by Dr. J. F. Payne for the Epidemiological Society of London. 1894.

Burnet, Bishop Gilbert. *History of His Own Times.*

City Remembrancer. 1769. Vol. 1.

Clarendon, Edward Hyde, Earl of. *Life.*

Clippendale, Dr. S. D. *A Medical Roll of Honour ;* physicians and surgeons who remained in London during the Great Plague. (Reprint from *British Medical Journal.*)

Cock, Thomas. *Hygiene,* or a Plain and Practical Discourse upon the first of the Six Non-Naturals, viz. : Air, with Cautionary Rules for the Preservation of People in this Time of Sickness, 1665.

College of Physicians. *Certain Necessary Directions* for the Cure of the Plague, as for preventing the Infection, etc. By the King's Majesties Special Command, May, 1665. (Reprinted in †.)

Creighton, Charles, M.D. *History of Epidemics in Britain.* 1891. *Social England,* vol. iv., pp. 603–46.

Defoe, Daniel. *Journal of the Plague Year.* 1722. *Due Preparations for the Plague.* 1721.

Diemerbroeck, Isbrandus. *Tractatus de Peste,* Arnheim. 1646. Extracts from Diemerbroeck's book were trans-

lated into English and published under the title of
Several Choice Histories, etc. of the Plague, in 1666.

Directions for the Prevention and Cure of the Plague Fitted
for the Poorer sort. 1665. Anonymous. Of small
interest. Dr. Payne, Boghurst's editor, suggests that
Mr. Coniers, at the Unicorn in Fleet Street, who is mentioned in the pages, and probably was an apothecary,
is the author.

Echard. *History of England.* 1707–20.

Ellis, Sir Henry. .*Original Letters*, 2nd Ser. vol. 4. Contains certain letters by Stephen Bing and J. Tillison in
Harleian MSS. 3,785.

Evelyn, John. *Diary.*

Gadbury, John. *Londons Deliverance Predicted;* in a
Short Discourse on Plagues in General. 1665.

Garencieres, Theophilus. *A Mite Cast into the Treasury* of
the City of London ; A Discourse on the Plague. 1665.

Golgotha; or, a Looking-Glass for London. With an
humble Witness against the Cruel Advice and Practice
of Shutting up unto Oppression. By J. V., grieved for
the Poor, who perish daily hereby. 1665.

Graunt, John. *Natural and Political Observations upon
the Bills of Mortality,* 3rd Ed. 1665. *Reflections on the
Weekly Bills of Mortality.* 1665. (Reprinted in †.)

Harvey, Gideon, M.D. *A Discourse of the Plague*, etc.
1665.

Historical Narrative of the Great Plague at London in 1665.
Lond. 1769.

Hodges, Nathaniel, M.D. *Loimologia,* sive Pestis Nuperæ
apud Populum Londinenseum grassantis narratio. 1672.
This valuable book was written in 1667, and an English
translation by Dr. John Quincy was published in 1720.
Letter from Dr. Hodges to a Person of Quality, May, 1666.
(Reprinted in †.)

Intelligencer and *Newes*, 1665–6. Roger L'Estrange's
bi-weekly newspapers.

Kemp, W. *A Brief Treatise* of the Nature, Causes, Signes,
Preservation from, and Cure of the Pestilence. 1665.

Kephale, Richard. *Medela Pestilentiæ.* Theological Queries
concerning the Plague ; also Method for curing that
Epidemical Distemper. 1665.

Lamentatio Civitalis, or London's Complaint against her
children in the country, shewing her desolatenesse
Blaming their unkindnesse . . . towards her. Also a
brief account, how many died in the years 1592, 1603,
1625, 1630, 1636, 1637, 1638, 1646, 1647, 1648 with this

present year 1665. Likewise several preservatives against the infection. Lond. 1665.

Londini Lacrymœ: or London's complaint against her fugitives. 1665. (A satire in verse.)

London Gazette, 1666.

London's Dreadful Visitation; Or, a Collection of all the Bills of Mortality for this Present Year, etc. By the Company of Parish Clerks of London. 1665.

Londons Lord Have Mercy Upon Us. 1665. (Broadside, many reprints. A single folio sheet with similar name was published in 1637.)

London's loud cries to the Lord by prayer: made by a Reverend Divine. With an account of several modern plagues . . . in London . . . continued down to August 8th, 1665. Lond. 1665. (Broadsheet.)

Lyson, Rev. Daniel. *Environs of London,* 1792–1811.

Mayoral Proclamations (printed) in British Museum Library, Pressmark 21. h. 5. Others, more numerous, are in manuscript in Guildhall " Journal."

Mead, Richard, M.D. *A Short Discourse concerning Pestilential Contagion.* 1720. Eight subsequent editions.

Middlesex County Records, vol. 3.

Munk, W. *Roll of College of Physicians of London,* 1878.

Nicholson, Dr. Watson. *The Historical Sources of Defoe's " Journal of the Plague Year."* 1919.

Notes and Queries (see indices).

Orders Conceived and Published by the Lord Mayor. (Undated. [1665.] Reprinted in † and by Defoe.)

Orders formerly Conceived and Agreed to be published by the Lord Mayor and the Aldermen of the City of London and the Justices of Peace of the Counties of Middlesex and Surrey concerning The Infection of The Plague. And now Re-printed and published by Order of the Honourable House of Commons. Lond. 1646.

Overall's *Index to Remembrancia of the City of London.* 1878.

Oxford Gazette, 1665–6.

Patrick, Rev. Symon. *Autobiography.* 1839.

Pepys, Samuel. *Diary,* ed. by H. B. Wheatley.

Reresby, Sir John. *Memoirs.* 1734.

Royal Proclamations (State Papers, Various, vols. 11 and 12, at Public Record Office).

    1665, *April* 26. Seamen of colliers trading between Newcastle and Sunderland and London to be free from the King's press.

    May 24. Proroguing Parliament from June 21 till a time to be appointed.

June 14.   Prohibiting Barnwell Fair, near Cambridge, by reason of danger of further spread of the Plague.

June 23.   Prohibiting St. James's Fair at Bristol.

June 28.   Requiring disbanded officers or soldiers who served in the armies of " the late usurped Powers " to depart from London and Westminster.

July 6.   For observance of a general fast throughout the kingdom " for removal of this heavy judgment " of the Plague.

July 26.   Removing the Exchequer from Westminster to Nonsuch.

Aug. 7.   Prohibiting Bartholomew Fair, Smithfield, and Stourbridge Fair.

Aug. 27.   Prohibiting Howden Fair, Yorkshire.

Aug. 30.   Further proroguing Parliament to meet at Oxford on Oct. 9th.

Sept. 21.   Prohibiting Wantage Fair.

Sept. 26.   Postponing Nov. fast which fell on All Saints' Day to Nov. 8.

Sept. 26.   Adjourning Michaelmas Law Term from Westminster to Oxford.

Nov. 10.   Prohibiting Boston Fair.

Dec. 21.   Prohibiting Bristol Fair.

1666, *Jan.* 5.   Removing Exchequer from Nonsuch to Westminster.

Jan. 12.   Adjourning Hilary Law Term from Westminster to Windsor.

Jan. 17.   Proroguing Parliament to April 23.

April 6.   Proroguing Parliament to Sept. 18.

May 25.   Prohibiting Barnwell Fair.

Aug. 6.   Prohibiting Bartholomew and Stourbridge Fairs.

Sept. 26.   Prohibiting Gravesend Fair.

Sharpe, Dr. Reginald.   *London and the Kingdom*, vol. 2.

Shutting up Infected Houses, as it is practised in England, soberly debated.   Anonymous.   1665.

Statutes of the Realm, 1st Jac. I., ch. 31.

Smyth, Richard.   *Obituary of Persons he knew.*   1849.

Sydenham, Thomas, M.D.   *Observationes Medicæ civea Morborum acutorum historiam et curationem.*   1676. Contains this famous physician's paper on the Plague, which is reprinted in the English editions of his works.

The Run-awayes safe refuge : or the penniless pilgrims' answer to their miserable comforters their fellow citizens in London.   1665.   (Broadsheet.)

Thomson, George, M.D. *Loimotomia*, or the Pest Anatomized. 1666.

Victoria County History of London. (Ecclesiastical section.)

Vincent, Thomas. *God's Terrible Voice in the City.* 1667. (Many editions.)

Wilcox, *Petition of Charles* (British Museum Library, Pressmark 816, m. 9).

Willis, Thomas, M.D. *A Plain and Easie Method for preserving those that are well from the infection of the Plague.* 1691. (This was written in 1666. The writer's more familiar *De Febribus*, etc., was first published in 1659.)

MANUSCRIPTS.

Bishopsgate Institute Library. *Genealogical MSS. relating to Lord Mayors.*

British Museum, MSS. Department. *Addit. MSS.* 4,182 (Court's stay at Salisbury) ; 4,376 (City of London Plague Orders since Henry VIII.) ; 5,810 (Symon Patrick's Letters) ; 10,117 (Rugge's " Diurnal ").

Egerton MSS., 2,603, fo. 4.

Harleian MSS. 3,784 and 3,785 (Letters to Dean Sancroft).

Stowe MSS., 152, fo. 113 ; 840, fo. 46.

City Corporation, Guildhall. Records Department. *City Accounts*, 1665, *passim.*

Journal (of Common Council), vol. 46, *passim.*

Old Bailey Sessions Papers, 1665[–6].

Repertory (of Court of Aldermen), vol. 70, *passim.*

Duke of Buckingham to Lord Mayor, 1664, June 27. (Original Letters.)

Guildhall Library MSS. No. 270. *Payments for Relief of the Poor during the Plague.*

No. 295. *Services of Dr. Pecke.*

No. 359. *Sickness and Pest-house bills.*

Lambeth Palace Library MSS. *Carthe Mis.*, vol. 6.

Private Collections. (The page references given are to the published Calendars of the Hist. MSS. Comm.)

Bath, Marquis of (4th Rep., 229).

Chester Corporation (8th Rep., 387b).

Clare College, Cambridge, p. 115.

College of Physicians (8th Rep., 229a).

Denbigh, Earl of, part 5, p. 6.

Finch, p. 404.

Gawdy (10th Rep., part 2, p. 163).

Heathcote, p. 199.

House of Lords (7th Rep., p. 560).

Le Fleming, p. 37.

Leicester Corporation, p. 439.

Montagu of Beaulieu, Lord, p. 167.

Portland, Duke of, iii. 292, 293, 294 ; iv. 146.

Salisbury Corporation, p. 245.

Stewart, Captain, p. 111.

Verulam, Earl of, pp. 59–60, 214.

Woodchester Priory.

Also see 6th Report, pp. 336, 336b.

Public Record Office. *Privy Council Register*, vol. 58,
passim. (For Scotland, see printed Calendar of *Acts of
Privy Council for Scotland*, 3rd ser., vol. 2.)

State Papers Charles II. (See Calendars State Papers
(Domestic), 1664–5, 1665–6, 1666; Addenda,
1660–70.)

Treasury Books. (See Calendar, 1660–7.)

Society of Friends, Devonshire House, Bishopsgate. *Swarthmore MSS.*

Transcripts of London (Quaker) Burial Registers.

Vestry Minutes, Churchwardens' Accounts, etc., mostly in
the various Metropolitan Borough Councils' Offices and
for City at Guildhall Library ; Burial Registers in the
various churches or Guildhall Library.

Westminster City Hall. *Plague Accounts of St. Margaret
Westminster.* (This invaluable record, compiled with
studious care, merits special attention, being far more
detailed than are the like records of other parishes.)

INDEX

ABERGAVENNY, LADY, 55
Acton, 15, 185–6
Additional Aid, 197, 302
Admiralty Court, 66
Advertisements of Plague cures, 36
Air, belief in infection of, 154, 237, 247, 249.
Albemarle, George Monck, Duke of, 25–6, 55, 81, 137, 177, 186, 202n, 237–8, 244, 277, 300, 305–6, 308–10, 313–4, 329 ; decides to stay in London, 69 ; tomb, 306 ; visits to King, 306, 308–9 ; Duchess of, 305
Aldermen, 4, 12, 36, 45, 63–5, 67, 84, 87–8, 91, 95, 124, 146, 169, 210, 237, 277–9, 314 ; dead by plague, 6, 88, 279n, 312 ; fines, 287 ; indemnity of, 85 ; orders to, 27, 77, 81, 130–1, 286 ; to stay in London, 77, 84, 169 ; to tend sick, 104
—— Backwell, 313 ; Bide, John, 215, 279n ; Browne, Sir W., 214 ; Jermyn, John, 287 ; Noel, Sir Martin, 215, 279n ; Peake, Sir W., 86 ; Robinson, Sir John, 166, 278, 289 ; Turner, Sir W., 86 ; Vyner, 313
Aldersgate, 14, 159
Aldersgate Street, 117–8
Aldgate, 96, 212, 269 ; plague pit, 152–3
Allen, Anne, 311
Allhallows Bread Street, 18, 216
Allhallows Honey Lane, 245
Allhallows London Wall, 282
Allhallows Staining, 87
Allhallows-the-Great, 228
Allhallows-the-Less, 277
Allin, John, 128n, 141, 203–4, 229, 255–65
Allway, Jane, 52
Almanacs, 2

Alordin, John, 52
Amen Corner, 37, 62
Amsterdam, 246, 349
Anabaptists, 18
Angel Court, 256
Angier's fume, 35–6
Annus Mirabilis, 255
Apothecaries, 9, 16, 51, 86, 203, 206n ; deaths among, 37, 206, 268 ; payments to, 287 ; Bernard, Francis, 162 ; Boghurst, William, 13–5, 98, 99n, 116, 125. 128n, 155–6, 158, 193–4, 247 ; Harmon, Edward, 86, 206 ; Johnson, William, 37, 203 ; Slade, 290 ; Stokes, 114
Apollo Smintheus, 248
Apparitions in sky, 1, 3
Apprentices, City, 121
Arlington, Lord, 25–6, 35, 69, 81, 299
Arras, Dr., 303
Artillery Ground, 212, 225
Ashbridge, Arthur, 282
Askew, John, 150–1
Assizes, 63–4, 86, 311–2
Astrologers (see also Allin), 2, 3, 257 ; predictions by, 2, 12 ; Edlin, 2 ; Gadbury, 14 ; Lilly, 2, 40–1
Astronomy School, Oxford, 302
Athens, Plague at, 299
Athias, Rabbi Moses, 180
Austen, Rev. Samuel, 225
Austin, Rev. Samuel, 150
Austin Friars, 88
Austin's Anatomy of the Pestilence, 98, 111, 183, 256
Ayloff, Joseph, 68

BACILLUS pestis, 247, 250
Backwell, Alderman, 313
Baldwin's gardens, 99n
Bangor, Bishop of, 50
Bankside, 132
Barker, John, 146

Barking, 201
Barrett, Henry, 149
Bartholomew Fair, 194, 326
Barton, 323
Basing Lane, 323
Basinghall Street, 80
Basingstoke, 322
Bastwick, minister, 190, 226
Bath, 141 ; Earl of, 25
Battle, 324
Baxter, Richard, 15, 91, 154, 186, 222
Bayswater pest-field, 319–20
Beak Street, 283
Bearbinders Lane, 21, 89
Bearers of the dead, 29, 52, 104, 113, 134, 177–8, 183–5, 213, 268, 271, 276
Beech Lane, 145
Bedel, Gabriel, 97
Bedford, Earl of, 54
Beggars, 36, 280, 292, 313–5, 333
Bell Alley, Westminster, 44
Bell, John, 278
Bellman with dead cart, 30, 80
Bergen, attack on, 240, 305
Bermondsey, 32, 186
Bethlehem (see Hospitals)
Bhagavata Parana, 249n
Bide, John, 215, 279n
Bills of Mortality (for full-bill of 1665, see facsimile facing page 320), 12, 23, 34, 39, 44, 57, 132, 147, 182, 195, 214–5, 219, 300, 329–30 ; extracts from Bills of 1665, 30, 58, 63, 65, 80, 92, 95, 119, 170, 207–8, 232, 236, 241–2, 266, 270, 272, 274, 280, 312 ; deaths in 1666, 253, 317, 325 ; for years before 1625, 5–7 ; for 1625, 7 ; for 1631, 12 ; for 1640–7, 7 ; for 1664, 5, 13
—— collections of, 62, 278, 321 ; falsification of, 16, 76, 92–3, 115, 131, 251 ; first compiled weekly, 5 ; five worst weeks, 245 ; Hyde's misstatement of, 179 ; method of preparing, 17–21 ; origin of, 5n, 20 ; parishes contained in, 134 ; price, publication of, 58 ; proportional deaths in City, Liberties and out-parishes, 123
Bing, Stephen, 94, 223, 225, 289
Bird, William, 186
Birds " infected," 245–6, 249
Bishopsgate (see St. Botolph)
Black Death, 7, 8, 44, 252

Black Eagle, 117n, 217–8
Blackwall, 34, 201, 270
Blackwell Hall, 322
Blague, Margaret, 163
Blemell, Rev. John, 228n
Blithe, Samuel, 81
Blizard, Thomas, 149
Bloomsbury, 27, 101
Board of Green Cloth, 301
Boghurst, William (see Apothecaries)
Boldnesse, John, 220
Bolnest, Dr. Edward, 147
Bonner, Joseph, 105n
Booker, Daniel, 105n
Boreman, Rev. R., 29
Bread, prices of, 123
Brentford, 169, 209, 241
Brentwood, 100
Brewers Company, 215
Bridewell, 190n
Bridgewater Square, 145
Bristol, 175, 199, 288, 322 ; population of, 13
Britains Remembrancer, 49n, 255
Broad Street, 63, 88, 178
Broadsides, 103–4, 219–20
Brockhurst, Francis, 51
Brode Lane, 18
Brokers of the dead, 220–1
Brouncker, Lord, 70, 292
Browne, Sir Anthony, 99 ; Sir William, 214
Brush, Edward, 21
Buboes (see Medical, symptoms)
Buck, James, 60, 62
Buckingham (bearer), 184
Buckingham, George Villiers, Duke of, 4n, 26
Bunhill Fields, 181, 211, 287
Burge, John, 132
Burials of plague victims (see also Plague Pits), 36, 39, 118, 132, 180–2, 231, 304, 314–15
Burlington House, 119
Burnet, Dr. Alexander, 56, 203, 207, 230 ; Gilbert, 56
Burwell, Dr., 303
Buryers, 46, 113, 118, 177, 184
Busby, Dr., 49
Butchers, plague among, 183, 230, 269
Butler, Lewis, 216

CAMBRIDGE, 80, 290–1, 323–4
Cannon Street Ward, 87
Canterbury (see also Sheldon), 322 ; Archbishop's license to practice medicine, 41, 203, 291 ; wills, 159

Carnarvonshire, aid from, 198
Carpenters Company, 129–30, 215
Carriers, country, 137, 284
Cartaret, Sir George, 170, 199;
    Lady, 100, 230, 241
Castlemaine, Lady, 298, 300
Catherine of Braganza, Queen, 1,
    26, 170, 289, 307, 309, 311
Cats, destruction of, 59, 85, 248
Census of 1631, 11
Certificates of health, 36, 136–7,
    333
Chalfont St. Giles, 255
Champney, Thomas, 277
Chancery Lane, 21, 60, 258
Charing Cross, 120, 209
Charles I., King, 97, 120–1, 141, 180,
    299; plague at accession, 7, 37,
    339n
Charles II., King, 23, 26, 36, 46, 49,
    64–71, 181, 289, 291, 305n, 314,
    321; at Hampton Court, 67, 169,
    308–9; at Oxford, 172, 298–9,
    302, 305–9, 338, 351; at Salisbury,
    169–72; at Sion, 66–7, 311;
    at Whitehall, 1, 24, 309–11;
    letters to Lord Mayor, 169, 202;
    sees Lord Mayor before depar-
    ture, 81; subscriptions to relief,
    195–6
Charles, Jonas, 35
Charles Street, 54–5
Charms against plague, 3, 163–4
Charterhouse, 7n, 167
Chatham, 319, 322
Cheap, ward of, 87
Cheapside, 98, 287
Chelsea, 82; Hospital, 326
Cheshire, plague in, 8, 143
Chester, 288; Bishop of, 326;
    Edward, 227
Chief Justice, 23, 314
Chiffinch, Tom, 317
Chilton, Henry, 62
Chislehurst, 226
Chiswick, 49
Chrisolitus, " Dr." Stephanus, 98
Christ Church, Oxford, 289, 302
Christ's College, Cambridge, 323
Churchwardens, 47, 85, 105n, 106,
    313; dead by plague, 149, 186,
    276–7
Churchyards, 39, 139, 245, 281,
    314–5; 320; fires in, 210
Churchyard Stairs, 208
Cibber, Caius Gabriel, 135
City Cash (see Relief)

City Chamberlain, 289; Coroner, 5,
    134, 189, 243; Marshal, 118, 173;
    M.P.'s, 302; Sword Bearer, 279
Clapham, 169
Clare College, Cambs., 80–1, 323
Clare Market, 33
Clarendon, Lord Chancellor (Edward
    Hyde, Earl of), 26, 38, 119, 179,
    271, 299, 301–2
Clark, Rev. William, 226
Clarke, Henry, William, 276
Clayton, Dr. (prescription), 97
Clements (Quaker family), 18
Clergy, flight from London, 62, 148,
    221; who stayed in London, 29,
    148–9, 223–6; dead by plague,
    225–6, 263, 312
Clerkenwell (see St. James Clerken-
    well)
Clifford, James, 223
Cloth, trade in, 322
Coaches, 59, 292; hackney, 75, 101,
    240, 285; stage, 57, 284
Coal ships and supplies, 201
Cobb (minister), 262
Cocke, Captain, 267
Cock Pit, St. James's, 69, 306
Coffee-houses, 52
Coelifolium, 259–61, 263–4
Coffins, 174, 192, 210, 212, 231, 239,
    267; church, 148
Colchester, plague at, 18n, 200, 285,
    319, 321–2
Cole, Peter, 219
College of Heralds, 291
College of Physicians (see Physicians)
Collins, Thomas, 97
Collyer, John, 277
Colman Street, 290
Comets, 1, 3, 14, 22, 265
Cominges, Count, 12, 26, 244
Common Council, 77, 169, 278, 287;
    Hunt, 102
Commons, House of, 7, 75, 302–4;
    no Members dead, 312
Companies, City, 21, 88, 129–30,
    215–6; assessment for relief, 130;
    Brewers, 215; Carpenters, 129–30,
    215; Drapers, 167; Goldsmiths,
    129, 215; Haberdashers, 83;
    Merchant Taylors, 167, 210;
    Parish Clerks, 18, 58, 147–8;
    Pewterers, 215; Saddlers, 216;
    Salters, 287; Tackle Porters, 10;
    Vintners, 11, 215; Woodmongers,
    122
Constable, Richard, 116

Constables, parish, 23, 28, 47, 85, 106, 132, 304, 313–4
Conventicle Acts (see Statutes)
Coombe Farm, 143–4
Cooper, Edward, 293
Corn, bounty on, 199
Cornhill, 219, 326
Cotes, Edward, 62
Courts, Lord Mayor's, 85, 145, 313 ; of Requests, 81 ; Sheriffs, 85, 313
Covent Garden (see also St. Paul Covent Garden), 54–5, 70, 291, 331
Cowes, Isle of Wight, 143
Coxe, Dr., *Divertions against ye Plague*, 52
Craven, Earl of, 34, 49, 70, 82, 137, 185–6, 290, 306, 314–5 ; on evils of Plague measures, 317–18 ; gift of pest-field, 319–20
Craven Hill Gardens, 319–20
Creechurch Lane, 180, 181*n*
Creswell Street, 146
Cripplegate Ward (see also St. Giles Cripplegate), 87, 144, 196*n*
Cromwell, Oliver, 339*n*
Crooked Lane, 40, 214
Cross of plague, blue, 48 ; red, 22, 24, 56, 72, 103, 274, 315, 334 ; printed, 129 ; white, 267, 315, 334
Cross (divine), 227
Cross Lane, 99*n*
Crosse, Robert, 50
Crowder's Well, 9, 146
Crumwell (dog killer), 102
Customs House, 187, 199

Dagenham, 138, 241
Dalton, George, 244
Dartmouth, 288
Darwin, Erasmus, 278*n*
Davies, Alexander and Mary, 50, 51*n*, 284
Dawson family's deaths, 8
Dead Carts, 30, 51, 104, 107, 118, 132, 134, 178, 184, 244, 266, 280
Deal, plague at, 321
Deanery of St. Paul's, 155–6
Defoe, Daniel, v., vi., viii., 39*n*, 49*n*, 72–5, 83, 105–6, 134–5, 153, 161, 192*n*, 196*n*, 200, 246, 257, 271, 282, 330, 353
Dekker, Thomas, 6, 191–2
Deptford, 138, 200–1, 239
Derby, 289, 323
Devonshire, Earl of, 294
Diemerbroeck, Isbrandus, 268, 353

Disinfection (see Fumes, Gunpowder, Tobacco, Water)
Ditches, 11, 34, 42, 146, 251 ; town ditch, 27
Ditton, Kent, 193 ; Cambs., 323
Doe, Sir Charles, 65, 73
Dog Yard, 99*n*
Dogs killed, 51, 85, 101, 104, 248, 341
Dolben, Dean of Westminster, 50, 67
Doolittle, 228
Dorchester, 140, 172
Dover, 64, 140
Downing, Sir George, 285
Drapers Almshouses, 167
Drury Lane, 21, 33–4, 44, 70, 256
Durham, plague in, 323
Dyer, William, 226

East India Company, 187–8
Edwards, Rev. Richard, 226
Eley, John, 105*n*
Elizabeth, Queen, 5, 6, 32, 37, 78, 79*n*, 88, 129, 144, 251, 269, 339*n*
Ellwood, Thomas, 189
Epitaphs, 162, 271, 284
Epsom, 187, 218 ; wells locked, 140
Eton boys smoking, 156
Evelyn, John, 14, 26, 65, 200, 218, 239, 267
Everard, Charles, 215
Eversden, Henry, 97
Examiners, 45, 47, 78, 105, 318, 334
Exchange (see Royal Exchange)
Exchequer, Royal, 187, 292, 309
Excise, 187 ; farmers discharged of rent, 200
Executions, 64, 233*n*, 311
Eyam, plague at, 293–7

Fairs, 194–5, 324, 326 ; Bartholomew, 194, 326
Fancott, Ralph, 105*n*
Fast days, 66, 94–5, 170, 208, 288, 335
Feasts prohibited, 129, 286 ; Goldsmiths', 129
Fees of Homage, 170
Feilding, Lord (letter to), 233*n*
Fells, Margaret, 117 ; John, 105*n*
Fenchurch Street, 56, 63, 240, 326
Fetter Lane, 227
Finch, Sir Heneage, 50
Finch Lane, 80
Finsbury Fields, 33, 145, 211
Fires in streets, 104, 236–8, 241, 243, 347
Fisherton, 171–2

Five Mile Act, 228–9, 265, 303

Fleas as plague carriers, 247, 250

Fleet Lane, 213 ; Prison, 42 ; River, 9, 42, 213, 275–6 ; Street, 21, 42, 86, 91, 97, 276

Fleetwood, Recorder of London, 88

Flesher, Joseph, printer, 73–4

Flight from London, 2, 12, 23, 45, 49, 53, 56–60, 62, 91–6, 104, 137, 154, 188, 197, 265, 273, 310, 316, 327 ; of the Court, 66–71, 80, 101, 208, 298–9, 310

Foster, Robert, 216

France, ports closed, 144 ; war with, 326

Francis, William, 214

Franklin, Rev. Robert, 227

French remedy, fatal effects of, 236

Frederick, Sir John, M.P., 302

Friends (see Quakers)

Frosts (see Weather)

Fryth (Rye solicitor), 203, 257–8, 261–2

Fudge, " Lying," 217

Fumes, fuming, 35–6, 51, 139, 142, 155, 194, 285, 333

Funeral processions, 131, 175, 232, 258

GADBURY, JOHN, astrologer, 14

Gale, Marie, 43–4

Gaol delivery, 63–4, 85, 174, 311

Gavell, Philip, 105n

Geere, John, 29

Gervise, Edward, 149

Gifford, Mary, 311

Gloucester, 143, 152

God's Terrible Voice, 228

Godfrey, Sir Edmond Bury, 68, 70, 81, 197

Gold, medicinal virtues of, 3, 97, 126, 263

Golden Coast, 10, 155

Goldsmiths Company, 129, 215

Goodchild, John, 48

Goswell Street, 282

Gracechurch Street, 59, 118, 240, 279, 285

Grandchester, 323

Grant, Dr., 48

Grass in streets, 230, 238, 267

Graunt, John, 12, 19

Gravesend, 200–1, 217–8, 319, 326

Grays, 201

Gray's Inn, 60

Great College Street, 42

Great Ejectment, 225, 257

Great Fire of London, vii, 252–3, 306, 326

Great Plague in London (see also Medical) : first signs, 13 ; outbreak in St. Giles-in-the-Fields, 14, 23–4, 27 ; spread of, 40 ; in Westminster, 41–4, 52 ; pesthouses equipped, 38–9, 47, 89 ; flight from West-end, 53, 57–62 ; flight of Court, 66–71 ; plague orders issued, 72–8, 81, 84–5 ; doctors appointed, 86–8 ; epidemic plague in City, 90, 103, 167–8, 176, 210–16 ; flight from City, 91–5, 188, 223–6 ; quack remedies 96–9, 163–4 ; plague officers, 17–8, 105–13 ; evils of shutting up houses, 107, 114–6 ; mortality in City, Liberties, and out-parishes, 123 ; public gatherings prohibited, 129–32 ; plague piper, 134–5 ; plague in country, 136–44, 321–6 ; vast mortality in Cripplegate, 144–52 ; clergy and ministers dead, 150, 225–6, 263, 312 ; soldiers moved out, 164–5 ; Court at Salisbury, 170–2 ; plague among Jews, 179–81 ; among Quakers, 181–2, 189–90, 217–8 ; living burials, 183 ; decay of trade, 186–8 ; poor relief, 195–9, 286–90 ; trade leaves Thames, 199–202 ; doctors dead, 203–7 ; post-mortem on plague victim, 128–9, 203–6 ; churches closed, 221–5 ; death spread by infected, 223 ; grass in streets, 238, 267 ; fires in streets, 236–8 ; worst week of plague, 243–5 ; origin, spread, and modern knowledge of plague, 246–54 ; letters from London, 255–65 ; decline of plague, 266–8 ; Stepney's death roll, 270 ; in Clerkenwell, 272 ; in St. Bride's, 275–6 ; return of refugees, 280, 284–5, 291–3, 312 ; Court at Oxford, 298–300, 306–8 ; Oxford Parliament, 301–4 ; King returns to Whitehall, 311 ; last of plague, 317, 321–4 ; full bill, 325

Great Turnstile, 27

Greenwich, 60, 65, 143, 200, 217, 291 ; Navy office at, 70, 100, 187, 202 ; plague at, 201

Gresham College, 63, 292

Grimes, John, 151, 227

Grubb, John, 105n

Grunman (divine), 227
Gunpowder, 155
Gutter Lane, 98
Gwynne, Nell, 42

HABERDASHERS Company, 83
Hackett, Bishop John, 289
Hackney, 34, 186, 214
Haggerston, 215
Haigh, N. B., 136
Hale, Sir Matthew, 2, 3
Halfield, Anthony, 52
Hall, Francis, 98 ; Bishop, 326
Hallam on Estimates, 303n
Halsall, Queen's Equerry, 171
Hampstead, 93, 185 ; Judges' Walk at, 86
Hampton Court, 67-8, 307-8
Hand Alley, 282
Hanson, Sir R., 278, 311
Harcourt, Lord, 331
Hare's foot charm, 163
Harford, Rev. Anselm, 241
Harley, Sir Robert, 300
Harlingdon, 148
Harper, James, 105n
Harrison, Dr. Randolph, 225
Hatton Garden, 86, 99n
Haymarket, 119
Hayward, Sir Richard, 122
Hearne, Thomas, 156
Henchman, Humphrey, Bishop of London, 49, 54, 66, 224-5, 315, 324
Henrietta Maria, Queen, 64, 196
Henrietta Street, 54-5
Henry VII., King, 6 ; VIII., 6, 37, 42-3, 78, 79n, 146, 251
Herne, Samuel, 80-1, 138
Hewer, W., 241
Hickes, James, 141, 155, 299
Hicks Hall Sessions, 64
Highgate, 93, 185
Hinder, John, 105n
Hippocrates, 45n, 97-8, 237
Hobman (churchwarden), 105n
Hodges, Dr. Nathaniel (see Physicians)
Hog, Eliza, 134
Holborn, 21, 27-9, 33, 35, 101, 268
Hole Haven, 4
Holland, plague in, 3, 4, 246, 257 ; war with, 4, 22, 53, 64, 67, 69, 144, 199-200, 217-8, 240, 246, 285, 292, 301-2, 326
Hollar, 42
Holmes, Mrs. Basil, 282
Holywell Mount, 282

Hooke, Robert, 218
Hooker, Sir William, 278-9, 311
Hookes, Ellis, 117, 190n
Horton, Rev. Thomas, 226
Hospitals (see also Pest-houses), 320 ; Bethlehem, 162, 190n, 210-11, 214 ; Kingsland, 19, 162 ; St. Bartholomew's, 19n, 51n, 108, 162-3 ; St. Thomas's, 51n, 162, 211, 291, 331 ; Southwark, 19, 162
Hounslow, 142, 209
Howe, Marshall, 296
Hoxton, 80, 138, 145, 214
Hull, 304
Hurlock (parish clerk), 216
Hyde, Edward (see Clarendon)
Hyde Park, troops in, 164-5, 291
Hyett (Vintners Co.), 215

INARD, DR. TRISTRAN, 38
Indian Plague Research Commission, 247, 249, 250n
Infant Mortality, 330
Inmates (lodgers), 25, 28, 84, 124, 313-4, 316, 318, 334
Inns of Court (see Gray's Inn, Lincoln's Inn, Temple)
Intelligencer (see Newspapers)
Ipswich, 141, 200, 319, 324
Islington, 29, 34, 185, 228, 245
Italy, plague in, 233n

JACOBS, DR. JOSEPH, 179
Jackson (Keeper of Newgate), 189
James I., King, 7, 10, 32, 46, 78, 79n, 146, 339n
Janeway, Abraham, 150 ; James, 227
Jeake, Samuel, 257, 261-2, 264
Jegon, Richard, 68, 70
Jester, the King's, 170
Jews, 18, 179-82 ; burial ground, 180-2, 231
Johnson, William, 37, 203
Journal of the Plague Year, v, vi, 72-5, 105, 330, 353
Joyce, John, 170
Judges, no deaths of, 312
Justices of the peace, 16, 35, 45, 60, 70, 86, 114, 137, 214, 277, 314-6, 317, 329, 333, 335 ; no deaths among, 9, 312 ; orders by, 23, 25, 28, 34, 37, 45-6, 104 ; to stay in London, 68

KEMP, W. (Brief Treatise), 45, 99n
Kensington, 34, 283
Kent, plague in, 140, 322

King Edward Street, 166
King Street, Westminster, 43, 55, 65
King's Bench, orders by, 23, 47
King's Evil, 172
King's Lynn, 324
Kingsland hospital, 19, 162
Kingston, Rev. Richard, 274–5
Knells for the dead, 80, 158, 178, 209, 230, 234, 275, 310, 342–3
Knightley, Rev., 226
Knightsbridge, 34, 44, 245, 283*n*

LAMBETH PALACE, 70, 198, 224, 353
Lancashire, no plague in, 323
Lane, Rev. Peter, 226 ; Richard, 159
Law terms at Reading, 7 ; at Oxford, 187, 301, 308–9 ; at Westminster, 309, 311 ; at Winchester, 7, 66 ; ordered at Windsor Castle, 309, 311
Lawrence, Sir John (see Lord Mayor)
Lawson, Admiral Sir J., 65
Laystalls, 9, 33, 146, 315, 333
Leadenhall Street, 187
Leicester, 141
L'Estrange, Roger, 4, 40, 63, 93, 95–6, 131, 176, 216, 277, 300
Letters, 141–2, 256, 299
Lichfield, 141
Lilly, William, 2, 40–1
Lime in churchyards, 36, 314–5, 334
Lincoln's Inn, 60, 221
Lincoln's Inn Fields, 54
Link-bearers, 52, 209
Llewellyn, Peter, 215
Lloyd, Simon, 198
Loimologia, 161
Lombard Street, 215, 230
London, Bishop of (see Henchman) ; efforts to restrict size of, 144 ; population, 12–3, 246
London Pest-house, 37
London's Dreadful Visitation, 62
Londons Lamentation, 139
Londons Lord Have Mercy on Us, 219–20
London's Remembrancer, 278
Long, Sir Robert, 59
Long, Rev. Timothy, 225
Long Acre, 33, 39
Long Ditch, Westminster, 41, 43–4
Long Lane, 80
Lord Chancellor (see Clarendon)
Lord Chamberlain (see Manchester, Earl)
Lord Mayor, 4, 18, 21, 25–6, 36, 45, 63–5, 67, 69, 75, 236, 314, 333, 344 ;

court, 85, 145, 313 ; dead by Plague, 6
Lord Mayor, Bludworth, Sir J., 277–9, 311, 322, 324 ; Hills, Sir T., 6 ; Lawrence, Sir John, 25–6, 70–1, 73, 95, 177, 187, 329 ; character, 82–4, 278 ; feast, 26 ; orders by, 26, 81, 94, 105, 131, 137, 176, 198, 285 ; retirement, 277–9 ; Rawlinson, Sir T., 326*n* ; Rowe, Sir Thomas, 210 ; Stokker, William, 6
Lord Mayor's Remembrancer, 244, 279
Lords, House of, 302–4, 326 ; no peers dead, 312
Lothbury, 54
Lowndes, Richard, 97
Luckeyne, Rev. Thomas, 148–9
Lutener's Lane, 99*n*

MAGISTRATES (see Justices)
Maidstone, 322
Malpas, plague at, 8
Manchester, 288
Manchester, Earl of (Lord Chamberlain), 25, 55, 69, 172, 299
Mandrill, Rev., 226
Mann (examiner), 52, 105
Marley, Henry, 150
Marsh, Ralph, 215
Marvel, Andrew, 304
Marylebone (see also Pest-Houses, St. Giles's), 38, 282
Matthews (cure-seller), 98
Medde, Dr. Theodore de, 97
Medical aspects of Plague, 113–4, 116, 243, 246–54, 314 ; bacillus pestis, 247 ; climate, 251–2 ; medicine at Restoration, 11, 16–7, 35 ; disappearance of plague, 253 ; doctor's day, 161 ; fleas and rats, 247–50 ; hospitals, 162 ; " infection " of air, 154, 237, 247, 249 ; nursing, 108–11, 158 ; origin of plague, 247 ; physicians appointed, 86–8, and discharged, 313 ; plague little infectious, 250 ; pneumonic plague, 250 ; postmortem, 128–9, 203–6, 261, 335–8 ; prescriptions, 11, 36, 59, 125 ; preventive measures, 36, 79, 105, 237 ; quack practitioners, 96–9 ; repeated attacks, 213 ; symptoms : (blains) 126, (buboes) 126–7, (carbuncles) 127, (tokens) 127–8, 157 ; treatment in 1665, 117, 125–6, 193 ; venereal disease, 19, 99

Memorials of plague, 162, 281, 284
Menasseh Ben Israel, 180
Merchant Taylors Company, 210 ; School, 167
Meriton, Rev. John, 226
Merton College, Oxford, 289
Meynell, financier, 313
Middlemore (examiner), 105
Middlesex Street, 204
Middleton, Com. T., 233
Mildenhall, 116
Mile End Road, 180, 270
Mill Ditch, Westminster, 42
Millet (Pewterers Co.), 215
Mills, Rev., 293
Milton, John, 255, 290
Minchinhampton, 288
Mompesson, Rev. William, 294–6, 329
Monck, George (see Albemarle)
Money, disinfection of, 193–4, 295, 349
Monmouth, Duke of, 55, 307
Montagu, Lady Mary, 329
Montagu of Beaulieu, Lord, 137
Moorfields, 145–6, 209, 211–2, 265
Morais, Abraham de, 180
Moravian Chapel, 227
Morice, Secretary, 25, 69, 262
Morley, Daniel, 159
Morton, Edward, 243
Mount Mill, 282
Munk's *Roll of College of Physicians*, 205
Myddleton, Hugh, 10
Mywell, Alderman, 323

NAVY OFFICE, 70, 100, 187, 202, 238
Needham, Benjamin, 151
New Exchange, 97
New Oxford Street, 27
New River Company, 10, 254, 280
New Street (St. Bride's), 275, (Bishopsgate), 282
Newbury, 137, 299
Newcastle, 201
Newgate Gaol (see Prisons)
Newgate Market, 166, 183, 269
Newington, 34, 245
Newport, Isle of Wight, 142
Newport, Lord, 49, 55, 197
Newspapers, 4, 216 ; *Intelligencer*, 4, 40, 56, 63, 92, 96, 300 ; *Newes*, 4, 25, 95–6, 277, 300 ; *Utrecht Couranter*, 144
Newton-street, Holborn, 35
Nichols, John, 216

Nicholson, Dr. Watson, vi, 72–3
Noel, Sir Martin, 215, 279n
Nonconformity (see also Conventicle Acts), 217, 223–5, 257, 323 ; deaths among ministers, 150, 152, 227, 262 ; Five Mile Act, 228–9 ; heroic work by ministers, 149 ; in vacant pulpits, 225 ; plague's influence in establishing, 227–8
Nonsuch, Exchequer at, 187
Nore, Fleet at, 64–5
North, Roger, 43
North Allerton, 288
Northamptonshire, plague in, 143
Northumberland, plague in, 323
Northumberland, Duke of, 66, 298
Norwich, 13, 324
Notification of deaths, 17–20
Nottingham, 325
Nunes, Isaac Alverez, 180
Nurse-keepers, 45, 100, 103, 107, 126, 157–8, 177–8, 184, 271 ; at Poole hanged, 140 ; crimes by, 108–11, 158

OGLE, EARL OF, 312
Old Bailey Sessions, 64, 174, 311–2
Old Street, 88, 146
Opdam, Admiral, 64, 65n
Orders Conceived and Published, vi, 72–9, 81, 105–6
Oriel College, Oxford, 289
Origin of Plague (see Medical)
Ormonde, Duke of, 25–6
Osbaldston (parish clerk), 216
Outram, Rev. Dr., 226
Oxford, 141, 162, 172, 298–301, 306–9, 338, 351 ; ball at, 307 ; law term at, 187, 301, 308–9 ; Parliament at, 7, 67, 187, 228, 265, 301–4, 328
Oxford, De Vere, Earl of, 55, 301
Oxford Gazette, 309
Oxford Street, 282

PALL MALL, 43, 101
Parish clerks, 18–20, 93, 147, 221 ; deaths among, 148–9, 182, 186, 216
Parish Clerks Company, 18, 58, 147–8
Parliament (see also Statutes), 45, 69, 75 ; adjournments, 22–3, 57, 67, 186 ; migrations of, 7 ; at Oxford, 7, 228, 265, 301–4, 328 ; at Salisbury, 7 ; members dead by

plague, 7, 312 ; no money vote for plague, 46, 197
Parliament Square, 44
Passon, William, 56
Paternoster Row, 321
Patrick, Rev. Symon, 70, 226, 239–40, 253
Pechell, Rev. John, 225
" Peculiars," Primate's, 177
Peine forte et dure, 17, 311
Pembroke, Earl of, 170–2
Pentecost Lane, 166
Pepys, Samuel, 2, 13, 28, 41, 48, 53, 65, 80, 131, 166n, 167, 200, 238, 240, 245, 266–7, 277, 279, 305, 324 ; anticipations of death, 208 ; August *Diary*, 208–9 ; false Bills, 93 ; first sight of red cross, 44 ; on flight from town, 57–8 ; grave-yards, 281 ; at Greenwich, 100, 202 ; hare's foot charm, 163 ; on plague-stricken town, 100–2, 230, 267, 321 ; periwig, 285 ; plays, 327 ; public fears, 137–8, 191, 317 ; return after plague, 291–3 ; shut-ting up houses, 176–7 ; sick spread plague, 233 ; watches departure of Royal Court, 169 ; on weather, 252, 284
Periwigs, 285, 300
Pest-field, Lord Craven's, 319–20
Pest-houses, 24, 37, 81, 100, 104, 114, 138, 140, 192, 304, 315–18, 327, 334 ; institution of, 37 ; pro-cession of cured from, 232 ; Cam-bridge, 319 ; City of London, 38–9, 47, 88–9, 287, 319 ; Poole, 140 ; Portsmouth, 170 ; St. Giles-in-the-Fields, 25, 38, 192, 316 ; St. Martin-in-the-Fields (Soho), 38–9, 192, 316, 319 ; Salisbury, 171, 319 ; Tower Hamlets, 165 ; Westminster, 38–9, 43–4, 47–8, 51, 192, 316, 319
Pest House Row, 88
Pest rate (see Relief)
Peterborough, 324
Petersfield, 324
Petticoat Lane, 204, 336
Petty France, 42
Petty, Isabella, 174
Petty, Sir William, 218
Pewterers Company, 215
Peyton, Sir Thomas, 28
Phillips (divine), 226 ; John, 277
Physic School, Oxford, 303
Physicians (see also Apothecaries, Surgeons), 9, 17, 25, 51, 62, 86, 106–7, 114, 157, 193, 243–4, 248, 268, 287, 312–3, 335 ; deaths among, 87, 203–7 ; rewards to, 70–1, 290 ; appointed for plague service, 86–8 ; flight of, 62
Physicians who stayed in London, Allen, Thomas, 291 ; Astell, Jeremy, 290 ; Baker, Sir John, 291 ; Barbone, 87 ; Barwick, Peter, 224, 256, 290 ; Bayard, 207, 252 ; Bernard, Francis, 162 ; Bolnest, Edward, 147 ; Bravo, Joseph Mendez, 180 ; Brookes, Humphrey, 87 ; Burnet, Alexander, 56, 203, 207, 230 ; Butler, Nicholas, 291 ; Conyers, William, 206 ; Davis, Nicholas, 88 ; Day, 204–5 ; Deantry (or D'Awtry), Edward, 88 ; Fife, 291 ; Glover, John, 87, 203 ; Grant, 48 ; Hodges, Nathaniel, 11, 13–4, 21, 86–7, 98–9, 104, 108, 207, 238, 244, 252, 286, 329 : (appointed City Physician) 86, (doctor's day) 160–1, (on bad nurses) 110, (on Plague) 125–6, 128, 154n, 157, 213, 233–5, 246, 266, (on shutting up) 116, (tablet of) 162, 284, (on venereal disease) 99 ; Inard, Tristran, 38 ; O'Dowd, 203 ; Paget, Nathan, 290 ; Parker, 87, 206 ; Peck, 287, 290 ; Starkey, George, 203, 205–6 ; Thomson, George, 3, 163, 204–6, (post-mortem by) 128–9, 204–5, 335–8 ; Wharton, Thomas, 291 ; Witherley, Sir T., 86–7, 104
—— other physicians, Alston, Sir John, 62 ; Creighton, Charles, 5n, 79, 279n, 330 ; Coxe, 52 ; Diemer-broeck, 268, 353 ; Garencieres, Theophilus, 113 ; Glisson, Francis, 290 ; Goddard, Jonathan, 292 ; Harvey, Gideon, 353 ; Hilmy, Fouad, 250n ; Kitasato, 247 ; Liston, Glen, 249 ; Mead, Thomas, 154n, 219, 353 ; Merritt, 62 ; Micklethwaite, 162 ; Petrie, G. F., 250n.; Ponteus, John, 19 ; Skander, Riad, 250n ; Sydenham, Thomas, 62, 273, 353 ; Terne, 162 ; Todd, Ronald, 250n
Physicians, College of, 16, 35, 62, 86, 88, 98, 107, 161–2, 203, 206, 290, 328 ; advice by, 11, 36, 79, 86, 146, 155, 237 ; prescriptions 11, 36–7 ; robbery at, 62–3
Piccadilly, 38, 119
Pick, William, 204, 336

Pierson, Rev. Richard, 226
Pillulæ Pestilentiales, 274
Piper, the Plague, 134–5
Pistor tomb, 284
Plague (for epidemic of 1665–6, see Great Plague ; see also Black Death, Medical aspects, Statutes, Sweating Sickness), 5, 11 ; bubonic, 126, 250 ; " Harbourer " of plague, 88 ; in Bible, 248*n* ; leaves Europe, 253 ; segregation, 37
—— at or in, Amsterdam, 246 ; Baltic, 330 ; Egypt, 250 ; Greece, 236–7 ; Holland, 3, 4, 246, 257 ; Hong Kong, 247 ; India, 247–9 ; Italy, 233*n* ; Marseilles, v, 74, 253, 330
—— epidemics in England, in 1532 and 1535, 5*n* ; in 1563, 5*n*, 6, 236 ; in 1574, 1578–82 and 1583, 5*n* ; in 1592–3, 5*n*, 7, 88 ; in 1603, 5, 6, 45–6, 191–2, 236 ; in 1625, 7, 8, 11, 37, 45, 49*n*, 54, 130, 237, 251, 255 ; in 1636–7, 11, 47 ; in 1640–7, 5, 7, 8, 22, 38, 47, 75, 94 ; plague in 1664, 4 ; after 1666, 329–31
Plague pits (see also Burials), 20, 39, 48–9, 104, 134, 147, 182, 184–5, 211, 281, 287 ; Aldgate, 152–3 ; Bishopsgate, 282 ; Broad Street station, 178 ; City Road, 283 ; Fulham, 283 ; Golden Square, 283 ; Kensington, 283 ; Liverpool Street station, 210–1 ; Marylebone, 282 ; Moorfields, 282 ; Mount Mill, 282 ; St. Brides's, 276 ; St. Giles-in-the-Fields, 29, 90 ; St. John's Wood, 283 ; Shadwell, 282 ; Shoreditch, 282 ; Soho, 283 ; Southwark (Deadman's Place), 258–9, 282–3 ; Stepney, 270, 282 ; Wapping, 282 ; Westminster, 47 ; Whitechapel, 282
Plague Ship in Thames, 217–18 ; at sea, 217–18*n*
Plague Water, 100, 331
Plaistow, 186
Player, Sir Thomas, 289
Playhouses, plays, 6, 54, 327, 346
Playter, Sir William, 68
Plymouth, 217, 288
Poole, Dorset, 140, 172
Poor rate (see Relief)
" Poore's plague," 28, 313
Population (see also Bristol, Norwich, London), of England in 1669, 13*n*
Portlington (divine), 223

Portsmouth, plague in, 4, 170, 233, 246
Post Office (see also Letters), 155, 239, 299
Post-mortem on plague victim, 128–9, 203–6, 261, 335–8
Potter, Francis, 2
Predictions of plague, 2, 99, 262
Press Gang, 201
Preston, 288
Prisons, 287 ; Fleet, 276 ; Gate-house, Westminster, 119 ; Ludgate, 161, 190 ; Newgate, 17, 56, 175, 189–90, 202, 217, (last delivery before plague) 63–4, 174, (first after) 311, (plague in) 5, 117, 311–2, (Quakers in) 117 ; Poultry Compter, 190, 226 ; White Lion, 119 ; Wood Street Compter, 190
Printers dead of plague, 216
Pritchett, Rev. John, 148, 152
Privy Council, 68–9, 88, 322 ; committee of, 24–5, 69, 317 ; for Scotland, 137 ; orders by, 4, 11–2, 23–5, 34, 36, 38, 47, 51, 66, 68, 76, 107, 114, 142, 301, 313–4, 317–9, 333–5 ; at Hampton Court, 68 ; at Oxford, 301 ; at Salisbury, 186, 202 ; at Sion House, 67 ; at Whitehall, 23–5, 66, 70, 326
Proclamations, Mayoral, 26, 85, 104*n*, 129–31, 176, 238, 286, 313 ; Scottish, 136 ; Royal, 66, 144, 173, 186, 194, 269
Pullar, Philip, 146
" Pulpits to let," 223
Pyne, Elizabeth, 148 ; Nicholas, 147–8, 216

Quacks, quack remedies, 3, 25, 35–6, 96–9, 122, 126, 236
Quakers, 18, 21, 117–9, 181, 189–90, 209, 217–8 ; burial ground, 18, 118, 181–2, 231, 244 ; in Newgate, 117–8, 189–90, 217 ; on ship Black Eagle, 117, 217–8 ; fund for relief, 118 ; transportation of, 189–90, 217
—— Bidle, Ester, 117 ; Dickenson, Christopher, 117 ; Ellwood, Thomas, 189 ; Fells, Margaret, 117 ; Hookes, Ellis, 117 ; Latey, Gilbert, 118 ; Parker, Alexander, 118 ; Travers, Anne, 117 ; Trigg, Hannah, 190 ; Whitehead, George, 118, 217, 329, 352

Quarantine, 4, 28, 76, 330–1; at Thames ports, 4
Quarterman, Dr., 303
Queenhithe, 209; Ward, 25, 82

RACQUET COURT, 275
Rain in London (see Weather)
Rakers, 85, 104, 154, 210, 315
Raleigh, Sir Walter, 7, 88
Ramsay, William, 167
Ratcliffe, 200, 209, 270
Rats, 59, 158, 247–50, 252–3
Rawlins, Thomas, 277
Rawlinson, Daniel, 326
Raworth, Rev. Francis, 225
Reader, Nicholas, 186, 216
Reading, law term at, 7
Red cross (see Cross of plague)
Red Lion Yard, Walbrook, 160
Registration of death, 17–20
Relief, public, 36, 113, 130, 132–4, 287–90; by City cash, 130, 197–8, 286–7; collections for, 66–7, 130, 196–8, 288, 324; charity, 46, 49, 50, 169, 196–7, 286; City's gift to out-parishes, 288–9; funeral gifts, 50; pest rate, 47, 87, 91, 130, 195–8, 286, 335; poor rate, 47, 91, 195–8, 335
Repas, Denis de, 300, 307–8
Reresby, Sir John, 134–5
Return of refugees to London, 279–80, 284–6, 292, 312
Rhodocanaces, Constantine, 97
Richmond, 81
Roberts, J., printer, 73; (divine) 227
Robinson, Sir John, 166, 278, 289
Rochester, 322
Rogers, Tom, 156
Romilly, Sir John, 320
Roscoe Street, 182
Rotherhithe, 34, 200, 329
Rowe, Sir Thomas, 210
Royal Court, at Hampton Court, 67, 308–9; at Sion, 66–7; at Oxford, 172, 306–9; at Salisbury, 162, 169–72, 179; at Whitehall, 54, 57–8, 65–6, 312
Royal Exchange, 54, 56, 94, 101, 209, 230, 240, 268, 279, 285, 312; closed, 102
Royal Mint, 279
Royal Navy, 141, 201, 233, 271, 308, 314; plague in, 202
Royal Proclamations (see Proclamations)
Royal Society, 12, 63, 163, 218, 290

Royston, 323
Rugge's " Diurnal," 93, 184
" Rules and Orders," 318–9, 333–5
Rupert, Prince, 67, 145, 196
Rye, 141, 203, 206n, 257–9, 265, plague in, 263

SABBS, PETER, 68
Saddlers Company, 216
St. Abb's, Oxford, 299
St. Alphage London Wall, 122, 133, 197, 225
St. Andrew Holborn, 9, 21, 29, 32, 40, 90, 242, 268, 275, 289
St. Andrew Undershaft, 87
St. Anne Blackfriars, 87, 241
St. Anne and St. Agnes, 226
St. Augustine, 225
St. Bartholomew's Hospital, 19n, 51n, 108, 162–3
St. Benet Fink, 197, 225, 245
St. Benet Gracechurch, 87
St. Benet Paul's Wharf, 221, 226
St. Benet Sherehog, 123, 245
St. Botolph Aldersgate, 216
St. Botolph Aldgate, 151–2, 228, 242, 268
St. Botolph Bishopsgate, 30, 152, 211, 242, 268, 277
St. Bride, 9, 87, 113, 220, 226, 275–6
St. Christopher-le-Stocks, 221, 226
St. Clement Danes, 9, 13, 21, 33–4, 39–40, 63, 113, 137, 193, 214, 277, 320
St. Dunstan-in-the-East, 65, 221, 277
St. Dunstan-in-the-West, 21, 29, 87, 276
St. Dunstan Stepney, 34, 226, 245, 253, 270–1, 275; mortality in, 145, 242, 270, 274, 276
St. Faith, 225
St. Gabriel Fenchurch, 56
St. George Hanover Square, 320
St. George Southwark, 226
St. Giles Cripplegate, 9, 29, 32, 144–52, 177, 196n, 214, 216, 253, 258, 275–7; mortality in, 27, 30, 147, 150, 152, 242, 268, 276
St. Giles-in-the-Fields, 5, 13–5, 19, 20n, 21, 23–5, 27–30, 32–3, 37–9, 55, 63, 80, 85, 89, 90, 105–6, 193, 252; church, 27, 34; mortality in, 5, 21, 30, 65, 90, 242, 268, 276; pest-house, 25, 37–8, 192, 316; pits, 29, 90; riot in, 24; rookery, 28
St. Gregory, 225

St. Helen Bishopsgate, 83, 87, 228, 277, 291

St. James Clerkenwell, 30, 113, 268, 271–2, 274–5

St. James Curtain Road, 282

St. James Duke Place, 87

St. James Westminster, 320

St. James's Palace, 1, 101, 239

St. James's Park, 43, 69, 101, 164

St. James's Square, 43

St. James's Street, 119

St. John Evangelist (City), 123, 245, (Marylebone), 282

St. John Wapping, 282

St. John's Wood, 283

St. Katherine-by-Tower, 270

St. Katherine Colman, 87, 227

St. Katherine Cree, 87, 132, 277

St. Leonard Shoreditch, 153n, 225, 243, 270

St. Margaret New Fish Street, 159, 277

St. Margaret Westminster, 34, 41–5, 49, 50–2, 55, 59, 67, 105n, 106, 113, 132, 196, 252, 284, 289; mortality in, 45, 113, 242

St. Margaret's Lane, 55, 215

St. Martin Ludgate, 87

St. Martin-in-the-Fields, 13, 19, 29, 33–4, 40–1, 43, 55, 102, 252, 319–20; mortality in; 65, 242, 268; pesthouse, 38–9, 192, 316, 319; whipping post, 40

St. Martin's Lane, 34, 215

St. Mary Aldermanbury, 222, 225

St. Mary Aldermary, 216

St. Mary-at-Hill, 112n

St. Mary Axe, 244

St. Mary-le-Bow, 216

St. Mary Magdalen Milk Street, 168, 228

St. Mary Savoy, 34, 39, 55, 193

St. Mary Staining, 150n, 225

St. Mary Whitechapel, 242, 269–70

St. Mary Woolchurch, 21, 26, 40, 134

St. Mary Woolnoth, 226

St. Matthew Friday Street, 123, 226

St. Michael Bassisshaw, 216, 226, 291

St. Michael Cornhill, 226

St. Olave Hart Street, 87, 93, 100, 167–8, 292–3

St. Olave Silver Street, 277

St. Olave Southwark, 242, 256–65

St. Paul Covent Garden, 13, 19, 20, 34, 39, 70, 133, 193, 226, 239, 320

St. Paul Shadwell, 282

St. Paul's Cathedral, 54, 94–5, 148, 196, 223, 225, 241, 289

St. Paul's Churchyard, 25, 97

St. Peter Chepe, 214

St. Peter Cornhill, 6, 7, 167

St. Saviour Southwark, 226, 242

St. Sepulchre, 9, 241–2, 275

St. Stephen Colman Street, 87

St. Stephen Walbrook, 162, 284

St. Thomas Apostle, 277

St. Thomas's Hospital, 51n, 162, 211, 291, 331

Salisbury, 7, 67, 162, 169–72, 179, 186, 202, 298, 319, 322

Salters Company, 287

Sancroft, Dean, 156, 176–7, 203, 224–5, 256, 289, 352

Sandwich, Montagu Earl of, 53, 240, 305

Sasportes, Jacob, 180

Savile, Sir George, 294, 295n

Savoy (see St. Mary Savoy)

Saul, Daniel, 271

Scarvel, Richard, 174

Schools, closed, 84, 122; Charterhouse, 7n, 167; Christ's Hospital, 27, 166, 190n; Merchant Taylors, 167; Westminster, 47, 49

Scotland (no plague), 136

Seamen, 201, 317; dead of plague, 202, 271

Searchers of the dead, 17–20, 45, 76, 104, 106–7, 116, 131, 157, 182–4, 318, 334; oath of, 18n

Sedan chairs, 51, 104

Seeling (Pewterers Co.), 215

Seething Lane, 100, 238, 292

Sermons, violence of, 222

Seward Street, 282

Sextons, 17, 29, 149, 167, 178, 182, 234, 271

Sheene, Christopher, 105n

Sheldon, Gilbert, Archbishop of Canterbury, 50, 70, 95, 186, 196, 224, 326

Shelford, 323

Sherbourne, 142

Sheriffs, 82, 86; courts, 85, 313; Doe, 65, 73; Hanson, Robert, 278, 311; Hooker, William, 278–9, 311; Waterman, 65, 73, 84

Shipping, French ports closed, 144; little trade on Thames, 199–202; quarantine, 4, 136, 330; plague in ports, 143, 246

Shoreditch (see St. Leonard's)

Shrouds for dead, 51

Shutting up of houses, 20, 23–4, 37, 51, 56, 59, 78, 106–12, 114–19, 124, 130, 157, 173–7, 202, 209, 213, 216, 239, 256, 274, 297, 317–8, 327 ; forty days' term, 37n, 76, 107, 315, 318

Signs (see also Taverns), Black Boy, 97 ; Blazing Star, 96 ; Golden Heart and Anchor, 324 ; Green Dragon, 98 ; Greyhound, 97 ; Lamb and Ink Bottle, 25 ; Ship, 24 ; White Lion, 97

Sion House, Isleworth, 66–7, 311

Skelton, Samuel, 150

Slaughter-houses, 36, 166, 269

Slums, 32–3

Sly, John, 96

Smallie, Edward, 214

Smith, Peter, 260

Smyrna, plague at, 246

Smyth, John, 105n ; Obituary, 148 ; Rose, 8

Soho (see Pest-houses, St. Martin's)

Sothern, Fernando, 149

Southampton, 140, 143, 217n

Southampton, Wriothesley Earl of, 25–7, 69, 101

Southcote, Sir Edward, 139

Southwark, 30, 32, 45, 204, 264, 267–8, 282–3 ; hospital, 19, 162

Southwell Deanery, 294, 297

Spitalfields, 269, 271

Spring Gardens, 120

Stanley, Rev. Thomas, 294

Stanton, William, 105n

Stapleton, goodwife, 112

Statutes, Conventicle Acts, 21, 189, 217, 229 ; Five Mile Act, 228–9, 265, 303 ; Plague, 1st Jas. I., 12, 45–6, 78, 303 ; Additional Act for Plague, 304 ; Quarantine, 330–1 ; Subsidy, 302–3

Steelyard, 268

Stepney (see St. Dunstan) ; High Street, 270

Stinking Lane, 166

Stocks, St. Martin's, 40

Stow, John, 269 ; Nicholas, 44

Strand, 21, 34, 97, 118, 253, 305 ; procession of cured in, 232

Stratford-atte-Bow, 186, 322

Streets, cleansing of, 26, 36, 154, 315 ; cries, 84, 121–2, 231 ; filth in, 11, 315 ; fires in, 104, 236–8, 241, 243, 347 ; kennels, 36 ; paving, 26, 154

Stuart, Mrs. " La Belle," 307

Sudbury, Suffolk, 227

Surgeons, 86, 107, 157, 203, 233n, 314, 335 ; deaths among, 147, 203, 206n, 233n, 314 ; duties of, 76 ; payments to, 287 ; Arbilleur, Lawrence, 290 ; Boone, Henry, 162 ; Fisher, 38 ; Fox, Thomas, 151 ; Gray, Thomas, 86, 162, 206 ; Higgs, Edward, 287, 290 ; Turpin, Thomas, 162 ; Waters, J, 147 ; Westwood, Josiah, 14 ; Woodall, 162

Sutton, Surrey, 284

Swansea, 288

Sweating Sickness, 6, 88

Sword Bearer, City (also see Lord Mayor's Remembrancer), 279

Tackle Porters, 10

Tattersall's Gate, 283

Taunton, 288

Taverns, 25, 84, 122, 171 ; Angel, 240 ; Bull and Mouth, 117–8 ; Cock, 91 ; Heaven and Hell, 41–2 ; King's Head, Oxford, 301 ; Mermaid, 326

Tayler, Deputy, 151

Taylor, John, 220

Temple, 60–2, 97, 275 ; plague deaths in, 61–2, 190n

Thames, River, 43, 57, 85, 156, 169 ; deserted state of, 199–202, 239 ; ice in, 14, 284 ; plague ship in, 217–8 ; quarantine, 4 ; quays, 122 ; suicides in, 214 ; waterman, 241, 268

Thames Street breweries, 121, 153

Thieving Alley, 44

Thompson (Bailiff), 50

Thomson, Dr. George (see Physicians)

Thomson, Sir William, 187

Three Nuns Court, 153

Throckmorton, Rev., 226

Tilley, John, 19n

Tillison, John, 156, 176, 203–4

Toad amulets, 3, 163, 259

Tobacco, 47, 155–6, 323

" Tokens," plague (also see Medical aspects), 127–8, 157

Tothill Fields, 47–8

Totnes, 288

Tottenham, 80

Tottenham Court Road, 27, 34

Towcester, 299

Tower Hamlets, 39, 165–6, 221 ; Hill, 240 ; Stairs, 240

Tower of London, 164, 166, 217, 268, 278–9 ; plague in, 39, 165–6

Town guards, 137, 142

Trade, decay of, 153, 186–8, 284–5 ;

on Thames, 199–202 ; with Scotland prohibited, 137
Trevelyan, Sir G. O., 135
Trig's " great cordial," 96
Tunbridge Wells, 224
Turner, Rev. Edward, 227
Turnor, Sir Edward, 186
Tyburne, 10, 42
Tyne towns infected, 143

UNDERWOOD, JAMES, 68
Unicorn's horn, 3, 126
Upton, Nathaniel, master of City pest-house, 64, 89
Utrecht Couranter, 144

VAN GOGH, 94
Vauxhall Gardens, 101, 119
Venereal disease, 19, 99
Very Valuable and Scarce Pieces, 73
Vicars, George, 293
Vincent, Rev. Thomas, 58, 70, 108, 110, 168, 212, 222, 226, 228, 230, 245, 329
Vincent Square, 47
Vintners Company, 11, 215
Vintry, 11, 18, 148, 215
Vurles, James, 149
Vyner, Alderman R., 313

WAKEFIELD, 288
Wakeman, Rev. Edward, 226
Walbrook, 86–7, 145, 160, 162, 245
Walker (divine), 227
Wall, John, 150
Wapping, 221, 282
Warcupp, Edmond, 68, 70, 81
Wardmote inquests, 77, 84, 286
Warrington, 288
Warton, Thomas, 68
Watchmen, 44–6, 103, 106–7, 157, 177–8, 184, 280, 334 ; woman, 113
Water supplies, 10, 33 ; New River, 10, 254 ; wells, 9, 51, 146 ; disinfection by, 194, 295, 349
Waterman, Sir George, 65, 73, 84
Watermen, Thames, 156, 241, 268
Watling Street, 118
Weather, frost, 13–16, 284, 306, 309, 320 ; heat, 207, 244, 251–2 ; rain, 15, 207, 241, 251–2 ; snow, 281 ; wind, 207, 252
Weavers, 145–6
Weedon, Henry, 51
Welcombe, 135
West End (Hampstead), 185
West Ham, 186, 216

Westhall (Suffolk), 227
Westlake, Canon, 45, 55
Westminster, 7, 13, 14, 21, 34, 41–5, 58–9, 67–8, 101, 105–6, 145, 173, 238, 245, 268, 278, 285, 289, 292, 308–11, 319–20 ; Abbey, 41–2, 44, 55, 59, 245, 306, 317n ; Dean (Dr. Dolben), 50, 67 ; ditches, 42 ; great bell of, 245 ; Hall, 41–2, 208, 311 ; New Chapel (Christ Church), 48, 59 ; Palace of, 245 ; pest-house, 38–9, 43–4, 47–8, 51, 192, 316, 319 ; School, 47, 49
Weymouth, 172
Wheeler, Sir William, 68
Whetstone Park, 28
Whipping Post at St. Martin-in-the-Fields, 4
Whitaker, Margaret, 108
Whitechapel, 29, 32, 153, 174, 204, 242, 269, 282
Whitecross Street, 147, 214
Whitehall Palace, 1, 40, 43, 55, 57–8, 65–6, 68, 70, 101, 164, 180, 238, 307, 309–11, 317, 321
Whitehead, George, 118, 217, 329, 352
Whitfield, Nathaniel, 215
Wilcox, Charles, 165–6
Wiley, William, 277
Wilkins, Dr., 218
Williams, Thomas, 98
Wilton Hayes, 171–2
Winchester, 322 ; Admiralty Court at, 66 ; law term at, 7
Winchester House, 54
Winchilsea, 260
Windsor, 81, 309, 311 ; plague precautions at, 6
Windsor Terrace, 283
Witches, trial of, 2, 3
Wither, George, 49n, 211, 255
Wolsey, Cardinal, 10, 37, 185
Woodchester, 288
Woodmongers Company, 122
Woolwich, 100, 138, 143, 200–1, 209, 265, 267, 291
Wren, Sir Christopher, 270n, 303
Wyborne (churchwarden), 277
Wycombe, 306
Wynde, William, 137

YARMOUTH, 142, 200, 246
York, 171, 173 ; Duchess of, 49, 169, 196, 309 ; Duke of, 65, 67–8, 81, 173, 298, 308
Yorkshire, plague in, 323
Younge, Walter, 167